The New Welfare Bureaucrats

The New Welfare Bureaucrats

Entanglements of Race, Class, and Policy Reform

CELESTE WATKINS-HAYES

University of Chicago Press   Chicago & London

CELESTE WATKINS-HAYES is assistant professor of African
American studies and sociology at Northwestern University. In addi-
tion to her faculty appointment, Watkins-Hayes is a Faculty Fellow at
Northwestern's Institute for Policy Research.

The University of Chicago Press, Chicago 60637
The University of Chicago Press, Ltd., London
© 2009 by The University of Chicago
All rights reserved. Published 2009
Printed in the United States of America

16 15 14 13 12 11 10   2 3 4 5

ISBN-13: 978-0-226-87491-3 (cloth)
ISBN-13: 978-0-226-87492-0 (paper)
ISBN-10: 0-226-87491-5 (cloth)
ISBN-10: 0-226-87492-3 (paper)

Library of Congress Cataloging-in-Publication Data

Watkins-Hayes, Celeste.
    The new welfare bureaucrats : entanglements of race, class, and
policy reform / Celeste Watkins-Hayes.
        p.   cm.
    Includes bibliographical references and index.
    ISBN-13: 978-0-226-87491-3 (cloth : alk. paper)
    ISBN-13: 978-0-226-87492-0 (pbk. : alk. paper)
    ISBN-10: 0-226-87491-5 (cloth : alk. paper)
    ISBN-10: 0-226-87492-3 (pbk. : alk. paper)
    1. Public welfare administration—United States. 2. Social case
work—United States. 3. Social service and race relations—United
States. I. Title.
    HV91.W375 2009
    361.60973—dc22

                                                      2008048164

FOR MY FAMILY

Contents

Acknowledgments

I accrued many professional debts and personally treasured moments throughout the development of this project. The support of several people carried me through the peaks and valleys and stretched me in ways that I never expected. I probably would not have become a scholar without the personal mentorship of Johnnetta B. Cole and the faculty of Spelman College, who first encouraged me to consider the proposition that I too could have a career in the world of ideas. It was Dr. Cole who also taught me that just as the old African proverb reminds us that, "It takes a village to raise a child," so too does it take one to fashion an academic. My scholarly village-building that started at Spelman continued at Harvard, where I was fortunate enough to have a dissertation committee that truly represented a team of "stars," both professionally and personally. I often tell people that if you can get someone like Katherine Newman in your corner, you will receive nothing short of a lifetime of mentorship from someone who once told me that she considered it "professiorial malpractice" to offer anything less. Kathy possesses that perfect blend of passion for the discipline and love for her students that pushes us to our best work. I often find myself repeating many of her nuggets of professional advice to my own students. William Julius Wilson was a key reason for my coming to Harvard, and I could not have completed my degree without him. He gave me my first research assistantship, allowed me to serve as his teaching assistant for two years, and made sure that I had all of the advocacy, intellectual poise, and professional guidance that I needed to do the kind of work that I wanted to do. He also wrote a letter of introduction that provided entrée into the Massachusetts Department of Transitional Assistance, the field site on which this book is based. Barbara Reskin provided invaluable and much-appreciated advice, encouragement, and excitement about my work and was a phenomenal resource of sociological instruction as I carved out ideas. She brings a fire to the field that I seek to emulate. Despite their stature (and very busy schedules), Kathy, Bill, and Barbara always had time and an encouraging word for me, and I will forever be in their debt.

My village expanded throughout my time in graduate school as I developed friendships with an outstanding group of scholarly "big brothers" and a "big sister": Karyn Lacy, Mario Small, Omar McRoberts, and John Jackson (who arrived as a post-doc). I thank them for our ongoing conversations as we continue to think out loud about our work and how to craft the professional trajectories that will truly make us happy. Mathematica Policy Research Inc. provided summer support as I wrote my dissertation proposal, and the Multidisciplinary Program in Inequality and Social Policy at Harvard offered outstanding graduate training. I must also express appreciation to the Brookings Institution, where I served as the Robert W. Hartley Dissertation Fellow during a critical year of writing. Joyce Ladner as well as R. Kent Weaver and the rest of the team working on the Welfare Reform and Beyond Project allowed me to bounce ideas around and provided steadfast encouragement. The National Science Foundation provided that last critical grant that allowed me to revise the manuscript at the National Poverty Center at the University of Michigan—Ann Arbor. There, Sheldon Danziger offered fantastic mentorship and ensured that this sociologist kept her word to write a book that spoke to an interdisciplinary audience (no one wields the "track changes" feature on a PC better). I was also honored to be in the presence of Sandra Danziger and Kristen Seefeldt, key figures in the field of welfare reform implementation who offered helpful feedback and good cheer during my time at Michigan. Finally, the University of Chicago Department of Sociology provided the perfect intellectual home while I was on sabbatical from my faculty appointment and graciously allowed me to enter a cocoon to get the final revisions completed. One of my favorite parts of my time there was the regular meeting of my writing group, which provided clear and brilliant counsel on chapters 1 and 4 of this book. I am more grateful to its members—Cathy Cohen, Michael Dawson, Mario Small, and Martha Biondi—than they could ever know.

One sometimes hears horror stories about the grueling first years as an assistant professor. Although they were challenging, I could not have asked for better or more enthusiastic support. I therefore sincerely thank my colleagues at Northwestern University in the departments of African American Studies and Sociology, the Institute for Policy Research, and across the university. They collectively and individually did whatever they could to ensure that I had the resources and confidence to see this project to completion. Special thanks to Mary Pattillo, Richard Iton, Barnor Hesse (whose concept of entanglements is borrowed for this book's title), Gary Alan Fine, Jeff Manza, and Ann Orloff, who read and commented on chapters of the manuscript. Along with Darlene Clark Hine and Aldon Morris, they offered sage advice as I established my footing as a new faculty member. Mignon Moore and Sandra Smith read chapter 4, and I thank them for their very insightful comments and excitement about my work. A very special word of gratitude goes to Kathryn Edin, who generously read the entire manuscript and offered extremely useful comments. Joe Soss, Evelyn Brodkin, Zeke Hasenfeld, and the community of scholars working in the area of policy implementation in welfare offices also deserve my heartfelt appreciation. This has proven to be an outstanding collective for a young scholar to join (and yes, it truly is a community), and I will always treasure their willingness to include me in the conversation by extending various invitations for dialogue and debate my way.

It is never easy to allow a researcher to enter into what we might call one's sacred space of the everyday and begin asking questions, but the administrators and staff of the Massachusetts Department of Transitional Assistance proved to be extraordinarily generous. I suspect that this is because these professionals were curious to gain an outsider's fresh perspective on what has been their life's work. Although they often heard observations that were difficult and challenging, they were always invested in dialoguing with me and trying to determine how to improve their work. Notably, Bruce Goodro, Director of Program Assessment, read every single word of the manuscript (including footnotes) and offered thoughtful suggestions, probing questions, and a passion to ensure that I both "got the story right" and produced an engaging read. He definitely has a future as an editor in a publishing house should he ever desire a career switch. I always wanted my work to possess both scholarly rigor and practical value for the "real world," so I believe that those interactions with Bruce, other DTA administrators, and the frontline staff as I tested my arguments with them went a long way toward that goal. So for access into their work lives, for their candor and openness during my data collection process, and for making me feel excited to come into the field every day, I sincerely thank them.

There were also many "behind the scenes" that helped to constitute my village. Doug Mitchell is quite the legendary editor in academic circles, so I will always be grateful for his warmth, astuteness, encouragement, and excitement from those first moments when I pitched the project to the final edits of the production process. Doug was also able to secure phenomenal anonymous readers who offered such brilliant feedback that I wish that I could reference them by name here. Tim McGovern, Mary Gehl, and the rest of the University of Chicago Press staff lived up to their reputation as a powerhouse press, and I consider it an honor for me to have them publish my book. A version of chapter 4 appears in the May 2009 issue of the journal *Social Problems*. I thank the anonymous reviewers for their very helpful feedback and editors Amy Wharton and Ted Chiricos for allowing the chapter to appear in this book. Thank you also to Sherra Merchant, Margo Strucker, Angela Salvucci, Bridget Eckstein, and AAA Office Services in Chicago for their wonderful transcription work. Special thanks also to William Barnett and John Raymond for their diligent editing. Thanks to Yondi Morris, LaShawnDa Pittman, Jean Beaman, and Marcella Wagner for research assistance over the years that kept my multiple research projects afloat simultaneously. And a very special thanks to Marisol Mastrangelo, who not only made the charts in appendix B her singular obsession for almost a year, but offered some of the most thorough and cheerful research assistance that one could hope for. Finally, I should note that this material is based upon work supported by the National Science Foundation under Grant No. 0512018. Any opinions, findings, and conclusions or recommendations expressed in this material are those of the author and do not necessarily reflect the views of the National Science Foundation.

Finally, and most importantly, I thank my parents, Walter and Harriett Watkins, for encouraging me and for instilling in me the drive, commitment, intellectual curiosity, and desire to find joy in my work. I thank my sister, Ché, for always being there and for setting a wonderful example of success through both substance and style. My appreciation also goes to the Watkins, Drake, Crawford, Hayes, and Stoute families for their love and support. I thank my childhood friends— Jennifer Campbell, Lorri Pearson, and Eboni White—and my college buddies—Johnita Mizelle, Laurel Beatty, Malene Dixon, Shari Hicks-Graham, Robin Young, Nia Castelly, Iman Hobbs, and Stacey Abrams—

for their love, laughter, and brilliance. I must also thank those friends who reminded me of the importance of stopping to smell the roses as I moved from place to place while writing the dissertation and eventually the book: Nikole Richardson, Blessed Chuksorji-Keefe, Modupe Akinola, Ardenia Gould, and all of the women and men whom I count as dear friends and supporters throughout the country. And my eternal love, devotion, and gratitude goes to my husband, Rejji Hayes, who has been my rock, my best friend, and my confidante from the earliest stages of this project.

Introduction: Do Street-Level Bureaucracies Matter in a Post-Welfare Era?

In the waning days of August 2005 the United States experienced one of the deadliest and costliest natural disasters in its history. Hurricane Katrina surged along the coastlines of Mississippi, Alabama, and Louisiana, destroying homes, businesses, and community agencies and eventually causing several breaches in the levees that protect the city of New Orleans from nearby lakes. With over 80 percent of this metropolis and many of its neighboring parishes under water within days, the drowning of the "Big Easy" contributed to over fifteen hundred deaths reported to be the direct and indirect results of the hurricane and its aftermath (Dyson 2006; Brinkley 2007; National Hurricane Center 2007). Over a million people were displaced, and thousands of men, women, and children were reportedly missing for months on end (Brinkley 2007). Weeks after Katrina's arrival, Hurricane Rita would make landfall in Texas, Louisiana, and other areas along the Gulf Coast, adding an estimated $11 billion to the $81 billion in damages attributed to Hurricane Katrina.[1]

These natural disasters, particularly Hurricane Katrina, revealed what some called an "unnatural" disaster, a slow and dilatory response from local, state, and federal governments to evacuate, provide critical supplies to, and protect some of its most vulnerable citizens. What became apparent to many were two stark realities. First, as more advantaged families boarded up their homes, packed their belongings into SUVs, and headed for airports, hotels, and the secure homes of relatives who were out of harm's way, the abject poverty of many of the area's most marginalized left them without the wherewithal to mount such nimble relocations. Twenty-eight percent of New Orleans residents were living in poverty at the time the storm hit, and the Center on Budget and Policy Priorities (Sherman and Shapiro 2005) estimates that 54 percent of the city's poor households did not have a car, truck, or van at the time of the 2000 census.[2] The tragedy offered the stark revelation that socioeconomic class informs people's agility during not only everyday but also extraordinary emergencies. Many impoverished families would be left to confront Katrina's wrath with buckets, a few bottles of water, a paltry supply of food, and perhaps the physical ability to climb upon rooftops when things got too dire. Observers wondered aloud, "Why didn't these people just leave when they heard about the hurricane?" Others answered, "Where could they go and how would they get there?"

Katrina and Rita revealed a second disturbing truth. As thousands huddled on rooftops and in makeshift rescue boats, crowded into a New Orleans Superdome that would quickly turn unsanitary and unsafe, witnessed uncollected corpses drifting down city streets that had become toxic rivers, and looked into television cameras to beg for all manner of help, Americans saw their government in action, or, perhaps more problematically, in its ineffectiveness. At the federal, state, and local levels, government's preparedness, responsiveness, and investment in those literally and figuratively left behind left much to be desired. It quickly became difficult to reconcile the boasts of accomplishment by government officials with the (mostly black) sea of faces seen suffering for days straight, raising suspicions early on that "Katrina," as it had become known, was taking on a distinct and disturbing racialized tone.[3] From news reporter Anderson Cooper to rapper Kanye West, many openly questioned the commitment of politicians and bureaucratic officials to those who occupied the lowest rungs of the economic and social ladder. "Where was the leadership? Where was the plan? And who was ready to implement and act?" became collective cries that reverberated around the world.

Such a disaster exposes that behind "faceless bureaucracies" are networks of individuals who bring their own experiences, knowledge, beliefs, attitudes, agendas, priorities, skills, and shortcomings to bear in the distribution of the public's resources. The bungled bureaucratic mobilization before and after the hurricane could be viewed simply as a case of massive administrative breakdown, as government officials' delays, hesitation, and confusion exacerbated the pain, suffering, and frustration of a random cast of disaster victims (Schneider 2005). However, anyone who wanted to divorce "the social" from our understandings of government and its dealings, to avoid bringing contentious issues such as race and class into our discussions of how public institutions work, was given pause by what unfolded in August and September of 2005. Poor families made up the lion's share of those left behind, and African Americans represented about one in three people living in the areas left most vulnerable and eventually hit hardest by the hurricane, despite making up just 12.5 percent of the U.S. population (Sherman and Shapiro 2005). Regardless of the various motives and intentions of public officials, what the preparation leading up to and the aftermath of Hurricane Katrina demonstrated is that seemingly remote government bureaucracies become vital and highly personalized institutions in the eyes of a public that demands and desperately needs resources. The rights of citizenship—uniform on paper, but varied in practice—become interrogated and contested as individuals attempt to lay claim to "help," broadly defined. Studying the inner workings of government's organizational arms, those physical and social environments where policy is created or dismantled, asserted or ignored, altered or stalled, reveals a great deal about not only the successes and limitations of public policy but also about those of human beings.

Welfare offices represent a conduit through which these sociological dimensions of policy implementation can be explored. The public's reactions to these are themselves telling. Almost invariably, when I tell people that I study welfare offices, I am met with a blend of curiosity, concern, and perhaps even a bit of thinly veiled hostility. "What is it *really* like inside these places?" they ask about the agencies charged with dealing day in and day out with those described as "the truly disadvantaged," "the underclass," "the poorest of the poor," or simply "those people." How are they remaking a welfare system that almost everyone agreed was deeply flawed? Are they up to the challenge? And how do people end up working in a place like that anyway?

I became interested in studying welfare offices largely because of their notorious reputations. While serving as a graduate research assistant, I was dispatched to a local branch of a national nonprofit agency that did social service and community advocacy work. It had recently joined the growing ranks of newly minted providers of "welfare-to-work" programs popping up all over the city. As 1996 welfare reform was only a few years old at the time, the agency saw this as an opportunity to serve the thousands of local families who stood to be jettisoned from the rolls once their now-time-limited benefits ended. My mentor's instructions were to "hang out there and see what they're doing," eventually resulting in a report about the program that represented my first foray into applied research and an academic paper about the women's experiences after the program that committed me to inequality scholarship (Watkins 2000). Yet as I got to know the women in the program—who were being taught "soft skills" and résumé crafting to play up undervalued talents such as cooking and hair braiding and strategically veiling gaps in their employment histories—someone kept entering into our conversations, seemingly taking up residence in the women's economic and familial lives and eventually in my own mind. Welfare caseworkers are sometimes described in heroic terms, but more often are portrayed as apathetic evil-doers. I became fascinated with them and with the behemoth agency whose policies they carried out.

In many ways, welfare offices represent the quintessential bureaucracy. Populated with what Michael Lipsky (1980) famously termed "street-level bureaucrats" who directly provide public services to citizens, these individuals' use of discretionary power constitutes a unique form of political influence as they reshape public policy through their everyday decision making on the job. In welfare offices, civil servants are expected to fit the complicated, ever-changing, often heartbreaking, and sometimes distorted accounts of low-income women (and men) into categories and then to use these classifications as the basis upon which to dispense cash and in-kind resources. In some ways, welfare offices have elements of what sociologist Erving Goffman (1961) termed "total institutions," where personal identities and histories are downplayed and discipline is a highly valued commodity. *Turn in the forms, show up in the office when we call, go to work when we demand it—* these are a few of the many directives that clients explicitly and implicitly receive when they agree to accept public assistance. Establishing and maintaining the bureaucracy's ability to maintain control over the interactional agenda becomes paramount, as caseworkers use service delivery to evaluate and regulate various aspects of their clients' economic and domestic lives.

Justifying such an institutional structure, with its heavy reliance on hierarchical bureaucrat-client relationships, often involves appealing to long-standing mandates of welfare offices: institutional efficiency and effective supervision of the poor. In few government agencies will you find its observers so invested in curbing waste, fraud, and abuse, and this obsession has clear moral, racial, gender, and class overtones. The desire to provide economic sustenance to low-income families is tempered by an underlying assumption that, out of necessity or corruption, people will lie and finagle to gain more of the public's resources than they are entitled to have. Adding another layer of complexity is the assumption that those who come to welfare offices have engaged in some kind of problematic behavior to warrant their attendance. Their choices—about work, marriage, sex, childbearing—face explicit and implicit scrutiny in ways that their more economically and socially privileged brethren rarely encounter. The impersonality that we typically associate with bureaucracies is complicated by these very personalized associations. Thus, when a researcher casually mentions that she studies welfare offices, she almost certainly will be asked, "Have they finally been able to kick all of *those women* off the dole? Are they still letting people cheat using *my* tax dollars? And can they stop these women from having babies they can't afford?"

For others, welfare offices represent a distinctly different possibility of what government can be. These "poor support" agencies, to borrow a term from economist and former Clinton administration official David Ellwood, are expected to react sensitively to the chronicles of their clients and not merely to relegate them to numbers and stereotypes. These institutions symbolize the public's desire to help those who have been unlucky in the combination lottery and foot race that is the American capitalist system. Those with such philosophical convictions are deeply saddened that so many remain unable to realize the American Dream. They have a nagging suspicion that who lands on which rung of the social ladder is far from random and contradicts what we tell ourselves about how "anyone can make it if they try." The expectation is that welfare offices will be the way stations for these individuals, places where they will find the financial support, emotional encouragement, and practical tools they need to turn things around. For those who cannot, these agencies are counted on to provide the ongoing support necessary for parents to raise their children with their basic needs met. In short, welfare institutions exist to reduce the number of families going hungry while living in the richest country on the planet. Hence, this same researcher is also likely to be asked, "Are those places really helping people so they can feed their kids? And what happens if somebody can't find a job? They don't let them just end up on the street, do they?"

These concerns may seem contradictory, but in fact they reflect a long-standing tension in the country's debate about the poor and our collective responsibilities for creating institutions that will respond to their needs. On the one hand, the idea of not assisting society's most vulnerable—particularly children—troubles most people. On the other hand, many will also say that they want to discourage certain behaviors and encourage others in exchange for the help. We hear public demands that government be more accountable for protecting families, while others charge that the state too often turns a blind eye to free-riding and does not vigilantly curb what they see as a bloated social welfare system. This paradox is not new; the United States has debated its responsibility to the poor from its inception. Government policies reflect some of the incongruities in these public debates, and the social, economic, moral, political, and practical implications of these policies have filled volumes of research papers and books.[4] In recent years, calls for measurable performance accountability, increased privatization of social welfare programs, and devolution raise new questions about how to shape human services to reflect these political tides (Marwell 2007). In fact, this conundrum is shared by many industrialized countries as they determine how to structure their social welfare systems in ways that are responsive to the emerging macro-structural demands of neoliberalism, increasing employment among women, and rising immigration while addressing the micro-level needs of individuals in families and workplaces within their borders (Haney 2002b; Korteweg 2006; Jewell 2007; Esping-Andersen 1999).

Under the backdrop of a highly contentious political fight between President Bill Clinton, a Republican-controlled Congress, key political appointees, and outside advocates, the passage of the 1996 Personal Responsibility and Work Opportunity Reconciliation Act (PRWORA) represented the culmination of many a political promise that had been offered from both the Left and the Right over more than a decade to massively restructure the American welfare system. PRWORA set a new and definitive tone in the stance that the United States assumes toward aid to the poor, that of time-limited assistance.[5] Temporary Assistance for Needy Families (TANF) replaced the Aid to Families with Dependent Children (AFDC) program and provides cash assistance, in-kind resources, and work opportunities through block grants to states, which have the flexibility to develop their own welfare programs within certain parameters.[6] Work requirements, mandated participation in child support enforcement, and sanctions for noncompliance with rules are now standard fare in most welfare offices. Increasing the employment and earnings of needy families, reducing welfare caseloads, and enforcing child support collection are now the central focuses of local welfare systems across the country.

More than ten years since the passage of PRWORA, some key findings are emerging about the effectiveness of welfare reform. Several indicators point to a lowering of the rolls nationwide (from almost five million families in 1994 to just under two million in 2005), increased work among some low-income mothers (especially those never married), increased child support collection, and even a period of falling poverty rates.[7] To be sure, the booming economy of the mid-late 1990s and other key policy changes around that period such as the increase in the minimum wage and the expansion of the Earned Income Tax Credit (EITC) also critically contributed to these shifts.[8] Many have nevertheless concluded, using various measures, that welfare reform, at least in the short term, has "worked" and can be crowned an overwhelming success (Haskins 2006). Political scientist Lawrence Mead (2004) branded as a triumph in the political and administrative history of government bureaucracies Wisconsin's trailblazing efforts to implement a welfare reform that involves a "help-with-hassle" approach that makes increased demands on clients and subjects them to close supervision to ensure that work and other obligations are fulfilled in exchange for assistance.[9] Welfare agencies across the country that followed suit with tweaked combinations of similar policy measures are being widely congratulated for having finally figured out how to get people off public assistance and into jobs.

But there are skeptics. Although these gains are certainly noteworthy, they feel somewhat hollow and even incongruous in the wake of dogged realities that remain a part of the nation's fabric. Our collective attention span may move away from 1996 welfare reform, but Katrina's stark and disturbing images of poverty and race intertwined remain etched in the minds of many. Everyday reminders continue to plague any celebrations over PRWORA's success as we continue to witness high levels of deprivation and desperation in communities across the country. Poverty rates remain stubbornly high among both welfare leavers and stayers, and many continue to cycle between welfare and low-wage jobs with few opportunities for mobility (Urban Institute 2006).[10] Child poverty rates increased from 2000 to 2004 after a dramatic drop in the 1990s. Scholars and journalists are also increasingly complicating the overwhelmingly favorable assessment of welfare reform by documenting the everyday struggles of low-income families both on and off the rolls, suggesting that the results they are experiencing under the restructured system of government assistance are mixed at best (Abramovitz 1999; Danziger and Seefeldt 2003; DeParle 2004; Hays 2003; Munger 2002).[11]

Questions therefore abound about the inner workings and effectiveness of the "new and improved" welfare offices.[12] A cadre of welfare implementation scholars have challenged rosier depictions, contending that the conversion of local welfare agencies to fully complement the service needs of impoverished families has been only partial (Brodkin 1997; Meyers, Glaser, and MacDonald 1998; Meyers, Riccucci, and Lurie 2002; Lurie and Riccucci 2003; Lurie 2001; Riccucci 2005; Danziger, Sandfort, and Seefeldt 1999; Danziger and Seefeldt 2000, 2003; Sandfort 1999, 2000; Morgen 2001; Hays 2003). They identify multiple problems: a lack of sustained support for those in the labor market, difficulties preparing current recipients for entrée into the job market, and few tools to address "harder-to-serve" clients with multiple barriers to economic self-sufficiency, such as physical and mental health problems, learning disabilities, illiteracy, histories of abuse, and drug and alcohol dependency. Although these researchers often point to fundamental flaws in policy, they ultimately identify operational explanations for how these shortcomings go systematically unaddressed: extremely high caseloads; an overemphasis on rapid-employment services at the expense of tailored and in-depth case management; and a workforce ill-equipped to effectively identify and respond to client skill deficits, health issues, and other barriers to employment. Writing about Wisconsin, *New York Times* writer Jason DeParle (2004) offers an assessment that differs from Mead's by suggesting that substantial administrative waste and service-delivery failures have taken place under the state's welfare contracting system, staffed by employees who do not always have the training, wherewithal, or will to engage clients on the level that many policymakers intended. Others conclude that, in many offices where dual responsibilities exist under the same roof, the new work-focused environment "has not replaced the older AFDC agency operational goals of minimizing eligibility errors and ferreting out fraud and abuse; rather, it has been added onto the AFDC culture" (Gais et al 2001, 63; also see Beckerman and Fontana 2001; Danziger, Sandfort, and Seefeldt 1999).[13] This simultaneous "help" and "hassle" approach has actually generated misalignments and conflicts in service delivery for caseworkers as they pursue the often contradictory goals of improving clients' economic circumstances while policing heavily against dependency and fraud. These dual administrative ambitions of addressing complex familial needs while adhering to demands for speed, accuracy, and benchmark enforcement often operate at cross purposes, creating a gulf between the service missions of these agencies and the circumstances of their clients.

These matters certainly give us pause if ever we are tempted to relegate antipoverty policy to a lower priority on the nation's agenda or to argue that welfare offices no longer matter in the lives of the poor. The aftermath of Hurricane Katrina and related events remind us that the philosophical intricacies of prescribed policies matter little to people in crisis. In these moments, they look to intermediaries on the "front lines" to translate those abstractions into concrete resources and services. In this book I will attempt to respond to the questions that I get from people from all walks of life about exactly what it's like inside perhaps these most polarizing yet critical of intermediary institutions: local welfare offices. Although welfare may be "reformed" in many people's minds, organizations that are intimately involved in addressing the needs of the poor remain exceedingly relevant and necessary. They serve important symbolic and instrumental functions in the lives of those who find themselves seemingly forever on the margins. We therefore still have many questions to answer and solutions to uncover to make these institutions part of the bridge over the gulf between what we want to be as a nation and where we actually are—politically, socially, culturally, and economically.

Concomitantly, there is overwhelming evidence to suggest that the administration of welfare and other public services designated for or disproportionately used by socially marginalized groups has historically been informed not only by policy shifts and administrative challenges but also by the social divisions that undergird society and its institutions. Racial prejudices, gender norms that distinctly regulate women as mothers and workers, and moral assumptions that parse out the "deservingness" of various groups to receive public assistance have conspired to transform welfare offices into social environments in which groups continually engage to reinforce, contest, or circumvent existing inequalities (Katz 1996; Nadasen 2005; Trattner 1999; Abramovitz 1996; Gordon 1994; Orleck 2005; Kornbluh 2007). For example, as appendix A makes clear through its overview of the history of welfare administration, blacks and other racial minorities were for decades subjected to the excessive regulation of their work and domestic lives in exchange for benefits or were utterly denied state resources through policies and procedures—both formal and informal—that disqualified them (Quadagno 1994; Neubeck and Cazenave 2001; Bell 1965; Piven and Cloward 1971; Brown 1999).[14] Recent work suggests that decisions and practices directed toward clients within welfare agencies continue to reinforce social hierarchies by deploying power differentially and distributing resources to clients unevenly on the basis of social group

9

memberships and statuses, even if the policies and procedures are ostensibly designed to be more fair and equitable (Gooden 1998; Schram et al. 2009; Schram, Soss, and Fording 2003).

Under the backdrop of these social and administrative histories, PRWORA asked welfare offices all over the country to change their DNA—their makeup, how these institutions define themselves, and how others see them. The policy change did not just attempt to shift the public identity of welfare mothers in politically and culturally loaded ways—from "recipients" to "workers." It also gave welfare offices the opportunity to fundamentally shift their prevailing organizational models, and it provided the professionals who staff them the chance to alter how they conceptualize and organize their work. To go solely from cutting checks and managing the endless reams of eligibility paperwork to helping low-income mothers (and some fathers) find employment and live with a reconfigured and far less extensive social safety net was, and continues to be, a daunting task. In addition, as welfare workers strive to meet policy goals, welfare reform's massive shifts have opened the door for bureaucrats to grapple with how racial and economic inequalities shape the lives of their clients when they leave the welfare office, stunting the opportunities that the policy assumes are widely available. Rarely, however, do we ask frontline workers to talk candidly about these issues and to ponder how major policy shifts as well as inequalities within and outside of their institutions affect their work. Could it be that these social debates and conflicts commingle with actors' assigned professional roles and systematically help or hinder the kind of change necessary to realize certain policy ambitions? Stated differently, even in social welfare's restrictive current environment, are there varieties of interests and investments on the part of street-level bureaucrats that fundamentally shape how they interpret and operationalize their new institutional roles within distinct environmental contexts?

The formulation of workers' *professional identities,* their connection to bureaucratic discretion, and their relationship to the larger social context in which they are embedded is the central concern of this work. In this book I wrestle with the following guiding questions: How are professional identities constructed, and how are they informed by both institutional and environmental dynamics? Do the social locations of organizational actors (e.g., race, class, gender, community residence, and so forth) inform their professional identities? How does this become incorporated into how institutions work? How does the interweaving of professional and social identities shape institutional transformation and the administration of the public's resources through service delivery?

It is my contention that professional identities are informed by *both* organizational cues and social group memberships that carry significance inside and outside the institution, and these identities are articulated and systematically performed through the exercise of bureaucratic discretion. Identities—both social and professional—are the missing pieces in the explanations of the implementation of welfare reform specifically and public policy more generally. This limited attention to the evolution of professional self-conceptions has caused us to underestimate the degree to which *how* street-level bureaucrats think of themselves—as professionals, members of racial groups, women, men, and community residents—shapes *what* they value, what they emphasize, and how they negotiate distributing the resources of the state to clients. This is not a deterministic endeavor; one cannot assume the concerns, attitudes, and behaviors of service providers simply by virtue of their social group memberships. Rather, these social locations suggest an ongoing interchange between personal and collective experiences, on the one hand, and environmental and institutional dynamics, on the other, generating a complex professional self for individuals that is *informed* rather than *determined* by these social categories. As such, the untold story of welfare reform should reveal how its implementers have drawn upon various investments and interests to remake the welfare system in ways that reflect *their* ideas about how their jobs, workplaces, and clients are to be transformed.

I should say at the outset, however, that this book is not about the mechanics of how welfare offices went about implementing PRWORA.[15] Rather, it uses the case of welfare reform to investigate how "the social" complicates an ongoing process of institutional change. To answer the questions posed above, I focus almost exclusively on welfare caseworkers. Based on past and current research, we know a great deal about clients' perspectives on these institutions (Nadasen 2005; Orleck 2005; Hays 2003; Soss 1999; Lens 2007), but the voices of street-level bureaucrats, highly important social actors in their own right, often go ignored. They labor to translate our abstract policies and political debates into tangible services and resources. Their worksites are not simply the places where the benefits are allocated, the work requirements enforced, and the time clocks managed. This book will demonstrate that in welfare offices the politics around defining professional roles and group interests give rise to distinct interpretations of what "helping the poor" looks like. How street-level bureaucrats locate themselves inside and outside of these institutions, and the groups to which they feel loyal, will be shown to affect how they formulate strategies to address a myriad of client needs. In many cases, this ranges beyond those duties for which social welfare workers are "officially" responsible.

Policy implementation of the sort undertaken by welfare offices can therefore be characterized as a series of negotiations by street-level bureaucrats as they wield (and are subject to) power in the service of their own self-definitions. Poverty relief will be shown to be just as much about the social positions and investments of street-level bureaucrats as it is about the social locations and conditions of clients. As a result, although the welfare rolls have been pared down and many mothers have found work—due in no small part to the expanded eligibility and compliance benchmarks of the policy—competing interpretations of the "new welfare bureaucrat" have generated inequities in how the welfare system now looks on the ground.

More specifically, as a significant policy shift, 1996 welfare reform has created opportunities for street-level bureaucrats to rethink, redefine, and represent a host of intertwining identities. In using the term "identity," I note the cautions of sociologist Rogers Brubaker and historian Frederick Cooper (2000), who have criticized the overuse and lack of specificity of the term. I borrow from them in order to operationalize the term identity and submit that street-level bureaucrats create "self-understandings [that] shape social and political action" in important ways (9). Competing interpretations of their occupational roles have, however, provoked clashes among the caseworkers implementing the current poor-support system about what the agency ultimately should become as an institution and who welfare bureaucrats should become as professionals. These debates have been intensified by ancillary dynamics as employees' social group memberships and subsequent commitments—on the basis of race, class, gender, and community—have taken on fresh salience in the process of implementing the new law of the land. Buoyed by the increased opportunities to engage with clients as a result of the "work first" policy thrust that emphasizes probing familial dynamics and barriers to work to achieve desired policy outcomes, frontline workers are making strategic decisions about how to integrate multiple and at times competing professional, political, and personal interests into their service delivery in ways that sometimes advance and sometimes undermine policy goals. Although the agency at the highest level has largely failed to detect or question such maneuvers, they have informed the welfare implementation process on the ground.

This book therefore uses the empirical cases of two local welfare offices to explore, in my terms, "socially situated bureaucrats" in "catch-all bureaucracies."[16] Each chapter explores a distinct dimension of their work lives in order to tease out how professional and social identities intersect to shape how individuals conceptualize and perform their labor.[17] I establish the book's analytic scaffolding by first immersing readers in the bustle of the Staunton and Fishertown offices of the Massachusetts Department of Transitional Assistance in chapter 1's opening and closing in order to quickly show the gravity (and occasional levity) of the issues bureaucrats face. (To protect the anonymity of my research subjects, all names used in this book, including Staunton and Fishertown, are pseudonyms.)[18] By integrating Michael Lipsky's conceptualization of *street-level bureaucrats* with Brubaker and Cooper's notion of *situated subjectivity,* I advance a notion of *situated bureaucrats* (Lipsky 1980; Brubaker and Cooper 2000). Situated subjectivity is defined as "one's sense of who one is, of one's social location, and of how (given the first two) one is prepared to act" (Brubaker and Cooper 2000, 17), and I suggest that this subjectivity gives rise to a general framework through which each bureaucrat approaches her job. One of the book's central points is that bureaucrats' discretionary acts are in fact far from a set of random, independent, unrelated of-the-moment decisions prompted by organizational events but instead represent the products of a worker's complex but systematic professional identity (an identity that is partly malleable to organizational dynamics but also largely constituted through individual and group-based social experiences).

Overarching professional frameworks through which to do the job of service delivery are particularly important in *catch-all bureaucracies,* institutions whose work is intimately tied to responding to a variety of individual- and family-level issues and concerns that are directly or indirectly related to severe economic and social disadvantage. A well-rehearsed professional identity—seasoned with social experiences as a result of one's racial, gender, class, community, and other group memberships—can withstand the kaleidoscope of issues that clients bring to their doorsteps. I do not wish to imply that all crises are addressed and brought to graceful conclusions in catch-all bureaucracies. Nor do I want to suggest that catch-all bureaucracies represent the institutional arm of a robust social safety net. Rather, clients approach these institutions *in spite of,* or perhaps more accurately, *because of,* the reconfigured and porous social welfare system. What results is often a loose, partially improvised patchwork of services and interactions that reflect the attempts of situated bureaucrats to integrate the seemingly contradictory impulses of surveillance and support that undergird the public's ambivalence about this population in a way that resonates with their own socially constructed professional identities. This set of social processes helps to constitute what Gubrium and Buckholdt call "the social organization of care in human service institutions" (1982, ix).

Those interested in gaining a more in-depth understanding of the historical trajectory of welfare casework as a profession and tracing how many of the bureaucrats in this study came to work for the institution are encouraged to review appendix A before proceeding to the book's empirical findings. Numerous texts have tracked the evolution of the welfare system from its inception and caseworkers' roles in supporting and regulating the contours of work, family, and citizenship for poor women (Katz 1996; Nadasen 2005; Trattner 1999; Abramovitz 1996; Gordon 1994; Neubeck and Cazenave 2001). But the goal of appendix A is to trace public welfare work's ancestral roots in social science research, social work, and volunteer charity. In so doing, I suggest that welfare workers historically have been active players in contests over their own professional legitimacy and futures, the appropriate roles of women in not just the receipt but also the administration of public services, and the terms under which racial minorities enter into government work. In short, disputes over boundaries and access—professional, community, racial, gender, and class—have long been central to the formation of street-level welfare bureaucrats and, in turn, to the internal workings of welfare offices. As policy shifts and societal events usher in prescribed changes to their formal roles, these actors in turn negotiated professional identities that reflected their debates about the contours, opportunities, and limits of not only poor support but also the work involved to carry out such ambitions. The narratives of how the majority of caseworkers in this study came into this line of work reflect the transition of the job from one rooted in professional social work in the 1960s to one that attracted low-skilled workers (including former recipients) who could conform to the increasingly clerical demands of the job in the 1970s and 1980s. Appendix A's final section also provides more detail on many of the policies under way in the Massachusetts version of TANF. Those interested in gaining a sense of the demographic composition of the research sites, or learning more about the methods of this study, are encouraged to review appendices B and C respectively.

Chapter 2 examines how policy implementers' interpretations of their professional roles shape what they do and the service received by clients. By building on the concept of *situated bureaucrats,* I argue that much of the variation in service delivery that we observe among street-level bureaucrats—often generically characterized as "worker discretion"—is actually the operationalization of differing professional identities that workers create to implement public policy. Caseworkers generate perceptions of clients, the agency, and their work that help them to create methodical frameworks for doing their jobs, and these frameworks feature toolkits that offer caseworkers the practical resources to reconcile "who they are" with what they believe the institution expects of them. To *efficiency engineers,* successfully implementing welfare reform means taking clients through a series of finite steps; they see themselves as guides and enforcers in this progression and follow strict prescripts to implement policy with an eye toward speed and accuracy. This identity encourages workers to continue to see themselves as the claims processors of previous incarnations of the job, albeit with a new set of requirements to track as a result of welfare reform. For *social workers,* successfully implementing the current welfare policy means advising clients on a wide range of options and resources, delving deeper into their personal lives, and responding to them when they hit barriers, great and small. What many in the office call "social work" stresses coaching, networking clients to a variety of social services, and providing tailored support to implement policy. Social workers do not expect to be able to fix all of the problems that clients present, but they do see it as part of their job at least to try.

Chapter 3 explores why these disparate professional identities emerge within welfare offices and the role of the agency itself in the creation of this variation. I argue that because welfare officials have not invested enough in the professional development of their workers in the postreform era, they have unwittingly contributed to the disparities in service delivery outlined in the previous chapter. The two competing occupational identities that workers have established—efficiency engineering and social work—were informed by organizational cues that suggested that each might be legitimate. Subscribers to the latter model of in-depth case management are encouraged to adopt this approach as a result of the rhetoric coming out of central office around client support, a job title change for frontline workers to include the phrase *social work,* and a revised worker evaluation system that, on paper, encourages workers to help clients create transformative changes in their work and personal lives by helping them to leverage resources. On the other hand, the human capital realities of the staff, the administrative hurdles to creating such a sweeping policy change, and the actual implementation of the evaluation system, with its focus on accuracy and efficiency, have suggested that a very different model is in play. *Efficiency engineering* emphasizes speed in processing and the use of the policy's eligibility and compliance requirements to regulate access to cash assistance and work-related resources. By not consistently implementing a coherent incentive structure and other organizational cues to make the professional model of choice explicit, the organization, in effect, rewards efficiency engineering while creating expectations that workers should become social-work-like case managers. Further, a third professional model has emerged. *Bureaucratic survivalists* are those organizational actors whose identity is grounded in the notion that insofar as the agency, its mission, and its debates over how they should perform as professionals is concerned, they will invest in the system (and its clients) only minimally. Each of these models has its own social norms, incentives, risks, and drawbacks, and frontline workers deploy their own logics to decide which of them they will pursue.

Chapter 4 explores how ideas about race, class, gender, and community shape the formulation and operationalization of the professional identities of black and Latino street-level welfare bureaucrats in what I term the Staunton office of the newly named Massachusetts Department of Transitional Assistance. In particular I ask how their social backgrounds, occupational experiences, and political attitudes shape their conceptions of their work and their interactions with minority clients. I demonstrate how black and Latino social welfare workers balance institutionally vested power and their (relatively) privileged class standing against the subordination inherent in their historically disadvantaged racial status. Minority supervisors and caseworkers make strategic choices about whether and how to inject issues related to race, class, and gender into the service-delivery process, armed with a broader array of tools and edicts under the new policy regime and a fair amount of influence by virtue of their class and professional locations. A few vigorously seek to divorce these social identities from their interactions within the organization and their interpretations of the broader implications of their work. For these bureaucrats, there is noticeably less integration of their professional identities with their social consciousness. However, the majority of black and Latino respondents actively use welfare reform and their interactions with minority clients to engage in a unique kind of street-level activism by igniting the points of solidarity, as well as the fault lines of difference, within their racial communities. They leverage racial, and at times gender, commonality to communicate the social goals and political motives of welfare policy and attempt to use occupational authority and social status to articulate why minority clients should adopt a certain set of behaviors. As these bureaucrats simultaneously communicate their support and challenge clients of color through a variety of techniques, they deploy in-group politics in powerful ways to pursue moral and political rescue missions grounded in racial-group-centered ideologies.

Chapter 5 focuses specifically on what I name the Fishertown office, where the predominantly white community in which its welfare workers live is experiencing significant demographic changes. I use this case to show that white caseworkers similarly use the welfare office as a lens, and potential medium, through which to view and address group-based concerns. As low-income families find themselves "priced out" of large urban centers and seek affordable and available housing in "outskirts" towns and midsized cities, receiving communities such as Fishertown are seeing their numbers of racial and ethnic minority residents grow. The city's welfare office takes on special significance in this migratory trend, serving as a symbolic and substantive institutional gateway as the poorest of these families transfer their cash assistance, food stamps, and Medicaid cases so that they can be administered within the host community. I explore how Fishertown staff members are addressing the question of how best to incorporate migrants from nearby central cities into their caseloads and service-delivery strategies and what this says about the integration of their professional identities and perceived racial, class, and residential interests. I show that, when street-level bureaucrats see the institution as a reflection of the community in which they both live and work, perceived negative changes in the client caseload are seen as threats to both the organization and to the community at large. Caseworkers and organizational leaders express their concerns about community change and racial diversity by framing newcomer clients, and their professional responsibilities to them, in discourses tied to service delivery. This analytic reimagining of the importance of environmental context in the self-understandings of situated bureaucrats suggests, as it did in the previous chapter, that dynamics around race, class, and neighborhood change register in their professional identities in often subtle but critical ways. These individuals in turn deploy bureaucratic power as a filter through which to interpret, and sometimes as a tool to protect, defined group interests.

Lastly, I explore how my findings relate to many of the theoretical, policy, and programmatic debates that have emerged as a result of welfare reform specifically and larger institutional changes to public human-service bureaucracies more generally. The case studies of the Staunton and Fishertown welfare offices uncover many of the politics that drive the delivery of services to low-income families. I posit that many of these dynamics are applicable in a variety of institutional settings and therefore demand further analyses and responses. The changing uses of institutions in the lives of the most socially and economically marginalized begs the question of how race, class, gender, community, and professional orientation complicate institutional processes in ways that may bolster or undermine particular policy efforts, empower or disempower clients, and strengthen or weaken the effectiveness of street-level bureaucrats. If allowed to go unaddressed, emergent conflicts embedded in these dynamics can continue to breed inequities in service delivery in ways that further hamstring our efforts to create institutions that play productive roles in the lives of our country's most vulnerable. In essence, my goal in writing this book remains the same as it was when I first visited that welfare-to-work program in Boston—to offer a theoretically informed, empirically rich analysis, a scholarly chemical reaction of sorts, mixing sociology, African American studies, policy studies, and public management scholarship in a way that more fully accounts for the complexities of public bureaucracies today.

ONE

Situated Bureaucrats

Locating Identity in Catch-All Bureaucracies

At 3:25 p.m. on a blisteringly cold Friday in February 2006, Sharlene Roberts throws open the waiting room's heavy oak door, leans out, and summons her last client to join her in the labyrinthine client service area of the Staunton Office of the Massachusetts Department of Transitional Assistance (DTA). Sharlene has worn a path around the office all day, with me hot on her heels, shuffling a parade of exhausted-looking mothers and bundled-up children into her cubicle, frequenting her supervisor's office to collect signatures of approval, and copying stacks of submitted documents bearing witness to her clients' progress in meeting their work, job training program attendance, or community service requirements. A nearby fax machine spits out paperwork from landlords testifying to who occupies their tenements, bank records exposing fledgling account balances, child immunization certifications, and other details of the lives of low-income families. When she isn't running around, Sharlene diligently wades through a tidal wave of information, feeding it into her computer as she sips on a large bottle of lemon-lime seltzer water.

Kim Purcell, the day's last client, gathers her son in her arms and follows Sharlene to the first empty cubicle in the client service area. Why bring her all the way back to my office if I don't need to? Sharlene reasons. "What can I do for you?" Sharlene asks as we take our seats. She silently braces herself, hoping for a quick resolution so she can return to the stack of still-to-be-processed papers that awaits her.

"My mother is in the mental hospital because my brother was abusive to her. He held a knife to me and my baby's throats. I can't stay there," Kim confesses stoically. "I'm requesting emergency housing. I called around to some shelters, and I couldn't find anything except all the way in Greenfield."

"Who is your worker?" Sharlene asks.

"You," Kim responds. With almost 150 current cases and some twenty recent applicants out gathering the verification documents needed to gain access to the welfare rolls, it isn't surprising that Sharlene doesn't know Kim.

It won't be easy to meet Kim's request for emergency housing at 3:30 on a Friday afternoon. Clients such as Kim are typically sent to the homeless unit in a DTA office across town for placement, but few shelters will have beds available this late in the afternoon. Getting to the other office before 5 p.m. on public transportation will be an obstacle in itself. But Sharlene knows that she is required to do something, particularly since Kim reports that she fears for her safety.

Sharlene's supervisor, Ida Lubelle, agrees, but wonders whether finding a shelter is the solution. "Wait," Ida says before Sharlene leaves the impromptu consultation we left Kim to attend. "What about a restraining order? If she's on the lease and he's not, she can call the police and kick him out. Why hasn't she tried that? Somethin' ain't right. Are you sure it's not a boyfriend?"

Sharlene returns to Kim with the restraining order suggestion. Kim is reluctant to involve the police—what would happen to her brother? "Besides, when my mother gets out, she's going to let him back in the house, and then he's going to be mad."

When Kim's mother was admitted to the hospital, an assigned social worker contacted the Department of Social Services (DSS) to report elder abuse. DSS instructed Kim that she and her son could not continue to stay in the same home because her brother was a hazard to both of them. "I'm in danger of losing my child because of him," Kim laments.

"Okay, come with me," Sharlene commands. She escorts Kim to the enclosed cubicle of one of the agency's domestic violence (DV) specialists, introducing them and closing the door behind her as she turns to leave. "So you're done with that client?" I ask. "Yeah, probably," Sharlene responds. "The domestic violence people will take care of it now." We return to Sharlene's cubicle for more paperwork.

About fifteen minutes later, the DV worker wanders into Sharlene's cubicle with Kim and her son in tow. Sharlene has already moved on.

During her brief meeting with Kim, Sharlene's telephone voicemail maxed out and a client she had seen earlier faxed in her GED program attendance record to prove that she is meeting the requirements for the state's version of TANF—the Transitional Aid to Families with Dependent Children (TAFDC) program. She now waits for Sharlene to lift the department's sanction against her and reinstate her cash benefits. Ida has left a note that Sharlene's client Tracy called, leaving messages in both Ida's and Sharlene's voicemail boxes. The welfare office, Tracy reports, has miscalculated her food stamp benefits and she has instructed Sharlene to "Please fix this." "I hate when they do that—'Fix this'— ordering me around," Sharlene comments with irritation. Ida and Sharlene were working through the calculations to find the reputed discrepancy when Kim, her son, and the domestic violence worker entered.

"There are no shelters available in the city," the DV worker announces to Sharlene, stepping away and leaving Kim in the cubicle with no apparent resolution. Kim, with Sharlene and Ida noticeably occupied, offers to wait somewhere else. "No, you're fine," Sharlene comments. Kim takes a seat, trying to remove the baby's snowsuit while he teeters on her lap. The DV worker returns in fifteen minutes and suggests that Kim wait in the empty cubicle across from Sharlene.

As Kim relocates, tears begin streaming down her face, making her Sharlene's third client to cry that day, overwhelmed by nothing in particular and everything at once. It happens at that critical moment when clients become aware of the gap between their needs and what the welfare office can offer. The DV worker leaves for a few minutes and then returns to Kim's makeshift waiting room with pen and paper, interrupting this show of emotion to ask Kim about other places she might stay. Jotting down a few notes, she proposes that Kim and her son move back to the office's front waiting room until they resolve the matter. It is the last time that Kim will see the DV worker. She still has nowhere to go.

Another fifteen minutes pass and Ida wanders back into Sharlene's cubicle after checking on her other supervisees, asking after Kim. Sharlene shrugs and suggests that Ida check with the DV worker. Ida returns five minutes later, visibly aggravated, and announces that the DV worker has left for the day. "What did she tell the client?" Ida demands to no one in particular.

Sharlene and Ida retrieve Kim from the waiting room and escort her once again to Sharlene's cubicle. As they move Kim from place to place within the office, they replicate in eerie miniature her experience in the broader social services system as she is shuffled from agency to agency, bureaucrat to bureaucrat. Ida asks Kim a series of questions, trying to understand what the DV worker told her.

"Did she fill out any paperwork with you?" Ida asks.

"No, she just took notes," Kim responds.

"Did she tell you about available shelters? Did she call around?" Ida asks.

"Yes, and she told me that only Greenfield was available, the one I called before. But it's too far. I need to be able to see my mother," Kim explains.

"And what else did she say?" Ida asks.

"That was it," Kim shrugs.

"Is your name on the lease of where you live with your mother?"

Kim nods in the affirmative. "Okay, thank you," Ida says, turning and heading to the office of the assistant director (AD). Evidently, the DV worker wasn't supposed to leave without resolving the matter. Perhaps, by recommending the Greenfield shelter, she thought she had.

In the AD's office, Ida airs her frustration with the DV worker and then moves on to Kim's dilemma: "At 4:30, the chances of her getting emergency housing are slim. Especially because her name is on the lease, a homeless shelter will likely not accept her because technically she has a place to stay. If she calls the police, the police will put her in a hotel that she won't want to stay in. It'll be terrible."

Another twenty minutes pass as the AD places a call to the DSS worker assigned to Kim's mother's case. Kim waits silently in Sharlene's cubicle as her son grows increasingly restless. After Sharlene entertains the boy with an assortment of funny voices and completes some last-minute paperwork—approving a slot in a job search program for a client who has agreed to fulfill a twenty-hour per week attendance requirement in exchange for an extension of her twenty-four-month time clock for cash benefits—she clears her desk and positions her purse and coat for departure. Kim sits staring at nothing in particular, looking dejected and fatigued. "Now we're just in waiting mode," Sharlene reassures her. They sit in silence as Kim's eleven-month-old baby enjoys juice and Cheerios produced from his mother's baby bag, unaware of and unfazed by his family's crisis.

At 4:51 Ida returns to Sharlene's cubicle. "Kim, do you have any relatives? Because I know that we can't place you today."

After thinking for a few moments, Kim volunteers that she has an aunt in Norton with whom she could possibly stay.

"Is your brother on medication?" Ida asks, abruptly shifting gears.

"No, but he should be. He sells drugs," Kim answers.

"When did he last start acting up?" Ida inquires.

"He's always been like this, but he hasn't done anything since January. So most likely I can get in a shelter?" Kim presses.

"We're trying, dear. You being on the lease is an issue we're looking into. We have some calls out. But, regardless, there should be a restraining order. In case you see him out, you need some protection. What does your mother say about all this? She must be beside herself."

"She's upset, but my mother will let him back in the house. No matter what he does. And he's been to jail," Kim offers, subtly reasserting her reluctance to involve law enforcement.

"How long was he in jail?"

"Ten months. He got out in September."

"How old is he? Is there a probation officer or someone who can help you with him? I know he's your brother, but he can't wreak havoc like this. He needs some counseling or something."

The women continue to talk as Ida tries to convince Kim that she and her mother need more support to address the situation. Kim appears to take in Ida's advice about what should be done—a restraining order, a call to his probation officer, perhaps a therapist who might be able to medicate him—but has yet to agree, seemingly pondering the implications of each intervention for her family. Ida gives a sympathetic and motherly nod, continuing to process potential solutions in her mind. Satisfied that she has offered all that she can, she saunters back to the AD's office, returning us to the waiting game. Ida emerges at 5:10. "We're going to have you go to your cousin in Norton over the weekend. But come back on Monday and we will try to place you somewhere. And think about what I told you."

Kim rises and gathers her son in her arms, her energy low and her expression not changing. She mumbles her thanks to Sharlene and Ida and leaves to wait for the bus in the dark February winter, an hour-long trip to Norton ahead of her.

––––––

It's been said that one of the most profound human needs, what we often crave after food, water, and shelter, is to be heard. In moments of quiet desperation and personal pleas for support, what each of us desires is to have someone listen to our hopes, our needs, and our frustrations and perhaps even to respond in a way that improves the quality of our lives. This book speaks to how that need to be "heard" permeates a particular government institution and creates a unique set of opportunities and challenges for those who implement its policies and for those who try to utilize its resources.

On that wintry Friday afternoon, the women charged with helping Kim, a young mother anxious to find safety for herself and her child, are faced with a set of implicit questions and choices. A client approaching the welfare office reporting that she is homeless due to some traumatic event is not unusual for any of these bureaucrats.[1] But their responses are blends of formalized procedures and the "real world" improvisations that must be invented when the client shows up too late on a Friday to be sent to the agency's homeless unit, the domestic violence worker leaves earlier than her colleagues expect, and the client resists the initial prescriptions of the bureaucrats who suggest that she get a restraining order and go to a shelter far away from her crippled (but valued) support system. Sharlene's interpretation of the bureaucratic demands of the job dictate that her involvement in Kim's situation be precisely defined, emotionally contained, and ultimately delegated to specialized co-workers. Ida, on the other hand, performs a series of steps until it becomes clear that the bureaucracy has no more to offer Kim except to suggest that she stay with extended family and return on Monday when the bureaucratic apparatus is prepared to churn for another week to help her find housing. Ida even allows the encounter to wander into territory in which she is troubleshooting around the root of the housing crisis, the turmoil within Kim's family. For a few moments, she takes on the role of adviser and confidante, perhaps not fully grasping Kim's apprehension but clearly trying to engage in a broader conversation about what Kim might do.

In this book I seek to uncover the intricacies that lie beneath the surface of encounters like these by exploring how street-level bureaucrats create professional identities to help them "hear" clients and do their jobs. How do they produce presentations of their prescribed occupational roles? How do these reflect their individual interpretations of the responsibilities they feel and the goals they believe are worth pursuing within the strict parameters of service delivery and the expectations placed on them by clients and other agency actors? As we come to know Sharlene, Ida, and their co-workers over the next several chapters, we will see that how these bureaucrats understand themselves as professionals, and who they are and are *not* willing to be for the sake of the agency, its clients, and the surrounding community is paramount. It represents how they position the work that they do within the lives that they lead. It forms the scaffolding around which employee discretion, the central idea in Michael Lipsky's classic *Street-Level Bureaucracy* and its descendants, is built. The self-definitions of organizational actors are expressed strategically and reverberate deeply, and they speak to the very essence of an organization. Bureaucrats' professional identities will be shown to make crucial differences in terms of both how client needs are identified and addressed and the tools and tactics that organizational actors deploy to pursue certain goals. As each employee makes choices that define the expanse and depth of the bureaucracy's reach as she interacts with families in crisis, she exemplifies how individual actors shape, and are shaped by, the institutions in which they work. Bureaucracies, therefore, are powerful entities in the lives of not only the clients who receive services but also of the individuals who staff them.

The arguments offered in this book encourage us to read bureaucrats as *socially situated* actors who bring personal conceptions of their occupational roles, as well as investments based on their social group memberships, into policy organizations. They use those experiences and perceptions as filters in part to answer questions about the future of their profession and how they should adapt in times of policy and institutional change. By locating bureaucrats within particular social, political, community, and economic contexts, we gain an even better grasp of how they define and do their jobs, accounting for dynamics that previously remained hidden in our institutional analyses or that were generically categorized as "worker discretion." A question such as "Who am I as a professional?" should no longer be considered overly cerebral; it speaks to the ability of an individual to articulate an understanding of the organization's purpose and her role within it, to execute policy and procedures on the basis of that understanding, and to withstand internal and external critiques to her approach (Albert, Ashforth, and Dutton 2000; Whetten and Godfrey 1998).[2] In the aggregate, the *professional* identities of bureaucrats can contribute to, or diminish, the constitution of an *organizational* identity designed to provide the overarching framework of the institutional enterprise. Identity dynamics can fuel perceptions of difference as well as differences in perception within institutions, igniting varying behavioral choices among actors that can bolster or delay how institutions execute organizational changes and stabilize conflict (Gioia et al. 1994; Gioia and Thomas 1996). The inherent battles over identity in organizations exist long after the cosmetic changes involved in organizational transition have taken place and frequently are still being waged as institutional observers and stakeholders have declared the success or failure of a prescribed change.

Identities can be described as self-perceptions that are informed and defined by individuals' associations and memberships within various social groups (Tajfel 1982). Identity formations emerge out of individuals' attempts to classify themselves and others, to articulate a shared sense of group distinctiveness and prestige, and to highlight out-group salience (Ashforth and Mael 1989; Tajfel and Turner 1985). Professional identities represent relatively stable and enduring constellations of attributes, beliefs, values, motives, preferences, and experiences that individuals use to define themselves in an occupational role (Schein 1978; Ibarra 1999). They mark the relationship between individuals and their institutional environments. Professional identities are assumed to develop over time and to be somewhat pliant as varied experiences and critical feedback are incorporated: "The beauty of identity and identification concepts is that they provide a way of accounting for the agency of human action within an organizational framework" (Albert, Ashforth, and Dutton 2000, 14). If the *job designs* or *professional roles* of welfare caseworkers are dictated by organizational leaders, *professional identities,* as interpretations of these roles, are developed by street-level bureaucrats themselves. These individuals read institutional cues that address their purpose and objectives and then infuse their own meanings, goals, and commitments to create day-to-day capacities for action. Along with illuminating the broader institutional context in which street-level bureaucrats such as Sharlene and Ida operate, in this chapter I make a case for using identity frameworks to explore the massive changes under way in human service institutions as a result of significant policy changes such as the 1996 welfare reform.

Rethinking the Bureaucratic Imperative in the Era of PRWORA

Despite the recognition that local welfare offices are crucial if imperfect buffers against even harsher economic and personal circumstances for millions like Kim, these bureaucracies are perhaps best known by their tarnished reputations. Posited for decades by many researchers, policymakers, and the general public as passive enablers at best and active contributors at worst to poor families' economic deprivation, political disempowerment, social isolation, and even nonnormative behavior, these agencies are thought to represent the institutional manifestations of what many believe is wrong with our larger system of organized provision of educational, medical, and financial assistance to the needy (Mead 1992; Bane and Ellwood 1994; Ellwood 1988). Conventional wisdom hardened over the years around the idea that welfare offices were particularly "sticky," slow and resistant to change despite policy shifts that tried to introduce a work-focused system through the WIN (Work Incentive) program, the JOBS (Job Opportunities and Basic Skills) training initiative that was part of the Family Support Act of 1988, and the state welfare experiments that federal waivers encouraged in the 1990s (Meyers, Glaser, and MacDonald 1994; Holcomb et al. 1998; Rogers-Dillon 2004). Kane and Bane's (1994) widely cited analysis of pre-PRWORA welfare offices suggested that these agencies emphasized benefit-eligibility determination and rule-compliance enforcement above all else and in fact discouraged employment among low-income mothers through agency practices that saw it as adding tiresome complexity to the paperwork necessary for eligibility determination.

These perspectives were likely buoyed by the cultural significance that welfare offices have assumed over the years as not only scholarly research but also journalistic and even fictional accounts described what was happening within these poor-support agencies. Competing values and goals—the autonomy of the individual versus the desire for community protections, the virtues of work versus the primacy of the family—constitute these institutions, producing at times contradictory narratives of their inner workings and social relevance (Ellwood 1988; Hays 2003). In some analyses, such as in Michael Harrington's harrowing rendering of the lives of poor Americans in his 1962 book *The Other America*, welfare offices and their emissaries are depicted as economic lifelines:

The aging woman in New York called her social worker on the telephone. She was in tears. Her check had not come from welfare on the expected day, and she was terrified that she had been cut off, that now she would literally face starvation. Her life, like those of many in her situation, was suspended by a thread from the city's welfare system. The social worker was her symbol of hope. (109)

Of course, the intrusive, patronizing welfare office—that of the midnight raids of previous decades in search of evidence of a "man in the house" and the present-day questions about absent fathers for child support enforcement—is also very much a part of our picture of what goes on within these institutions. Who could forget the scenes from the 1974 movie *Claudine* in which Claudine, Diahann Carroll's Harlem single mother, and her children scramble to hide the evidence of her under-the-table job as a maid, their battered television, and her budding romance with the garbage man, Roop, played by James Earl Jones? If discovered, these would all be perceived as "luxuries" that called Claudine's financial need into question. As Claudine's white caseworker enters the domestic space of nervous black faces for a home visit, a whole history of supervision and punishment of poor black single mothers hovers over the encounter. Claudine and Roop's decision to continue their relationship unearths a backlash from the welfare department—Claudine is humiliated, her family almost torn asunder, and her relationship nearly destroyed by the power of the bureaucracy.

In other portrayals, welfare offices are represented in a very different light, taking on a less vital role in the everyday consciousness and material lives of the poor. Jason DeParle's widely read analysis of the political and practical journey of 1996 welfare reform and its impact on the lives of three Wisconsin mothers illustrates this view. When asked about their impressions of welfare reform when it was first introduced, DeParle was taken aback by the women's ambivalence. Welfare, and the agencies that administered it, were hardly at the forefront of the women's concerns:

Even accounting for some false bravado, it is hard to square such studied indifference with the tenets of the national debate. From a distance, the threesome seemed the very definition of dependency. Together they had been on welfare for twenty-seven years; they had moved to Milwaukee just to get the benefits they now stood to lose. They appeared to embody the one assumption that the partisans on both sides shared—that the program was central to recipients' lives—which made conservatives so keen to restrict it and liberals so afraid of its loss. But as Angie and Jewell saw the world, if the money was there, they were happy to take it; if not, they would make other plans. With welfare or without it, Angie said, "you just learn how to survive." (2004, 156)

How do we reconcile these vastly different conceptions, and how should we be thinking about these institutions in the post-AFDC era? Although describing distinct decades in welfare service delivery and varied configurations of federal and state policy, all of the scenarios presented above seem at once perdurable and current. They also appear to capture the inner workings of a variety of public bureaucracies, not just welfare offices. All suggest the difficulties that low-income individuals experience as they struggle to be "heard" in environments that seem to encourage anything but. Taken with perhaps their most common indictment—that of being mired in a "red tape" orientation—the use of the term "bureaucrat" is perceived by many as an epithet, hinting at incompetence, mediocrity, and impersonal service. As such, the phrase "government agency" often conjures up images of an inefficient, unwieldy, highly hierarchical administrative system bereft of innovation, change, and flexibility.

Still, social constructionist scholars would challenge any temptation to reduce encounters within welfare offices and similar institutions to being simply about conflicts over the distribution of a set of financial resources. These are locales of political struggle, "fraught with ideological conflict," that reinforce societal norms and symbolic statuses (Haney 2002b, 14; Soss 2000). As locales where "the poor make their most pressing claims, negotiate the policy decisions that affect them most directly, and come face to face with the state's capacity to punish or protect," Joe Soss (2000, 1) argues that welfare offices teach client "claimants" valuable lessons about politics in ways that shape their broader political orientations and perceptions of government as a whole. This is just one example of the body of work that asserts that by communicating and regulating the definitions and obligations of citizenship through the distribution of state resources, of womanhood by making their access to state resources dependent on their status as mothers and now workers under neoliberalism, and of race by differentially providing access to public resources, welfare offices engage in highly symbolic and elaborate work. This is perhaps best summarized by sociologist Lynne Haney's contention that these institutions and the welfare regimes under which they operate "set social boundaries; they determine which groups fall inside the redistributive sphere; and they structure who gets which resources and on what terms" (2002b, 12).[3]

Welfare offices therefore cannot be neatly classified as economic lifelines, "take-it-or-leave it" government resources, the "Big Brother (and Sister)" of America's poor, or as oppressively complex and time-consuming bureaucratic juggernauts. They can be all of these, and their relationships with the people they serve often weather different tones and intentions at various points in time. These entities continue to provide necessary services and financial resources to millions of families—and they insert themselves into their work and family lives in sometimes protective, frequently highly invasive ways. They are only one of several sources of economic survival for low-income families—existing alongside family, friends, intimate partners, workplaces, nonprofit community agencies—and they exert inordinate amounts of power over the time, decisions, and resources of poor mothers (Edin and Lein 1997; Domínguez and Watkins 2003). They enforce certain social expectations on poor women and subject them to moral scrutiny in ways distinct from what is often faced by their middle- and upper-class counterparts—*and* they also have ways of being markedly absent and detached during crucial moments in their clients' lives. In short, these institutions, and the bureaucrats who staff them, are at once symbolic and instrumental, peripheral and central, as they impart lessons about what the poor can expect from government.

Perhaps the greatest and most underexplored significance of these agencies is the role they play in moments like the one described between Kim and the Staunton office staff. We typically associate welfare offices with their most popular program—Temporary Assistance for Needy Families, formerly Aid to Families with Dependent Children — and we assess the success and ongoing relevance of these agencies through the effectiveness of this program. But what Kim's story highlights is the way in which individuals are approaching these institutions to address needs far outside of the cash benefits, child care vouchers, and job search help that have become the story of welfare reform. Well beyond the world of time limits, work requirements, and sanctions, Kim approaches the welfare office because, as she see it, *there is no place else to go.* When family is tapped out, friends may later reveal vulnerabilities, and the money is dry, welfare offices exist as *catch-all bureaucracies,* government agencies called upon to be societal arms of "help," broadly defined.[4] In light of ongoing debates about the conditions and causes of poverty, these institutions remain central to our understanding of how those most economically, socially, and politically disadvantaged navigate macro-level societal transformations as well as micro-level conditions and struggles. How bureaucrats bring their own interpretations and investments to encounters with these families therefore is critical: as public servants they continue to represent our collective capacity to respond to some of our deepest societal challenges, but now do so under a climate of increasing debate about their relevance, missions, and functions as professionals.

The Catch-All Bureaucracy

What do I mean by "catch-all bureaucracies," and why should they be considered a unique subset within the population of government agencies where goods and services are distributed directly to the public? Michael Lipsky (1980) famously defined *street-level bureaucracies* as institutions where government workers interact directly with citizens and exercise substantial discretion in their jobs. However, it would be a mistake to lump all street-level bureaucracies together—harboring the inaccurate assumption that they contain similar levels and kinds of social meaning and subsequently face similar organizational dilemmas. What separates catch-all bureaucracies from other street-level bureaucracies—such as Departments of Motor Vehicles, city halls, or public services in the most affluent communities—is how the micro-level manifestations of personal struggles with economic deprivation are readily apparent within their borders. As clients wrestle with poverty's causes and consequences, they in turn bring a myriad of concerns and situations into these institutions, placing unique demands on the employees who work there.

Although catch-all bureaucracies may set out to implement a specific set of policies and distribute a finite set of resources, clients often challenge these institutions to address more complex problems by bringing a range of issues to their doorsteps. With the advent of welfare reform and similar policy shifts, the collective insistence of the public and policy that impoverished mothers juggle care work and low-wage employment introduces an additional set of complications for clients as they navigate those demands in their respective communities. For a disproportionate share of the clientele, racial stratification's consistent imprint on economic, housing, and educational opportunity structures further compounds and adds complexity to their challenges (Wilson 1987; Massey and Denton 1998). Human service institutions whose clients are exposed to a range of individual-, family-, and community-level issues that are directly or indirectly tied to being at the bottom of the societal ladder are therefore transformed into catch-all bureaucracies. They become the "first responders" in that they often offer a bare minimum of services for families in immediate crisis and the "last resorts," leveraged when no other options remain. Because the challenges are so great, and the alternative resources so few, catch-all bureaucracies take on unique roles in the lives of disadvantaged families, even if their circumscribed organizational missions and policy mandates are simultaneously trying to limit clients' reliance on them and increase the demands made on these individuals.

As noted in the introduction, I do not wish to imply that all crises, particularly those that fall outside the prescribed ambit of social welfare agencies in the current PRWORA era, are addressed and brought to graceful conclusions in catch-all bureaucracies. My use of the term of "catch-all" delineates the range of issues and concerns that *clients* bring to the doorsteps of these agencies rather than the range or quality of the *services* that these agencies offer to clients. Human service organizations that routinely offer limited or low-quality services to impoverished families are still catch-all bureaucracies if clients manage to introduce their challenges into the organizational milieu in ways that shape service delivery. Institutions that target marginalized groups for service delivery (welfare offices, housing authorities) are examples of catch-all bureaucracies as are agencies in which external dynamics disproportionately send disenfranchised groups through their doors such as child welfare agencies, juvenile detention centers, and public health clinics. In sum, if Lipsky's notion of "street-level" is meant to signify both the location of the bureaucrat-client encounter and the power of the frontline worker to shape policy, "catch-all" is meant to signify the range of issues that clients bring to the process. Both are critical descriptors as we try to understand the parameters and scope of service delivery within particular institutions.

There is an irony here. Under the current "work first" era of welfare policy, the missions of catch-all bureaucracies are supposed to be more tightly focused than ever. With the end of welfare as a cash entitlement program for low-income families, increasing privatization of social services, and diminishing support for economic redistribution policies, many see the whole point of welfare reform as diminishing rather than expanding families' reliance upon these institutions (Mink 2001; Piven 2001). Clients such as Kim are approaching welfare offices at a time when the social safety net offers few guarantees. Yet under the Personal Responsibility and Work Opportunity Reconciliation Act, bureaucrats are introduced to a wider swatch of client concerns precisely *because* so many of the problems facing low-income families are no longer formally addressed by the social welfare system. Further, TANF, the policy's flagship program, provides time-limited cash assistance and in-kind resources that are directly tied to work. This means that, more so than under previous regimes, bureaucrats are expected to acquaint themselves with their clients' struggles outside of the office in order to put together the right package of resources to get them back into the labor market. The onus therefore, is increasingly on caseworkers to determine whether and how to engage with clients whose lives are laid bare under the backdrop of ticking time clocks and strict work requirements.

Identity in the Study of Human Service Organizations

My understanding of the professional practices of welfare caseworkers is informed not only by welfare implementation scholarship but also by the body of work on social processes within an array of human service organizations. Medical providers (Kleinman 1996), residential treatment centers (Gubrium and Buckholdt 1979), prisons (Thomas 1984), juvenile court systems (Jacobs 1990), educational institutions (Maynard-Moody and Musheno 2003; Horowitz 1995), and other sites face many of the same issues negotiating the relationship between professional identities and institutional mandates, and a great deal of rich, mostly qualitative accounts suggest that bureaucrats are quite effective in creatively articulating and operationalizing their professional roles.[5] These researchers part ways with structuralists who see organizational actors as interchangeable entities subject to heavy institutional constraints that severely restrict their behavior. Discretion in that view, to the degree that it exists, is thought to be generated in an institutional vacuum, developed out of a gap between formal mandates and organizational uncertainties and restricted to the occasional deviation from institutionalized norms. Organizational theorist Richard Hall offers this perspective: "When a new member enters the organization, he is confronted with a social structure . . . and a set of expectations for . . . behavior. It does not matter who the particular individual is; the organization has established a system of norms and expectations to be followed regardless of who its personnel happen to be" (1977, 26).

I suggest in this work that professional and social identities form a mutually constitutive relationship with discretionary practices, and together they generate a great deal of flexibility in the performance of professional roles within bureaucratic milieus. Discretion emerges in part from what bureaucrats "bring into" the organization and add to the institutional mix. This interacts with client dilemmas and organizational mandates, encouraging bureaucrats to assess and reassess their boundaries, goals, motives, and investments to actively decide just what function they will serve with a particular client in a particular moment. As bureaucratic discretion represents what political scientist Robert Lineberry calls a "continuation of policy-making by other means" (1977, 71), this interchange between professional identity and discretionary choices proves to be quite powerful in the determination of who gets what level of access to which services, information, and treatment within bureaucracies. As Mark Jacobs's work on probation officers in the juvenile court system illustrates, creative and discretionary maneuvers are absolutely critical in public agencies when bureaucrats decide to "immerse themselves fervently in the drama of their clients' lives, exercising remarkable personal resourcefulness to counteract the evasive practices of others" (1990, 2). Running up against bureaucratic constraints and contradictions as well as deliberate dodging and absolutions of responsibility among related agencies, street-level bureaucrats adopt informal means to fulfill formal duties. When incorporated into what Sherryl Kleinman (1996) calls a cherished "moral identity," professional identities can support individuals' investments in "doing right" through their work even if it means adopting contradictory interpretations of what this means or even ignoring embedded institutional inequalities in favor of frames that support a certain professional self-conception.

What became apparent during my fieldwork was that identity—how bureaucrats articulate who they are as professionals, members of racial groups, and community residents—continually serves as a lodestar for organizational actors in the midst of institutional transformations, helping them decide what they will and will not do as things constantly change and resettle around them. This is particularly important in catch-all bureaucracies, which are often "explicitly in the business of structuring and reconfiguring [the] personal identit[ies]" of their clients, which are often deemed troubled by policymakers, the public, and bureaucrats themselves (Gubrium and Holstein 2001, 2; Loeske 2007). As identities are both functional and representational, how bureaucrats navigate these dynamics, attempt to shape conceptions of their work, and offer behaviors consistent (or not) with their perceptions inform how policy is systematically reworked on the ground. Identity, therefore, has the potential to function as a mechanism of institutional and programmatic stickiness or change in policy organizations. In the offices in this analysis, identity will be shown to be crucial to the operation of casework relationships and a generator of organizational variation. As such, the construction and performance of professional identities are not simply symbolic exercises; they have consequences for clients in terms of what they receive from service organizations and when and how services are rendered.

Examining Identity in the Everyday: Methods in the Study of Human Service Organizations

Organizational ethnography is an ideal way to explore the intersection of professional and social (e.g., racial, gender, class) identities and to capture the various forces bearing down on individuals as they attempt to balance the expectations of multiple constituencies while carving out their own views about how their occupational lives should look. Moreover, as we place these processes within the context of the new welfare system, Paul Hirsch and Michael Lounsbury (1997) tell us that "the details of micro-level action are needed to explain how macro-level institutions change" (412). The aggregate weight of these struggles over the kind of professionals that frontline workers should become as a result of the restructuring of the welfare system speak to both the successes of local offices' implementation of this current poor-support regime as well as to the intractable problems that remain. Borrowing from famed organizational ethnographer John Van Maanen (1979), my aim was "to come to grips with the essential ethnographic question of what it is *to be* rather than *to see* member[s] of [this] organization" (539).[6]

Thirty-three employees of the Staunton office of the Massachusetts Department of Transitional Assistance and thirty employees from the Fishertown office form the respondent pool from which study data were drawn. Because many of the dynamics described in this study—including the articulation and advancement of interests not directly related to welfare policy—are not advertised functions of these rationalized bureaucracies, I had to find ways to tap into these often difficult-to-observe events. One-on-one interviews in which service providers had opportunities to describe and reflect upon their actions helped to tell a story about how they understood their work.[7] Over a nine-month period between 2000 and 2001, I interviewed sixteen caseworkers, six supervisors, three office administrators, and two special operations (SO) staff members in the Staunton office and nineteen caseworkers, six supervisors, two administrators, and two SO staff members in the Fishertown office.[8] As these institutions are dynamic, made up of ever-changing policies as well as always-unfolding politics, intentionalities, and interests among actors, I returned to the Staunton and Fishertown offices in 2006 and 2007, respectively, to complete a second round of fieldwork.[9] After spending hundreds of hours talking with and observing frontline office staff, I interviewed eight key administrators in the DTA's central office in Boston in 2007 in order to apprehend the "big picture" issues surrounding my analysis as well as to learn more about the ongoing process of trial and error in which administrators were engaged as they guided the operationalization of state and federal policies.[10]

Data presented in this book are also derived from direct observations of employees' activities. This allowed me to explore not only what these individuals said about their work but also what they did. I sat for hours with caseworkers as they did their jobs, observing client-caseworker meetings where services were delivered and other daily work activities such as completing paperwork, making phone calls, and meeting with supervisors.[11] I also spoke with caseworkers before and after their client meetings about what I was going to see or had seen, and I informally chatted with clients during their meetings with caseworkers if the situation was appropriate. At other times, I would sit in the office waiting rooms or behind the check-in desks with the clerks, asking questions and observing the flow of the office. Finally, I sat in on staff meetings and engaged in lunchroom and hallway "water cooler" chats with staff members about their day and the latest events in the office.

Lastly, I conducted archival research, analyzing service delivery manuals and documents, client case documents, institutional literature on welfare reform, and worker performance evaluation documents. Here my aim was to examine how the documents produced by the agency portrayed welfare reform as a policy shift and how they affirmed certain models of professional identities for workers and deemphasized others. In an agency predicated on "paper," I was particularly interested in what documents helped to drive the everyday events of the organization—serving as frequent topics of discussion among institutional staff and offering directives for "the way things should be done." I was curious as to whether and how workers rebuffed those formal sentiments and maneuvered the welfare system's documentation apparatus to advance certain goals, to protect themselves against charges of ineffectiveness, and ultimately to operationalize their professional identities.

As an urban sociologist, I found that Staunton was an easy choice as a research site. The office is the result of the merger of several welfare offices in one of the state's most populous cities. It funnels a geographically and racially diverse staff and client base into an urban location to administer TAFDC. In March 2001, 44.4 percent of the office's caseload family heads were black, 35.0 percent Hispanic, 15.9 percent white, and 4.3 percent Asian. At that time, 48 percent (fifteen) of the office's TANF caseworkers, application screeners, and Employment Services Program (ESP) workers were white, 26 percent (eight), black, 19 percent (six) Hispanic, and 6 percent (two) Asian, and the office staff grew even more diverse by the time I conducted the second round of fieldwork five years later.[12] Staunton has six white and two African American supervisors of work units that administer the TAFDC program. This office is located on one of the city's busier thoroughfares, sandwiched between office buildings and warehouses filled to capacity. It serves a clientele that comes from a variety of communities in the area, who can access the office via a sprawling public transportation system. In 2000–2001, as the city enjoyed record low unemployment, employers were eager to place many welfare recipients in burgeoning service-sector jobs in the area. The Staunton office's location in a thriving metropolitan area offers its clients employment opportunities, social services, and other urban conveniences that, while by no means exhaustive, are in much shorter supply in Fishertown. Yet the office's clients also face challenges as a result of the surrounding city as rents and other cost-of-living indicators make it among the most expensive places to live in the state.

For my second site, I considered selecting an office located in a rural part of the state for comparison purposes, but I was ultimately drawn to Fishertown because of its liminality. Fishertown is a not a small rural town, with a quaint little welfare office that services locals or draws clients from nearby communities. Nor is it in a booming metropolis on the order of the Staunton office. Fishertown, as it soon became clear, is wrestling with its middleness. Betwixt and between insularity and growth, the city struggles to maintain its parochial feel while striving to develop a small but powerful fraction of the kind of economic clout that the state's largest cities wield. It is located in a high-unemployment region of the state, full of shuttered factories. Fishertown enjoys a relatively low cost of living compared with Staunton; visitors looking to stay at the poshest hotel in town are directed to the mid-priced chain hotel, located in a nearby city. Fishertown had long been a destination town for European and Cambodian immigrants, but its recent transformations have been created by an influx of migrants from more urban parts of the state, introducing a range of new issues into the Fishertown community that will be explored in later chapters. The demographic and economic compositions of both Staunton and Fishertown therefore make them compelling research sites, allowing me the opportunity to tell a story about policy implementation in two very different local contexts.

The two offices share important similarities by virtue of being in the same state and governed by the same state laws and regulations. Both the Staunton and Fishertown offices are charged with implementing the state's welfare policy on the ground, and their employees are subject to the same systems of performance monitoring, evaluation, and institutional rewards and penalties. Massachusetts continually consolidated offices as rolls went down, ensuring that most caseworkers across the state have similar caseload sizes and that most offices employ similar numbers of staff. Both the Fishertown and Staunton offices have a staff made up of a director, three assistant directors, and approximately five to eight work units that administer TAFDC (each composed of three to five caseworkers and one supervisor).[13] Although they were not the focus of the study, both offices have separate work units staffed with government workers that solely administer food stamps or the Emergency Aid to the Elderly, Disabled, and Children (EAEDC) program.[14] The mission of TAFDC workers is to aid clients in acquiring resources for their families both in the short term and in anticipation of the time when they no longer rely on the welfare system. Because of these similarities, the first few chapters of this book will focus on intraoffice variation within the Staunton and Fishertown sites, while later chapters will more directly compare and contrast these institutions based on their different environmental contexts.

I should note that my focus is on the processes that drive these institutions and produce variation in service delivery rather than on how the actions taken by street-level bureaucrats directly influence client outcomes. In this regard, I follow the lead of many implementation scholars who focus on what Norma Riccucci (2005, 2) calls "organizational outputs," the delivery of welfare benefits and services to clients. There are several reasons for this emphasis on the actual work of the organization rather than on client outcomes. First, multiple factors potentially shape whether a client finds and keeps a job, uses up her time-limited allotment of benefits, avoids sanctions, or accomplishes any of the other goals of welfare reform. Clients interact with multiple organizations in addition to the welfare office—such as training programs, employers, and child-care centers—in order to pursue certain outcomes, so it would be difficult to discern just which institutional levers lead to which particular results. In addition to these organizational mediators, clients' individual, familial, and community circumstances, resources, and barriers also play critical roles in determining whether a client fulfills a certain policy goal. A truly rigorous analysis of the impact of organizational dynamics in welfare offices on client outcomes will likely need to involve an experimental study design or a large-scale survey of caseworkers and clients that tracks both of these groups over time.

I should also point out that the perspectives highlighted in this book are drawn from employee rather than client perspectives on the internal workings of welfare offices (Van Maanen 1979). Countless books and articles take on the latter responsibility and very deftly present the experiences of welfare "leavers," "stayers," and those in between as they acquire resources, protect themselves from extensive state regulation and stigmatization, struggle with their disadvantaged institutional position, and grapple with the imprint that this form of state involvement leaves on their lives outside of the institution (Hays 2003; DeParle 2004; Soss 2000). However, my goal from the outset was to conduct an in-depth analysis of socially situated bureaucrats within catch-all bureaucracies and the processes that drive the particular ways in which they present themselves to clients and implement policies. Many have observed that this "black box" approach is problematically in short supply in current work on organizations (Reskin 2000; Vallas 2003).

Lastly, it is my hope that those reading this book, but perhaps most importantly the respondents who accepted me into their workplaces and their lives, feel as though I got the story "right."[15] They may quibble with my interpretations of certain facts, ideas, or opinions presented to me, but it is my hope that this study's participants indeed feel "heard" and will begin to engage in a process through which they can find ways to make this a constructive and helpful document to improve the work that they do. I take the work undertaken by what I am calling catch-all bureaucracies very seriously—the experiences of Kim and countless others whom I observed still echo in mind. And I believe that it is crucial that we offer scholarship that serves as not only a sociology *of* but also *for* these institutions.[16] Kim and women like her are counting on us to constantly work to make things better in that regard.

The Institutional Terrain of Postreform Welfare Offices: A Deeper Introduction to the Research Sites

Having opened the chapter in the Staunton office, it is fitting that we end it in Fishertown as a way of setting the context in which situated bureaucrats construct and operationalize their professional selves. The Fishertown office of the Massachusetts Department of Transitional Assistance is situated on the first floor of a converted textile mill, a large edifice that once supplied jobs for hundreds of industrial workers. Fishertown's mill-based economy has all but disappeared, leaving several of these large multistory brick buildings abandoned in the middle of a once-thriving manufacturing center. Fishertown has struggled, largely unsuccessfully, to revitalize its economic base. Its unemployment rate has traditionally remained stubbornly higher than the statewide average. The majority of the city's mill space has been converted to offices, small-scale industrial parks, and commercial spaces that house discount shopping centers. Other buildings remain shuttered. The ironic symbolism left behind by the former occupants of the Fishertown DTA office lends itself to a variety of political interpretations. Whether viewed as a bureaucratic "factory" that "pulverizes" its targets in exposing and crushing ways, produces dependents through the repetitive nature of service delivery and the ongoing provision of resources, or transforms individuals into "polished" workers through sustained pressure, this agency now serves as a "people processing" facility (Prottas 1979; Hasenfeld 1972).

The physical space, the structure of service delivery, and the mixture of new and old policies all suggest that there is a new game in town. "Because DTA emphasizes temporary assistance," its mission statement notes, "recipients are encouraged to participate in education, training, and job search activities which promote responsibility and self-sufficiency."[17] From a client's first visit, the office works to present very clear messages about what she can expect from both policies and service delivery. The ambition is to convey that these institutions represent revolutionary new approaches to how they have assisted families than they did in decades past. Even though welfare reform is now over ten years old, the "newness" of the regime is consistently reinforced. They are "about work," not dependency; jobs, not handouts. They feed clients a steady diet of these themes to convey this shift: the importance and expectation of work, parental accountability, and the temporary nature of welfare. The office and its actors seek to "jolt" clients into recognizing this current regime so that they will accept its demands and respond appropriately. This is done not only by the "carrots" and "sticks" embedded in policy but also by the prescripts of service delivery— the rules of engagement that define the boundaries between clients and workers.

A caseworker's preparation for the presentation of a professional self to clients begins before they even interact face-to-face (Goffman 1959). Morning tends to be the busiest time in the office, particularly Monday mornings. In addition to visiting cubicles to catch up on the latest events of their co-workers' lives—the children who will soon be getting married or having children, tales of unusual feats accomplished to arrive to work on time, and other exchanges that mark another day or week on the job—caseworkers busy themselves reviewing client files, looking over their calendars to learn which clients are expected to pay them a visit, and assessing daily memos from the central office that command them toward certain actions: *see these clients whose benefits are scheduled to end, close these cases, follow up on these red flags.* Most caseworkers theorize that morning's faster pace is because clients know that this is when fewer clients will be ahead of them, and many are stopping by the welfare office early to get business out of the way on their way to work or training programs. Other clients are scheduled to appear in the mornings as caseworkers try to reserve their afternoons for paperwork and part-time caseworkers depart for the day between 1 p.m. and 3 p.m. Providing another perspective, Jane Braddock, a Fishertown caseworker for over a decade, ventured that Monday mornings are so busy because clients "have had all weekend to screw their lives up, and now they need us to fix something. I know it sounds bad, but it's true." Lost electronic benefit cards that allow recipients to access their benefits and weekend job loss are common Monday morning problems.

When a client enters the front doors of the office, she must be careful not to be so presumptuous as to step directly to the front desk, even if there is no line ahead of her. She is told, either by a placard or by the front-desk clerk, to pause a few feet from it and wait to be called forward. Being viewed as disrespectful or impatient by a clerk could result in an unpleasant experience, since the front-desk clerk helps to determine how much time a client spends in the waiting room. Orderly rows of padded electric-blue chairs face the front desk, occupied with clients, their partners, friends, and children. Posters line the seafoam green walls surrounding the waiting room. They carry unmistakable messages of 1996 welfare reform: *Looking for work? TANF ending? Time [limit] running out? What will you do when your time limit is up?* The signs advertise job placement centers in the city and training programs that offer to teach participants how to be everything from a certified nurse's assistant to a data processor. Other posters announce that GED programs are available and list phone numbers for further information. Legal Aid makes its presence known through flyers suggesting that if a client feels mistreated by the welfare department, she should call immediately for representation.

But perhaps the most potent display of the message expressing current policy is reflected in a poster with a black-and-white photograph of a wide-eyed child asking, *"Mommy, will we always be on welfare?"* The prescribed answer is plastered across the bottom: *Work: Your Way Up. Give Your Kids a Reason To Be Proud.* Displayed prominently in offices throughout the state, the poster signals to clients the importance of a temporary, rather than permanent, spell on welfare. The moral is reinforced by connecting welfare receipt with disappointment, and work with hope, in a child's eyes. Responsible motherhood, it contends, is about economic self-sufficiency.

A client in the Fishertown office is greeted by one of the two front-desk clerks. The variation in their greeting styles is clear. Steven Moss communicates a professional yet friendly tone, suggesting the colloquial and small-town feel of Fishertown. He often greets clients by name: "Hello, Ms. Miller. What can we do for you today?" Having worked in the office for more than a decade, he knows most of the clients, although the increasing influx of newcomers from nearby cities makes the recognition harder. "It's okay to have a good experience here," Steven explains. "You could be in their shoes tomorrow. Wouldn't you want someone to be nice to you?" Steven is empathetic and sympathetic, gently telling a woman who had recently suffered a house fire that she would not qualify for benefits because she has no children and is not disabled. He immediately suggests that she try the local Red Cross: "Go and see if they can help, and remember, you've got your life. My mother was burned out, that big fire on Syracuse Street. Remember that one? Just like with her, you survived and that's what's important." As the point of entry, Steven tries to convey that the Fishertown welfare office is the friendly neighborhood agency, ready to take on the role of a catch-all bureaucracy.

Margaret Johnson, who began working in the office just a few years after Steven, takes a different tack: professional yet commanding. She inquires "May I help you?" assertively and abruptly as she manages the activities of the waiting room. She rarely refers to clients by name and does not chat with them. To Margaret, it is imperative to communicate to clients that the waiting room is extremely busy and that it would be a mistake to engage in lengthy discussions about their problems. She is quick to point out that, while Steven has been reprimanded by management for his extensive conversations with clients, she manages an extremely efficient waiting room. "I'm not their counselor," she explains. "It's not that we don't care, but there's nothing I can do about it. So why tell me, especially when the phones are ringing off the hook?"

The client can provide several responses to Steven's and Margaret's offers of assistance. If she already has an open case with the welfare department, she will typically ask "to see her worker," meaning her welfare caseworker. For the occasional client who does not remember her worker's name, Steven or Margaret must retrieve the information, an annoyance since it slows down the waiting room management process as they wait for the computer to churn up the information. "How can you not know your worker's name?" Margaret will occasionally snap. The next question from the clerk is almost invariably whether the client has an appointment. Regardless of the answer, the clerk calls the caseworker and tells her or him, or the voicemail, the client's name and "call number." Call numbers are designed to protect the anonymity of clients, yet they symbolically reinforce the sense that clients are simply being processed through a large bureaucracy where their individual concerns and needs are irrelevant. Other offices, like Staunton, summon clients by their last names, sacrificing privacy. At the Fishertown office, the clerk hands the client a pink index card with the matching call number and tells her to "take a seat."[18]

As a catch-all bureaucracy, the office draws a cavalcade of individuals who make their way in front of Steven and Margaret on any given day. Although most are mothers applying for or currently receiving TAFDC, such clients are not the only visitors to the Fishertown DTA office. "Everybody's got an emergency," a part-time clerk would tell me as she tended to the front desk like a goalie at a soccer game. In a span of an hour, countless clients would report for meetings with their caseworkers, a man would wrenchingly announce that he is having a "bad day" after learning from the clerk that he would not qualify for emergency food stamps and thus couldn't see a caseworker, and the clerk would spend much of her time assuring an applicant recently released from prison that he would be seen soon so that a caseworker could assess his eligibility for food stamps and EAEDC to help out until he found work.

I spent hours with Steven and Margaret during my time in the Fishertown office. In many ways, they represented the disparate professional approaches to the human services that embody the central dilemmas in both of the offices that I studied. Steven had a very clear vision of welfare service delivery as a kind of "social work" that hinged upon personal connections and resource brokering. Margaret, on the other hand, was all about efficiency, the technical execution of connecting clients to workers, jettisoning those whom the office would not be able to assist, and engineering an "efficient waiting room." Certainly these had likely been their dispositions before welfare reform, but in this new era their approaches now seemed to have more urgency and consequence. Their butting of heads in many ways reflected the tension that I would witness throughout my fieldwork as caseworkers tried to discern their terms, boundaries, and aims as "new welfare bureaucrats."

As part of this remaking process, the use of physical space is a critical element of the boundary formation taking place within these institutions. Erving Goffman (1959) argued that two kinds of bounded regions shape social interactions and create the divisions between "audiences" and "performers": "front regions where a particular performance is or may be in progress, and back regions where action occurs that is related to the performance but inconsistent with the appearance fostered by the performance" (134). When clients are in the waiting room, or "front-stage," the adjacent client service area in which workers' desks are located serves as a backstage area. Although workers argue that access to the client service area is controlled due to safety concerns, the access restrictions also serve the secondary purpose of preventing clients from witnessing behavior among caseworkers that is not addressed to clients.

For example, a worker preparing to meet with a client with an unusual case that requires an intricate understanding of an obscure, rarely used aspect of policy may confer with a supervisor or co-worker to receive a quick tutorial while the client sits in the waiting room. When she meets with the client, however, she will act as if she is very familiar with the necessary procedure in order to present an air of competence and control. A worker may discuss a client with a co-worker, revealing opinions that she would never share with the client—the sad circumstances of the case, the peculiarity of a child's name, how "together" the mother seems, or how suspicious it is that she can afford to dress so nicely. Workers do not refer to clients by name when they discuss cases, preferring instead to use such generic pronouns as "she," "the daughter," and "the boyfriend." This aspect of workers' shared vocabulary helps to protect clients' privacy, yet seems to depersonalize the cases.

Meanwhile, the front-desk clerk will sometimes falsely tell a waiting client that her worker is with another client, attempting to quell any impatience. Clients repeatedly returning to the front desk to ask about the wait or to ask questions about services that clerks feel ill-equipped to answer are viewed as an annoyance by Margaret and Steven. As Steven explained, "the last thing you want is the natives getting restless, and you have to take the brunt of it because you're right there." In some offices, like Staunton, clerks are supported by the presence of security guards who are ready to quash any conflicts that might erupt or that might suggest a lack of order and attract the attention of the office's management. In this vein, the waiting room serves as the site of a constant struggle for control between clients and the front-desk clerks in the welfare bureaucracy. Front-desk workers manage the pace, noise level, and happenings of the waiting room, setting the terms under which business will be conducted. Clients, by challenging the waiting time and by frequently reasserting their presence before front-desk workers, push to have their time and needs respected by the organization. The power of the front-desk clerk is, however, circumvented by caseworkers, who ultimately decide when a client will leave the waiting room. Although hostile words are rarely exchanged this early in a client's visit, these tensions create a subtly adversarial tone between clients and the welfare office staff.

Behind the locked doors separating the waiting room from the client service area, welfare workers juggle their days as implementers of perhaps the most significant reform to social policy in decades. TAFDC workers, or temporary assistance social workers (TASWs), must organize a workload that, by most accounts, is staggering. In 2000 and 2001 Fishertown workers had, on average, eighty-five to ninety-five open cases. Staunton workers had, on average, ninety to one hundred open cases, and these numbers had increased considerably by my second round of fieldwork.[19] Workers tend to plan their days to have three or four appointments with clients, each expected to take between fifteen minutes and two hours. They use the rest of the day to process paperwork and deal with such additional organizational requirements as supervisory meetings. Almost daily, however, new applicants and clients with active cases come to the office without appointments expecting to see their caseworkers. From the clients' perspective, the workers' job is to deal with clients as their needs arise. After all, the business that they come to the welfare office to conduct has to do with their family incomes and resources. On the other hand, from the workers' perspective, the constant and unpredictable demands of their caseloads and the pressure to fit all of their responsibilities into tight schedules often frustrate them. They are then forced to surrender control over their work pace and daily agendas to accommodate clients and assorted emergencies. What workers often see as a lack of respect for their time by unscheduled clients is exacerbated by a large workload full of time-sensitive matters.

The majority of a caseworker's time is actually spent processing paperwork. This is one part of the job that makes it difficult to always present an informed and consistent front to clients, as information is constantly arriving that can alter a worker's script. For this reason, workers must "be on top of things" to determine how to respond to clients' questions and provide directives. They attempt to control this as much as possible by insisting that clients adhere to certain formalities. For example, clients will be told that information regarding their cases should be reported quickly and accurately and that their workers' time must be respected. Clients should return phone calls and paperwork from their caseworkers promptly, call for appointments (as coming to the office without one does not guarantee a timely visit with a caseworker), and notify their workers immediately if they cannot make an appointment to avoid potential sanctioning. Clients' grants can be reduced or their cases closed completely for failure to show up for an appointment without calling.

The time limits and heavily touted emphasis on work introduced a new sense of urgency in welfare offices in the 1990s, and they also generated even larger amounts of paperwork. The massive quantities of documentation are perhaps the most telling sign of the degree of surveillance to which not only clients but also workers are subjected. Caseworkers' capacity to manage the tidal wave of information signals their level of professional competency, and the documentation of all of their transactions and client interactions testify to their efforts to "cover their bases." Client documents directly and indirectly related to welfare reform are constantly filtering into the office, from client pay stubs, to training program attendance records, to eligibility verifications.[20] The worker must process paperwork quickly so that her clients consistently and appropriately receive (or lose, if now ineligible) cash benefits, subsidized child-care vouchers, transportation assistance, and any other services that clients are accessing through the welfare department. In addition, the worker regularly receives from her supervisor lists of clients whom she should track down because their names emerged in Department of Revenue, Internal Revenue Service, or Department of Motor Vehicles computer-generated records documenting potential unreported wages, the collection of government benefits in another state, unreported automobile ownership, or unreported lottery or court settlement winnings. Even a report that a client simply *applied* for a job has to be investigated to ensure that unreported wages are documented. The central welfare office also generates lists of clients showing time-limit decreases that require caseworkers to close cases or meet with clients to discuss options for cases pending to close within the next few months: Are they looking for a job? Do they want to try a different training program? Do they intend to apply for an extension of their time clock for good cause? Clients also frequently call their caseworkers throughout the day to ask questions, return messages, respond to mail they have received, find out why they were sanctioned, or report changes to their cases. The worker must always be poised to provide the appropriate response or remedy to the client query. For this reason, the unorganized worker has a particularly difficult time on the job. With frequent interruptions, she must be ready to pick up and drop projects at a moment's notice and then remember where she left off when she returns to the issue. Errors represent money lost—for the client or the state.

Because of numerous time demands, even the most routine case-management tasks can become drawn-out affairs for both clients and workers. This creates a constant push-pull between clients, who want tasks completed in the least amount of time so that they can leave the welfare office and access resources for their families, and workers, who must juggle several projects and client demands at once. For workers, the job becomes all-encompassing; it requires the stamina to quickly shift focus and recite policy without hesitation. When clients call to ask about services, some workers are able to tell them immediately and precisely what documents they will need to bring with them, and a few are even able to fire off what paperwork is missing from the particular client's file without looking at it. As Camilla Suarez, a Staunton case-worker explained, "this job takes over your mind to the point that all you know are rules and cases."

Meetings with clients require preparation work, much of which the worker does just before the case conference. The worker reviews the client's records to determine whether or not she is exempt from the policy's time limit and work requirement; how much time she has on her benefit clock; whether all of the necessary verifications have been turned in; whether there are any "red flags" in the case that could create an error in payment; and what the goals of the meeting should be. The meeting could involve a case review, a case closing, a case opening, or a case reopening. The meeting could be designated to discuss the client's plans after welfare, an application for an extension on the client's TAFDC benefit time clock, or services that the client may need to get back into the labor force. Regardless of the purpose of the meeting, the worker must assemble all of the necessary documents that she and her client will complete in the course of the interaction and determine an agenda. Then, she is ready.

Every four to six minutes, the door connecting the waiting room to the client service area flies open and a worker leans out and calls a number. Clients come forward, exchange pleasantries (or frustrations about the wait), and then follow their workers through a maze of cubicles to the appropriate stations. Here, the backstage becomes the front-stage where the bulk of service delivery will take place. The client service area is noticeably calmer and quieter than the waiting room. However, along with this, clients sacrifice privacy as most of what is said between them and their workers can be heard in the surrounding cubicles and walkways.[21] Workers conduct client meetings in their four feet by six feet cubicles, a cramped space with a desk, several filing cabinets, a computer, and stacks of folders containing case files and paperwork. Many workers decorate their spaces with a combination of work program flyers and photocopied cartoons espousing the frustrations and mundaneness of work. "Sometimes the dragon wins . . ."

reads one taped to a file cabinet, complete with a drawing of a defeated knight, his shield and sword hanging listlessly. Other file cabinets feature photos of clients' children and have boxes of toys lying right next to them. Just about every caseworker's cubicle has a state-supplied calendar tacked to the wall, with the paydays and holidays when the office will be closed highlighted in bold black ink.

The client takes her seat in a straight-back chair directly across from the worker's desk and settles her children in adjacent seats if she brought them to the office. She will be expected to keep her children occupied and quiet during the course of the appointment. Once the worker, client, and children are settled, the business begins.

TWO

Not Everyone Has the Same Bag of Tricks

Identity Discord, Discretionary Toolkits, and Policymaking in a Changing Institution

Camilla Suarez has a bachelor's degree in social work and had worked in the Staunton TANF office for just two and a half years when I met her in 2001. When she joined the welfare department, her ambition was to "save the world," but the day-to-day realities of the job have lowered her sights a bit. "To me," she explained, "[the job is] more data entry. It's paperwork and guidelines . . . benefits— approved or not approved. Time limit—yes or no. Have you met the criteria?" Camilla contends that the way the job is set up precludes her from practicing the kind of social work that she was trained to do:

Case maintenance and eligibility [determination] is a good 75 percent of your job. . . . You don't really have time to sit down and work with people. You deal with people and you may hear their problems, but there's only an extent to which you deal with it. "What can we do to get you to a job? What do you need?" If they tell you about their problems, you can only talk to them for so long. And then you don't really see the person. If they just started twenty-four months [of benefit eligibility], you're only going to see them every three months. Some clients, once a month, tops. By then, they've probably lost all their motivation, you're starting back at step one every time, you're never progressing. . . . You need to be there for

49

them continually, but that's not my job here. The job itself, with all the [case] main-tenance, is not designed to be in-depth social work.

With so many tasks (and ninety-one open cases), Camilla addresses concrete issues such as child care and transportation with a voucher for subsidized services, but tackles nothing more complicated than that. Clients mandated to work receive a voucher to attend a local job pro-gram.[1] Camilla worries that such a limited focus creates a barrier be-tween her and her clients. Indeed, she acknowledges that her posture is to be highly suspicious of them and to assume that most are trying to game the system. In an effort to guard against welfare fraud, abuses of any benevolent leanings she might display, and those clients who are "full of excuses" about why they can't work, Camilla vigorously polices for incomplete, contradictory, or incongruous stories. She re-counted her interaction with Tina, a new client and mother of a nine-month-old baby who moved to the city that month in order to be closer to her family:

I'll admit that the job has sapped me of some compassion. Once in a while will come a case where you're like, "Wow," but not often anymore. So this case today, the nineteen year old. She moved here from Puerto Rico on the twenty-first or twenty-second and she's already in the welfare office applying on the twenty-seventh. She's four months pregnant with a second baby by the same father. Apparently, he's still in Puerto Rico; they're not married. In my head I'm thinking, "She's well trained in the system of welfare." Her aunt or mother here probably called her and said, "Why don't you move here and you can apply for welfare and let the government pay for you?" . . . I swear they must give classes out there for welfare 101, how to pass the intake process or something.

Camilla then added that in such a case she recommends what is known as "front-end detection" of the suspicious request for assistance, a process in which an Investigations Unit worker will either pay Tina a surprise home visit or contact her landlord to corroborate who is liv-ing with her before she is allowed access to the TANF rolls. Camilla suspects that the father of Tina's children has moved with them and is providing financial support. In most cases, a client's completed hous-ing verification form, listing the household members and a landlord's signature, suffices. But Camilla opts for the more vigilant tack.

Camilla assigns responsibility to "the job" for her distrustful and terse approach with clients. As the next few chapters will show, her claim is valid to a great extent: working with clients is a demanding undertaking and efficient case processing and effective fraud detection are certainly highly valued by the organization and a hallmark of how it defines "good casework." Further, the high caseload that each worker oversees goes largely unaddressed due to understaffing problems, making lengthy interactions with clients where a connection can be forged a near impossibility. But Camilla ultimately makes a choice about how to interact with her clients, one that she discerns is best for her ability to do her job. Other colleagues will trust a client's word and the submitted verification documents or wait for damning evidence before they launch a formal inquiry. For her part, Camilla routinely uses the Special Investigations Unit to monitor clients. She has formulated a professional orientation that guides her general approach to her work and helps to define how she wields her discretionary power. This tack of detachment and skepticism, with a simultaneous focus on speed and precision, in turn shapes her service delivery and how she implements policy on the ground.

For other employees of the department, this persona is awkward. More than sixty miles away in Fishertown, a day with Martine Neves is a study in bureaucratic creativity. The DTA office is most certainly a catch-all bureaucracy from Martine's perspective, and her job is to help clients gather up as much of the social safety net as possible. She and her client Shaunte sit in Martine's cubicle one spring afternoon, organizing the avalanche of paperwork Shaunte brought to try to prove her eligibility for cash assistance. Her newborn son Amir, asleep in a portable child seat at her feet, occasionally rouses from his slumber to find his mother trying to line up the paper trail that authenticates the last several months of her life. Her main offerings of documents for today's meeting are three of her boyfriend Lorenzo's pay stubs testifying to a meager income over the last few months and a letter from his employer certifying that Lorenzo took two weeks off to help Shaunte with the baby (and thus received no pay for that time).[2] Martine imagined that Shaunte did not want to expose Lorenzo to the Department of Revenue's child support enforcement process, complete with garnishments to his paycheck that mostly go back to the state, and recommended instead that they apply for benefits as a burgeoning two-parent family. As a result, Lorenzo's financial information also comes under the direct scrutiny of the office.

The problem, Martine explained, is that two weeks are still unaccounted for in the income documentation that Shaunte is presenting. "What you can do is bring the pay stub in," Martine offered, "or if you've got the employer ID number, I can find it myself. But everything else is here. You did good, Shaunte. You brought me what I needed. But they will be looking for that pay stub. I'm sorry." Until Shaunte returned with the missing document that completed the story of Lorenzo's gross pay of $330 a week to support a family of three, they would not be able to access services from the state.

Shaunte listened intently, struggling in vain to hide her disappointment. This was her third visit to the DTA office with verifications tucked under her arm, each time hoping that she would have enough to satisfy "them." She had first visited without an appointment, requesting to sign up for benefits. Martine was accepting all the walk-in clients that day, met with her briefly within a day packed with meetings, explained what documentation she would need for benefits, and sent her on her way. Shaunte, on maternity leave from a job as a substitute teacher, resurfaced with just about everything she needed, but opted to return a third time with Lorenzo's income verifications once the child support issue surfaced. Now, without this last pay stub, Shaunte's application would continue to maintain its "pending" status.

The irony is that Martine is almost positive that Shaunte's family will not be eligible for cash benefits. Even as Shaunte confessed that paying rent was a challenge that went largely unmet this month as they redirected their paltry funds toward the baby's needs, Lorenzo's income will likely put them over the eligibility limit. Martine imagined the struggle that awaited them, leaning on friends and family until Shaunte finished her maternity leave and returned to work. "But you are a family," Martine offers after warning Shaunte of the likely impending denial of cash benefits once her application finally does go forward. "You try to do. You just gotta keep trying to do."

I was puzzled by the interaction. If Martine knew that Shaunte was likely ineligible, why go forward with the process—taking the application, having Shaunte scrounge for verifications, spending her own time with the exercise? Wouldn't most workers do the quick budget calculations, see the writing on the wall, and suggest that Shaunte visit the food stamp unit down the hall where the threshold for eligibility was more generous? Martine's contrarian strategy reveals the complexity of these bureaucracies. After Shaunte left, Martine leaned toward me and quietly let me in on her plan: "I'm going to put their application in anyway. It will be denied, but we can give them medical benefits. That way, they will get something. She and the baby already have Mass Health. I could have sent her down to the food stamps unit so that they could just get that, but if I do it this way, they'll still get food stamps, but *he'll* get Mass Health too. Now, he'll get covered too." A month or so after Shaunte submitted the last of the documents, Lorenzo could count himself among the medically insured.

One can easily forget that Martine and Camilla work for the same state agency, are implementing the same set of rules, and are working with clients in similarly dire economic straits. These caseworkers imagined their clients' lives outside the walls of the welfare office very differently, reading different motives into clients' actions and subsequently using different organizational tools to address them. For Camilla, remoteness and even doubt are important parts of her professional toolkit, allowing her to "cut through the bull" of clients' stories and ensure that they are not "pulling a fast one." Her assumptions about how Tina learned about welfare—"they must give classes out there for welfare 101"—appear grounded in a narrative that low-income families are not simply sharing useful information among themselves but are in fact colluding to conspire against the system. Although she concedes that there may be a legitimate need for survival resources, Camilla's view is that clients also often dissemble to get as much from the system as possible and that part of her job is to expose these contrivances. Camilla's professional orientation would feel completely contradictory to the way that someone like Martine routinely operates and how she believes she should implement the same set of policies. "My question," Martine offers, "is what can I do to help them out, make it a little easier."

In these moments, Martine and Camilla use their professional authority to expand and restrict the everyday functions of public policy and the reach of organizational processes, and they possess the ability to produce variation within and between their institutions. In both the Fishertown and Staunton DTA offices, bureaucrats like Martine and Camilla coexist in an often unspoken and sometimes uneasy contest over how to function as social welfare workers operating under an unprecedented context of time-limited, work-focused public assistance. As those outside local offices have by and large pronounced PRWORA a legislative and administrative success and moved on to other matters, what remains are public bureaucrats who still hold divergent ideas about how to grapple with the extensive and difficult demands of the job. As we become privy to the experiences of clients such as Tina and Shaunte, we see how Camilla and Martine's respective differences matter in consequential ways as they work out what "helping the poor" looks like and present what they each believe is the best way to "be" in the organization. In this chapter I take up the following questions: What are the elements of disparate professional presentations such as these, how do they emerge within the agency, and how do these deviations shape organizational processes such as service delivery in ways that may reinforce or buffer existing inequalities experienced by clients?

In this chapter I examine how policy implementers' interpretations of their professional roles shape what they do. By building on the concept of *situated bureaucrats* introduced earlier in the book, I argue that much of the variation in service delivery that we observe among street-level bureaucrats—often generically characterized as "worker discretion"—is actually the operationalization of differing professional identities that workers create to implement public policy. Caseworkers generate perceptions of clients, the agency, and their work that help them to create methodical frameworks for doing their jobs, and these frameworks feature toolkits that offer caseworkers the practical resources to reconcile "who they are" with what they believe the institution expects of them. In other words, these discretionary toolkits help workers implement policies in ways that reflect their occupational goals and personal commitments while trying to satisfy the demands of the institution. The disparate professional identities among welfare bureaucrats in Staunton and Fishertown are organized around diverging views of three central questions: How should they define "client self-sufficiency"? How broad should the assistance be to help clients get there? Should clients be able to help define workers' professional roles? *Efficiency engineers* tend to be more rigid in how they define client self-sufficiency, possess a narrower view of how expansive the agency should be in addressing broader client needs, and resist clients' attempts to bend workers' professional identities toward client preferences and agendas. *Social workers,* on the other hand, tend to be more expansive in how they approach helping clients achieve self-sufficiency, possess a wide interpretation of the areas in which they should intervene to assist clients, and demonstrate a greater willingness to allow clients to help them co-create their professional identities based on their charges' economic and personal needs. Because these professional identities and their accompanying discretionary toolkits are such powerful and systemic entities, they are likely better targets for effecting organizational transformation than the individual actions and decisions of these socially situated bureaucrats.

Discretionary Power within Catch-All Bureaucracies

Researchers have long argued that discretion is an important aspect of life in street-level bureaucracies (Galligan 1990; Hawkins 1992; Campbell 1999; Lipsky 1980; Prottas 1979; Maynard-Moody and Musheno 2000;

Brodkin 1997). Individuals leverage personal agency and authority granted by the institution and tailor their applications of bureaucratic mandates. For instance, human service workers with more sympathy toward clients have been found to provide higher benefits and more service referrals in both survey and experimental studies (Kroeger 1975; Scott 1997). Others show that welfare caseworkers use their social networks to link select clients to choice jobs (Livermore and Neustrom 2003). Clients who are deemed a suitable fit within a particular service environment, who exhibit greater levels of need relative to those with similar economic resources, who are knowledgeable about how to navigate the bureaucracy, and who garner the sympathy of their caseworkers often receive higher levels of service, while clients who are seen as more troublesome receive fewer services (Peyrot 1982; Goodsell 1980, 1981; Tripi 1984; Scott 1997). Because street-level bureaucrats are rarely subject to constant supervision as they interact with the public, discretion becomes an important ingredient in policy implementation that can produce both positive and negative consequences for clients.

Previous studies generally treat discretion as a mechanism that fuels organizational variation, a product or enabler of loosely coupled systems whereby each discretionary event preserves its own logical separateness and independence (Weick 1976). Camilla exercises her discretionary power by wielding the agency's surveillance apparatus while Martine opts to pull a different set of levers to engage its resources for client support. We therefore often think of discretion as situation-specific and institutionally embedded, a vehicle for leveraging, brandishing, or adapting organizational mandates to the conditions of the environment while facing immediate institutional challenges. The problem with this construction is that it encourages us to focus on the decisions made— the deployment of the Special Investigations Unit versus the filing of an ineligible applicant's claim for cash assistance in order to get health benefits for her partner—while ignoring the sociological and political bases through which workers like Camilla and Martine make these discretionary decisions. In failing to chart the overarching frameworks within which bureaucrats operate as they make these choices, researchers, practitioners, and policymakers often emphasize the *outcomes* of what is often a sophisticated social *process* of service delivery and policy implementation. As a result, much of our attention—in both scholarship and practice—hovers around targeting the individual decisions of situated bureaucrats rather than addressing the conceptual framework that shape their organizational actions and subsequently bolster or thwart ongoing efforts toward organizational change.

Discretionary toolkits denote and organize the capabilities, perceptions, resources, and choices that organizational actors have at their disposal to shape institutional actions and outcomes. Socially situated bureaucrats manage discretionary toolkits that include tangible resources such as a menu of programs and services that can glean monetary and in-kind goods for their clients, intangible resources such as contacts with other institutions that may offer assistance, and what we might call *stylist devices,* actors' techniques for doing their jobs in particular ways including interaction styles, strategies for connecting interpersonally with clients or for asserting bureaucratic distance, and tactics designed to drive home policy messages. This provides a knowledge base made up of both articulated policy rules and tacit knowledge that forms a kind of "common sense" for how to do the job (Giddens 1993; Campbell 1999). Discretionary toolkits are constituted in part by the social meanings and motivations that organizational actors draw upon when they adopt, or seek to adopt, certain behaviors, providing a philosophical "glue" that holds one's knowledge base together. Informed by personal experiences, political and social beliefs, and their cumulative understandings of clients and the institution, these cultural entities help to inform and frame social interactions.

The discretionary toolkit framework is rooted in the widely cited work of cultural sociologist Ann Swidler (1986) that conceptualizes culture as a toolkit that molds behavior into "strategies of action" by providing actors with a set of beliefs, ritual practices, habits, skills, and styles that they draw upon to interact with the social world. What Swidler describes as "unsettled" cultures create new or revised strategies of action.[3] In these periods of cultural change and structural revision, ideologies—explicit, articulated, highly organized meaning systems—shape behaviors until they become familiar and ritualized. If professional identities—as expressed professional self-understandings that guide actors' behaviors and help them to convey their places within the institutional environment (Ravasi and van Rekom 2003)—help workers construct professional standards (and vice versa), discretionary toolkits help individuals operationalize these conceptions in uncertain times until they become familiar work routines.

By leveraging their discretionary toolkits in various ways, workers can align how they perform their assigned organizational tasks with their personal professional orientations. In welfare offices, these tools can add up to important resources such as advice, service agency referrals, advocacy assistance, customized information about available resources such as daycare, extra time for clients to deliver eligibility documents before negative actions are taken, and maneuvers that make it easier or more difficult for clients to jump through some bureaucratic hoops. Such identity strategies therefore may produce vastly different experiences for those seeking assistance. Caseworkers can dramatically affect how policy is communicated, resources are divvied up, and rules are enforced.

It is difficult to pinpoint workers' professional identities simply by looking at a snapshot of their activities; a multitude of strategies in different contexts and circumstances are used to carry out their work. In the Staunton and Fishertown TANF offices, all caseworkers function as gatekeepers and resource brokers at different points in time. All act as enforcers and coaches. All engage in claims processing (to approve, deny, reinstate, or end a case) and what might loosely be called social work. But with the toolkit model we can acknowledge inconsistencies and variations among and within individual *patterns* of behavior. "People may have in readiness," Swidler contends, "cultural capacities they rarely employ; and all people know more culture than they use" (1986, 277). The analytic challenge becomes determining the patterns by which formulated professional identities shape discretionary actions and vice versa. Whether operating in a "settled" or "unsettled" culture, individuals leverage some sets of beliefs and behaviors more frequently than others and gather a dependable set of tools, ritualized practices, and skills in order to function.[4] Professional identities allow socially situated bureaucrats to assert their understandings of what their occupational roles represent and how they should do their jobs in the face of institutional complexity. Discretion, in this sense, serves as a mechanism for managing one's professional identity. Over the next several chapters, we will see how this allows workers to operationalize and perform their understandings of the kind of professionals they should be in the service of not only institutional but also personal, occupational, and political goals and commitments.

Welfare Service Delivery after Reform:
Social Work or Efficiency Engineering?

PRWORA ushered in an unsettled period in welfare offices. Longstanding practices and approaches to service delivery were disrupted, and the tools workers had at their disposal to do their jobs were revamped. High-level administrators coupled the mantras of work, personal responsibility, and independence with expanded power granted to caseworkers with the hope of reorganizing how local welfare offices function, how staff members interact with clients, and how workers think about their jobs. As the next chapter will show in greater depth, institutional leaders established, along with new policies and procedures, new structural mechanisms in order to encourage workers to revise their strategies of action. From these arrangements, workers assembled their discretionary toolkits, pulling from a range of acceptable behaviors in order to select those tools that would best reflect their sense of who they were (and were not) as professionals. As each worker reformulated her own professional identity in the post-AFDC era, she in turn revealed her investments, commitments, strengths, and weaknesses as an organizational and social actor.

It is widely acknowledged that welfare work after reform remains riddled with contradictions that reflect the tension that exists between a counseling role and that of the efficient, rules-observant bureaucrat. To be a welfare worker means to have the authority to allocate critically important resources to low-income families, yet operate in an institutional environment full of constraints (Lipsky 1980; Maynard-Moody and Musheno 2003). Workers must balance their idealistic interpretations of the job with pragmatic realities, creating not a singular professional identity but a variety of interpretations.

Casting Divergent Paths to "Self-Sufficiency"

Most caseworkers that I observed articulated, in accordance with the rhetoric of welfare reform that prescribes work and only temporary welfare use, a common professional purpose related to "client self-sufficiency."[5] It was not the case, however, that workers agreed with administrators or each other on how to interpret and operationalize this. They worried foremost about the feasibility of meeting all of the expectations around client services, institutional bookkeeping, and rule enforcement placed upon them, and this in turn informed how they defined an opaque term like "client self-sufficiency."

I detected that workers created two distinct framings of the job. We might think of them as poles on a professional continuum, reflecting a range of differences in terms of how workers conceptualize and organize their work, theorize their clients' problems, and assert their own responsibilities and capacities. Just as sociologists often "conceptualize gender as an interactional accomplishment, an identity continually renegotiated via linguistic exchange and social performance," situated bureaucrats engage in similar identity work (Cerulo 1997, 387). With their identities socially constructed through interactions with clients and colleagues, workers deploy different sets of knowledge, shared understandings, rituals, and practices that represent orientations toward either *social work* or *efficiency engineering,* and these identities in turn shape service delivery.

One group of bureaucrats in the Staunton and Fishertown DTA offices very clearly defines itself as *social workers,* and these actors articulate a mission around not only serving but also advocating for their clients through their work. Although formally trained and licensed social workers remain a rarity among welfare caseworkers, by asserting such an identity through both what they call themselves and how they describe and conduct their work, these individuals advance a distinctly professionalized interpretation of their occupational role. John O'Reilly, a worker with sixteen years in the department, clearly saw his job as social work and challenged the notion that it was not:

I have been dying to say this: I do social work. To me, social work is referring people to the resources that I have in order to make sure that they are self-sufficient. A lot of the people in this office said that it's not social work that we do, but it is. I mean, it's always supposed to be social work. If somebody told me that they were having problems with their rent, or with their landlord, I'm doing a housing assistance placement agency referral, you are doing social work. If you advise somebody to take their GED exam or become a nurse's assistant, I think that's social work. . . . How many doctors have we had who come in and take the form and he reads it off and says, "Okay, this is what's up"? And he *tells* you what's wrong with you. And then there is a doctor who comes in and he asks you what the problem is and he sits and talks with you. And he listens to your situation and he *discovers* what the problem is. And then he works with you and even gives you names of specialists to go to. That's what I do, the second one. I'm the doctor and I refer people to specialists. That's social work!

For workers in this group, success is not defined simply in terms of enforcing program requirements and efficiently processing paperwork. Social workers talk about and try to actively pursue a broad but ultimately abstract notion of improved well-being for clients and their families and see this as *central* to their definition of client self-sufficiency. They envision client support as coming in many forms and see themselves as sounding boards, community resource brokers, and even motivational coaches for their clients. Social workers tend to approach the operationalization of welfare reform as holistic work with clients, even though these workers often aren't able to deliver on such ambitions because of limited resources and institutional constraints. Although they recognize the limits of what they can offer as time clocks tick and work requirements must be enforced, social workers nevertheless carve out techniques to act in ways consistent with how they define themselves as professionals. Loretta Esteban, who describes herself as a "social worker," talked at length about how she values finding ways to encourage clients in order to make the job more rewarding:

At least the pretty part [of the job], when you go out and you can tell a girl, "But you already have your GED. Go to community college. Do this, do that." Or somebody who got to the eleventh grade, but never got to graduate: "I can give you a voucher, you can take a GED test. You might pass it. You got to eleventh grade." So in those instances, when the client says, "I might pass it," and I give them the voucher, I tell them, "You have nothing to lose." And that's one occasion, whenever I encourage, I like it. In those instances when they accept it, when they take the test and they pass it, and they move a little bit higher, that's a reward that you don't get in the paycheck.

Loretta's advice is often personalized, supplemental, and therefore highly discretionary. Attending community college, while likely beneficial to clients, is not a part of the state's "work first" approach. Clients are not prohibited from attending—work-mandated clients are free to go to college as long as they also fulfill their work or training program attendance requirements and clients without work mandates are free to go as well (albeit only for the first twelve months of a degree program if they are subject to the twenty-four-month time limit). Loretta's advice to clients that they go this route is therefore more reflective of *her* ambitions for her clients than it is of policy mandates. How she advises her clients affirms her professional identity as a resource-brokering "social worker" and coach to individuals in her caseload. It distinguishes her from many of her co-workers, while still allowing her to adhere to the bureaucratic demands of the office. Social workers likely displayed many of these styles and approaches prior to welfare reform, but as we will see in the next chapter, the new policy introduced rhetoric, resources, and other tools that these bureaucrats believe signaled that asserting this kind of a professional identity is absolutely essential to the successful implementation of policy.

Despite the strong convictions of John, Loretta, and those like them, a second occupational orientation is evident in the agency among those tasked with doing the same job. In fact, this group asserts who they are by asserting who they are not: social workers. Unwilling to buy in to the professional interpretation that their co-workers circulate that the job is and should be social work, *efficiency engineers* assertively demarcate their obligations to clients and limit their focus to fulfilling the technical demands of eligibility determination, rule enforcement, and referrals to employment centers that they presume do the "heavy lifting" of getting clients employment. That, they believe, will help their clients achieve self-sufficiency as their definition of the term hinges simply on them no longer being dependent on welfare. The toolkit of Lee Chen, a no-nonsense efficiency engineer in the Staunton office, is therefore quite different from that of John and Loretta. As her stock of strategies and resources to work with clients, she states the facts, informs them of the benchmarks such as time clocks and work requirements, and refers them to the local career center. This ultimately is a business relationship to Lee, and she believes that what she describes as clients' "personal problems" should not derail "the steps" for achieving self-sufficiency: "The purpose of the welfare reform is that they want everybody just to go to work, not be on welfare for a long time. . . . So make sure the teen [clients] really get the GED or diploma. And then, for everybody else, the next step should be, have them go to skills training. Know how to interview. Learn how to write their resume. Keep track with them. And keep—enforce them. Let them know that now, you know, you need this step. Then you need to get this step, then this step."

Efficiency engineers prize predictability, neutrality, and studied detachment in the job. This group, as the next chapter will show, also received new tools and resources to support this professional orientation under welfare reform. Although most social workers and efficiency engineers in the offices value and often demonstrate high levels of technical acumen and knowledge of policy, efficiency engineers are more likely to define this as the centerpiece of their work rather than as a skill that is of equal value to their interpersonal connections with clients. As Camilla explained in the chapter's opening, "the job itself, with all the [case] maintenance, is not designed to be in-depth social work." Efficiency engineers argue that the best way to help clients is to get their benefits to them as quickly as possible, not to try to solve all their problems.

It would be too simplistic to suggest that efficiency engineers, by definition, are not aware of or concerned about the challenges that their clients face. Rather, they have no illusions that their work is potentially transformative in their clients' lives. They see extensive involvement as not only logistically impossible but also as potentially irresponsible; they are by and large without the extensive training and expansive tools that these workers believe are necessary to address many of their clients' issues. The nuances among their clients are therefore largely unimportant as the main question before the efficiency engineer is whether or not these individuals are eligible for services and meeting the benchmarks that the current welfare policy lays out related to time clocks and work requirements. As an efficiency engineer, Sharlene, who we met in the first chapter, has a systematic and blunt approach:

When they're coming in, I tell them they have two years [of assistance] and to utilize the department while they can. We're going to pay for daycare and job training. . . . So try the programs that you want . . . because once the two years is up, we will do nothing for them. That usually works [with clients]. Usually that's helpful. Then you have some that don't want to do anything. I tell them, "The clock is ticking; you're still not doing anything." Once your time is up and we discuss your case and there are all these no shows [in job program attendance] then you're going to get denied [for an extension] and you can't get anything but food stamps and Mass Health.

Sharlene encourages clients to "shop" for training programs, which grants them the power to determine what path they will follow but also puts the onus squarely upon them to determine which among a set of programs—on which clients likely have little information—is of the best quality, provides the best chances of finding employment, and best matches their skill sets. Efficiency engineers tend to assume that outside vendors are providing high-quality services to clients, even though we know from several studies of welfare-to-work programs that this is not necessarily the case (Johnson-Dias and Maynard-Moody 2007; DeParle 2004; Hasenfeld and Weaver 1996; Iversen 2000; Anderson and Van Hoy 2006). Because most of the vendors are under contract with the DTA, efficiency engineers assume that "management" has the best sense of program effectiveness, and they subsequently focus their concern on whether or not the client "is in a program," generically conceived. This means that if clients aren't successful, they are expected to be proactive in finding something else to meet the requirement. Sharlene is not alone in the assumptions that guide her approach. Many of the efficiency engineers that I talked with and observed seem to hold this idea: once the office has provided twenty-four months of cash assistance, vouchers for day care services, and referrals to job programs, it has largely done its part and met its responsibility in helping clients with their transitions. Clients must step up. This view is central to the professional identities of efficiency engineers, who in turn center their energies on the technical demands of meeting the office's circumscribed obligations.

Nevertheless, it is not unusual for a strong normative sentiment to undergird the tenor of what both efficiency engineers and social workers say to their clients. Sharlene shares that if her cut-and-dried exposition of what clients should do during their two years of assistance is not getting across, she has other tools in her discretionary toolkit: "Then I try to say, 'How are you going to support your kid, your family? Don't you think it's better for them to see you leaving the house going to the program rather than sitting around the house watching television? They see, that's what you do, that's what they're going to do. 'Mommy don't do nothing so I don't have to do nothing.'"

Sharlene believes that using "tough love" that eventually tries to tap into clients' obligations as mothers is an efficient way to sell her prescriptions and to swiftly convince clients that they have a moral obligation to perform in a certain way. Both efficiency engineers and social workers undergird their discretionary toolkits with moral claims about how clients should behave as mothers and workers to try to remind them of the stakes. But whereas Loretta uses the potential for success to encourage a mother to pursue more education, Sharlene's articulation of failure as a job seeker and by extension as a mother underscores the seriousness and punitiveness of the power that workers deploy through their discretionary tactics. Her narrative of a "do-nothing" client is inconsistent with what we know about how welfare recipients organize their days (Edin and Lein 1997; Hays 2003; Seccombe 1998), yet it serves as an important tool that Sharlene uses to operationalize her professional role.

Differences between social workers and efficiency engineers were evident throughout both the Staunton and Fishertown offices. Many workers themselves agree that the service that clients receive largely depends on the worker assigned to their cases. Under welfare reform, this is even more evident as caseworkers have many more instances to engage with clients to create packages of services to help them meet policy goals. At times, it was jarring to see individuals with such different approaches operating side by side in the agency.

Perhaps the clearest example of this was when I observed caseworkers implement the requirement that nonexempt clients work a certain number of hours per week or engage in work activities such as training classes. Embedded in the approach of efficiency engineers is the belief that, with very few exceptions, their clients should and can work as both a normative and institutional matter. "The rules are the rules," one often hears efficiency engineers say, and they express very little apprehension about the spirit and expectations of the work requirement. They agree with their more social-work-minded colleagues that most of their clients have a variety of challenges related to work and family, but efficiency engineers tend to believe that these problems can be overcome, or at best relegated to the back burner in order to address the more pressing goal of providing for one's family. Many of their clients' problems can be solved simply by going to work, efficiency engineers believe, regardless of the realities of the low-wage labor market that may make it a very difficult place to subsist (Newman 1999).

This stance was evident during a transition plan meeting that I observed between Fishertown caseworker Jackie Ridge and her client Terry, a mother of eight- and ten-year-old sons. Terry had five months remaining on her time clock, and had been on and off of public assistance for about four years. She had been laid off from a job with a furniture-making manufacturer several years back and had struggled to find something that paid well enough to support her children. Terry was working between fifteen and twenty-two hours per week at a local discount store but quit, citing the difficulty of balancing an erratic work schedule with her children's needs. "It's too much," Terry explained. "My hours were crazy and when I had to stay 'til closing, I wouldn't get home until late. I kept telling them to just give me day hours but I got night hours all the time."

Jackie went no further helping Terry troubleshoot her child care situation so that she might be more successful in her next job, likely because the children were too old for almost all of the child care programs on the list that Terry hands to clients and even fewer have night hours. Jackie would, however, ensure that Terry's case file was up to date and that her benefits were quickly and fully reinstated. "The reason I called you in here," Jackie explained, "is first because I never got a work termination letter from you. You'll need to go back to your employer and get me that letter." While she spoke, she typed Terry's name and Social Security number into the computer. "I just need to make sure you didn't come up on Learnfare probation. I thought I saw your name on the list, but maybe not. . . . No, I don't see it. . . . Well, let's do your transition plan. You haven't found work, right?"

Learnfare probation would have indicated that one of Terry's children was truant from school.[6] If the problem continued, she would be sanctioned and her grant would be reduced. This was not true for Terry. Jackie slid the Transition Plan form across the desk to Terry. "Fill that out," she commanded.

The Transition Plan asked Terry what efforts she had made since the last Transition Plan meeting to seek training or find a job. Terry filled in, "looked in paper." She checked off that she was not currently working or in a training activity. She listed in the appropriate space the date, wage, and job title for her last job: Feb. 2001; $6.30/hour; cashier and stock clerk. Where the Transition Plan asked her why she wasn't in a training program or working, she filled in, "Looking for work." For the question, "What can you do at this time to increase your income and/or find a job?" Terry answered, "Look for more ads and go on interviews."

She completed the rest of the Transition Plan and gave it back to Jackie, who quickly scanned it for completeness but asked no follow-up questions in response to the brief answers that Terry had provided. Jackie quickly ran through a reminder of Terry's time limit and work requirement. They spoke no further about the kind of job Terry might want or how she planned to alleviate her child care problem. Jackie filled out a referral for the Structured Job Search program offered by the local career center. Jackie made copies, handed one to Terry and told her that she would "see her next time." Jackie had this to say about the meeting: "It's pretty black and white. She's not exempt from time limits and she is mandated to work. You do your Transition Plan. The client can put whatever she wants. Give her the referral and make sure she knows about her time limit. . . . You'll hear people say it's like an assembly line. You want to keep it 'in and out.' When you've got stacks of things behind you and stacks of things beside you, and phone calls and people coming in, you just want to do everything with a client as fast as you can."

When workers articulate their approaches to their work tasks, they are making statements about how they see themselves as professionals. By contending that the job is "black and white" and "like an assembly line," Jackie stakes out a professional orientation that deemphasizes personalized advising to address the challenges facing each client and asserts a more utilitarian (and arguably time-efficient) approach to service delivery. It is ultimately claims processing with limited resource brokering; more like record keeping and enforcement than "social work." She uses her discretionary power to carefully direct the interaction toward eligibility and compliance issues. Referring her to a job search center would be the extent of her welfare-to-work counseling, coaching, and support as Jackie focuses on trying to stay on top of her workload.

The narratives that efficiency engineers and social workers assign to clients' lives and selves—their interpretations of who they are, why they are in the conditions they are in, and what obligation the state has to address their needs—contribute to how they shape service delivery (Loeske 2007). Social workers tend to see clients' challenges as indicative of a system that is "rigged" against them from the start. It is not that they disagree with the principle that many of their clients should be working; rather, social workers part ways from their efficiency engineering colleagues on whether the supports—economic, personal, familial—needed by their clients are sufficient and whether it is their job as bureaucrats to be concerned. Social workers therefore spend a lot of time trying to protect their clients from these harsh realities or extending themselves to help clients access as much support as possible.

Unlike Jackie, who, as an efficiency engineer, tended to expect her clients to find their own solutions to their barriers to work, Martine is intimately involved in the troubleshooting process. During one afternoon observing Martine do her job, we met with Jenna, her client of the past three years. Jenna was facing one month left on her time limit, and Martine was growing increasingly anxious about Jenna's options. She informed Jenna, a thirty-year-old mother of a four-year-old son and ten-year-old daughter, of her time clock and saw job training as the best option to help Jenna prepare to survive after welfare. Referring her to one of the local programs wasn't enough for Martine; she also worked hard to persuade Jenna to fully invest in the process. As Jenna's time limit neared, Martine started delving deeper in their meetings— sometimes commanding, sometimes cajoling—to draw out of Jenna what she thought prevented her from landing a job. During the tense conference that I observed, Martine expressed her frustration: "Your time clock is winding down. You know that, don't you, Jenna? We've tried several different avenues of structured job search for you. None of these options have led to anything that has lasted more than a few weeks. What are your plans?"

Jenna nodded as Martine described the situation. "I want to get a job, but they don't pay anything," Jenna explained. Martine gingerly continued, lowering her voice and leaning closer: "What you have to keep in mind is that a job is a job. With the skills you have, the most you can get right now is a job paying $6 or $7 an hour. But it's a job. You have to work at a job to get a promotion or to get ready for a better paying job. You need to take care of your family. . . . You have to accept this. You can't make $15 an hour right out. . . . Let's talk about the interview. Maybe that's where you're getting stuck. You've got to sell yourself, you know. That is up to you."

Martine asked Jenna if she were dressing properly for interviews, expressing excitement about the job opportunity, and following up with a phone call to the employer. Jenna commented that she had a few skirts and blouses to wear and followed up with a phone call to her interviewer "most times." "I don't know what else to tell you," Jenna commented. "I'm trying, but nothing's happened so far." Martine continued: "You've been in this [job search] program forever and you are not getting anywhere. I'm going to call there and see what's going on. We're working together, you and me. We've got to find a program that is more aggressive because you'll have no time left and no job. This is not working."

Jenna nodded in agreement. "Fine," she commented. "I'll keep trying." Martine handed her a referral to keep her in the job search program for five more days. She also addressed Jenna's attendance problems in the program:

It is so important that we work together, Jenna, but I keep losing you, literally and figuratively. I feel like every time we meet, you're fine after and then when I find you again, nothing has changed for the better. My job is to make sure that you are okay financially. Are you concerned about that? Are you concerned about not having a job and being at the end of twenty-four months? Your chances of getting an extension are small. They look to see that you are in a job search program and that you go consistently. But you are having a problem sticking to a program. That won't look good.

Jenna repeated that she would try to do better. Martine asked how Jenna's children were doing and whether she had enough food in the house, handing her a referral to a local food pantry. Martine ended the meeting and walked Jenna to the door. "You have to keep in touch with me, Jenna. You have to keep trying." Martine said good-bye and returned to her desk, exhaling in exasperation and plopping down in her seat. Her frustration was palpable as I asked her to reflect on her work:

We are dealing with all these forces. I'll talk to a client and reach her. I'll end the appointment, knowing that I got through. Then a few weeks later, I see her again and she's down and apathetic again! We fight all those forces outside the office. . . . You tell them, "I'm going to help you. It's going to be okay." And then the forces— the boyfriend, the family, other people who say stuff to them, all of their problems, you know—those forces get them on the outside, get them when they leave these walls. That's probably why some workers don't even try. Just do the paperwork and that's it.

Martine concedes that co-workers with a different orientation might find it easier to do their jobs. But she has decided that she does not want to be that kind of caseworker. Besides, successes like securing health insurance for Shaunte's partner proved to her that she should be creative in how she thought about the parameters of the job, even if it wasn't easy. In her interactions with Jenna, this sense of professional identity produces motivational words and concerned questions about Jenna's enthusiasm, her food needs, and her appearance at interviews, among other things. Martine fully embraces the idea that, along with monitoring time clocks and processing eligibility paperwork, she will use her discretionary power to address "the whole client":

When welfare reform started, people thought, "Oh, God, we are really going to have to look at people seriously. We're going to have to be taking a holistic point of view." They [management] knew that they were going to have to change the job titles around. We became "social workers." I think somebody somewhere actually was right. Before you were checking for t's and i's, making sure the case is right . . . and when Transitional Assistance came in, it called for social work. You are very much involved with clients. You're assessing. You're setting goals. You are taking clients from point A to point B. So yes, there is a lot of social work, and yes, welfare did change. And I think it changed for the better, I really do.

During her interaction with Jenna, Martine is by turns frustrated and patient as she grapples with Jenna's impending end to welfare benefits. At the time, policy was such that Jenna would not have been sanctioned if she had dropped out of the job search program, but Martine felt compelled to keep encouraging Jenna to complete it as the time clock ticked.[7] She therefore engages in a time-consuming and emotionally taxing process. Organizational managers have complimented Martine on the level of client support she provides. But they have also stressed that Martine must still ensure that the documents for her eighty-nine other cases be completed and that she continually monitor whether her clients are meeting the benchmarks of welfare reform. In my observations, her resistance to these demands was unmistakable:

I don't care about the reports. Eventually I do them, but I'm always late. I've got clients walking in, phone calls, appointments . . . I don't rush them through. Everything else I think should be secondary. When I started, I [was] in food stamps. Even if people are just applying for food stamps, they are going to tell you everything about their life. Before welfare reform, I listened if I had time. With welfare reform, I think you *have* to listen. How else do you know what they need? When you are looking at everything with the client, you do become a social worker at that point.

The challenge becomes how to "help" clients, in whatever form workers deem reflective of their professional self-conceptions, within the constraints of the organization. Martine has to tweak how she thinks of herself as a professional as she struggles to meet the organization's demands. If she were completely focused on what she defines as "social work," she would be unable to meet her job requirements. Martine therefore plays a complicated and delicate role with clients, admonishing them that they "must work together" and offering support to people like Jenna, while simultaneously enforcing the more punitive aspects of reform. She recognizes that shifting in this way along the continuum of social work and efficiency engineering requires agility:

Implementing welfare reform has been difficult. You have to deal with the demands of the administration. You have to deal with the demands of recipients. The administration gives you a list with twenty cases that are going to close next month. They want to know what you're going to do with these people. Are you sending them to job search and are you ready to close the case? Have you seen them as often as you were supposed to? And then you've got these twenty people telling you, "I don't want to do anything. When my time ends, it's going to end and I'll find a job then." That's not enough for [me]; we have to make sure that this family is safe. I'm supposed to provide the services even after they go off for the first year . . . everything that's necessary to get them started again . . . referrals, all these follow-ups. So it's not like with welfare reform, the case closes and you say, "Good, it's out of my hair." I don't think I'm supposed to just let them go like that.

Conversely, efficiency engineers certainly had their own frustrations with how their professional identities were treated in the organization. In Massachusetts, the requirement that mothers of older children immediately find work and are subject to time limits adds a feeling of urgency that efficiency engineers can leverage to drive home their messages. Yet, the state's relatively liberal policy means that those who fail to fulfill their hourly obligations in jobs or work programs and are sanctioned can have their benefits reinstated after two weeks of compliance, whereas other states require clients to go a month without benefits or never reinstate them. Further, benefit extensions are routinely granted for those who exhaust their twenty-four months of benefits as long as administrators deem that clients are participating in a job search training program. These reprieves are something of a frustration for efficiency engineers who feel that some cases needlessly "drag on," as Lee put it, and that higher-level administrators remove some of the "teeth" from what they are trying to accomplish with clients.

Disparate professional identities among these welfare bureaucrats therefore have produced very different interpretations of how the policy goal of client self-sufficiency should be pursued. While efficiency engineers direct clients to find work, they heavily rely on the benchmarks of the organization to eventually move clients off the rolls. Promoting economic self-sufficiency to these bureaucrats means pulling the levers of the institutional apparatus to ensure that clients are either following the employment rules (or reaching their maximum period of benefits). For social workers, pursuing self-sufficiency is a more complex enterprise that involves addressing an unspecified variety of needs to try to get clients to engage in the labor market and improve their human capital, with less reliance on using the benchmarks of the organization as the standard by which they should advise their clients.

For the Good of the Client: Delineating the Boundaries
of "Help" as a Discretionary Device

The differences between efficiency engineers and social workers are more extensive than how they motivate clients for employment. The variation in professional identity also has implications for the tangible resources that clients are receiving and the bureaucratic surveillance to which they are subjected. Social workers deem qualities such as compassion and "a caring heart" to be critical in their work. Their relationships with clients are based heavily on trust, so they rarely use the more extensive measures of surveillance that are available in the organization such as dispatching the Special Investigations Unit to look into allegations of fraud or asserting their right to ask clients for supplementary documentation to corroborate any story that sounds fishy. They believe in "taking a client's word for it," barring any interference from their superiors, and they see this show of trust as a key resource in their professional arsenals.

With regard to the resources offered, medical disability supplements, or "supplements," as they are known by caseworkers, are applications for exemptions from time limits and work requirements due to clients' physical or mental disabilities. For social workers, supplements have become critical tools with the advent of welfare reform, as Ivy Scott, a Staunton office caseworker, explained:

I'm talking to a client and it seems like there's a disability. They say they really want to work, but "I keep wanting to just crawl into bed and curl up in a ball." I'll say,

"Maybe you're depressed and you need to get some help and you should fill out a supplement." Or if they're trying really hard but not getting anywhere very often it will come out that there's issues. I had a client who tried and tried but could not pass the math part of her GED exam. She didn't ask for it, but then another worker suggested, "Why don't you have her fill out a supplement?" She's exempt and it came back that she had both medical problems and a learning disability. She's now on SSI. A lot of people really want to work; they want to do what normal people do. The fact that they're having difficulties doesn't make them stop trying. I think you need to make the client aware that these things exist and they can make the claim if they want.

While the application spends months winding through the state system on its way to approval or denial, the client is able to "buy some time" as her benefit time clock stops. If the application is ultimately approved, she receives a longer term exemption, and the caseworker might then encourage her to apply for SSI. It has a higher bar for eligibility but, if approved, clients receive more benefits, and the caseworker can transfer the case out of the office. Ivy, who defined herself as a social worker in interviews, stays alert to potential disabilities among her clients, offers up the supplement with little prompting, and, in the case of the client above, even makes a preliminary diagnosis of depression that might feel downright irresponsible to an efficiency engineer. Her narrative about who her clients are becomes critically important. As she contends that many want to work but are simply unable, she sees her job as protecting clients from requirements of the office that she sees as unrealistic for them.

Social workers argue that they don't abuse the supplement option, but they concede that they use it much more liberally than some of their co-workers. Billie Viera, a Fishertown supervisor, credits welfare reform with giving her workers the power to make clients "do something" and move toward employment. She adds, however, that a cynical "gatekeeping" approach to the job often does a huge disservice to clients who face a myriad of challenges. Similar to Ivy's philosophy, the task of workers, Billie contends, is to use their discretionary toolkits to find ways to help those individuals and, in some cases, to protect them from some of the more unforgiving aspects of welfare reform:

The work requirement is that you have to find a job within sixty days and a client is saying emotionally, "I'm not ready." Emotion is not in policy. We are supposed to say, "Tough cookies, your days are being counted off as we speak." That's not a fair regulation. Some of our clients just aren't ready. We'll tell them, "Why don't you file a medical supplement?" That stops the clock the day that medical supplement is sent out. We use that an awful lot when you look at a person and you know that this person is not going to be able to get a job. I, as an employer, would not hire this person. . . . What we do, the savior, is the medical supplement . . . then their case is all set. . . . That's our biggest goal [in my unit]; that's what we're doing with most of our clients at this time.[8]

Medical disability supplements provide an important way for social workers to leverage their discretionary toolkits in order to advance their understandings of their professional identities. Of course, this raises the question of what qualifies Ivy and Billie to determine which clients are "ready" and which are not and therefore in need of a disability supplement.[9] The potential for abuse and discrimination certainly coexists alongside what Ivy and Billie define as critical decision-making power. Clearly, there is also a possibility for disparities to emerge between efficiency engineers and social workers in their offerings of supplements to clients. While Ivy commented that "I think some workers don't use [the supplement] enough," efficiency engineers, on the other hand, shared that they were reluctant to readily offer such an option. When they believed that disability exemptions were absolutely necessary or clients stated that they believed that they had a disability, efficiency engineers for the most part facilitated clients' access to the mechanism. However, as Sharlene, who is Ivy's co-worker in the Staunton office, commented, "We have [employees in this office] coming in here limping. We have people in here, diabetics, and they work. Why can't you work? Clients get a medical [supplement] and so it's a fraud. There isn't anything wrong with these people." To Sharlene, disability supplements have been abused by some clients and co-workers who seem to view "enabling" clients as part of the job. As efficiency engineers and social workers contest the use of this institutional mechanism, their professional identities and accompanying toolkits create disparate access to certain benefits among clients.

*Confronting the Agency's Reach: Clients Test
the Boundaries of Professional Identities*

Efficiency engineers are much more circumspect about the notion that the office should operate as a catch-all bureaucracy, welcoming all of their clients' troubles into the agency as their social-work-minded co-workers seem to do. They are much more protective of the hierarchy between clients and workers and view it is a way to maintain order and contain the uncertainties of the job. As such, efficiency engineers use interactions with clients as opportunities to reassert their professional identities and to clarify and reinforce the boundaries of their role.

For example, in the hours that I spent observing her, Lee's stance on who she is as a professional (and who she is not) is evident in how she does her job. In striking contrast to Martine's assertion, she explained to me that "we're not social workers. We are business workers, financial workers." When Lee is put into a position by clients where she is asked to offer counseling, extensive resource brokering, or "social work," she actively resists.

One Monday, Lee's client Steven visited the office, speaking in long sentences and peppering his statements with details of ongoing and considerable suffering. He was there to complete the paperwork to sign up for EAEDC, the state's cash assistance program for disabled and elderly U.S. citizens and legal immigrants who are not currently receiving resources from the Social Security Administration, a resource separate from the disability supplements available through the TAFDC program.[10] "I brought my birth certificate like you asked," he reported as he took a seat in Lee's cubicle for their meeting, pulling it from the inside pocket of his tattered black leather jacket and carefully unfolding it. Running his hand through his thick and wavy brown hair, Steven continuously shifted forward and back in his chair as he spoke to Lee.

Lee turned to her computer to determine what other documents Steven had yet to complete to prepare his application for assistance. As she read her screen, Steven shared his disappointment about not working in the past month and expressed frustration that his mind seemed to be slowing as a result. "These seizures," he lamented, "they are keeping me from getting out there."

As Steven continued, Lee pulled together a stack of paperwork from various folders in her tall filing cabinet. She nodded at Steven's ruminations. "Okay, I need you to sign the bottoms of these," she interrupted. "I didn't have you do them last time you came in to fill out the application." She briefly introduced each of them as she placed them in front of Steven:

This certifies that you have the right to know what financial assistance programs are available to you. This is certifying that you were explained the regulations for food stamps. This is your application for the assistance program. This is a medical report form that goes to the doctor so that they can release information about you.

This is a citizenship form where you are saying that you are a U.S. citizen. *This* is to show that you know that you must report any changes to the department within ten days. *This* is to show that you understand what happens if you lie to us. *This* is to say that you speak and understand English. *This* form says that you will apply for SSI and that you allow the department to get reimbursed if you end up getting SSI. We will take money out of your SSI checks.

As Lee passed each form to Steven, he continued to talk. Prison, he explained, had been hard for him as he served time for "punching someone" and then getting into a few fights while institutionalized. He reported that his seizures got worse while incarcerated because he wasn't given the necessary medicines after he was transferred from one facility to another. "I'm lost," he commented ruefully. "I can't get a job and I have these seizures."

"I understand, Steven," Lee replied, trying to redirect the conversation toward the pile of forms in front of him. "But my job is to help you get your assistance, so you have money coming in. Now, I'll need a landlord verification, something from your grandmother's landlord showing that you live there."

"My grandma's ninety-five now. That's good, right? She remembers you," Steven commented to Lee.

"Yes, that is good," Lee concurred as she persisted in trying to keep Steven focused on the task at hand. "I need you to write a statement explaining your housing situation, about the prison time, explaining how you are making ends meet," she instructed. "Put your name and Social Security number on the top."

"I can't see anymore hardly because they just let me have these seizures when I was in jail. They didn't give me my medication." Moments passed as Steven stared at the blank page that Lee provided him, "Now what am I supposed to write?"

"'To whom it may concern,'" Lee dictated, "'My name is blank and my Social Security is blank. I reside at'—write down your grandmothers' address—'with my grandmother'—and put her name. 'I was receiving SSI until July 29, 2002, due to seizures. I went to prison and was discharged on February 26, 2006. At the present, I have no income and no other resources.' Then sign and date it."

Steven carefully followed Lee's instructions. Lee turned to the computer as he wrote and typed into the space asking for narrative explanations of the actions taken with clients, reading aloud as she typed: *Client will need to have a doctor complete the medical report in 22 days, with the option of an 8-, then 15-day extension.* "You have to request the extension," Lee informed Steven. She turned back to the computer: *He will also have to complete a medical supplement form.* "Are you with me?" she asked. Steven nodded.

"Steven, don't forget that landlord verification form," Lee continued. "Or you can fill out a shared housing form to show that you live with your grandmother or you give me a utility bill with your name on it. I don't work on Fridays and we're closed this Monday. I won't be in this Tuesday. So when you bring everything in, leave it with the front desk."

Steven nodded and continued talking, venting about the prison system, his difficulties getting health care, and his belief that he was clinically depressed. As the stack of forms that Lee slid toward him got thicker, it was questionable whether Steven fully understood what he was being asked to sign. He did not stop to read them as he continued to talk. "If I did something wrong or if they were suing me, they'd have all of this information at their fingertips. But now, I got to give all the information again, all this red tape," he lamented.

"You talk so much!" Lee chastised. "Bring in the documentation so we can get this done. Okay?" Steven agreed.

"Now, do you have any more questions?" Lee asked. When Steven replied that he didn't, Lee rose so that she could escort him out. "Let's get your EBT card before they go to lunch. I don't want you to have to wait." Sensing that Lee would not be a willing audience (nor allow him to take such liberties with me), Steven followed Lee to the room where a staff member would take his picture and create an electronic card so that he could access his cash assistance and food stamps.

"They all want attention!" Lee concluded when she returned to her desk. "The EBT card station closed for lunch by the time we got there. I had to give him a little lecture. I told him, 'You talk too much. When you come in, you got to stay focused. I know you have problems and bad things have happened, *but I'm not a social worker.*'"

Lee continued to explain her interpretation of her occupational role: "Sometimes they get mad when I tell them that [I'm not their social worker]. One client said to me, 'You don't ask me about my problems.' I say, 'I'm not a counselor.' I like to keep it on business. I tell them, 'I don't have time to discuss all your problems . . . especially if you come in at four and the office closes at five. I have to decide if you are eligible and then open the case or decide to have you come back. . . . I need to focus on business.'"

Lee clearly defines herself as an efficiency engineer and uses the skills in her discretionary toolkit to guide the caseworker-client interaction toward that professional orientation. While some colleagues may try to engage their clients more deeply around their issues and concerns as they address their cash assistance needs, Lee's boundary-setting with Steven serves to assert her occupational identity and demonstrates what she sees as the function of the agency. It is *not* a catch-all bureaucracy, a place where clients can bring a myriad of concerns and worries to their doorsteps. Steven resists such a declaration, sharing details of his life in an apparent attempt to vent his anxieties, receive some level of emotional support, and perhaps even field suggestions from Lee on how to respond to his life's difficulties. His desire to engage and his expectations for the bureaucracy's functions are ultimately overpowered by Lee's desire to maintain control of the interview, protect her time in the face of a huge volume of work, manage Steven's beliefs about the kind of bureaucrat with whom he is interacting, and get him his benefits as quickly as possible. Of course, a motivating factor for Steven's presentation might have been his own desire to appear as a "deserving" and sympathetic client, but Lee gave few clues that such a performance was desired or even necessary. "My job," she asserts, "is to help you get your assistance, so you have money coming in." Steven's disclosure of his issues in fact serves as a distraction to Lee, who ends up advising him not about the issues that he reveals, but on how he should conduct himself more effectively in the TANF office.

Social workers tend to be more comfortable with the idea of the welfare office as a catch-all bureaucracy. They allow client needs to partially dictate where they will go as professionals, allowing the definition of social work to bend and stretch to meet the demands of each client. For example, social workers actively engage in interagency resource brokering for clients, even if the intervention is not directly tied to the work-focused goals of the office. Rather than providing a paper referral to a local agency, it is not unusual for these bureaucrats to also call the agency and speak to a favorite contact—introducing the client over the phone, articulating her needs, and asking whether the client might be eligible for certain services. Similar to the juvenile court workers in Mark Jacobs's (1990) study, social workers use their connections, clout, and abilities to articulate client needs in accessible and thus addressable ways to other service providers, something that efficiency engineers rarely do. They seldom declined clients who tried to demand more from their interactions than the strict parameters of the program dictated. This also meant that they spent much more of their time on tasks only marginally tied to welfare policy. Jennifer Stevens, a caseworker in the Fishertown office, explained her interactions with clients in this way:

> If clients have an issue going on, they'll call you, whether it's about the court system or anything. . . . Sometimes, if they don't have family that they can depend on, they will call you to just vent. I had a client in December [who] went to court and they told her she was going to go to jail for thirty days [for drinking and driving and later driving her son without a license]. So throughout the whole holiday season, she was calling me, and the girl suffered from mental illness, had bipolar disorder, was completely, like, beside herself, thinking she was gonna be sent to jail for thirty days. . . . And she would call me and I would just talk to her.

The stories of Lee and Jennifer show us two workers who don't just pull different discretionary levers; they have two very different understandings of who they are as professionals and the kinds of approaches and responsibilities that are embodied in that understanding. Critically, they also differ in the degree to which they will allow their clients to help set the service-delivery agenda and ultimately contribute to defining their professional identities. Efficiency engineers and social workers are subject to the same policies, job descriptions, and supervisory structures, but each makes a personal choice about the boundaries and contours of her job and what her clients can expect from her and the office in general. As a result, each uses a different discretionary toolkit in terms of how she leverages definitions of "client self-sufficiency," policy resources, and interpersonal styles to implement policy. This in turn creates variation in terms of the reach and function of these catch-all bureaucracies.

Do all of these differences amount to actual variation in the resources allocated? It is hard to make such an assessment without either an experimental or large-scale survey research design, where we can account for or even manipulate the myriad factors that determine clients' cash and in-kind benefits. Such an undertaking is beyond the practical resources of this particular study. We have, however, seen a few examples to suggest that there are some critical variations among these situated bureaucrats that appear to create disparities among clients in terms of their access to resources and experiences within these institutions. When Camilla decided to contact the Special Investigations Unit, as noted at the start of the chapter, she could have set in motion a series of events that shaped her client Tina's access to resources in ways Tina may not have experienced if her case had been in the hands of a worker who thought very differently about her professional role (and therefore did not wield the agency's surveillance apparatus in the same way). Regardless of the outcome of the Special Investigations Unit's scrutiny, Tina will presumably gain access to her benefits later than others who apply on the same day, turn in their verification documents at the same time, but don't have to undergo front-end detection. This chapter also suggests that even ancillary services, such as access to medical disability exemptions like those liberally deployed by social workers like Billie and Ivy, are being offered up differently, depending on the professional orientation of the caseworker. Recall Martine's intent to file a doomed application for a family in an effort to secure health care coverage for the father. Jane, an avowed efficiency engineer, describes how she handles similar scenarios:

We still see lots of new cases all the time. And a lot of them you won't see because they don't end up being eligible, because they have a little bit of something. . . . Most of them don't file the application, even though they have the right to. Because we'll tell them, you know, "You're this much over income." Even though it's a small amount. They know they're just gonna get a formal denial, so they don't wanna bother going through it. Without exaggeration, I'd say maybe a third of the applications I screen are like that.

Further, if we think of resource allocation not simply in financial terms but also as coaching and functioning as a sounding board, the resources offered by workers like Jennifer, Martine, and Loretta certainly differ from those offered by workers like Lee and Sharlene. These ethnographic data suggest that there are practical differences within the offices in terms of how clients are treated and their cases handled, which are determined at least in part by the professional identities that their caseworkers operationalize.[11]

The Role of Identity in Policy Institutions

Discretion, I have argued, is not simply the aggregate of varying bureaucratic choices at different points in time but instead represents the performances and products of a professional's self-conception. The findings presented in this chapter demonstrate that how caseworkers define themselves as professionals affects how they interact with clients and the services that they offer. Studying welfare caseworkers as situated bureaucrats who bring distinct interpretations of their professional roles to their jobs reveals the concrete and systematic ways that they exercise discretion in policy implementation. Discretion is not merely a product of random decision making; it is embedded in a certain interpretation of who clients are, what they should expect from institutions, and how these agencies should in turn define "help." Here I have parsed out several of the assumptions that guide these professional self-conceptions and their attendant toolkits, which workers then use to present competing presentations of service delivery. The interactions between these two elements—professional identities and discretionary toolkits—are powerful forces in the execution of public policy.

By locating themselves at various points within a logical space of competing professional identities, street-level bureaucrats make assertions about how they believe policy should be implemented. Debates among workers about their occupational missions are therefore settled (or unsettled) within organizational processes. What is apparent from these workers' narratives, along with my observations of their work, is that the resources and stylistic devices that they leverage to accomplish policy goals differ immensely. At issue is not just how one should implement policy but the very ontology of the organization for which they all work. To efficiency engineers, successfully implementing welfare reform means taking clients through a series of finite steps; they see themselves as guides and enforcers in this progression. Their ability to stay on top of bureaucratic processes so that they rapidly assess clients' needs and their persistence in steering interactions away from issues not directly related to fulfilling program requirements are the resources and interactive style that they bring to the table. As previously stated, for social workers, successfully implementing welfare reform means advising clients on a wide range of options and resources, delving deeper into their personal lives, and responding to them when they hit barriers, great and small. Social workers do not expect to be able to fix all of the problems that clients present, but they do see it as part of their job at least to try to do so.

Both of these stances come with downsides. On the one hand, social workers may intrude on sensitive issues without the training to properly address them and may oversell the degree to which they can be helpful given the constraints of the policy that they ultimately have to implement. Furthermore, as we will see in the next chapter, it is not unusual for them to fall out of favor with administrators as they deemphasize certain agency priorities. Moreover, their deliberate adoption of the dual roles of support and enforcement has the potential to be quite confusing to clients who may not be sure whether these individuals can be trusted to be good stewards of the information that they impart to bureaucrats who ultimately must enforce the rules.

Efficiency engineers, on the other hand, run the risk of "skimming the surface" with clients without ever properly addressing critical issues that might shape their success or demand serious intervention. In addition, efficiency engineers can create barriers between themselves and their clients that are actually counterproductive to the policy aim of getting the client back to work and off the welfare system. It is likely difficult to confide in a professional who makes it very clear that brevity and compliance are what is preferred from clients. Further, efficiency engineers appear to be less likely to think creatively about how to deploy the agency's resources to clients who are in dire economic straits.

For a segment of clients, the orientations of their workers and the disparities that lie therein will be inconsequential. Regardless of the style of the message and the scope of the resources, they will move from the rolls and into employment, struggle to remain in the system, or be unable to meet the program requirements and be forced to find other means of support. I believe, however, that for many clients the discretionary toolkits that their caseworkers bring to the job have serious implications for these recipients' abilities to gather the resources necessary to support their families in the short and long term. Particularly in light of recent literature on the experiences of postreform welfare recipients, much of their success depends on their access to information and referrals to assemble expansive webs of institutional support (Domínguez and Watkins 2003; Hays 2003; Small 2006). Before welfare reform, this variation was less consequential. Because there were no enforced time limits and work requirements were inconsistently and sometimes weakly enforced, having a worker who thought of herself as a "social worker" or who was particularly focused on efficient service delivery carried benefits but ultimately wasn't necessarily tied to one's economic fate.

My justification for an identity approach to the study of these institutions underscores Judyth Sachs's explanation for her work on teachers' professional identities. She suggests that "making these narratives public is a source for lively professional development. . . . Furthermore, it gives rise to a more active, spirited debate about policy and practice" (2001, 158). By making explicit how workers think about their jobs, we create opportunities for them to dialogue with organizational leaders, each other, and additional stakeholders about the emerging challenges of delivering welfare services, the changing nature of public assistance, and exactly what their professional interactions with clients should entail. In the next chapter I explore how these identities are formulated, the role of personal and institutional factors in this process, the complications that arise as workers move along a continuum of professional identities, and what happens when workers clash over their professional identities.

THREE

Reinventing the Street-Level Welfare Bureaucrat?

The Reformation of Professional Identities in Postreform Welfare Offices

In the more than ten years since Massachusetts initiated its own version of welfare reform, agency administrators have continued to fine-tune the TAFDC program. This constant refashioning has been influenced by a combination of internal assessments of best practices, mandates from federal and state policymakers, and a very influential and watchful legal services network that has successfully challenged various aspects of the state's welfare policy on behalf of impoverished families. In 2001, the advocacy community scored a significant victory in contesting what it saw as the DTA's disregard for the difficulties that learning disabled clients might face in fulfilling welfare reform's work and training program requirements. How could a mother with dyslexia, they asked, be expected to successfully compete in a work training program's classroom environment if other educational settings had responded poorly to her challenges? What kind of job search support should the DTA provide if many of the employment opportunities that were recommended require applicants to read with some proficiency, work a cash register, or complete other tasks that require them to interpret symbols or characters?[1]

As part of a settlement that would prevent subsequent legal action from the Department of Justice and the potential loss of federal dollars, DTA agreed to add to their client interview template the option for clients to participate in the department's Learning Disability Assessment. During the TAFDC application and recertification processes, caseworkers would read to clients a paragraph about the importance of diagnosing learning disabilities and present the possibility that appropriate services might be available. At the end of this litany, caseworkers would ask applicants whether they wanted to participate in a ten-question screening. If clients answered in the affirmative, caseworkers would navigate a computer program to administer the exam and, depending on the answers, refer clients to the state's Rehabilitation Center for further testing, diagnosis, and treatment. This information also would ideally be used to help caseworkers advise clients on the best possible job training programs and work opportunities based on their abilities. If a client replied that she would not like the screening, the application interview focus would shift back to her financial history.

Stanley Boyer of the Staunton office strongly supported this change. With over twenty-five years of experience as a welfare caseworker and a willingness to talk about his own dyslexia, Stanley could relate to the learning difficulties of clients. He felt that the agency had few resources in place to respond to such conditions. "We're guilty, all right, there's no doubt about it," he commented. Although he took issue with the department's rudimentary approach to the problem, Stanley saw the Learning Disability Assessment as a step in the right direction.

Stanley's endorsement of such an evaluation reflects more than his shared connection with clients. The Learning Disability Assessment would move Stanley and his colleagues one step closer to a professional identity that he prized, promoting a more holistic interaction with clients, marking TAFDC caseworkers as "social workers" and symbolically reinforcing an important occupational transition in the welfare office. Welfare reform sought to transform its street-level workforce from claims processors to welfare-to-work professionals. As the previous chapter demonstrated, ten years later caseworkers continue to grapple with exactly what this metamorphosis represents and demands. They have settled into disparate professional identities (and varying approaches to service delivery) as a result. The department's first step toward addressing the learning disabilities of clients represented an agency-wide cue to the "social workers"[2] that perhaps *their* interpretation of the assigned professional role would be supported and even promoted. For Stanley, this increased responsibility was not only in clients' best interests; it also improved the odds for occupational survival among DTA line staff: "We're trying to move the department in that direction. Absolutely. It's the right direction to go in. It's bringing back more social work to the job because the more we can bring back social work, the more secure our jobs are. If it gets to the point where [clients] can punch [their information] into the computer all on their own, there's no need for social workers."

As the Learning Disability Assessment was implemented, the occupational transformation that Stanley had in mind did not take place in every corner of the office. Several cubicles away sat his colleague Michelle Stephenson and Jasmine, a nineteen-year-old mother of an eight-month-old child. Jasmine was reapplying for benefits after spending more than thirty days out of compliance with the department's requirement that teen parents attend school. She attributed her spotty attendance and poor math scores in the GED program to her work schedule at a nearby clothing store, but her track record of detachment from school suggested that something else was awry. An undiagnosed learning disability was a plausible theory to explain her lack of engagement. Michelle chastised Jasmine on her attendance and grades with the tone of a protective older sister, reminding her that her child care voucher could be at risk. Michelle's eyes darted between the screen and Jasmine's one-inch-thick case file as she confidently clicked through the computer screens in the department's online case management system. Questions came in rapid fire. "Has your address changed?" "Where are the pay stubs from your job at the store?" "Who is living in your home now?" Finally, Michelle reached the latest addition to the client interview. "Do you have a learning disability?" she asked. When Jasmine shrugged and answered with a no, Michelle was at the ready with a form that testified to Jasmine's answer. "Okay, then sign this form," Michelle directed her as she promptly prepared to move to the child support portion of the interview.

The way that Michelle raised the learning disability issue is actually a violation of policy. She was supposed to read the paragraph, offer *screening*, and then ask a succession of diagnostic questions if Jasmine answered in the affirmative. Michelle's speedy and blunt approach, including her decision to ask Jasmine outright whether she had a learning disability, differentiates her approach from Stanley's in a critical way. In a later conversation with me, she endorsed a widely circulated and unapologetic interpretation of the agency's mission. "Clients," she once heard someone say, "are here to get their services, get their checks, and go home. That's it." Spending a lot of time with each of them to diagnose their challenges and to "do social work" was not Michelle's idea of what the job required.

Both Stanley and Michelle provide time-limited financial assistance and program referrals to help low-income clients find and maintain work. Both track eligibility-compliance benchmarks to ensure that clients are eligible for resources, and both discourage welfare dependency. Yet, the differences in how they *define* their roles are reflected in how they interpret organizational and policy directives, interact with clients, and implement policy. But why did these disparate identities emerge, with some people seeing the job as social work while others do not? And how do such distinct and at times competing self-conceptions coexist within one institution? In this chapter, I argue that because welfare officials have not invested enough in the professional development of their workers in the postreform era, they have unwittingly contributed to the disparities in service delivery outlined in the previous chapter. The two competing occupational identities that workers have established—efficiency engineering and social work—were informed by organizational cues that suggested that each might be legitimate. As these situated bureaucrats have interpreted the agency's competing messages about how they should think about their work, each has chosen a professional identity that suits her personal and professional goals and has worked to sustain that sense of self within the agency amid multiple and at times contradictory goals and directives.

Identity Formation in Institutions: A Conceptual Overview

Accountability measures and the formalization of procedures exert continuous tension on the discretionary power of street-level bureaucrats (Kroeger 1975; Aiken and Hage 1966). What Jewell (2007) calls the consistency versus responsiveness trade-off is endemic to these institutions. Although benefit amounts tend to be highly standardized and services routinized and structured, welfare caseworkers and supervisors are often able, little by little, to develop their own techniques and styles during client interactions. They deliver messages in particular ways, emphasize certain initiatives, and maneuver through bureaucratic rules, depending on their beliefs about what casework should accomplish (Maynard-Moody and Musheno 2000; Brodkin 1997). These discretionary practices and styles evolve in a changing bureaucracy as employees uncover new arenas in which to assert agency and lose control over others.

As I am attempting to connect these seemingly random discretionary practices and styles to workers' professional identities in order to highlight how these events are patterned, strategic, systemic, and socially constructed, it is important to explicate how bureaucrats' professional self-conceptions form in the first place. In his seminal book on roles and identity in organizational life, Blake Ashforth (2001) contends that actors' willingness to embrace some roles more readily than others depends on the significance that they assign to various identities. Subjective importance and situational relevance, what others have called accessibility and fit, are at least two of the factors that determine how salient a role is for an individual and how it will figure into her self-representation (Turner and Haslam 2001; Turner et al. 1994). A role that an organizational actor deems critically important or strongly in line with her goals, values, or other key attributes becomes highly central to her sense of self. The more subjectively important the role, Ashforth asserts, the more solidly articulated the identity tends to become, even if it is not widely shared. The formulated identity becomes highly instrumental in realizing goals. Situational relevance, on the other hand, refers to the "degree to which a given identity is socially appropriate to a given situation (i.e., a specific context, setting, or encounter)" (2001, 32). Ashforth surmises that "whereas subjective importance is defined by internal preferences, situational relevance is defined by external norms" (2001, 32). Subjective importance and situational relevance interact to determine the salience of a given identity for an organizational actor, shaping how it will be presented within an institution.

With the transformation of local offices that has accompanied welfare reform, researchers have focused primarily on cleavages between policy implementation strategies followed by the frontline staff and the complex realities of clients' lives (Hays 2003). But these are not the only sources of discord within welfare institutions. The assigned roles and emergent identities of caseworkers also have been contentious as various stakeholders have weighed in on how street-level welfare bureaucrats should do their jobs. Like most of the general public, caseworkers have also found themselves hearing the competing political messages about remaking the welfare system and supporting (and regulating) impoverished families. Like their organizational leaders, they too continue to be engaged in thinking through the form the restructured welfare system should take, how this new formulation should be presented, and how it should be reinforced. Like their clients, caseworkers are endlessly targeted for change and wrestle with whether the claim is true that the system demands more *of* them but offers more *to* them.

On many levels, welfare reform has granted to situated bureaucrats an opportunity to rethink, reformulate, and rearticulate their professional identities. Each therefore structures a professional self-conception that is both personally accessible and an appropriate fit within the agency. The complexities and tensions of these processes, and the role of organizational leadership in these reformulations and representations, are at the core of this chapter.

Walking a Mile in a Client's Shoes:
How Poverty Shapes Professional Identity

Although this chapter ultimately offers an agency-based explanation of the emergence, formulation, and reinforcement of competing professional identities within institutions, I do not mean to imply that other factors do not contribute to this process. The personal histories of poverty shared among a large proportion of the DTA workforce, for example, merit close analytic attention when examining how bureaucrats formulate and operationalize their conceptions of themselves as professionals. The Fishertown and Staunton offices have long had a contingent of workers who are single mothers, and over one-third of interviewed employees had histories of welfare receipt as adults or children. Others teetered on the brink of eligibility at some point in their lives. These experiences often inform their core beliefs about clients and how the service-delivery process should unfold. Although their personal histories may or may not be brought to the fore explicitly during interactions with clients, they often inform the stylistic approaches that these situated bureaucrats adopt in their communications. For Jennifer in the Fishertown office, trying to access subsidized medical insurance as a pregnant teenager over thirty years ago left an indelible impression:

I came into the office with my mother. Now, I was already married, but he left, 'cause we were sixteen and eighteen [years old respectively]. And we walked into an office, applying for medical assistance, and one of the receptionists said [coldly], "You're not eligible. You're your mother's responsibility." And it was very humiliating, and so my mother walked out with me and she said, "He's not gonna make you humiliate yourself like this," meaning my ex-husband. And I worked in a factory and I paid the doctor for my daughter to be delivered, which then was $350, but he gave me $150 off.

In part because Jennifer's first experience in a public aid office was as a benefits applicant rather than as an employee, she is strongly inclined to align herself with and protect clients. She petitioned to focus solely on teen parents such as she once was, determined to revise what young women experience when they come for help and to never inflict the humiliation she suffered on others. The sobering reality of how important a role her own family (and a charitable doctor) played in her ability to survive encourages Jennifer to model this for her clients:

I'm a fairly empathetic person. I try to just be a source of support. 'Cause I know how easy it can be to walk in someplace and have somebody make you feel worse or make you feel like there's no potential to do something different with your life. And you don't have to go on and on about it. Sometimes it's just a couple of words and just an attitude or an approach. I think a lot of the teens now, very few of them have that family support. And then they're in this situation, and if we're not there to give them the support that the program intends, then that's another loss for them. So I'm very comfortable with the caseload that I have and the job I do.

Jennifer clearly understands what "the program intends" in a particular way that appears to be aligned with how *she* wanted to be treated when she was that scared sixteen year old. For Jennifer, being a professional means bringing that experience to bear and using it not only to inform her interactive style as she distributes cash assistance but also to offer broadly defined "support" akin to what one can expect from a family member.

To be sure, for workers with a history of poverty, accessing a job in the welfare office signals an opportunity to give back for some, a simple irony for others, and a source of great pride that can easily turn into hubris for still others. As Laney Marino, a Staunton administrator, admits, "some of the meanest people are workers that I know were on assistance before. That really bothers me. I don't understand it. I've seen them and if they were ever my worker, I would not want them as my worker."

Indeed, I am often asked about bureaucrats who are former recipients themselves and whether they are more or less punishing with clients. Although this is a legitimate question, I worry that it is too simplistic. It tempts us to reduce these bureaucrats to caricatures—the once down-on-her luck caseworker with a heart of gold versus the haughty striver who doesn't understand why everyone can't make it just as she did. The personal histories of caseworkers often matter in more nuanced ways. Experiences with poverty often give workers a set of resources for their discretionary toolkits that can be marshaled with clients that co-workers from nonimpoverished backgrounds are less likely to wield. In the narrative that follows, Edna Singletary's account demonstrates how she deploys her history in a way that is layered and often unrecognized in previous research. As the story unfolds, we can see how this Staunton office caseworker who experienced welfare in her childhood sees herself as at once "just like" and very different from her client Monet, defying conventional categories of the benevolent versus punitive recipient-turned-bureaucrat:

I had this young girl who lives in the projects on Lyman Street. And Lyman Street, I lived on when my mother was alive and we were young kids. [The client] has her boyfriend living with her off and on, and I know that. I always ask her, "How's your boyfriend?" And she will say, "Oh, I'm trying to get him a job." I said, "Well, he needs to get up and get a job. Why are you [the one at the TANF office] doing all this?" So I had to get to her level because she was a transfer in from [another local office] and I don't know how [that office's] workers work, but they kind of give the clients a hard time. So she thought I was giving her a hard time when we talked over the phone. . . . And just last week I said, "Listen, Monet, I really don't know who you think you are talking to. You need to calm down or I'm going to hang up the phone." She said, "I'm not talking loud." I said, "I got the phone away from my ear and there is somebody standing outside my cubicle, and they can hear you." I said, "I want you to come in here at a specific time that we have scheduled." And she came in. We sat down and we talked. I said, "Where is it that you live?" So she said, "Detney Court." And I started laughing. I said, "Mm-hmm." She said, "Why'd you say that?" So to come down to her level, I had to tell her. "I was born and raised in that project." She said, "You were?" I said, "Yes." She said, "I can't even walk through there." I said, "If you're not into anything around there, you're safe. But if you are into something, you're not going to be safe." She said, "I took out the trash and somebody approached me and said, 'Where's so and so?' And I said, 'I don't know what you're talking about, I'm out taking out the trash.'" I told her, "That's what you tell them and keep walking." She said, "But I can't send my boyfriend out." I said, "Go out with him, you and your son and walk with him to the trash. Because it's not safe for a man in that area by himself. Walk out there so they will know that he is with you and your son and he is there periodically." She said, "You think I should do that?" I said, "Yeah. But is he into anything?" She said, "Oh, no. He is at home asleep now." I said, "Well, why isn't he out looking for a job? You need to tell 'your boo' that he needs to get up and go out. If you want me to give him some information, [I can]. Because he could be put on your food stamps." She said, "He can?" I said, "Yeah, but if he is working, I need his income." "But then that will reduce my food stamps," she said. I told her, "I'm telling you this 'cause you can do that. He is not the father of your child." She said, "But he's always there with [my son]." I said, "Okay, it's up to you." Even girls that say the father's not there and you can tell that they're lying, I say, "If he is in the house, let me know. He can be included but he has to follow the rules of welfare."

As Sharon Hays (2003) notes, public policies are translated into organizational rules and procedures around work and family that are then "sifted . . . through the practical concerns and moral ideals of welfare caseworkers" and meet the complex lives of low-income mothers and their children.[3] Here, intersecting social identities and investments related to gender, class, race, and community membership influence the articulation and performance of Edna's professional identity. Edna believes that some of her most effective tools for leveraging her discretionary power aren't what they teach at the new caseworker orientation or what her supervisors tell her to do, but what she has learned from her experiences on Lyman Street. We see in Edna's narrative several of the resources and qualities that constitute her discretionary toolkit, operating beyond the formal edicts of the agency. Her history doesn't simply shape certain attitudes about how she should treat clients or her feelings about their struggles; Edna's experience has given her *practical tools* for working with clients.

She provides a rich account of how she shapes the style and tone of her interaction with Monet as well as the tangible and intangible resources that she allocates during this organizational process. To be sure, their encounters vacillate between being confrontational and collaborative, typical of many of the exchanges that I observed. For her part, Monet showcases how clients are doing their own work in these interactions: deflecting stigma and challenging their presumed lack of power in their relationships with their caseworkers by periodically asserting themselves in their interactions. Edna's authority nevertheless prevails as she reminds Monet that she needs to restrain herself on the phone and to remember to whom she is speaking. Edna's decree that Monet's boyfriend should be looking for work, and her insinuation that it is unfair to Monet that she is the one who has to secure resources for them through welfare, could have offended Monet and underscores the inequality inherent in their relationship.[4] Edna's description of "coming down to her level" reinforces this point as Edna clearly sees a hierarchical distinction between herself and Monet.

What diffuses the situation is the two women's common history with Detney Court, emerging from Edna's decision to go outside of the formal service-delivery script. In such an interaction Edna deploys her class status as a tool to create both distance—she is someone who has "made it" and no longer has to contend with the same issues—and familiarity—she is someone who nevertheless has "been there" and can rhetorically level the playing field with the content of her message. That both women are African American creates a climate of intraracial exchange freighted with meaning, something that will be explored in greater depth in the next chapter. The women's shared history in this racially segregated housing project recalls the delicate dance that blacks from different class statuses perform in everyday interactions described by pioneering social scientists such as W. E. B. DuBois (1899) and in more recent work by Mary Pattillo (2007, 1999) and John Jackson (2000).

When Edna reaches out in this way, the tone of the interaction shifts and Monet feels comfortable enough to lower her defenses a bit and reveal her anxieties about her life outside the welfare office. Edna responds by pulling another tool from her discretionary repertoire; she empathetically counsels Monet that as long as she distances herself from the neighborhood's more dangerous elements, she should be safe. Monet also shares what is likely a foremost fear—the safety of her boyfriend. The irony is that in this interaction Monet reveals to Edna how and why the traditional gender roles have been reversed in her home, a central concern of welfare reform's chief architects. It is Monet who has the most immediate access to the state's resources such as cash benefits and employment support services. It is Monet who enjoys enough neighborhood safety to do routine tasks such as taking out the trash. It is her boyfriend who watches her son, yet is unable to safely take him outside due to neighborhood violence. And it will be Monet's actions that communicate to the neighbors that her family is not to be bothered because, as Edna affirms, "it is not safe for a man in that area by himself."

Monet takes in Edna's advice and Edna returns to her recommendation that Monet's boyfriend should be looking for work. It is not a policy mandate that Edna is called to enforce, but she nevertheless sees this counsel as part of her job and the service she provides, complete with its own social meaning and implications. Edna is reaching out to a family like the one hers used to be, residentially and socially, literally and figuratively. Even Edna's use of the slang term "your boo" to describe Monet's boyfriend and her question about whether he is "into anything" problematic affirms the forged informal connection and sisterly tone of the message. Yet, the interaction is a tightrope walk. Edna is also making an intervention into Monet's domestic situation in ways that call to mind how caseworkers throughout welfare's history have felt obliged to regulate various aspects of clients' lives, even if they weren't a part of formal policy mandates. As feminist scholars have noted, this involvement in both Monet's labor and domestic spheres reinforces certain gender norms for Monet and her boyfriend (Korteweg 2006; Monson 1997; Haney 2002a). What "good mothers" and "good men" do is encoded in her remarks: both should be looking for work regardless of any constraints in the labor market or at home. It is likely that only workers who deploy these kinds of tools most adeptly are able to walk this line without provoking a negative response from the client. Yet Edna's personal history and the content and tone of her advice likely make her able to intervene in this way and to be "heard" by Monet.

Edna finishes by returning to the more tangible policy-related resources in her arsenal—the opportunity for Monet's boyfriend to apply for food stamps as well. This is an opportunity that I saw few caseworkers offer to their clients, even though they are aware that many have live-in boyfriends. In short, Edna's willingness to use a wide range of tools from her discretionary toolkit to interact with Monet—her style of communicating, her license to offer advice about sensitive life topics, her choices of message, her willingness to incorporate her own history and life lessons, and her extensive knowledge of policy and her decision to share one of its least-publicized resources—affirms this critical piece of the story of socially situated bureaucrats in "catch-all bureaucracies." Organizational actors assert who they are through the work they do. Edna's professional identity is rooted in part in her social experiences, and such a distinct perspective becomes infused into organizational processes on the ground.

As caseworkers construct independent practices and images of their work, Edna's story shows us the importance of personal history as an instrument in the use of discretionary power. These experiences are distilled not only into attitudes and beliefs but also into the concrete tools that inform how workers view clients, how they believe they should interact with them, and what resources they can offer beyond formal policy mandates. Workers are powerful in this regard; they make choices about how their histories will inform, and be incorporated into, their discretionary toolkits. Over time, this process helps workers to formulate and reformulate professional identities that serve as overarching frameworks within which they do their jobs. As such, the relationship between discretionary toolkits and workers' identities is mutually constitutive: workers revise and reinforce their identities through their use of discretion, and their identities help shape what goes into their discretionary toolkits.

"Transforming" or "Benchmarking" Clients? The Battle over the Professional Identities of Postreform Welfare Bureaucrats

Personal histories—whether or not they include poverty—explain only part of the story of how professional identities come to be. They don't explain how we get the social worker and efficiency engineer models of the caseworker role because their influence on professional identity is highly individualized. They can't explain entirely why some bureaucrats emphasize brokering resources for clients while others stress gatekeeping. Nor do they help us to understand why and how these competing models are so enduring, leading to disparities in institutional outputs.

Over the course of my fieldwork, I began to see the important part that welfare's administrative system plays in the formation and maintenance of street-level caseworkers' professional identities. I use the term "system" to denote not only the two local offices that I studied but also the network of local offices with a central office at the helm. Both Fishertown and Staunton had social workers *and* efficiency engineers and both exhibited differences in service delivery *within* the local offices. Looking solely at each branch's office administrators therefore would not reveal how competing professional models came to be. Personality characteristics, occupational competencies, and disparate views on the part of workers about clients don't fully explain the variation either. These dynamics have presumably always been embedded in the Staunton and Fishertown staffs, but they haven't led to the differences in service delivery that we are now witnessing. Social-work-style case management and efficiency-based eligibility-compliance enforcement have coexisted uneasily in welfare offices for decades. Appendix A's historical overview highlights how these competing models have survived almost from the inception of welfare policy, and apparently there have always been bureaucrats with personal predilections toward one approach or another. But the models took turns as the preferred approach in local offices with each new rollout of reform over the decades. Immediately before welfare reform in the 1990s, most offices across the country unequivocally advocated the efficiency engineering model of the job (Brodkin 1986; Kane and Bane 1994). Social work was viewed as something that caseworkers could do on their own time, but it was absolutely not required in practice or as a professional identity that workers were to embrace. Welfare reform changed that.

Creating a Welfare-to-Work Professional

Although Massachusetts was a national pioneer in implementing some of the more stringent aspects of welfare reform in 1995—immediate work requirements for those whose children are a certain age, a 2.75 percent reduction in cash benefits for nonexempt recipients, and sanctions for failure to participate in a work activity—it did so in a relatively liberal-leaning political context.[5] Emergent policies likely represented the compromises struck between Republican governors William F. Weld (1991–1997), A. Paul Cellucci (1997–2001),[6] Jane Swift (acting governor, 2001–2002) and W. Mitt Romney (2003–2007), and the state legislature, which was controlled by Democrats during these periods. Moreover, the state's long history of legal protections for children and its very strong welfare-rights advocacy community pushed to temper some of welfare reform's most punitive features. It was a contentious fight, with DTA Commissioner Joseph Gallant sounding the battle cry, backed by Governor Weld, that the welfare system was badly broken. Only a waiver secured from the federal government would grant the flexibility necessary to make significant changes. Although central office administrators describe their leader at the time as "dogged in his determination" to change the welfare program, they took little convincing to concede that the existing system was failing to help the people it was meant to serve and needed reform. Although their benevolent assertions were rarely taken at face value by the local advocacy community, Jessica McDonnell, one of the state reform's chief architects, asserted that "I like to think that *we're* advocates for our clients, too." Her sentiments were echoed by Becky Thomas, a retired DTA official:

I think some would say, "You know, those people over there at DTA, they're so awful, they hate poor people." But I would say, "So wrong. We may look at how to help people differently, but this was not about hating poor people." This was about saying there's something wrong when you see the daughter of the woman that you worked with five years ago [now on the rolls]. Something's not right here. This is not helping people. Is this the perfect solution? I don't know, but I think our attitude was, "We're going to do something different; we're going to at least try something different."

Central office administrators describe the period around welfare reform's beginnings as a seemingly endless string of regulation-writing meetings, countless drafts of policy proposals that were negotiated in excruciating detail with their overseers in the federal government, and an aggressive public relations campaign to recruit service providers and employers to work with their clients. No one that I interviewed could recall any co-workers who left in protest, a marked difference from the contentiousness within the Clinton administration over welfare reform in a far more aggressively partisan policymaking environment (DeParle 2004). DTA created an ambitious plan for welfare reform that included launching its various components in their entirety simultaneously in all of the offices across the state. To raise the stakes even higher, the DTA launched its new behemoth computer system soon afterward to complement the administration of the new welfare program. Nonexempt clients' twenty-four-month-benefit time clocks started just one year later.

The remaking of street-level welfare bureaucrats, a goal coveted by central office administrators, ran a parallel course. Starting in the mid-1990s, the evolving organizational identity of the Massachusetts DTA was resettling around the notion that the welfare office provided temporary cash assistance but emphasized moving clients into the labor force and offering the supports to do it. For the benefit of both the public and office staff, administrators tried to reinforce the idea that DTA was a "helping" agency, fending off critics who argued that the agency was fundamentally punitive and had neither the know-how nor the desire to help clients in comprehensive ways. The DTA's evolving organizational identity, what members saw as the core, enduring, and distinctive features of their institution, became critically important to assert as part of the policy creation and implementation process (Albert and Whetten 1985). Not surprisingly, how rank and file caseworkers understood and performed their jobs became a crucial piece of the drive toward organizational transformation (Ashforth and Mael 1989; Elsbach and Kramer 1996; Dutton, Dukerich, and Harquail 1994). Administrators wanted the link between the new mission of the agency and workers' actions and approaches to be closely aligned. In other words, as organizational theorists have affirmed, central office administrators wanted to see a strong relationship between caseworkers' sense of DTA's organizational identity and image and their own sense of who they were and what they stood for as welfare professionals (Dutton and Dukerich 1991). Such a linkage would encourage a very personal connection between the subsequent actions of the organization and the individual motivations of workers. Bob Calhoun, a headquarters official, described his hopes for the professional identities of welfare bureaucrats down the chain of command in this way:

We need a workforce that is going to be more geared toward case management and helping people to address the special issues that they have, while at the same time having, as the overall goal, to help people find employment or to find traction that's going to help them escape poverty. That has not always been the message, and that needs to be repeated again and again as the overall objective of our work. It's not to reduce the caseload, it's not to have [caseworkers] function as [bank] tellers where the focus is entirely on the eligibility process; it's on the fundamental things that bureaucrats do within welfare agencies. That is something that we need to help them do more efficiently, but the overall goal is to help people out of poverty. And I think we're beginning to do that, and I know we need to repeat it more.

Adopting what Carolyn Hill (2006) calls *unified case management*, which integrates eligibility-compliance and welfare-to-work services in the duties of each caseworker, Bob and his colleagues had their choice of at least two different tactical approaches to implement this model on the ground. First, if the ultimate goal of reform at the national level was to reduce welfare dependency by decreasing caseloads and increasing employment, the Massachusetts DTA could push its local offices to utilize the expanding client-tracking apparatus in order to trigger exits. Using increased paper- and computer-based surveillance, caseworkers would be expected to ensure that policy-related bureaucratic mechanisms effectively "benchmarked" people off the rolls at the appropriate times. Time clocks would count down twenty-four months of assistance and then require caseworkers to manually close cases or oversee computer-generated automatic terminations when clients had effectively "spent" their allocation of public support. Sanctions would similarly reduce caseloads as the surveillance system flagged clients for Learnfare and other policy violations. Clients exempt from the work requirement but subject to time limits would experience welfare for the most part as they previously had, although now they were supposed to visit the TANF office to complete monthly transition plans until the twenty-four months of assistance ended. Clients subject to the work requirement would attend job search or training classes or work until their wages disqualified them, their twenty-four months ended, or they consistently failed to meet the weekly attendance requirement. Essentially, just by enforcing the rules and processing client data so that the office's surveillance system could mechanically manipulate clients' TANF grants, caseworkers could reduce their caseloads and satisfy a minimal definition of helping their clients become independent of welfare. Accurately and efficiently executing an eligibility-compliance model of service delivery that now includes time- and work-related benchmarks would qualify as an incarnation of unified case management.

A competing tactical approach to implementing unified case management exists, one that is inherent in Bob's description of his vision of the caseworker role. It engages a more far-reaching understanding of what it means to be a new welfare professional, tries to address the range of issues and challenges operating in the lives of clients in an effort to target barriers to work, and offers a broader package of "help" to clients to help them perhaps eventually escape poverty. While the prereform incarnation of casework focused on classifying and processing cases, this model would emphasize making substantive changes in the resources that clients have at their disposal in hopes of moving them from welfare to work and protecting those for whom this is not a feasible goal. Time limits and work requirements would not simply serve as benchmarks through which to measure eligibility and compliance at a given time. They would structure the parameters of holistic service delivery by giving workers an understanding of how long they have to work with clients and what behaviors must be incorporated into their service plans. Although caseworkers have neither the opportunity nor the capacity to respond to all of the structural and individual forces that affect their clients, they would now be expected to adopt the ambition of "working with the whole client" for the duration of their relationship. Their approach would be to ask more questions in order to triage clients' most pressing concerns and clearest barriers. Clients would be deemed "self-sufficient" not simply by virtue of the fact that they were no longer on the welfare rolls but because they were given the tools to find and maintain employment and to eventually escape poverty. For those unable to meet those goals, the agency would help them find other kinds of resources to survive, whether in the form of a disability exemption from time limits and work requirements or a move to a different government program. The overarching assumption, however, would remain that the majority of clients should and can work and are actively directed toward that goal by their caseworkers.

The expedient route likely would have been for the DTA as an institution to embrace the first, "benchmarking" model, but it instead chose to advance the second, "holistic" approach. This was possible in part because the DTA was not subject to the same intense pressure to massively reduce caseloads as in some other states because of its liberal-leaning state legislature and federal waiver. As Bob asserted, "the overall objective of our work is not to reduce the caseload, it's not to have caseworkers function as tellers where the focus is entirely on the eligibility process." Instead, DTA administrators opted to encourage a case-work style that they hoped would lead to caseworker-client encounters that were more transformational rather than routinized, particularistic, or instrumental (Meyers, Glaser, and MacDonald 1998).

To signal and reinforce this adopted professional model and to encourage caseworkers to think of their work differently, administrators sought to change not only workers' day-to-day tasks but also their orientations toward clients. Policies and procedures changed seemingly overnight and frontline workers were expected to catch up. Memos and newsletters announcing these large and small tweaks to the way that caseworkers were to do business, complete with messages from the commissioner about the importance of the task at hand, rained down from the central office on the local offices. The job titles of financial assistance workers were changed to *temporary assistance social workers.* Caseworkers' duties would now entail not only dispersing benefits but also supporting clients through complex welfare-to-work processes. As Jessica Stevens in the central office explained:

We were just concerned [for clients]. Really, what is your plan? I mean, part of what we tried to do with welfare reform is get people, from the minute they walked in the door, to have some sort of plan. That came along with the time-limited benefit nature of the program. You're going to have twenty-four months in a sixty-month period. And so what's your plan? You know, let us help you develop one, but you need to have a plan. Let's talk about your progress on your plan. And then especially, you know, we really geared up as people got closer and closer to the end of their twenty-four months because we were sincerely worried about what those people were going to be doing when they weren't eligible for assistance any longer.

The agency communicated these expectations and concerns to clients as well, who were notified via mass mailings from the DTA office, information sessions hosted by nonprofit agencies and the welfare office, and media coverage that stated that, while the welfare office would be much more strict, it also had loads of information about the latest job programs, employment opportunities, and other social services.[7] Although the in-house newsletter, *Transitions,* boasted that "Every job is 'a good job,'" the department seemed willing to help clients find good fits in the job market. These practices signaled to frontline workers just what kind of organizational change the department was embarking upon and how it expected the professional identities of the staff to follow suit. While caseworkers' assigned professional *roles* would now include the dual functions of rule enforcement and welfare-to-work support, the department's emphasis on in-depth casework to fulfill these tasks supported the idea that *who* welfare professionals would become within the organization (and for their clients) would also change in a way that stressed the personalized support piece of that role.

Perhaps the most important institutional signal that things were expected to change for street-level welfare bureaucrats was the central office's revision of its caseworker evaluation system. Caseworker performance reviews are conducted twice yearly by supervisors who then go over the results individually with each worker in their unit. The performance review framework is made up of twelve job duties, with brief descriptions provided for each. Supervisors rate workers on each duty with an "exceeds expectations," "meets expectations," or operates "below expectations" mark and provide feedback for improvement. Table 1 displays the duties for which workers are rated and the criteria for evaluation.

Added to long-standing measures such as *quality of casework* and *eligibility determination,* which emphasize neatness, accuracy, and efficiency, the office integrated performance benchmarks such as *recipient self-sufficiency* and *recipient assessment/reassessment, employment and transitional plan development* into their evaluation indicators. *Recipient self-sufficiency* is described as "the worker assists recipients who are subject to transitional assistance benefit time limitations to find jobs and to become self sufficient, as well as assisting exempt recipients, as appropriate." *Recipient assessment/reassessment, employment and transitional plan development* is defined in the following way: "The worker performs assessment/reassessment activities to determine recipient job readiness; initiates, explains, develops and amends employment and transitional plans; makes referrals; monitors participants; and authorizes Employment Support Services for his/her recipients. Initiates and follows up on recipient referrals to service providers, employers and other resources. Processes case management activities for both pre- and post-time limited recipients."

These major shifts in the evaluation structure align neatly with the work-focused goals of reform. Not only would workers' routine duties now differ but welfare reform would be expected to inspire a new orientation toward clients and the welfare enterprise. Although they would still track eligibility and rule compliance, the predominant prescription was that street-level bureaucrats would incorporate aspects of employment counseling, client advocacy, and resource brokering into their jobs. They would no longer exist simply as conduits through which clients accessed their cash benefits. The goals of these organizational changes

Table 1. Employee performance review system: primary job duties and performance criteria.

Duty	Performance Criteria
Eligibility Determination	The worker performs all eligibility determination activities accurately and timely so that applicants/recipients receive their correct benefits within established time frames.
Recipient Self Sufficiency	The worker assists recipients who are subject to transitional assistance benefit time limitations to find jobs and to become self sufficient, as well as assisting exempt recipients, as appropriate.
Recipient Assessment/ Reassessment, Plan Development Employment and Transitional Services	The worker performs assessment/reassessment activities to determine recipient job readiness, initiates, explains, develops and amends employment and transitional plans; makes referrals; monitors participants; and authorizes Employment Support for his/her recipients. Initiates and follows up on recipient referrals to service providers, employers and other resources. Processes case management activities for both pre- and post-time limited recipients.
SSI Conversion/Referrals	The worker assists in the achievement, maintenance, and improvement of the supervisory units' performance relative to Social Security Administration referrals and follow-up on EAEDC cases to maximize their conversion to SSI.
Quality of Casework	The worker performs transitional assistance casework in an accurate, thorough, and timely manner consistent with the Department's recipient employment mission.
Recipient Orientation	The worker performs orientation activities to insure that recipients are aware of their employment responsibilities under the Transitional Assistance Program and the resources that are available to help them find employment.
Attitude	The worker responds to recipient inquiries/requests in a professional manner, and seeks the establishment and continuity of courteous, cooperative and harmonious relationships with recipients, co-workers, and external agencies, while respecting the diversity of the populations involved.

Table 1. (Continued)

Duty	Performance Criteria
Communication Skills	The worker demonstrates an ability to listen, speak, and write in a manner that promotes understanding. Transmits information in a professional manner.
Management Information Systems	The worker utilizes and maintains available management information systems in a manner that insures that recipients' information is coded accurately and is up to date.
Reasonable Casework Expectations	The worker performs casework in a manner that is reasonable and consistent with the Department's policy and procedures, its recipient employment mission, and the collective bargaining agreement.
Food Stamp Casework	The worker performs Food Stamp casework in an accurate and timely manner consistent with the Department's employment mission for current, as well as former recipients.
Homeless Prevention	The worker performs casework activities that result in the early detection of housing problems and takes the appropriate steps that are necessary to prevent homelessness such as timely referrals to Housing Search Contractors.

were clear: Massachusetts sought to do more than simply benchmark clients off the rolls, letting time limits, work requirements, and sanctions essentially do the work of roll reduction for them. Instead, Massachusetts state officials wanted caseworkers to engage their clients using a broader set of tools. They aspired to see some level of transformation, no matter how minimal, in their clients' lives.

Meanwhile, as the idea of reforming the state's welfare system gained momentum in the fall of 1994, local administrators in the Fishertown and Staunton DTA offices increasingly felt that they were living in an institutional fishbowl. The contradictions that had long enjoyed an uneasy but secure existence within their offices were being destabilized and now served as influential justifications for welfare reform. What had been business as usual—continuously recertifying clients for assistance, not channeling many institutional resources toward addressing clients' barriers to work, and allowing employment to be a voluntary rather than mandatory effort among their clients—was officially up-ended in Massachusetts in 1995. Countless constituencies—the central office, client advocates, the press, friends and acquaintances of case-workers who kept hearing that "things were going to be different down at the welfare office," and of course clients themselves—seemed now to have a stake in how welfare bureaucrats did their jobs.

Although the philosophy, policies, and procedures driving welfare reform were viewed with much greater skepticism (and even hostility in some cases) in the local offices by frontline staff, many welcomed the vision of new professional identities for caseworkers promoted by Bob and the central office. Kieran Hannity, an administrator in the Staun-ton office, was optimistic when it became apparent that the new wel-fare system would dramatically change how workers functioned on the ground. Although Massachusetts ET Choices and previous incarnations of work programs had highlighted the importance of getting clients to work, the new TAFDC program would be *the* driving force behind how the office operated. "Although the legislation switch flipped like a light," Kieran explained, "we had to get [workers] thinking about a dif-ferent way to do their job. We got lots of training provided by outside vendors to the direct service staff and management to get us through this process [of] increasing awareness [of] how you work with people." Ostensibly, the organizational supports from the central office, such as the job title change, the revised evaluation structure, and the rhetoric coming down from the top promoting the notion of a new welfare bu-reaucrat, would go a long way toward convincing workers that a new day had arrived in the agency.

The Return of Social Workers in Postreform Welfare Offices?

This redefinition of their jobs to entail intensive resource brokering and social-work-like case management was particularly attractive to a great number of caseworkers in the Staunton and Fishertown DTA of-fices. They took the charge quite seriously, and interpreted the job title change that now included the phrase *social work* quite literally. They envisioned that their jobs would involve in-depth engagement with clients to address the challenges that they faced, advising them and connecting them to needed services. This was particularly attractive to some of the caseworkers who had initially thought that working for the welfare department would be like this when they were hired decades ago, before their expectations were met with the claims-processing realities of the job. Kelly Taub, a worker in the Fishertown office for nineteen years, explained that "many of us who came to work for this agency originally wanted to be social workers, thinking that we would be doing exactly what we are doing now. Sitting down, interviewing people, asking them questions, and asking, 'What can we do now for you? What can we do for your future to help you move on?' When the reform hit, we heard all this conversation that that's what we'd be doing, getting people independent."

In the period immediately before the mid-1990s reforms, the expectations that Kelly describes for her job would have been largely unrealistic. The model of casework that predominated in welfare offices when she was hired did not involve much social work in the traditional sense of counseling and referring clients to services to improve their overall well-being. "Getting people independent" would have been a worthy goal, and one that was encouraged through various incarnations of work training programs, but it would not have been the dominant model of casework. To this segment of workers, welfare reform and subsequent institutional changes provided an opportunity to reconcile the difference between what they had hoped their work would be and what it had evolved into over the years. By changing the evaluation process and their job titles to include the words *social work,* and by declaring that a big change was under way, these caseworkers believed that the welfare office was moving them in a different professional direction.

Others were more skeptical about the department's intentions around welfare reform and this highly touted shift in their professional roles, but they recognized the value in coming aboard and adopting the approach. Here's how Stanley finished the assessment of his job, the beginning of which we saw earlier in the chapter:

We have a system in this state where you can apply for food stamps through the computer. They're going to pilot doing that off the Internet totally, no worker involvement, no advocate, just [he simulated typing on the desk] you, the computer, and you're going to send your application to a welfare office. If that proves to be successful, there may not be a need for welfare workers anymore. You can send [the eligibility verifications] in afterwards through the mail. See, instead of having a social worker, everything would go to a processing center. It would be like an insurance claim, rather than a social worker function. I'm fighting the insurance claim model. . . . Technology will take [this job] away, unless you have enough soft services built in to make your job retainable. And that's the direction I'm going in.

As many of Staunton and Fishertown's street-level bureaucrats adopted and operationalized a professional identity centered around resource brokering and what they understand as social work, I observed them using their expanded purview under welfare reform to develop and solidify their accompanying discretionary toolkits, proactively seeking out more in-depth knowledge of the employment and social services in the area so as to be able to address an array of client needs. Flyers with the latest jobs programs are passed around and tacked to cubicle walls. Caseworkers chat informally in the hallways about which training programs lead to "good jobs" in the city for clients and which are a waste of time. They engage clients about what their lives are like outside of the welfare office. They address a broader swath of clients' concerns, offering up ideas on everything from after-school activities for teenage children to strategies for confronting unresponsive bureaucrats in the city's court system. In Staunton, when clients mention problems with housing or accessing other social services, it is not unusual for social workers to throw out suggestions for how clients might find help, leveraging the former Employment Services supervisor who has transformed herself into an indispensable guru of the city's resources for low-income families. I observed them attempting to revise the character and tone of the client-caseworker interaction in ways that represent these newfangled professional identities, providing motivational words to encourage clients to seek their fortunes in the labor market and "make a change" in their lives. In short, these caseworkers have developed a broad understanding of what they can influence within the agency and how they can work with clients. They are social workers, and this interpretation of their professional roles not only has the blessing of the agency but also its backing through a variety of institutional mechanisms.

The Reascent of the Efficiency Engineers

The organizational cues put in place by welfare administrations could give the impression that there is a whole new ballgame taking place in the Staunton and Fishertown welfare offices. The transition under way has proven to be less than seamless, however, and another, antithetical set of institutional cues engenders a very different presentation of a welfare-to-work professional. Although the stated goals of policy and the institutional signals previously outlined suggested that caseworkers should now structure their work very differently from what had characterized the "eligibility/check writing" days, several street-level welfare bureaucrats quickly surmised that there was only a loose alignment between the "talk" and the "walk." In fact, multiple institutional prompts told these workers that accuracy and efficiency in paperwork processing rather than coaching clients on employment, connecting clients to services and information, and doing "social work" ultimately would matter most in the organization. As a result, *welfare-to-work efficiency engineering* has become the institution's most strongly affirmed professional identity, and it has consequently been adopted by the majority of caseworkers. The implementation of the evaluation system and other organizational cues would express only weak and partial support for the *welfare-to-work social work* model.

The launch of BEACON, the sprawling welfare computer system, likely spelled doom for the social workers from the very beginning. One could make the argument that shifting the locus of the caseworker-client interaction from paper to a computer screen even further depersonalized the dynamic between the two groups, removing the last vestiges of connection that the massive increase in paperwork in welfare offices likely started years ago. This was actually only a small part of the problem. Rather, BEACON's major malfunctions and minor but frustrating technical glitches made the transition to electronic service delivery laborious, unpopular, and highly stressful for workers. In the central office, administrators focused most of their attention in the early years of the reform on trying to remedy BEACON's challenges and address the kinks in the new welfare policy under the glare of the media spotlight and the watchful eye of the advocacy community. Street-level caseworkers' professional development therefore was one of the first things to slip down the priority list of a beleaguered and inundated administration and line staff. Caseworker training sessions focused less on how to be a social worker and more on the new policies, announcing the latest changes, and getting staff up to speed on using BEACON. In many ways, these other priorities knocked the wind out of the transformation that welfare bureaucrats' professional identities were supposedly undergoing, encouraging them to shift their attention back to ensuring that the infant system functioned, and functioned as accurately and efficiently as possible.

Although the unfamiliarity with and commotion around BEACON and the state's new welfare policy eventually subsided, other cues signaled that there was a mismatch between the organization's outward support of one professional identity and the actual backing of another. Professional identities must be buttressed by an accompanying level of technical training consistent with how one understands the occupational task at hand. The adoption of a professional orientation based on resource-brokering or even social work assumed a level of training that most workers did not have. The vast majority of the department's caseworkers were hired during an era in which clerical skills were highly valued and the job was disconnected from social work (see appendix A for more details on this). The educational and prereform training backgrounds of workers, and the level of training provided by the department when welfare reform was introduced, favored the technical aspects of the caseworker job. Laney, a Staunton administrator, sees skill-level deficiencies as a problem in her office because welfare reform now requires different abilities in her workers:

I think some of the workers we have were promoted from clerical positions and they don't have the skills that they need to be workers now. They were promoted to the job when you were like a widget counter. For a while, they actually used to measure our work by saying, you change a [client] address [in our records], so you've got .3 hours of work credit. . . . Some people could do that. Whereas now, you have to be more of a social worker and more into referring people and getting them to where they need to be, and it's hard for them. They can't do it. I think that's a big weakness.

In a private firm, a sudden shift like this in the skills demanded would lead to turnover and workforce replacement, but the hands of central office administrators were for the most part tied. In the civil service, union-negotiated employment contracts are more durable, and in a climate of scarce resources—especially for a politically unpopular enterprise such as public assistance—large numbers of new hires or injections of dollars to improve the human capital of the staff continue to be unlikely. The skills issue has created challenges for the department among stakeholders as well. "The advocates," Laney explained, "are assuming or believe that the workers should know that these [clients] have problems, but the workers, a lot of them, don't have those skills to know or to understand that these people have problems." Diagnosing their clients' employment barriers and personal issues had never been part of their job descriptions.

The caseload size created another obstacle to staff members' abilities to transition their professional identities toward social-work-like case management. Local administrators in both the Fishertown and Staunton offices expected that each worker would have fewer clients to work with as they implemented reform. Kieran explains why that is so critical, considering the expectations placed upon the staff to be a particular kind of welfare bureaucrat: "Caseworkers could spend more time talking to the people and not feel as much pressure to have to move on because they have to see six more people today. Maybe with this they would only have to see three people today. So they could give more in-depth interviews and listen better. They could think it through better as to what they can offer or give better explanations instead of very short explanations or skipping it on certain issues. They'd be less stressed. You would get better service from [caseworkers] just feeling more comfortable."

In practice, workers who experienced significant declines in their caseloads could expect roughly the same number of new cases to be shifted to them. State budget cuts hit the agency hard, causing a wave of layoffs in 2003 that removed roughly one-fourth of the Staunton and Fishertown office staffs. The department offered early retirement packages to senior caseworkers and instituted a hiring freeze for approximately three years in an effort to cut costs. Some of the state's local offices, including Staunton, merged with other sites, and excess staff members were ushered out with severances and early retirement deals. Others were offered the option of saving their jobs by downgrading to thirty-hour work weeks, and many accepted four-day or five-day 7:30 a.m. to 1 p.m. shifts. Caseworkers who also serve as union representatives carry a reduced caseload, and an aging workforce means that medical leaves that render employees absent for days, weeks, and sometimes months at a time are not uncommon in Staunton and Fishertown. These challenges do not go unnoticed by workers, as Jane in Fishertown explained:

What we were told, going into welfare reform, is our caseload should not exceed seventy-three to seventy-eight, because we should be doing holistic dealing with clients. And instead my caseload is actually 150. So it makes it hard to do that aspect of it, because you can't do it all as one person. And they just keep adding more paperwork-type things [for us to do]. A lot of people retired. And they didn't replace anyone.[8] It appears they don't care to replace anyone [chuckles]. They haven't put anyone in our program. . . . I hate to go as far as to say they don't care—it certainly appears [chuckles] that they don't care. They're burning us out. Absolutely.

Although it's hard to know whether efficiency engineers would engage in more social work activities if there was less to do, the sheer volume of the workload limits what most workers can reasonably do with clients. For those with orientations toward social work, the flexibility and extra time required to fully realize their professional models has been severely curtailed.

These arrangements of bureaucrats' work hours and the regular reshuffling of caseloads to ensure caseload equity among co-workers mean that clients frequently interact with multiple staff members during their spells on TAFDC. This also makes in-depth case management difficult to sustain over time and encourages caseworkers to focus on tracking the benchmarks of whoever occupies the client chair at that particular time, being guarded with the office's resources because workers may not always know the full agency history of who is sitting in front of them. Often, the first few meetings with a client transferred from another office or from a co-worker's caseload within the office are all about simply trying to straighten out errors or fill in information gaps left by other workers: Is she missing documentation for child immunizations? Was her time clock paused for a pregnancy that has long since come to term? Is she supposed to be in a work program but still hasn't received a child care voucher? The project of client transformation that organizational leaders and many caseworkers envisioned becomes increasingly difficult to achieve within the organization's service-delivery structure. Few seemed more frustrated with the process than Kieran:

With the change in emphasis and providing more services and in-depth types of services, our caseloads are still too high to provide the services. We're providing them but not as good as we could. . . . I think we might be short-changed by not having some new blood and people who are younger. In the past, we did always have a group. We don't have that group now. That younger group of workers, in maybe a seven- or eight-year span, were the group most likely to leave [after the retirees] because things come up in their lives. The people that are here are a little bit older. So there's a gap.

With these human resource issues, the job has not moved in the direction that Kieran and others hoped that it would. Workers like Loretta, who described her investment in doing social work in the previous chapter, were hard-pressed simply to keep up:

Well, I try to leave things organized the night before. But in the morning, I try to prioritize . . . the voice message [mailbox] gets filled up pretty quickly. [I retrieve the messages] to give the opportunity for more people to leave messages. And maybe [by quickly calling back], I prevent them from having to come to the office. It makes [the job] easy in many ways if you keep [clients] informed, if you work the phone efficiently. . . . And then I print my workflow reports, whatever [issues] can close a case. Or whatever I have to process that day, because we have thirty days [for some things],[9] we have twenty-two days [for others], we have to wait five days [for other things], we have deadlines, many deadlines. And then I see if I have to send the client a reminder, call the client, or process a case. And then I go through the mail and through the faxes to see if people have sent me documentation for their cases. And in between [seeing] clients, you try to process cases as much as you can.

A worker too caught up in offering in-depth case management risks being buried under a case processing schedule of this magnitude and pace. While she is attending to the workload, Loretta will likely receive, approximately every thirty to ninety minutes, a message from the front desk that a client awaits her, or she might be interrupted by yet another phone call. Extensive engagement with clients in which Loretta can assess clients' barriers to work and strategically broker resources for them almost has to be shoehorned into her day. Her priorities have lately gravitated toward making sure that her clients get the right amounts of cash, food stamps, and child care vouchers at any given moment and that time clocks, work program requirements, and sanctions are effectively monitored.

Perhaps most tellingly, the professional identity the department ultimately prizes was indicated by the implementation of the formal evaluation system and the informal ways that supervisors addressed their caseworkers' performances in their day-to-day interactions. These cues have revealed just how management believes caseworkers should integrate their competing responsibilities. Although numerous measures have been put in place in the evaluation system to emphasize "softer" skills such as connecting clients to information and social services, coaching them on their welfare-to-work transitions, and helping them to address personal and environmental challenges, on closer inspection the uneven distribution of "teeth" that signals an institutional priority to caseworkers suggests that the old model of evaluation is alive and well, while the new is barely visible.

Supervisors reported having only vague criteria to measure the newer evaluation features. While they count the number of errors flagged by quality control in a year to measure *quality of casework*, supervisors have not used quantitative or qualitative data to measure *recipient orientation*, whereby caseworkers are judged on the degree to which they make recipients aware of employment resources available to help them. Also not heavily emphasized during the evaluation was the part of *Recipient Assessment/Reassessment, Employment and Transitional Plan Develop-*

ment that evaluates workers' appraisals of clients and their subsequent plans for in-depth casework. In addition, although evaluations account for the number of client complaints that a supervisor receives about a caseworker, a more representative sample of clients' opinions is not solicited to determine casework quality.[10]

Instead, supervisors invoke subjective and largely unsystematic criteria to evaluate workers on these newer elements of their performance. They admit that their attention is drawn mostly to whether their supervisees stay on top of their daily administrative tasks. Accurate and efficient paperwork management outweighs most evaluation criteria, with employment support and other social service provision existing as add-ons. Most supervisors I observed were able to outline many of the complex issues that their clients face in their welfare-to work transitions that go beyond the job placement program and child care referrals that workers routinely provided. However, the efficacy with which workers help clients address these issues, even in a limited way, plays no role to speak of in the enforcement of the evaluation system.

Conrad Dalton, a Fishertown supervisor for fifteen years with a total of twenty-eight years in the department, explained that, with the large caseload, he focuses on ensuring that his workers complete their paperwork rather than reviewing the content and quality of the client-worker interaction. He explained the aspects of the review process that he takes most seriously when evaluating his workers:

Well, when it's review time, you may look at errors. Like, if your worker has gotten some errors that were their fault, you would consider that. . . . You think about how speedy they are with their paperwork. With some of my workers, I can give them something and it's done like yesterday. Others, I gotta stay on top of because their stuff is always late. . . . like case closings and inputting wages [and training] program attendance and then computer hits like unreported income and Learnfare [monitors child school attendance]. You gotta stay on top of that and if a worker doesn't, I'll make a comment in the evaluation. . . . [Workers are] supposed to do transition plans [with clients] periodically and recommend job search, give a day-care voucher, whatever. You're supposed to ask [recipients] why they're not working and document the answer they give. There are forms that you have to fill out. I make sure they do the paperwork. But no, no one pores over a transition plan to see what the client said and what the worker said. There's too many cases for that.

Supervisors explained that their evaluations are scrutinized by office administrators, who report to the central office, who then report to the state legislature, the governor, and the federal government. What the department prioritizes, from the higher echelons down, has come to be emphasized in the execution of the evaluation system. Although the agency has tried to adopt an approach to unified casework that heavily emphasizes how well workers serve as resource brokers and engage in a style of in-depth case management akin to social work, leaders have signaled that they really expect caseworkers to focus on engineering efficiency. Administrators in the central office conceded that this is the case, as Becky explains:

We have always had a focus on error rates and quality of work and recognizing good quality work in terms of the performance measures that the federal government prescribes for us. Error rate is kind of ingrained in the professional identity of all staff. So even while we have an emphasis on employment and training, we are concurrently measuring performance in terms of accuracy of our work. Staff have always had this constant of focusing on eligibility. Today, it's primarily focused on the food stamp program, because that's the only program we're measured by the federal government for error, and we do very well.

Staunton supervisor Ellen O'Donnell explained how the department's focus on "accuracy and timeliness" translates on the ground: "It's funny, because one of the things I'm supposed to rate [is caseworkers'] social work skills. And I find that a very hard thing to evaluate. We're not really doing it. If you get an error that's found by [Quality Control] and it's your fault, you'll get an informal warning. If you don't set a case up timely, you'll get a letter and you have to explain why the case wasn't processed [in a] timely [fashion]."

Bob bluntly summed up how the professional transformation process was working: "We evaluate them as eligibility workers, and not as social workers or people who are more focused on helping a person escape poverty." It is a source of frustration for him and many of his colleagues. Despite their assertions that welfare reform was an antipoverty movement at its core, and their high hopes for transforming the caseworker role to meet that goal, for the most part the professional orientation of the staff has come to revolve around "benchmarking" clients.

Interview and observation evidence from caseworkers suggests that most clearly understand what really seems to matter within the organization. They have guarded their reputations in the office closely, as they know through their decades of service that the opinions of supervisors and co-workers can be hard to change. Because there is little flexibility in the provision of material rewards, normative rewards, such as being deemed a "good worker," assume a great deal of meaning. The most universal criterion for this title is that of the efficiency engineers: accurate and efficient processing of cases. In other words, as Sharlene explained, "getting your clients what they need, when they need it, and not screwing it up." Workers who have few documented processing errors, receive few client complaints, observe deadlines, and seem to have good rapport with their clients are highly regarded by supervisors because they both execute policy and limit the tension between clients and the office. Sharlene expounded on her assessment:

If you have a lot of [unreconciled computer matches], you're going to get a "[performs] below [expectations]." Getting all those intakes [new applications completed and submitted] in thirty days . . . doing the reports. You'll get a [computer] match, "This person is working [and the wages are unreported]" or sometimes "the 'I' is wrong there, it should be an 'E.'" They say the name is wrong. They check everything: Social Security number, the kid is two [changing mother's exemption status from time limits and work requirements], immunization things. Things you should check on a daily basis, but they're throwing everything at us so I don't check mine every day. But they still grade you on all that.

In fact, caseworkers who choose to play a more in-depth role with clients are not only less likely to be rewarded for these behaviors but sometimes feel that they are a source of stress for management. Loretta explained that although she does her best to focus on processing cases as quickly as possible, she does pause to counsel clients and invests a great deal of time helping them find resources and information that might address some of their challenges. She knows that this doesn't make her the most efficient worker and she worries that she is constantly being watched by supervisors who worry that she isn't placing enough emphasis on processing cases:

I might [get in trouble for it]. I sometimes feel like they look at me like, "Why are you doing it?" It's not like I see [clients] and I tell them the story of my life. I'm brief and concise and I just tell them there are options. But I continue to do my [work]. I don't stop and cross my legs and get a cigarette [laughter]. No, while I'm doing this and that, I'm giving them advice and I continue to do my things. Because I think I have had experiences in my life that make me more sensitive to the client. Otherwise, you will close down and I don't want to. Or it's just numbers. Some clients appreciate it and some don't. And I still do it. Which, like I tell you, it gives meaning to what I do . . . I don't really mind if I'm not all that popular with management, if I know that I'm doing a good job. I mean, my higher conscience.

To Loretta, the ultimate authority that shapes how she defines and performs her job is her own sense of self. Even if her professional identity ultimately doesn't feel supported by the agency, she is determined to sustain it within the parameters of the bureaucracy.

For efficiency engineers, the embedded and frequently unspoken signals about how they should organize their days speak volumes over the seemingly superficial modifications of job title changes, organizational rhetoric, and cosmetic changes to the evaluation and compliance structure. Through the everyday organization of their work, they forge their own response to the question of who they are as professionals. They have determined what they can and cannot influence in a way that stands at a distance from a social worker like Loretta. As interpreters of the contradictory organizational messages sent by the system, these bureaucrats opt to dismiss the notion that they are anything other than claims processors with a new set of benchmarks related to work and time limits. It is for these reasons that these bureaucrats assert that they are not social workers. As Ellen Maxwell of the Fishertown office pondered in her interview with me, "Is the job that we're doing social work? Not really, I don't think. It's more of an eligibility process, it's more rule enforcement and benefit claiming." With the ambiguities that they hear in the department's strident message about welfare reform's purpose (i.e., work, unprecedented work supports, and connecting clients to resources on the road to financial self-sufficiency) and an equally pointed set of messages that emphasize "old" goals (i.e., eligibility, check writing, and error-free benefit calculations), it is hardly surprising that workers must struggle with balancing mixed messages about the new system. Both emergent professional identities— social work and efficiency engineering—are simultaneously legitimized and delegitimized by various organizational cues. Out of the cacophony, caseworkers create and operationalize differing, although not entirely oppositional, interpretations of their professional identities.

When Identities Clash:
Role Conflict in Postreform Welfare Offices

Previous research cautions us against essentializing actors' experiences into stark categories or asserting that an actor exhibits one professional identity at all times (Sachs 2001; March 1994). Caseworkers may move between identities in particular contexts, with certain clients, and over time. They may occasionally improvise styles based on the circumstances in which they find themselves. They may even act in ways that are contradictory to their professional identities. "In times of rapid change," Judyth Sachs writes, "identity cannot be seen to be a fixed 'thing,' it is negotiated, open, shifting, ambiguous, the result of culturally available meanings and the open-ended power-laden enactment of those meanings in everyday situations" (Sachs 2001, 154, paraphrasing from the work of Kondo 1990, 24). Indeed, the line from identity to behavior is not always a straight one.

A more precise way to think about how caseworkers create and leverage their discretionary power, and how identity informs this process, is to explore how workers travel along a continuum of complex identities. "To understand the power of oscillation," sociologist Gary Fine tells us, "involves recognizing, first, the choices of which [individuals] are aware and to which they have access and, second, how these choices serve as a means of establishing boundaries" (2004, 9). Similarly, what James March and Johan Olsen (2005) call a "logic of appropriateness" is based on the idea that organizational actors assess the situations in which they find themselves, determine the kind of professional they understand themselves to be, and decide how professionals like themselves can and should approach certain situations. The obligations and rules that actors associate with a particular identity, however, may not be conducive to a preferred set of bureaucratic actions. "Action," they claim, "involves evoking an identity or role and matching the obligations of that identity or role to a specific situation" (951). This is often grounded in ethical beliefs about what the appropriate action should be. March (1994) argues in later work that because logics of appropriateness are imbued with such moral content, decision making is often steeped with emotion as actors navigate the institutional uncertainty produced by clients, co-workers, or events. Taken together, this assigns a great deal of institutional gravity to the discrete decisions of and conflicts among situated bureaucrats over professional identities.

A unified model of casework requires workers to perform tasks related to both benefits eligibility and welfare-to-work case management simultaneously. They are expected to be at once supportive and corrective, flexible and firm, all the while trying to create a coherent presentation of a professional self. It is therefore perhaps not surprising that such discord over how this should be done regularly erupts in postreform welfare offices as the administrative system separately emboldens each enterprise. For Kirk Andrews, a central office administrator, the onus is on caseworkers to figure out how to navigate this duality: "There is a tension between trying to make sure families are eligible for assistance and they're doing the things that they're supposed to do, but [also] trying to be supportive. That can be a difficult. . . . Establishing trust between a worker and a client in that situation is certainly a challenge. . . . To some extent, it's the nature of the beast in terms of the business that we're in."

Although each caseworker tends to present a professional self-conception that favors either social work or efficiency engineering, many caseworkers devise techniques for moving fluidly among professional selves, depending on the context. Sundra Jenkins, a Staunton caseworker, explains how she has had to temper what she describes as a highly sympathetic professional self in order to enforce the rules with clients who do not respond to her initial approach: "At the end of twenty-four months, some [clients] come very motivated, but sometimes you have to close your eyes and push the paperwork and say 'if you don't do this, your benefits are going to end.' It's kind of hard to do at times. I'd rather not do that because I don't see that as the type of person that I want to be. Nevertheless, I have to keep a job so I close my heart down and say, 'Sorry, Ms. Jones, this is what will happen in a month or two.'"

Sundra establishes emotional boundaries between herself and clients during difficult moments that challenge her self-understanding as a social worker. She recognizes that the agency expects her to have some level of investment in the organization's complex mission (including its tougher aspects) and to do the work necessary to move fluidly within this context. Although for Sundra a primary focus on efficiently and unemotionally engineering the implementation of policy is not reflective of "the type of person that [she] wants to be," it nevertheless increasingly has to become a part of who she is as a professional.

As a result of strategies like Sundra's, I found fewer examples of hand-wringing among workers than I expected about how to negotiate the contradiction of relating to clients as the proverbial "cop" and "social worker" simultaneously. Loretta contends that such an oscillation between identities in order to fit the institutional context has become less difficult for her to navigate over time. What facilitates this process for her are the coping strategies that she has devised and added to her professional toolkit. It is not a seamless performance; Loretta was moved to tears during our interview as she talked about the similarities between herself and her clients and her desire to do more for them. But telling herself that her clients are surviving by other means and that she must be less sensitive are her ways of easing the incorporation of a professional stance that is uncomfortable for her: "I have become more resilient. I used to be affected. The first time I had to close a case, I didn't sleep that night. And my supervisor told me, 'You're in the wrong field, girl. You have to close the case.' I was like, wow . . . what will they do? Then later, I have realized, particularly working in the city, that they sometimes work under the table, they'll survive, they'll survive. But in the beginning, I was totally in shock because I didn't know."

Of course, a handful of workers in both Staunton and Fishertown resist the ambiguity inherent in moving between professional orientations, occasionally opting to fight for the professional identity that they believe is best to do the job. Often citing accountability to a larger moral framework, some caseworkers see themselves as "doing right," even if it means being on the wrong side of management. Caught between caring for clients versus "caring for the organization" (Heimer and Stevens 1997), this moral imperative in the composition of professional identity represents what Sherryl Kleinman (1996) describes as the moral significance that people assign to and invest in their work. Ivy, a Staunton caseworker, tells the story of a client applying for benefits:

I did an intake. All my supervisors have been fairly easy-going—but he was on vacation and the supervisor I was going to while he was on vacation was very nitpicky. I had a battered woman who had been sent up here from Puerto Rico because of the battering. . . . Obviously there's a real issue. She had a job in Puerto Rico before she came up here. Well, I didn't have a work termination letter for obvious reasons: she fled the country. I'm thinking, "Well, obviously she's not working that job anymore, it's a long commute." Obviously she can't contact her job in Puerto Rico to request the letter [showing that] because the guy could find out where she is and she could die. So I turned in this intake. I had letters from the domestic violence shelter where she was staying here saying she could not contact Puerto Rico because they were fearful for her life. I had all these documents, and the woman supervising gives it back to me and says, "We don't have a work termination letter." So I looked at her and I said, "We're not going to get one." And she says, "Why not?" and I said, "Because I'm not putting my client's life in danger for a silly piece of paper when it's obvious she's not working because it's a too long a commute. . . . And I have a letter that she was on a leave of absence, so we know she's not still getting paid." And the woman says, "Well, we need that," and I said, "Fine." And I took the case back and I called up the shelter and I got in touch with this woman and I told her, "I can't get your case off the ground. She wants a work termination letter. My supervisor will be back in three days, I'll give it to him, it will be fine, don't worry about it, it will be open next week." He comes back Monday morning, he looks at [the other supervisor's] notes, and he says, "Why didn't she sign this?" So I told him and he says, "Oh, my God!" He took his pen and signed his name to it, submitted it, and [the case] was open the next day. . . . This case would never have opened if it had been left up to her. Her thing was, let's not bend the rules even if it's a stupid rule and it means nothing.

Not surprisingly, it is the social workers rather than the efficiency engineers who are more often compelled to fight these battles (just as they find themselves having to incorporate efficiency engineering into their work more frequently than efficiency engineers have to make concessions to social work in *their* work). The agency's efforts to protect victims of domestic violence were beefed up considerably after the event that Ivy describes, but the incident teaches us a great deal about the tensions in the agency. At stake is not simply the DTA's ongoing grappling with balancing its orientation toward "gatekeeping" versus "resource brokering" but also its continuing struggle over the motives and strategies that should drive new welfare bureaucrats. Ivy's aims might be summed up in the following way: protect the client, get the resources to her, and don't be afraid to circumvent authority if necessary. She sees herself as fundamentally accountable to this client, even calling her with an update when things went awry and letting her in on her plan to outwit the acting supervisor. Not surprisingly, Ivy asserts, "I don't care about the evaluation system. I know if I'm doing a good job." Luckily, her case accuracy and efficiency are considered top-notch by her supervisor, so he tends to "let her be." Nevertheless, the temporary supervisor was operating under a very different professional model and set of strategic aims: protect the agency's resources, provide resources to clients once eligibility requirements are met, and respect the administrative structure set up to ensure that this is done as accurately as possible. Accountability to the agency trumps the particulars of one specific case. Yet the agency's ambiguity ultimately allows Ivy to fight for her professional approach and to find an ally to make it work. At stake is not simply whether one bureaucrat's decision should trump another's; this conflict that Ivy describes represents the battle over the professional identity of the new welfare bureaucrat now under way in the postreform era. The clash with this supervisor over procedure mimics the struggles of social workers to endure as they try to assert their professional identities in a climate that privileges efficiency engineering.

The Third Way: The Survivalists

Why do conflicts over the professional identities of bureaucrats matter? Either model can produce bureaucrats capable of greatness or incompetence. Why is it significant that welfare offices have yet to resolve the tensions that have existed for decades, albeit prominently coming to the surface in the new welfare system with its dual aims of eligibility-compliance enforcement and welfare-to-work case management? As this and the previous chapter have demonstrated, these differences matter because they create disparities in service delivery that have the potential to shape the experiences and outcomes of clients. Had Ivy not had the moxie gleaned from her beliefs about what she should do as a professional, had Michelle approached the disability screening process differently because she understood it as part of her job to get to the bottom of her clients' barriers, and had Edna not thought it was not only appropriate but useful to bring her history in the Detney Court housing projects into her work, a victim of domestic violence seeking an escape, a mother struggling to meet a program requirement that she stay in school, and a woman trying to gain resources while keeping her loved ones safe might have had very different experiences in the welfare office—leaving with a different set of intangible and even tangible resources that could prove crucial for them and their families.

But unaddressed contradictions in institutional cues that continue to foster divergent professional identities are important for another reason. They have the potential to produce a third kind of bureaucrat. "Survivalists" are organizational actors whose identity is grounded in the notion that insofar as the agency, its mission, and its debates over how they should perform as professionals is concerned, they will invest in the system only minimally. Survivalists are least able to (or interested in) grappling with and negotiating the ambiguity inherent in the organization. Survivalists see neither purposeful assertions of efficiency nor heartfelt defenses of social work as relevant criteria of success in their approach. They ground their devotion, such as it is, in the prospect of retirement on the horizon should they remain in the job—a very narrow focus indeed, but one that helps them cope with institutional uncertainty. Apathy marks the bureaucratic survivalists' response to the agency's competing messages, the policy's misaligned incentives, the ongoing problems that clients bring, and the pressures of doing too much in too little time, effectively and efficiently. The problem with social workers and efficiency engineers, survivalists reason, is that they care too much—either about clients or about completing work tasks perfectly. They haven't realized that it is ultimately ineffectual to embrace either orientation. The agency (or the clients) will find a way to undercut you either way, survivalists contend. The lodestar that drives every decision, every action, is doing just enough to make it to the end of each day and, eventually, to retirement.

It would be easy to assume that survivalism is simply a function of an aging workforce, a natural progression of those who have given decades of service and are simply weary. Yet some of the staunchest survivalists are those who have the fewest number of years in the agency. Jane, an energetic efficiency engineer the first time I met her, was slipping slowly into a survivalist stance when I returned to the office years later:

I'm at a point where I don't know which way to go. I'm at a point where, in one-and-one-quarter years, I take medical [benefits] with me for life, and I'm hanging on by my fingernails to do that. And I just wanna get out of here while I still have my work ethic. Because I'm at a point now where to survive in this environment, you almost have to not care. The workloads are enormously high. My boss—who's great, she's a nice, nice woman. . . . But above that, they just torture you. They want perfection—which is great, that's a good thing. But they *less* than care about you. They have no concern for you as a person, as an employee, as anything. If you speak out, "Well, they mustn't be managing their caseloads right. So they need to figure it out for themselves."

From Jane's vantage point, the agency was asking her to become even more of an efficiency engineer, and she had little reserve energy to marshal. For someone who previously took such pride in her speed, accuracy, and thoroughness, the notion that she still could not perform the job up to par to meet the expanding demands of the agency was highly disturbing.

Social workers are also struggling with the temptation to become survivalists. They feel that their identities are threatened in different ways: the efficiency engineering side of the postreform environment seems to distance them further from the holistic approach that they think is best. Jennifer, the social worker who once described spending hours on the phone with a bipolar client who was facing jail time, was near the end of her rope when I returned five years later:

They've made our jobs even more about the sanctioning process, I think. I said, "I'm gonna go in there [in the interview] and it's gonna seem like I'm so cynical." And it doesn't have to be that way. I think when they come up with policy, they're just thinking—strict. It's like a punishment thing where "you're not doing this." They're not looking underneath the surface and seeing how we can approach the other issues that are facing the clients. Like, with teens, you can't just say, "You go to school or your case is gonna be closed. Then you get your GED and you're all set." Because for life it's not gonna work that way. And I think they should be making efforts to coordinate that GED program with programs that are about what teens are focused on, like self-image and the relationship problems. Because at that age, the relationship [with the boyfriend] is the focus. And sometimes, sadly, not the child, and not school, not themselves. And I think if you're looking down the road for what you want—a success in the long run, I think, is key. But we are so far from that . . .

Myrtle Scottt, a Fishertown caseworker, who had already slipped into survivalism, represents views that I found in both Fishertown and Staunton. She asserted that she entered the organization with a strong commitment to serving clients. However, years of jumping bureaucratic hurdles for few rewards, dealing with the intensity of what clients brought to her doorstep, and now the hypocrisy of watching one professional identity promoted while another was ultimately rewarded was proving to be too much for her. In the quote below, she is describing her frustrations with clients, but the central office, the legislature, co-workers, and office administrators could all be the objects of her aggravation. In fact, she took turns railing against them in the course of the interview: "It gets to the point where you really don't care anymore, you know, because you've heard every story. Although every once in a while one will crop up and they'll have some other excuse. But you've heard every excuse, every story imaginable and the sympathy goes out the window after a while. . . . Whatever I can do to make the job easier for me is what I do now. If you're entitled to it, you will get it. If you're not, you won't. That's the bottom line."

The breadth and depth of Myrtle's frustration suggest how, over time, survivalists become invested in being detached professionals—functioning on a basic level so as not to attract too much attention but certainly not sacrificing much toward either engineering efficiency or offering in-depth social-work-like case management. Her work performance, dictated by a professional identity that is detached from the organization, has become the minimum required at a moment when clients and the agency necessitate anything but.

Agency Transformation and the (Re)formation of Professional Identities

Institutional cues help to shape employees' understandings of who they are as professionals, and these messages contribute to or undermine the organizational change process by how they define and support the workforce expected to carry out the institutional transformation. Disparate organizational cues play an important role in the emergence of correspondingly disparate professional identities among organizational actors, leading to inequalities in outputs such as service delivery. We have seen variation in behavioral tactics and the range of what is addressed in client interactions among caseworkers at the DTA, and we have witnessed how messages are sent from the agency with respect to two competing approaches that took turns at being deemed not only appropriate but preferred. Each caseworker develops a steady state over time, a presentation of a professional self derived from the occupational models available. As welfare reform propelled to the forefront of public debate a range of competing political ideologies and social assumptions, DTA employees have been left to determine how to articulate a reasonably consistent set of messages about how its policies should be implemented.

Street-level bureaucrats trying to maintain their footing in the ebb and flow between these competing models ultimately have fashioned a variety of interpretations of their professional identities. What many in the office call *social work* stresses the use of coaching, networking clients to a variety of social services, and providing tailored support to implement policy. Subscribers to this model of in-depth case management are encouraged to adopt this approach as a result of the supportive rhetoric coming out of the central office, a job title change for frontline workers to include the phrase *social work,* and a revised worker evaluation system that, on paper, encourages workers to help clients create transformative changes in their work and personal lives by helping them to leverage resources. On the other hand, the human resources realities of the staff, the administrative hurdles around such a sweeping policy change, and the actual implementation of the evaluation system, with its focus on accuracy and efficiency, have suggested that a very different model is in play. *Efficiency engineering* emphasizes speed in processing and the use of the policy's expanding eligibility and compliance requirements to regulate access to cash assistance and work-related resources. This identity encourages workers to continue to see themselves as claims processors, albeit with a new set of require-

121

ments to track as a result of welfare reform. By not consistently implementing a coherent incentive structure and other organizational cues to make the professional model of choice explicit, the organization, in effect, rewards efficiency engineering while creating expectations that workers should become social-work-like case managers.

Several factors likely explain why individual workers are attracted to particular professional self-conceptions. As situated bureaucrats interpret the agency's competing messages about how they should conceptualize their work, they make choices that suit their personal and professional goals and work to sustain a sense of self. Presumably, workers have chosen roles that are in line with their moral objectives, values, and other key attributes (March 1994). Bureaucrats' personality characteristics and occupational competencies likely also play a role in determining which ones have become social workers and which ones have become efficiency engineers. Past experiences with clients and attitudes about who their clients are, why they are coming for help, and the resources to which they should subsequently have access are likely important as well. There was certainly evidence to suggest that social workers tend to see opposition and resistance to the agency as important and worthwhile; efficiency engineers, while not necessarily embracing the agency and its policies, believe that doing the job as assigned is highly important. Finally, it seems that, recalling Ashforth's (2001) contributions to our understanding of professional identity formation, the subjective importance that individual workers place on a particular role is likely key in determining why they gravitate toward a particular orientation.

So far, we primarily have been examining the assigned professional responsibilities of caseworkers in considering how they self-identify in their jobs. This tells an important part of the story of their identity formation and connects us to the various conceptual frameworks that have formed the history of welfare service over the years. In so doing, however, we have said little about the broader social context in which these actors are operating and its impact on their professional identities. The next two chapters therefore explore how social relations such as race, class, and gender intersect to inform the professional identities of street-level bureaucrats.

FOUR

Am I My Sister's Keeper?

Race, Class, Gender, and Community in Staunton

In a May 2004 address at a fiftieth anniversary commemoration of the *Brown v. Topeka Board of Education* Supreme Court decision, entertainer and philanthropist Bill Cosby made a controversial critique lamenting the ways in which the gains of civil rights activists were being eroded as a result of what he described as apathy, socially unacceptable behavior, and educational disinvestment within black communities:

No longer is a person embarrassed because they're pregnant without a husband. No longer is a boy considered an embarrassment if he tries to run away from being the father of the unmarried child. Ladies and gentlemen, the lower economic and lower-middle economic people are [not] holding their end in this deal. . . . Now look, I'm telling you. It's not what [whites] are doing to us. It's what we're not doing. . . . And that's not [my] brother. And that's not my sister. They're faking and they're dragging me way down, because the state, the city and all these people have to pick up the tab on them. (2004, 2–4)

Cosby's comments ignited a firestorm of scholarly and public debate about their validity and appropriateness, the spirit in which he delivered them, and the potential responses to issues that had so clearly vexed him.[1] What are the responsibilities of members of a community, one that is wrestling with some of the most complex social problems of our time? What behavioral expectations for its most economically disadvantaged remain part and parcel of a group's collective social uplift mission? As racism, sexism, and poverty collude to mire a disproportionate number of people of color in economic, social, and political marginalization, what roles should people of varied means within these communities play in the relief of profound social suffering? What grassroots strategies, privileged standings, and institutional positions are appropriate and necessary to leverage?

Such questions hover over catch-all bureaucracies, and the Staunton DTA office is no exception. The office funnels a geographically and racially diverse staff and client base into an urban location to administer the state's TAFDC Program. In March 2001, 44.4 percent of the office's caseload family heads were black, 35.0 percent Hispanic, 15.9 percent white, and 4.3 percent Asian. At that time, 48 percent (fifteen) of the office's TANF caseworkers, application screeners, and Employment Services Program workers were white, 26 percent (eight) black, 19 percent (six) Hispanic, and 6 percent (two) Asian, and the office staff grew even more diverse by the time I conducted the second round of fieldwork five years later.[2] When I first began the research for this book, implementing welfare reform in Staunton involved helping poor parents (mostly single mothers) negotiate a metropolitan economy that had tight labor markets. But there have been fewer employment opportunities in recent years, and persistent housing shortages and rising living costs remain. Additionally, the city's racially segregated schooling, housing, and employment environments challenge many clients' abilities to secure the kinds of opportunities that might lead to economic stability and eventual mobility.

The Staunton office's black employees, not unlike the commentators who chatted up the issue with great fervor from radio shows to corner barbershops across the country, were divided on Cosby's statements. Sharlene, who grew up working class in New York City, felt both implicated in a statement she heard Cosby make about the overprioritization of name-brand clothing and protective of her clients, who she sensed were the main targets of his message:

I don't think he should have stated that. I mean, not everybody has their kids wearing them high-priced sneakers. Not everybody in that category that he's belittling. . . . [not] all the black youth. That's his opinion. . . . So no, that's not everybody's opinion. . . . Yeah, he was talking about [people like] our clients. He was talking about our kids. You know, my kid is twenty-one years old. If he wears expensive sneakers, he works and gets that, you know? Does that make him what Bill Cosby's talking about? People talked about it [in the office] . . . they were saying that he shouldn't have said that, you know. And just because the clients are on assistance, don't make them a statistic. They're already a statistic when they come in here saying they're on the welfare roll. Don't make them feel bad about it. I mean, some people [are] on here for a reason. Some people are on and off. I didn't care for his comments.

As Sharlene pondered the question of "who fits?" among the group that Cosby targeted and condemned what she saw as the scapegoating and biting stigmatization of her clients, Timothy Murray, one of the few African American male caseworkers in the office, was more ambivalent about the remarks. From his perspective, there was "a lot of truth to it. But could it have been said different? I don't know. I mean, he didn't always have money either, you know what I mean?" Ida Lubelle, one of two African American supervisors in the office, shrugged, nodded, and offered her endorsement of Cosby's commentary: "I think he was right. People were mad at him, but he was right. I heard this radio show once when this young man was talking about 'stop waiting for a Black leader to come and save us because there isn't *one*. It has to be *all of us*.' That's how I feel. We all have to do our part. We gotta stop waiting for somebody to save us."

Ida, Sharlene, and Timothy are not detached elites, distanced residentially, socially, and professionally from poorer blacks and peering from on high at their failings and struggles. The lives of these working-class bureaucrats are entwined with the ones that Cosby describes, and they know it. Their reactions to this latest firestorm about class, behavior, opportunity, and uplift within black America are all the more significant because of the unique positions that these individuals share. They are a part of this racial community, one that seems perpetually engaged in critical debates about its political, economic, and social future; and they are also professionals within a state agency that seeks to simultaneously support and regulate some of the most disadvantaged members of this and other racial and ethnic groups.

In this chapter I explore how ideas about race, class, and gender shape the formulation and operationalization of the professional identities of black and Latino street-level welfare bureaucrats. In particular I ask how their social backgrounds, occupational experiences, and political attitudes inform their understanding of how they should do their jobs. As the Fishertown office had no black or Latino caseworkers or supervisors during my fieldwork, I focus on the experiences and attitudes of seventeen of Staunton's caseworkers and supervisors of color.[3] In light of ongoing debates within communities of color around a variety of social, political, and economic concerns, I am particularly interested in the encounters that black and Latino street-level bureaucrats report having with the black and Latino clients who are randomly assigned to their caseloads. In the next chapter I explore the intersections of the social and professional identities of white civil servants. These complementary analyses are critical in light of the recent shifts within welfare offices that have been documented in previous chapters. As caseworkers struggle to transition to a less rationalized model of service delivery under the current welfare system, the expanded drive to counsel, encourage, discipline, and connect clients to resources and networks opens up even more possibilities for workers to tailor and even personalize their messages to clients about work, family, and state involvement. Thus, there are many more opportunities for caseworkers to interject their own views and subjectivities into the caseworker-client interaction. This chapter and the next therefore consider how bureaucrats integrate their own multiple and interlocking identities and deploy them in efforts to shape institutional dynamics in policymaking agencies.

To be sure, this chapter does not set out to examine whether black and Latino bureaucrats—male or female, working class or middle class—allocate monetary resources differently to clients of color or are more likely to push for certain concessions related to time limits, work requirements, or other policies within welfare offices. Nor does this chapter explore whether clients are more likely to leave welfare for work if their caseworkers are of the same or different background with regard to race, class, or gender. Such questions will prove beyond the scope of the data on which this discussion is based.

Rather, by looking at the discourses that caseworkers of color elect to use during their interactions with clients of color, I show how intraracial dynamics inform bureaucratic processes within local welfare offices. Caseworkers and supervisors of color engage in "racialized professionalism" as they integrate race into their understanding and operationalization of their work and their goals for what it should accomplish. A few respondents vigorously seek to divorce the issue of race from their interactions within the organization and their interpretations of the broader implications of their work. For these bureaucrats, there is noticeably less integration of their professional identities with social group consciousness. However, I show that most of these service providers actively deploy race (and class and gender) by shaping the content and tone of their interactions with clients of color in ways that reflect both key priorities in welfare reform implementation and intra-group politics within black and Latino communities. They make strategic choices about when and how to inject their racial group concerns into the service-delivery process, armed with a broader array of tools and edicts under the new policy regime and a fair amount of power by virtue of their class and professional positions. They leverage racial commonality to communicate the social goals and political motives of welfare policy to black and Latino clients and attempt to use occupational authority and social status to articulate why these clients should adopt a certain set of behaviors. As these bureaucrats simultaneously communicate their support and challenge clients of color through a variety of techniques, they deploy in-group politics in powerful ways to pursue what they see as moral and political rescue missions grounded in group-centered ideologies.

The next section of this chapter builds on previous work on race in the workplace and introduces how we might conceptualize the role of race specifically and intersectionality more broadly in minority workers' interpretations of their professional roles in public bureaucracies. I set the political, social, and occupational context in which minority welfare caseworkers and supervisors are operating by exploring how they view their own status as professionals within the agency. I then examine how these bureaucrats understand the political and social context in which their clients of color function as they navigate the current welfare system. This backdrop helps us understand the relational context in which the power dynamics between bureaucrats and clients of color unfold. Finally, I explore how race, class, and gender emerge as shaping elements during interactions between the two groups, influencing the practice of welfare casework and the messages that are conveyed as services are delivered.

Intersectionality at Work:
Racialized Professionalism in Public Bureaucracies

Previous research on race in the workplace has extensively documented how race influences the hiring and promotion prospects of workers (Neckerman and Kirschenman 1991; Nkomo and Cox 1990; Pager and Quillian 2005); workforce composition (Reskin et al. 1999); pay rates (Barnum, Liden, and DiTomaso 1995; Reskin 2000); job-acquisition tactics and resources among would-be employees (Newman 1999; Royster 2003; Smith 2005); and everyday interactions among colleagues who must come together to pursue organizational goals (Foerster 2004; Smith and Calasanti 2005). Race continues to influence how individuals are slotted into work institutions as well as their experiences as they navigate institutional hierarchies that place blacks and Latinos at a disadvantage (DiTomaso and Smith 1996; DiTomaso, Post, and Parks-Yankee 2007). Researchers have tracked these inequalities among employees of varying occupational skill levels and institutional positions, including low-skill, blue-collar, and white-collar workers in the higher echelons of corporations (Anderson 1999; Bell and Nkomo 2001; Collins 1997; Thomas and Gabarro 1999).

This research is not without its gaps. First, how does race contribute to how workers of color themselves interpret their professional roles? We know a great deal about how blackness and other minority statuses are perceived by employers and co-workers. Racial ideologies are often *imposed* on workers of color as they negotiate these work environments (Neckerman and Kirschenman 1991; Waldinger and Lichter 2003). But we know less about how these actors are in fact strategic as they navigate experiences and perceptions of racial inequality in ways that are often informal. These individuals must determine for themselves what significance they believe their racial backgrounds should play in how they understand their work and its functions (Dhingra 2007). For example, racial group consciousness and group solidarity may operate as key organizing principles for how street-level bureaucrats of color integrate their professional and social locations. Group consciousness shapes and is shaped by actors' political attitudes as it integrates "in-group identification with a set of ideas about the group's status and strategies for improving it" (Chong and Rogers 2005, 350). Group solidarity—composed of self-identification with the social group, a sense of closeness to one's group, and a belief that one's fate is linked to that of the group—also may inform whether and how bureaucrats bring the issue of race into their jobs (Dawson 1995).[4] As potential sources of cultural pride, collective responsibility, or in-group concern, racial group memberships can thus be *actively deployed* by workers of color to pursue perceived group-based aims within workplace institutions in ways that, according to Pawan Dhingra (2007), both resist and support stratified social patterns. As such, racial systems do not only "bear down" on employees; race can also be tactically leveraged by these same individuals to help form the basis of professional identity.

Second, how is a professional self-conception informed by race and also shaped by class and gender? The term "racialized professionalism" represents the integration of one's racial identity into one's understanding and performance of work: beliefs about what workplace activities should accomplish, tools leveraged to meet certain goals, interpretations of organizational processes, and strategies for how the racial dynamics of the environment should be navigated. Although race is the organizing category of focus in this analysis, we will see that other dimensions of identity intersect with race to help produce the microinteractions, professional trajectories, and occupational concerns of street-level bureaucrats. As scholars engaging in intersectional analyses have argued, race, gender, and class cannot be reduced to individual attributes that are measured and assessed for their separate contributions to various institutional outcomes (Simien 2007; McCall 2005).[5] They interact with and shape one another in ways that create distinct constraints and opportunities for individuals and groups within organizations (Acker 2006). Regardless of background, individuals operating in a raced, gendered, and classed work environment must locate themselves within institutional hierarchies and make choices about how they will explicitly or implicitly leverage, challenge, downplay, or disavow these categories in order to pursue certain goals.

Third, how is racialized professionalism shaped by the specific dimensions of street-level bureaucracies? Scholarship on race in organizations focuses almost exclusively on private rather than public firms; but institutional motivations are likely to differ based on firm type, and work products and processes are accordingly driven by public policies. This gap is surprising as public-sector employment has been an important avenue for expanding the black and Latino middle classes, and thus plays a significant role in the labor market experiences of racial minorities (Greene and Rogers 1994; Hewitt 2004). At the same time, the very policies that these individuals are called upon to implement often have their own racialized histories, discourses, and motives behind their political support or opposition (Fox 2004; Gilens 1999; Hancock 2004). Nevertheless, there is little scholarship on how the interlocking social locations of bureaucrats of color inform questions of access, accountability, opportunity, support, and regulation in this institutional context. Gail Lewis's (2000) work on Afro-Caribbean, African, and south Asian government social workers in the United Kingdom is a notable exception. She links these workers' access to the field to the increasingly widespread public belief in the 1980s and 1990s that poor black and south Asian families required social regulation through social work, and that it should be done by professionals of color who can offer "ethnic knowledge." Yet while Lewis's conceptualization captures how race is subsequently positioned by these workers as a source of solidarity and support for clients of color, she places less emphasis on parsing out the roots of the regulatory impulses that these social workers also direct toward their charges. These workers' assertions of power potentially arise not only from demands placed upon them by the institution but also from imported class- and gender-based cleavages that also may be part of these communities of color.

At the heart of the notion of racialized professionalism is the assertion that social identities such as race, class, and gender inform professional identity, one's interpretation of one's assigned professional role. These individuals read institutional cues that address their occupational purpose and objectives and then infuse their own meanings, goals, and commitments to create day-to-day capacities for action. How and to what extent professional identities are informed by social identities is the central concern of this chapter.

The Professional as Personal:
How Biography Informs Racialized Professionalism

Beginning in the 1960s, political and social pressures led many government bureaucracies to diversify their workforces and ensure that their staffs better reflected the demographics of their clientele. Many have since recognized that staff members of government agencies, especially the 'street-level bureaucrats' who provide direct services (Lipsky 1980), are important social and political actors serving a variety of symbolic and substantive functions. Their visibility, the relationships they forge with the public, and their ability to navigate the expectations of a wide array of stakeholders are all thought to help bridge the divide between agencies' missions and the needs of constituents. Hence many bureaucratic outposts have become sites where nonwhite workers serve multiple informal roles in addition to that of formally implementing public policy. Street-level bureaucrats of color also exist as economic beneficiaries of racial inclusion (Burbridge 1994; Collins 1983), resource brokers for what Mary Pattillo (2007) calls "race-mates" in economically deprived communities, social regulators of poorer members of their racial communities (Lewis 2000), and counterexamples to the white bureaucrat–minority client service dyad that often dominates our assumptions.[6]

In the Staunton welfare office, although bureaucratic "middleness" is experienced by all street-level welfare workers by virtue of their simultaneous positions of power and subordination vis-à-vis clients and administrators, this is in many ways heightened for employees of color. Black and Latino bureaucrats must balance institutionally vested power and their (relatively) privileged class standing against the subordination inherent in their historically disadvantaged racial status. Their relative financial stability—via union-negotiated salaries, benefits, and pension packages—contrasts with the economic instability of their race-mate clients. Clients from their racial groups disproportionately make up the rolls, and their faces and images are most often invoked during political and public debates that lament the waste of the social welfare system and the personal choices of those on the bottom of the economic ladder (Gilens 1999; Hancock 2004; Lubiano 1992). At the institutional level, it is ironic that the clout to which black and Latino employees have access is in a government bureaucracy that has historically rendered many clients of color as powerless (Lieberman 2001; Neubeck and Cazenave 2001; Schram, Soss, and Fording 2003). Furthermore, these staff members monitor, assist, and police not only poor clients of color but also poor white clients who, although less economically advantaged, may enjoy skin-color privileges that they themselves do not possess (McIntosh 1988). This paradoxical position of privilege and disadvantage in an agency with such a distinct political character contributes to an environment of racial and class complexity for these "middlemen" and "middlewomen" of color (Pattillo 2007).

Perceptions of their own standing within the institution represent a key piece of how black and Latino bureaucrats interpret the intersection of their professional and social locations. Foremost for these employees is maintaining the measure of economic security that the job provides. For all but a few, their own lower-middle-class status is the result of a fairly recent climb up the socioeconomic ladder. Most were low income or working class before landing a job at the welfare office. Sundra's story is not unique among her cohort of co-workers who came to work for the office in the late 1980s. An African American caseworker and a single mother herself, she occasionally tells clients, "I understand your struggle because I'm of the same struggle." Her account of how she came to work for the department after a stint as a child care worker reveals a personal history with the welfare system plus economic anxieties that tether her to the agency and its stability: "My marriage fell apart and I had to support myself and my son. At that time, I didn't have a lot of skills. I had to make some goals for myself and I started off [receiving] welfare. I was able to go back to school. I used that to my advantage. . . . Because ultimately I was afraid of being fifty [years old] and working at McDonald's. That has always been my fear."

Maintaining the economic foothold that these bureaucrats have achieved requires that they navigate the institution effectively, including its racial politics. Ida embodies this blend of formidable influence and calculated silence. Ida was born in the segregated South during the 1950s. Her mother received welfare during part of Ida's childhood after they moved north. Ida earned a bachelor's degree in social work and has worked for the welfare department since 1978. Coupled with her second job working twenty hours per week at a residential facility for low-income, at-risk children, Ida and her husband have been able to carve out a stable middle-class existence largely by working in state social service agencies. With an interaction style that dispenses motherly advice, girlfriend-like anecdotes, and what many agree is a commanding knowledge of the ins and outs of welfare policy, Ida enjoys a degree of inclusion that makes her an informal opinion leader in the agency. Such a privileged standing didn't come easily. She was promoted to supervisor in 1992, an accomplishment made possible by "working hard, staying out of mess[es], and making sure I don't let them [management] mess with me." I asked Ida what role, if any, she believes her racial background plays in her job. Ida attributes her professional success to a judicious workplace survival strategy in which racism's potential grasp never escapes her thoughts:

I am often encouraged by my co-workers to be a part of the group. I seem to be in the loop on things. I don't even have to leave my office; a lot of times, people just come to me and tell me something so that I always know what's going on in the office, policy or gossip. I pull my share and stay out of mess[es]. I don't try to dump it on anybody. We [workers of color] get that stigma sometimes, "Well, they're not pulling their weight." They're not going to be able to say that about me because I'll do my share, and yours if I have to, to get the job done.

For Ida, racialized professionalism means guarding against racial stereotypes and devising strategies to reduce the chances that her race will negatively shape her work opportunities and institutional reputation. Success in the organization means both exceeding job expectations and making sure that she is ensconced in informal information-sharing networks, including those of the office's all-white top-level management team.

Since two out of eight supervisors in the office are people of color, and a collegial atmosphere is almost uniformly reported among the staff, strategies such as Ida's for integrating into the welfare office's work environment seem successful. Yet despite the efforts of Ida and her colleagues of color to demonstrate that they can defy stereotypes and successfully perform as welfare professionals, the power that the organization grants them is tempered by what these employees describe as stymied opportunity and subtle indications that their symbolic footing within the agency is not as secure as they might desire. When the topic of seeking promotions within the organization came up, Ida described the limited number of minorities among the department's senior management as a source of frustration and discouragement: "Well, they will only let you get so far. That's why I don't even apply for management jobs anymore. You're telling me with all these people of color, there is not one qualified for one of those jobs? I know a lot of people that applied—nothing. So I just do my job and they don't bother me."

Blacks and Latinos expressed similar levels of dissatisfaction with their promotion prospects in the agency, and they talked more frequently about the centrality of race, rather than other social characteristics such as gender or immigrant status, in shaping their opportunities. The department's employees of color tend to be frontline workers in the local field offices that administer benefits and have direct contact with the public rather than office administrators or officials in central headquarters where the higher paid and more prestigious positions in the statewide system are located. Carlos Salazar, a caseworker who migrated to the state from Puerto Rico, could barely temper his frustration:

When you see a job posted [in the organization] and it pays over $40,000,[7] no matter how good you sell yourself, they always find a skill for you not to get it. If you have what they're looking for, go to central office and you'll see all the Anglo whites.[8] They have a big title but know nothing. I go on one, two, three interviews and they hire someone else. They say, "You're so good." Well, then, give me the job. I've been sharing that information with my co-workers and supervisor [of color] and they tell me the same thing. "I applied for this job and this job, and I never got it," they tell me. Then they find out that someone else of a different color skin got it. They hire a few [people] of color just to cover it up.

Latino and black employees weren't the only ones who noticed that so few of the department's senior managers are people of color. Vicki Hawthorne, a white Staunton supervisor, was proud of both the ethnic and language diversity of the frontline staff; however, on the issue of the mobility of her co-workers within the organization, she stated: "[Race] is a very difficult subject. It's hard because in this particular office there are no black or African American management staff. It's totally white. And I don't know how black workers feel about that. You know, since I'm white also. I know that in other offices they do try to have a mixture of people in management staff. They have wanted to have diversity, rather than have such a top-heavy, white management staff, but unfortunately they haven't managed it here."

By and large, the Staunton staff members of color contend that they do not apply for higher-status positions with optimism.[9] The 2005 promotions of Constance Lewis and Leena Boggs, two of Staunton's black female employees, to management positions in other offices within the welfare department function as a racial Rorschach test, disproving the contention that race matters for some and serving as exceptions to a pernicious rule for others. Constance's own words in 2001 suggest a bitter irony—promotion is possible for those with the persistence to keep trying, but it is not without its hidden injuries: "Well, being a black person in any profession where you are going to be thrown predominantly with white people, the levels of what you can get are different. I worked in various social service and human resource jobs, and I have my own battle scars."

The challenge to professional authority did not always come from management or co-workers. The politics of social support and social regulation within the human services suggest that providers are regularly in positions whereby they must function as proverbial "good cop" and "bad cop" simultaneously with clients. These positions are not inherently contradictory, as they offer both assistance and discipline. Yet they are both ultimately stances of power, and the race of both the provider and the client complicates this dynamic. As Edna describes, white clients occasionally challenge the hierarchy that places workers of color in positions of authority over them, although this tension has subsided considerably as many of these clients have had to come to accept the increase in the number of human service providers of color in the last few decades. As is the case with all of her co-workers, Edna's institutional power, which could appear either vast or constrained depending on the situation, is juxtaposed against the racial power relations of both the institution and the larger society:

When I came to this office, my first few clients I got gave me a flashback to [my old office]—their attitude towards me being a black woman. They couldn't come out to disrespect in this era like I went through before, but you could feel the vibe or how they spoke to you. Some whites [from the farther out areas] refuse to come to this office. But it's only a few that I have problems with in regard to the race aspect of it. I think they are getting over it. Because with me anyway, some of them see that

I follow my rules and regs and that's what we have to do. And yes, they will follow up and call my supervisor and find out that I am telling you the same thing that my supervisor is telling you. You still go through that, but not as much.

Regardless of occupational path, black and Latino employees' own experiences around race and institutional power distinctly influence their perceptions of how the agency operates and where they fit in as professionals. Their position as street-level bureaucrats of color paradoxically grants and limits their power, generating simultaneous allegiance to and leeriness of the organization. As the next two sections will show, this relationship shapes how they wield their institutional clout. As they protect their hard-won economic stability, the lessons gleaned from personal experiences contribute to how black and Latino bureaucrats assess the social and political context in which their racemate clients operate and how they in turn should respond.

The Professional as Political:
How Welfare Politics Inform Racialized Professionalism

I knew who it was going to target more. Even though I know numbers-wise, more of them [whites] are on. But when I heard about it, I thought about how it was going to affect people of color.

TIMOTHY, AFRICAN AMERICAN, TWENTY-YEAR VETERAN CASEWORKER

The quote is Timothy's response to a question I posed about what he thought when welfare reform became law. As we will see, most black and Latino bureaucrats in Staunton hold clear beliefs about the juxtaposition of racial and economic inequality, and these attitudes inform their views of the welfare policies they implement in sometimes surprising ways. Many respondents identify on some level with the struggles their black and Latino clients face.[10] Timothy goes on to describe how he believes race affects the employment prospects of his clients of color:

Last hired, first fired of those who do want to go to work. There's what you call institutional racism in this state. There are some things that still haven't changed; they just have another label on them. Take a white boss. Everything he reads in the paper about a black or a person of color is negative. Watches the news, everything he sees about a black or a person of color is negative. I come in and apply for a job. I don't care if I wear an *eight-piece suit,* I don't have a snowball's chance in hell of getting that job because everything that you've just seen about me in the last twenty-four hours has been negative. Clients experience some of that.

135

Timothy was asked to describe how race operates for his clients. Yet in his answer he casts himself as the protagonist, the eager job seeker—suggesting that Timothy shares some sense of the economic vulnerability of clients of color despite his government job. At the same time, some black respondents worry that black clients do not do enough to disprove the negative reputations assigned to black employees by employers and that this has implications for other blacks (Kennelly 1999; Kirschenman and Neckerman 1991; Moss and Tilly; Newman 1999; Smith 2005; Waldinger and Lichter). Lionel Williams, an African American caseworker, joins Timothy in reflecting on his status as a black man in the labor market to describe the opportunities and barriers facing black clients, intertwining the personal, political, and professional:

People have asked me how I feel being the only or first black to do whatever. I never thought I was any different than anybody else, and I think that's the attitude that you should have. I think unfortunately there are not enough people who think like that. A lot of blacks don't feel comfortable being the only minority in a work setting, and I don't understand. They want to quit. . . . You should be a pioneer because if this works out for you, and you're a valuable employee, then that means if you recommend somebody, then that person comes highly recommended because of who you are. If you turn around and run out the door, that's gonna make it difficult for anybody else that comes through here that's a minority. Because they're gonna remember the experience with you. . . . It's the stereotype that we face day in and day out as minorities that we're slackers. . . . I know that there's racism out there. I know if you take the necessary steps to meet it head on, you can overcome that. I think our people are just beaten down and they don't want to compete. . . . If you're an African American, forget about it. You're not going anywhere.

Given these concerns about how minorities fare in the labor market, caseworkers of color do not implement the time-limited work-first policy without some trepidation. Topping the list of concerns is the quality of the jobs most clients are getting. Sundra finds herself funneling clients into the fast-food jobs that she previously described fearing might be her own fate. She criticizes the tough policies that she implements and worries about the practicalities of how clients are making ends meet:

There are times when the people [with] the power to make changes don't consider the little people . . . how we can bring this family from welfare to work. But you figure overall with the economy and the minimum wages, it's hard. The cost of living is so high. You just feel helpless in trying to help [clients]. No matter where you try to direct them, you know there's a wall and eventually they're gonna hit it and fall down. . . . The old saying is, 'Pull yourself up by the bootstraps.' But suppose you don't have any shoes?

Nevertheless, despite worries about the low-wage labor market, the black and Latino workers that I interviewed generally offered up arguments *in support of* the recent changes in the welfare system. They unanimously agreed that prejudice and other racial inequalities faced by clients of color make it more difficult for them to succeed, but they largely view these as barriers that could and should be overcome. Camilla, whose parents emigrated from Costa Rica, commented that "there is a way out; welfare is not the answer. I know it's harder and especially harder when you have children, but you can do it. It's not a matter of months but you can do it. [Being a woman of color] even then, you can." Black and Latino bureaucrats described specific aspects of the policy such as time limits, sanctions, and work requirements as important tools to encourage clients to follow agency directives and to emphasize the temporary nature of welfare services. Caseworker Veronica Ramirez emigrated from the Dominican Republic and has worked for the department for eleven years. She views as a weakness the department's forgiving policy toward sanctions that make them relatively easy to remove through two weeks of compliance with the rules: "Clients are not getting the message that you have to do [what we ask], and you are going to be sanctioned if you don't do it." Lionel described his frustration that clients balk at the low-wage jobs that they are often offered to fulfill the work requirement: "Nobody wants to start at the bottom. Everybody wants to start at the top, and that's not how it works. You've got to prove yourself first." These bureaucrats believe that government bears a responsibility to help those who cannot find work, but almost all those interviewed are largely uncomfortable with the idea of public cash support over an indefinite period of time. In this respect, they are very similar to both the majority of their white co-workers and previous literature that documents the views of welfare workers about reform (Hays 2003; Danziger and Seefeldt 2000).

Staunton's street-level bureaucrats know the economic and social realities confronting those leaving welfare and have lived with the policy long enough to witness some of its shortcomings. They've seen clients of all skill levels return to the rolls, unsuccessful in navigating the rigors of the low-wage labor market even after some periods of economic stability. But caseworkers' logic is that just about anything is better than long-term welfare, and clients need to keep trying unless they are physically or mentally unable to work. Timothy commented, "Whether it be unemployment, SSI, Social Security, [welfare], thank God that there's a safety net. And there will always be a permanent underclass, trust me on that. But let it be a trampoline and not a hammock." These bureaucrats had already been implementing the current policy for five years when I entered the field, and very few policymakers were calling for its abolishment. In fact, many policymakers point to the massive decline in the rolls and increased employment among low-income mothers to argue for even tougher requirements. Black and Latino political leaders have not taken up the mantle of reforming welfare reform, and grassroots activists are increasingly turning their attention to living-wage campaigns, immigration debates, and efforts to increase the minimum wage. Pushing clients to see the writing on the wall and move away from the welfare system are arguably realistic responses to the hard actualities of the current regime. The dire conditions of their clients, these bureaucrats argue, require blunt intervention.

For a handful of the bureaucrats of color interviewed, support for welfare reform is not simply a professional opinion about what is best for the majority of their clients or a regurgitation of the organization's mission. It is a political calculation as well. These employees express general support for welfare reform *because* of its racialized implications. Undergirding their beliefs is the assumption that the welfare system has broad implications not only for their clients but for minorities in general. It therefore bears a personalized meaning for these bureaucrats, even if they themselves have never been on assistance.

Political scientist Michael Dawson (1995) contends that African Americans often share a sense that their fate is linked to that of other African Americans, and there is some evidence, albeit less robust, to suggest that Latinos also share a sense of linked fate with other Latinos (Dawson 1995; McClain et al. 2006; Miller et al. 1981; Sanchez 2006).[11] "The historical experiences of African Americans," Dawson argues, "have resulted in a situation in which group interests have served as a useful proxy for self-interest" (77). Those who express high levels of linked-fate consciousness believe that the collective social standing of their racial group affects their personal possibilities for advancement.

Carlos's attitudes toward the welfare system illustrate this linked-fate perspective. After arriving from Puerto Rico with few resources, he took classes to improve his English language skills, attended a local community college for a year, and then studied business administration at a local university. Within seven years, he had a bachelor's degree and a job screening welfare applications. Yet his transition was not easy: "When I moved to the U.S., my whole world fell because I grew up believing things about America and how we are a part of the U.S. When I finally came here, it was a complete lie. They don't want us. . . . That affects us a lot because when we are there [in Puerto Rico], we feel we're a part of the U.S. When we come here, it's no, no, no, the people don't want us here. They say, 'If you don't speak English, go back to your country!'"

Although the racism that he experienced in the United States surprised Carlos, he quickly deduced that the government program for which he was now working had a racial politics all its own. He realized that when people talked about welfare, they seemed to be talking about people who look like him. His family has never been on welfare, but he feels implicated in its racialized vilification. Over time, the actual and perceived racial composition of the welfare rolls has become highly political in Carlos's mind, an association that he considers crippling not only to clients in the welfare office but also to him. Challenging that perception is something of a personal mission: "Every worker here, whether white or black, is in the same boat when it comes to that. We all get people from our same ethnic group, and I like to remind people of that." As Carlos integrates his sense of racial-group consciousness into the workplace, the demographic composition of the office's caseload has a social meaning that informs how he interacts with colleagues and understands his role as a professional.

When welfare reform was announced, Carlos's concerns about individual clients' fates were overshadowed by his focus on the group-level implications of the new law. Carlos reasoned that since the presence of Latinos and blacks on the rolls had already been demonized, restructuring their ties to the welfare system could be best in the long run: "Many years ago, you could be on welfare forever and that happened from generation to generation. Since the reform came, and I'm glad, you have to go in and out. In that way, it does good to our community and the people receiving the aid. When I talk about 'community,' I'm not talking about the Hispanic community only. Who are 'my people'? Everybody of color, people coming from other countries, different races and ethnicities."

This sense of pan-Hispanic and even pan-minority solidarity is a filter through which Carlos evaluates the policy he now implements. In Carlos's mind, the transitional emphasis of the new welfare system has the potential to liberate people of color from the pernicious grasp of dependency and revise the public narrative about minorities and the welfare system. In this sense, how Carlos discusses the demographics of the caseload with co-workers and evaluates the latest welfare policy goes beyond his role as a departmental employee; his focus places him squarely in the role of a member of a racial community. As such, Carlos's integration of his racial and professional identities is manifested as a political project.

Upon closer inspection, we see that Carlos's views on reliance on the welfare system by people of color is both gendered and classed: the unique needs of poor mothers of color are collapsed into what Carlos believes is "good for the community," and his belief is that these women should define themselves as labor market participants rather than as stay-at-home caretakers. His linked-fate framework reveals pitfalls identified by many observers of black politics. This investment often leads to further marginalization of the least powerful members within communities of color as the public representation of "group interests" is historically more reflective of the goals of its privileged members (e.g., middle class, heterosexual, male) (Boyd 2006; Cohen 1999; Gaines 1996; Ginwright 2002; McBride 2005; Pattillo 2007; Reed 1999). The extent, forms, and context of an all-encompassing pan-ethnic Latino linked fate has also been challenged by researchers who conclude that the notion of "interests" on the basis of race and ethnicity is fraught with qualifiers, contradictions, and contingencies (Jones-Correa and Leal 1996; Masuoka 2006; Segura and Rodrigues 2006; Stokes 2003).

Despite these complexities, many of the black and Latino street-level bureaucrats in this study hold ideologies about their racial group and its conditions and use these beliefs to interpret the social and political context in which their clients of color operate. To them, racialized professionalism includes injecting not only personal experiences but also political beliefs around race into their reading of their work. They reason that their racial communities are better served when the policy is administered with an eye toward a larger moral and political rescue mission: they bring a sense of racial group solidarity and consciousness to their service delivery in order to encourage their more disadvantaged race-mates to engage in certain behaviors.

Role Models, Regulators, or Both?
How Racialized Professionalism Informs Service Delivery

Staunton's top-level administrators explicitly discourage anything but a neutral stance toward clients in the service-delivery process, yet black and Latino frontline employees are hard pressed to keep group consciousness from making its way into their work. These views and behaviors are not easily classified as biases in favor of clients of color at the expense of white clients. Nor do these workers express preferences to work with clients from their own racial group to the exclusion of others (nor does the agency match them in that way). Rather, black and Latino street-level bureaucrats are responding to the economic and racial environments in which they find themselves and making choices about whether and how to explicitly inject race into the service-delivery process. Welfare reform has assigned greater obligations to clients and street-level bureaucrats to put strategies in place to help clients succeed without long-term public assistance. With this have come new opportunities for caseworkers to shape organizational processes, including how they communicate policies using their own worldviews.

Veronica and Sharlene, who are Dominican and African American respectively, stand as two of the few Staunton welfare professionals of color who dismiss the notion that their dealings with black and Latina clients differ from those they have with white clients. Their strategy is to try to be "apolitical" in thinking about their work and welfare's racial implications, and they frown upon the idea of invoking racial politics of any kind on the job. It is not that they consider race a nonissue, but they see clear limits to the idea of unity in the name of racial sameness. Politics, they reason, is best left to politicians and administrators who send orders down to the local welfare office. Both describe being preoccupied with the heavy demands of the job and highly value impartiality, even detachment, in their work with clients. I observed that, as efficiency engineers, the women focus solely on whether clients qualify for benefits and services or are meeting policy expectations. Besides, Sharlene reasons, policy is policy, "regardless of whether you are black, white, green, whatever." For Sharlene and Veronica, race is, and should be, understood as an implicit rather than explicit part of their professional identities.

Sharlene had learned to adopt this stance the hard way. She chose to deemphasize the issue of race in her encounters with all of her clients because she believed that it rarely turned out well when the issue was brought to the forefront. The real casualty, she felt, was her sense of professional legitimacy should race become explicit in an interaction with a client, regardless of any well-meaning intentions she may have. She began relaying a recent incident before I had even completed my question:

INTERVIEWER: Has race ever been an issue in terms of—?

SHARLENE: Of course. I had a [white] client who e-mailed the commissioner. She wanted expedited food stamps; I told her she wasn't eligible. And she wrote a letter. I leave at 1:00 most Fridays. She said she came in at 12:00 and there was nobody in the lobby but blacks, African Americans, and Spanish people. And the [front-desk clerks] told her that I was gone. Now, she didn't come [in at 12], we checked. It was actually 3:00. So she said that the two Spanish clerks was talking Spanish and laughing at her. She don't speak Spanish—how does she know what [the clerk] was talking about? And [the letter went on to say] how they had her waiting in the lobby too long and she was afraid. So—and how she called me three times and I didn't call her back that day. She [said] she felt that her case wasn't going to be opened quickly because she had a black social worker.

INTERVIEWER: And she put all of that in the letter?

SHARLENE: She put all of that in there. [The assistant directors] came and [the director] came, and they gave me this letter. And [one of the assistant directors] said, "Sharlene, just read it with a grain of salt." So when I read it, I got pissed off. Because when you come in, I don't see no color. My job is to help you. And she don't feel that she should be seeing, you know, black [caseworkers]. I didn't like that.

Not only was Sharlene disturbed by the content of the letter but the idea that she had to meet with management "to discuss how she *felt*" about the racialized incident was particularly frustrating. Even though the office managers encouraged her to discount it, Sharlene knew that her interaction with a client had been noted, from central office down to her direct supervisor. Further, the notion that this client might have felt as though her complaint had been effective was more than Sharlene could stomach. She considered having management remove the woman from her caseload, but instead opted "to make her see that I'm not this person that she wrote in her letter." Even in the face of such an antagonistic moment, Sharlene remained invested in disproving the white client's stereotypical construction of her, ceding a degree of power to her white accuser.[12] As a result of incidents like that, and in order to avoid a reputation for partiality or to incur the scrutiny of management, Sharlene felt that the best way to survive in the organization was to try to ignore race, seeing it neither as a hindrance nor as a tool in service delivery.

The majority of black and Latino frontline workers, however, do not assert this level of professional detachment. A sense of group consciousness often translates into a racialized understanding of the welfare system and the unique issues facing clients of color. They find assisting all clients valuable, but the fact that many are people of color advances the social significance of their work. Lionel commented, "I think that every time [black clients] have a success story, people might say otherwise, but I think you really feel good about that." Carlos opined that his accent and brown skin were deterrents to his landing a professional job for many years before starting his current state job. Working for the welfare department affords him the opportunity to both serve others and be in a place where his ethnic background is seen as an asset by his clients: "I wanted to be a social worker and I like to help people. I always use the opportunity to educate my people. . . . Yes, clients of color have certain expectations of you because you're a person of color. When Hispanic people come, even if they speak English, they want a Hispanic worker. They think it's cultural [that] we'll communicate better, which is true." I frequently observed Carlos offering to serve as a translator between clients and his co-workers, even when the client had brought her own translator or knew some English. Consistent with findings from previous research on black neighborhoods, Carlos, Lionel, and many of their co-workers use state-bestowed authority to funnel resources to those members of their community who haven't been able to overcome some of the obstacles that they have (Boyd 2006; Pattillo 2007). From their perspective, welfare casework has social resonance in part *because* of their racial backgrounds, and these bureaucrats do not want to completely disentangle their racial identities from their professional identities.

Black and Latino bureaucrats assert that they lack the power needed to change agency rules or deliver a different set of services to clients of color. To protect their own institutional and economic standing, they try to avoid appearing partial to their own racial group because, as Sundra explained, "I have to keep a job too." What Gail Lewis (1996) calls the "exposition of social proximity" can be asserted by both service providers and clients, and it can serve as a source of both connection and tension. It becomes a tightrope that bureaucrats who opt to adopt this more overtly racialized (and classed and gendered) posture must walk. For example, while we saw Edna extend herself to her client Monet with tailored advice on how to make it in Detney Court in the previous chapter, she nevertheless has to balance that support with boundaries that she communicates to clients who similarly share her racial, class, and even residential background:

People that I grew up with never knew that I worked for the department. So I went through that pressure when I came over [to the new office], like, "Oh, who do you think you are?" Or some that say, "Oh, I haven't seen you in years, Edna, and this is what you've been doing?" And I went through peer pressure at an older age from people that I went to school with down in the [neighborhood]. They are behind a desk talking to me, trying to get whatever benefits, and I have to tell them the rules and regs and they would get up and say, "Did you forget where you come from?" And I would say, "I lived in the [neighborhood] for years; I will never forget where I came from." A couple of them took it to heart, remembered what I said and then gave me respect after that. I am doing a job and I have mouths to feed just like you have mouths to feed. So respect me as a worker doing my job and I will respect you as a client of mine that wants to feed their children.

It would be easy to dismiss these clients' tactics as attempts to use race as a point of connection in order to test agency rules. Welfare caseworkers of all races and ethnicities report that each racial and ethnic group within the caseload seemingly holds a perception of which groups the system favors, and they want their providers to turn the tables to their advantage. However, what Edna describes are highly symbolic moments whereby intraracial and professional obligations are tested against each other within the institutional context. This suggests that the welfare office is viewed by some minority clients as a white-controlled space, despite its diversity. Edna is seen as operating on the wrong side.

Despite these tensions, many black and Latino employees nonetheless find ways to weave together a style of interaction that, while articulating the expectations of the institution, conveys another set of messages. Although they do not directly influence the size of a client's check or whether she is mandated to go to work, these bureaucrats clearly infuse tailored, discretionary advice and guidance into their interactions with certain clients.[13] All clients receive attention and resources, but clients of color receive a message that goes beyond the standard language of time limits, work requirements, and sanctions from these workers.

Anna Korteweg (2003) points out that welfare recipients are simultaneously designated as detached workers, marketable mothers, and dependent citizens who are expected to become independent worker-citizen subjects under the new welfare regime; much of the discourse in welfare agencies now focuses on this drive. Black and Latino workers are explicitly and implicitly injecting race into this project in order to encourage race-mate clients to invest in the process. For instance, Louisa Portes, a Puerto Rican caseworker, explains how she describes the department's training and education opportunities. Although bureaucrats most often reserve these tailored messages for members of their own racial groups, Louisa joins Carlos in invoking pan-minority solidarity in the service-delivery process:

When I come across a Latina [client], I always say, "You can do it. It's possible. My parents were on welfare when I was growing up. I remember the poverty that I grew up in, and I didn't want that for myself or my kids. The only way out is education.[14] Even if it's a GED, an entry position is better than being on welfare. I've been able to go to school and achieve things that I know are out there for me; it's not easy. But it's there to be grabbed and had." I've tried to stress to the clients. Blacks, I tell them the same as Hispanics. Somehow I try to convey to them that because of who we are, we have to be a step ahead of everybody. We are black and Hispanic and always thought of as inferior. We have to be a step ahead.

Louisa explicitly frames the economic issues embedded in welfare policy to Latina and black clients in racialized terms and draws upon her own biography to link the professional, the personal, and the political. Connections made on the basis of sameness give way to a politics of group consciousness that Louisa then translates into the work setting. Louisa's message of racial social uplift is woven into her service delivery as she advocates challenging stereotypes of minority inferiority by staying a "step ahead" through work and education. Intertwined is a class discourse that is centered around encouraging clients of color to engage in "bootstrap climbs" similar to the one that she offers up as her personal narrative. Although it is beyond the scope of this book to systematically determine whether these messages lead to outcomes for clients that differ from those that would happen if their caseworkers were white or bureaucrats of color who did not engage in such strategies, Louisa believes that they resonate with clients:

I feel comfortable that I've had successes with my approach. I haven't had many, but even now there is a person who is in charge of the Entrée Program, Hispanic woman. She used to be my client. She was going to school struggling, but she went through. That's a success that makes me feel good. She actually used [welfare] the right way, as a stepping-stone. I encouraged her and gave her the support and here she is. When I see her now she has a smile and can't take it away because she's on the same side as I am and even making more money than me. In that respect, I feel proud that a Latina is in a good position.

If we believe, in the tradition of Lipsky's *Street-Level Bureaucracy* (1980), that public policy is created in daily interactions between bureaucrats and clients, intracommunity political discourse becomes part of the policy implementation process within these institutions. One might argue that, by promoting behaviors that are in line with the goals of welfare reform, black and Latino bureaucrats are simply reflecting agency priorities rather than engaging in politically informed racialized professionalism. However, these employees' messages reveal common themes about black and Latino political mobilization. Success is referenced as a shared experience among race-mates, not simply the effective implementation of policy priorities. These workers emphasize actively resisting racial exclusion, triumphing over adversity, and proudly representing "the community." As we saw with Louisa, it is not uncommon for them to highlight their similarity to clients in their interactions, asserting social distance to serve as an example of how far one can go.

Black and Latino bureaucrats engaging in this strategic integration of their professional and racial identities are not unwilling to use their power to regulate. Their interventions therefore can be paternalistic or collaborative, condescending or supportive, even all at the same time, depending on the orientation of the bureaucrat. However, they almost always leverage notions of in-group or pan-minority racial solidarity in powerful ways to articulate why a client should adopt a certain set of behaviors. These bureaucrats of color take liberties to express views to black and Latino clients that they wouldn't necessarily express to white clients because, as Timothy explains, "sometimes you have certain white people that will say, 'How dare you talk to me like that?' But with blacks and people of color, that's not the problem. I encourage all of the clients, but yes, there's a familiarity there, things you can say to people of color." One could interpret this as confidence that actions taken with minority clients won't be policed within the agency in quite the same way that interactions with white clients might be. But Timothy assumes a kinship based on his racial identity and working-class background that he can then incorporate into his repertoire of policy implementation tools and leverage in service delivery to help punctuate his message about welfare reform. For him, this policy communications strategy represents a smooth merger of his racial, class, and professional identities:

[When welfare reform happened,] I thought, how can I as a worker use this? What can I do to empower clients of color to help themselves? I tell them, "I used to watch cowboys and Indians when I was little. And the cowboys would be riding up the path and the Indians would be lying up in the rocks, getting ready to ambush them and kill them. And I used to run up to the TV as a child and pound on it and shout, 'Watch out, watch out, it's a trap!'" And then I look back at them [clients] and say, "And I say that same thing to you now," [whispering] "Watch out, watch out, this is a trap! And I'm frustrated if you're not hearing me. . . . Don't get comfortable. Hang around people of like kind, it doesn't mean that you're better than [them]. If you're trying to be a truck driver, hang around other truck drivers. If you want to do real estate, hang around real estate agents. Hang around people who you want to be like. Don't hang around people who are on welfare. Water seeks its own level." Just trying to educate them, because there's a saying that goes, "My people are destroyed for lack of knowledge."

Timothy's "cowboys and Indians" homily reveals some of the complex implications of these moments. On the one hand, his depiction of the welfare system to clients of color is grounded in a sincere passion for this population and genuine concern for their well-being. Putting aside his assignment of people of color to the role of (white) cowboys and the welfare system to that of the (exotic) Indians, Timothy views his tale's heroes as individuals in constant danger of unanticipated hazards. As an observer with a bird's-eye view of the potential outcome, his task is to warn. "I am my sister's keeper," he explains. "I tell them, 'Don't play into their hands. You know what they say: Don't be a stereotype. You got to beat them at their own game.'"

Timothy's sermon is also grounded in assumptions that reveal that racialized professionalism is both classed and gendered. To Timothy, receiving welfare is a blemish.[15] The idea that welfare recipients should distance themselves from other welfare recipients is somewhat unrealistic, considering the dense intraclass networks that low-income mothers leverage for child care, social support, and other critical resources (Domínguez and Watkins 2003; Stack 1974). Timothy references truck drivers and real estate agents, occupations that require costly training that most of his clients cannot afford without assistance. These jobs also exist outside of the fast food, nurse's aide, and low-level retail jobs that most of these women will likely be offered. At the center of Timothy's prescriptions are directives aimed at modifying the individual behaviors of poor women of color to encourage them to exit the welfare system as quickly as possible.[16]

Comparisons between the styles of female and male bureaucrats of color should be made cautiously because of the small number of respondents (fourteen women compared with just three men), but some careful observations are in order. Notably, although both groups are trying to convince clients to find work and limit their time on welfare, black female and Latina bureaucrats appear to adopt a different tone and set of tools than their male counterparts. They are more likely to reference their own experiences as welfare recipients or single mothers of color and offer themselves up as examples to their clients that they too can escape the welfare system (see also Korteweg 2003). Having "been there," they deliver messages stressing the importance of using human and economic capital as tools to nurture children, and they explicitly argue that the way to empower themselves as mothers is to work outside the home to climb a difficult but ultimately rewarding labor-market ladder. Michelle, an African American caseworker for almost two decades, describes telling her personal story to clients over the years:

"I've been there. I was on welfare . . . I'm not embarrassed to tell you where I started out at." I tell them, "Look at me. I graduated from high school, and I [went to] college. . . . If I can do it, you can do it. And you have more tools to work with than I had to work with at that point. You can do it and do it better. I'm here to help you as much as I can . . . My son is in college now. He's in his third year." [With black female clients] I find myself trying to do more of that for them. . . . I'm there for [all my clients]. But sometimes I have tendency to lean a little bit more [with black female clients] because I see how far we struggle to get there. Plus I'm black too and I can relate more to them than I can relate to the white[s] or the Hispanics.

Similarly, Loretta, a Venezuelan woman who came to the United States in 1996, believes that her Latina clients are receptive to the maternal messages that she reserves for them, distilled from her own history of poverty and welfare use. "I feel just as proud if they do well, regardless [of race]," she commented. "But with the Spanish girls, particularly that are younger, I feel like I'm kind of more like a mother." She describes welfare reform as a "necessary evil" and views it as her obligation to help clients get all of the services and advice that they can in order to prepare for the time when they can no longer rely on the office. In contrast to the pan-minority assertions of some of her co-workers, Loretta tries to motivate her Latina clients by drawing contrasts between them and "other" welfare recipients of color who she believes are not as respectable:

I got [Latina] girls that were very rowdy. They were raised with girls of color in their urban population. And they have the same swing, the same talk. I feel like I can tell them, "Don't you want to do better? Do you want to be on welfare all your life? And your kids on welfare all your life? Don't you want better money than this?" And I tell them many times, they probably can quote me, "I'm telling it to you, like if you were my daughter." They understand that I am telling them for their own good.

Conversely, male bureaucrats tend to target what they perceive as clients' negative behaviors and engage in harsher scolding. Challenging clients to help protect the public image of the race and consider the consequences of their actions for the racial community at large appears to be a more popular tactic among male bureaucrats. For example, Carlos tells his [mostly female] clients of color: "[Welfare] is only to help you until you get on your feet. Don't try to be a parasite or what the system wants you to be. Don't be dependent on this. . . . What will you tell your children that grow up in this country and they learn to survive just on a minimal income also? This is only to keep *us* under the foot, dependent." The politics of the job intersect with intraracial politics, and Carlos uses the power that he commands in the welfare office to direct race-mate clients toward the outcome that he thinks is best.

The multiple factors that influence whether clients follow the edicts of welfare reform are both institutional and individual. Their welfare-to-work transitions are marked by ebbs and flows and peppered with success and failures, opportunities and closed doors, "good" and "bad" choices, resource constraints and underutilized resources, and personal limitations and agency breakdowns (DeParle 2004; Edin and Lein 1997; Hays 2003; Korteweg 2003; Watkins 2000; Newman 1999, 2006; Seccombe 1998). Yet when clients engage in behaviors that these bureaucrats deem counterproductive—having another baby, quitting a job that seemed like a good opportunity—the tone of the rescue mission can become even more severe. Bureaucrats' structural critiques of the labor market and the paltry resources offered to low-income women yield to clear messages that recipients are ultimately responsible for improving their own situations and are expected to fully invest in the welfare-to-work enterprise. Workers of all races share these views about clients of all races. But for many workers of color, the stakes can feel higher when it's a member of their own racial group. Timothy described his related frustrations with a frankness and tenor that seemed more prominent among the male caseworkers in this analysis:

It kills me [when they have] a bunch of kids and different "baby daddies." I sometimes ask [clients] to write the fathers' names down, so they can see it on paper. So they'll get it. How are you going to give "your best" away so easily? Instead of going 1, 2, 3, 4, 5 to 10 [in a relationship], they go from 1 to 10, just like that. And I hear them, "My man is doing 8–10, 3–5 [years in prison]." He ain't your man! He's somebody else's man around here and probably somebody else's woman up there. Unless he is snoring in your face, he ain't your man! Don't give away "your best" for nothing. I hear other clients—all of their baby daddies are in jail or on drugs. "What are you attracting?" I'll ask them. "Are you picking them or are they picking you?"

When Timothy's initial efforts prove ineffective, he may move his interventions in directions that are increasingly radical, disapproving, and invasive. Asking clients to write down the names of their children's fathers is not standard protocol; caseworkers verbally solicit this information from clients and type it into the computer for the child support enforcement process. Timothy's motives and methods—which also include asking clients about the wisdom of their choices about intimate relationships—are informed by a notion of racialized professionalism that transcends the boundaries of standard caseworker-client protocol. In fact, his lecture on family formation goes beyond the immediate policy concerns of welfare reform: child support enforcement and discouraging childbearing while receiving state support through family cap rules. Timothy is also targeting the women's *choices* of partners and the multiple paternities of their children. Even the quality of these relationships—the wisdom of going from "1 to 10" so quickly and having a relationship with an incarcerated partner—receives Timothy's attention.

In these interactions, black female clients are left unprotected from the harsher policing efforts of slightly more privileged blacks.[17] Their stigmatization, their minimal political clout, and the power imbalance between them and street-level bureaucrats likely make them reluctant to openly contest this morality policing. Timothy reports that few clients have responded to him with indignation: "You still get some of those old-school [blacks] saying, 'Even though I'm here applying for cash assistance . . . you can't talk to me that way.' So you have to be careful."[18]

Black and Latino Government Intermediaries in the Post–Welfare-Reform Era

The emphasis to date on how racial minority groups are incorporated into and represented within welfare offices has produced extensive scholarship on client experiences (Gooden 1998; Schram, Soss, and Fording 2003; Piven and Cloward 1971; Katz 1996). But the presence of racial minorities among the power-wielding ranks is also part of the story of how social policy is formulated and reformulated on the ground. Although we typically think of influence in terms of electoral politics, Peter Eisinger reminds us that "bureaucratic power provides opportunities to gather and interpret the information that underlies political decision making, to shape and establish choices on which elected officials act, to implement laws passed by elected bodies, and to shape the very character of the public workforce through internal procedures for recruitment, hiring, and promotion" (1982, 769; see also Lipsky 1980). Access to bureaucratic power thus theoretically provides individuals with opportunities to advance a variety of institutional, personal, and even group interests that influence, and are influenced by, how actors choose to interpret their professional roles.

In previous chapters, we saw that welfare reform, as a policy and organizational shift, created an environment in which many street-level bureaucrats revised their professional identities and infused those interpretations into their implementation of policy. This chapter considers how race, class, and gender inform this thesis by helping to shape the formulation and operationalization of the professional identities of black and Latino street-level bureaucrats. It shows that these employees strategically integrate their professional and social identities by drawing upon occupational experiences, personal histories, and political attitudes to determine how they should do their jobs. "Racialized professionalism" represents these employees' formulations of what workplace activities should accomplish in terms of both the immediate sphere of policy implementation and bureaucrats' broader ambitions for their racial groups. It involves the creation of discursive tools to pursue these goals and a unique lens through which to interpret organizational processes (Dhingra 2007).

Racialized professionalism is a concept that contributes to our understanding of the profound dilemmas facing professional people of color who are asked to both support and discipline race-mates within institutions. It is perhaps best understood as a three-step process that takes place at the level of the institution, the macrostructure, and the microinteraction. On each of these levels, I found few differences between the black and Latino bureaucrats in this study. First, individuals assess their perceived institutional power to pursue certain outcomes. For the black and Latino bureaucrats in the Staunton TANF office, the dominant forms of power operating in the economic, political, and social spheres provide a backdrop for their experiences as welfare office employees. Their presence and reportedly positive experiences at work evince the department's progress in hiring a workforce more reflective of the community it serves. With decent salaries and considerable job stability, they benefit from almost a century of struggle to integrate the public employment sector. Yet these individuals must remain vigilant against the possibility that their opportunities might be shaped or stymied by their race (King 1999). As "middlemen" and "middlewomen" in terms of both their institutional and societal positions (Pattillo 2007), black and Latino bureaucrats endure perceived racial inequalities within the agency and demonstrate institutional loyalty to maintain their somewhat precarious economic stability. This likely encourages them to restrict their efforts for minority clients to the range of acceptable behaviors within the institution, offering an adapted brand of social work.

Second, these bureaucrats engage the political and social context of the policies they implement, offering support and critiques that shape their views on how they might use their discretion to administer policy. Black and Latino bureaucrats—informed by environmental conditions, political objectives, and personal strategies for navigating racial inequality—assess welfare reform as a policy that has disproportionate implications for members of their racial groups. Although they have concerns about the new law of the land and how it affects poor blacks and Latinos, these supervisors and caseworkers ultimately champion the policy. This is not simply a case of bureaucrats obediently following the will of the institution; many have their own political and social motives for supporting the new system and hope that it will improve clients' quality of life as well as the collective standing of their racial groups. As such, perceived group interests are key drivers of racialized professionalism.

Third, bureaucratic actors choose whether and how to operationalize a perceived set of racial group interests in the course of service delivery. In other words, they strategize about how they want to use race as a tool to do their work. As professional identities intersect with distinct interpretations of the social meaning and implications of one's racial position, many black and Latino frontline workers attempt to use their occupational authority and social status to pursue certain political, personal, and professional goals that are grounded in group-centered ideologies. Legal scholar Kimberlé Williams Crenshaw writes, "People of color often must weigh their interests in avoiding issues that might reinforce distorted public perceptions against the need to acknowledge and address intracommunity problems" (1991, 1256). In Staunton, black and Latino bureaucrats use the caseworker-client interaction as an alternative space to address perceived intragroup concerns related to work, family, and state involvement with individual clients of color.

For these bureaucrats, mere organizational presence is not enough; they rely on their dual status as both community insiders and agents of the state to build relationships with clients and direct them toward these goals. The focus on advice giving as a key component of welfare casework allows black and Latino street-level bureaucrats to intervene in the lives of their clients of color in distinct ways, but guards against charges of bias and allows them to adhere to the expectations of the institution and protect their own standing. These actors see their interventions as liberatory in that they seek to alleviate the social and economic suffering of poorer race-mates and facilitate their independence from a relationship with the welfare system that, while perhaps necessary in the short run, they view as potentially damaging to both their clients and the racial community at large. As such, the choices of these bureaucrats do not unilaterally unduly influence policy implementation, but, in this case, complement them.

Of course, despite respondents' assertions of the primacy of race in informing their professional experiences and discursive tools, there are multiple identities at play here. An intersectional analysis, Evelyn Simien (2007) asserts, "rejects the separability of identity categories, as it recognizes the heterogeneity of various race-sex groups" (265). We saw how racialized professionalism is heavily influenced by class and gender, which helps us to understand variation among bureaucrats in terms of how and why they deployed racialized, gendered, and classed discourse during service delivery. Bureaucrats' assimilationist leanings favor clients entering the low-wage labor market, adhering to normative practices around childbearing, and limiting their use of welfare benefits. Although these interactions create opportunities for cross-class interracial connection and empowerment, they also can further marginalize clients with already limited power who rarely have the opportunity to challenge these directives during these exchanges. Women of color therefore disproportionately find themselves as both the recipients of support in the name of racial solidarity and the targets of gender- and class-based social scrutiny and regulation in ways that likely differ from what the men in their lives or white clients experience. These bureaucrats' simultaneous positions of disadvantage and privilege therefore complicate any assumption that matching black and Latino caseworkers to clients from their racial groups will offer a uniformly more beneficial approach to service delivery.[19]

This chapter also has revealed some of the longer-term implications of welfare reform as it becomes institutionalized within offices. Catherine Kingfisher (1996, 2001) observes that workers and recipients could be viewed as "co-members" in the welfare system; both receive very limited resources from a heavily regulated system that carries great social stigma. Yet welfare workers, despite often being women themselves, reproduce ideologies about the proper roles and behaviors of women through their interactions with clients. Some see recipients as violating "the rules" by having out-of-wedlock children or by raising children without fathers. These dominant gender ideologies, coupled with bureaucratic controls, constrain efforts toward caseworker-client solidarity and alliances that might undermine or transform the agency. Thus workers and recipients operate from structurally antagonistic positions, blunting the prospects for gender- or class-based alliances that could challenge the system.

A similar dynamic may be occurring between workers and clients of color. We certainly saw evidence of caseworkers of color asserting particular racial, gender, and class ideologies about the behaviors necessary for mobility that sometimes elicited negative reactions from caseworkers when clients failed to adopt what was prescribed. In addition, the embrace of welfare policy may have been partly a reflection of workers' relative impotence to dismantle major obstacles to change for their clients. Without the resources to heavily intervene in their clients' lives, discourse becomes a central tool for workers in their quest to facilitate upward mobility. Ideology, in this sense, is adopted to fit the demands of the job—a job that workers themselves need to maintain their own economic stability. In many ways, black and Latino bureaucrats, presumably like many of their clients, have adapted and yielded to a welfare system that places much of the burden of change on the behaviors and fortunes of clients. As clients confront work opportunities shaped by their skin color, gender, and/or economic disadvantages, these caseworkers and supervisors are ultimately unable to protect them. Their politically pragmatic messages offer a brand of policy implementation tailored to help clients of color navigate these realities; yet the aims and tactics of these social uplift missions, as well as any problems in the welfare system itself or in the low-wage labor market, go unchallenged.

Ultimately, did these bureaucrats "help" minority clients? The answer hinges upon how one defines "help." Depending on political persuasion, some might argue that these workers offer tailored case management that regulates and supports behaviors toward appropriate ends. Others will accuse them of making scapegoats of their race-mates while negotiating the larger structural problems and behaviors that are represented across the entire caseload, not just among blacks and Latinos. The bureaucrats surveyed in this study may well have done both.

They assessed the political current and steered their clients toward possibly better lives, but they have also failed to criticize a set of reforms that still leave a disproportionate number of people of color mired in poverty.

Arguably, these events reflect bureaucrats' own class stories and are very much in line with the strategies they have adopted for navigating the welfare system as professionals (and in some cases, as former clients). They offer clients lessons learned, not simply for leaving welfare but for navigating state and economic systems from a position of disadvantage. They are not abstract recommendations, but tactical and perhaps world-weary instructions of calculated silence, resilience in the face of socioeconomic striving, assimilation into the demands of the state and the mainstream labor market, and acceptance of both these entities' limitations. As such, this analysis tells us a parallel story about the mobility narratives offered by black and Latino street-level bureaucrats as well as their prescriptions for "bootstrap climbs" among their clients of color.

FIVE

Race, Place, and Politics

Negotiating Community and Diversity
in Fishertown

Welfare reform was implemented in one of the best economies in recent memory. The national unemployment rate
continued on a steady decline starting in 1992, decreasing
from 5.4 percent to 4.02 percent between 1996 and 2000.[1]
The 2001 unemployment rate in Massachusetts hovered
at 3.7 percent, less than half the rate of 9.1 percent a decade earlier.[2] The combination of tight labor markets and
welfare reform policies encouraged great increases in labor
force participation among single, and especially never-
married, mothers. Although the figure had been on the
rise since 1992, the number of never-married mothers in
the labor market experienced its biggest jump from 1996
to 2000—from 49.3 percent to 65.8 percent (Proctor and
Dalaker 2002). Significant reductions also took place in
the poverty rate, with 27.9 percent of female-headed families in poverty, compared to 35.8 percent in 1996, when
welfare reform was enacted on the national level.

Most poverty scholars focus on the benefits of such a
strong economy: increased employment opportunities for
low-skilled workers, declining welfare rolls, and an overall
reduction in poverty. There are, however, often downsides
to this kind of economic climate. Rising living costs and
escalating rents mean that many low-income families, regardless of their employment status, find themselves un-

able to find and maintain affordable housing in central cities. Neighborhoods that once housed working-class and low-income families can gentrify or simply raise housing costs, leaving few options in the private real estate market and long waiting lists for Section 8 and public housing. The National Low Income Housing Coalition reported in 2001 that an extremely low-income family in Massachusetts could afford monthly rent of no more than $489, while the fair market rent for a two-bedroom unit was $1,033.[3] The coalition estimated that the state's "housing wage" (the wage at which it is possible to afford such rents) was $19.86 an hour that year. Although many of these estimated costs are significantly offset by Section 8 and public housing assistance, housing affordability remains a daunting challenge for many central city families. Urban Institute scholar Sheila Zedlewski (2000) writes, "This reflects the interactions between two forces affected by the strong economy: higher incomes generally increasing families' purchasing power, but stronger housing demand increasing housing prices and rents in many areas."

Trina Miller, a thirty-year-old African American mother of two girls, aged six and ten, was one of thousands of low-income single mothers experiencing the mixed blessings that a robust metropolitan economy brought—employment opportunities, yet difficulties finding an available, affordable, and safe place to rear her children. Born and raised in the inner city, Trina was looking for better residential options than the public housing project where she and her children had spent the last four years. Her housing complex had become crime ridden and dangerous and Trina feared for the safety of her ten year old during her trips outside to play with friends. Trina's attempts to move to a different part of the city had proved unsuccessful. She was told by the housing authority that she would face at least a yearlong waiting list to move to another public housing development or to receive Section 8 housing assistance. The private rental market offered few options for a single mother on a meager welfare check. Trina had cycled between welfare and intermittent work in various service-economy jobs over the years: grocery store cashier, video store clerk, and office building cleaning lady. Her latest job, working twenty to thirty hours per week at a day care center for $6.75 an hour in 2001, was supplemented with food stamps and welfare benefits when her pay stubs did not put her over the income limit. Trina began hearing from more than one friend that "folks were moving out of the city in droves," to places like Fishertown, a working class community known to have affordable and available housing for low-income families. When the Fishertown Housing Authority reached her name after just a three-month wait, Trina quit her job, packed up her family, and moved sixty miles away to the midsize city. She was placed in the Woodley Commons housing project. As she explained to Terri Acosta, the new welfare caseworker assigned to her recently transferred case at the Fishertown DTA office, "the place seemed to have better opportunities—cheaper places to live that were cleaner and safer. Plus, I heard your money goes farther here."

Welfare bureaucracies do not operate in a vacuum; environmental context matters. Historically, the decentralized nature of AFDC administration has meant that state and local welfare officials have been able to help counteract the unique vulnerabilities created by their local economies as they distribute government relief. At their best, localized welfare services armed workers with the discretion to ensure the safety and well-being of children, tailor welfare services, and make certain that public funding was used appropriately. At their worst, welfare officials discriminated as they interacted with clients, and poor families were often caught in the crosshairs of brutal political battles between federal and state policymakers over poor support (Gans 1995).[4]

Street-level bureaucrats interpret and interact with environmental conditions in other ways as well. How these individuals understand "community," with its various nuances and implications, contributes to bureaucrats' investments and concerns. In the previous chapter, we saw how a race-based definition of community shapes how minority street-level bureaucrats integrate their professional and social identities. In the case of the Staunton office's black and Latino caseworkers and supervisors, memberships in marginalized racial groups create the space for, and often even compel, these individuals to interpret the distribution of institutional power, the implications of public policies, and the best strategies for policy implementation through the lens of a multifaceted understanding of their professional roles. We observed how that perception of community instills a sense of responsibility and desire among the majority of these workers to pursue certain goals and engage in tailored interactions with minority clients that are outside of the formal service-delivery script. (See Pattillo 2007 for how this operates in a neighborhood context.) Of course, class and gender inform and therefore complicate how these bureaucrats understand what is "good for the community"; and, taken with race, we witnessed how the reinforcement of these beliefs represents moments of both solidarity with and regulation of less-privileged race-mates. What is critical to carry into this chapter is the notion that socially situated bureaucrats align themselves with certain communities inside and outside the welfare office, and this informs their interpretations of their roles and challenges as professionals. Bureaucrats' professional identities are therefore informed in part by the concerns, histories, and interests of the communities in which they are embedded.

In this chapter I focus specifically on the Fishertown office, where the predominantly white community in which its welfare workers live is experiencing significant demographic changes. As a companion to the previous chapter, I use this case to show that white caseworkers similarly use the welfare office as a lens, and potential medium, through which to view and address group-based concerns. As low-income families find themselves "priced out" of large urban centers and seek affordable and available housing in "outskirts" towns and midsized cities, receiving communities such as Fishertown are seeing their numbers of racial and ethnic minority residents grow. The city's welfare office takes on special significance in this migratory trend, serving as a symbolic and substantive institutional gateway as the poorest of these families transfer their cash assistance, food stamps, and Medicaid cases so that they can be administered within the host community. I explore how Fishertown staff members are addressing the question of how best to incorporate migrants from nearby central cities into their caseloads and service-delivery strategies and what this says about the integration of their professional identities and perceived racial, class, and residential interests. I show that, when street-level bureaucrats see the institution as a reflection of the community in which they both live and work, perceived negative changes in the client caseload are seen as threats to both the organization and to the community at large. Caseworkers and organizational leaders express their concerns about community change and racial diversity by framing newcomer clients, and their professional responsibilities to them, in discourses tied to service delivery. This analytic reimagining of the importance of environmental context in the self-understandings of situated bureaucrats suggests, as it did in the previous chapter, that dynamics around social identities (race, class, neighborhood change, and so forth) register in their professional identities in often subtle but critical ways. These individuals in turn deploy bureaucratic power to serve as a filter through which to interpret, and sometimes as a vehicle to protect, defined group interests.

A Gateway Community:
Race, Migration, and Ethos in a Changing Community

Most of Fishertown's long-term residents can trace their roots to Portugal and a handful of other European countries. Many are just second- and third-generation immigrants themselves. As long as the textile mills were running, housing was affordable, and strong ethnic networks lent their social support, this was a sustainable process of immigrant succession. Robert Cordeiro, a Fishertown caseworker of Portuguese descent who went to the local high school and worked in the textile mills before being employed by the department, described Fishertown as made up of "very ethnic neighborhoods. The French section, the Irish section, the Polish section, it's always been a great ethnic city, a lot of ethnic diversity." This strong affiliation with relatively recent ancestry in Europe contributes a great deal to the community culture of Fishertown.

Although it has a population of about ninety thousand, Fishertown has a colloquial, small-town feel. Nancy Greene, a white special operations worker, once worked in the DTA office of a nearby city. Comparing her experiences in the two offices, she observes, "Having grown up in Fishertown, my friends [then] are still friends . . . there's something very parochial about it. When I was going to school, there was one person of color that graduated out of a class of eight hundred." Almost all of the workers in the Fishertown DTA grew up in the community—with just a few from nearby towns—attending the local public high school or the Catholic schools in the area. Most who attended college studied at one of the many institutions within Massachusetts, often just forty to fifty miles from home.

In recent years, Fishertown has struggled to regenerate and maintain an economic base. Residents clearly see the area's economic situation and their ability to survive it as a defining characteristic of their community identity. Stan Fonseca, the head of Community Cares, one of the city's largest nonprofit social service organizations, has made it his mission to help Fishertown's families weather the area's economic storms. Born and raised in the area, he describes how Fishertown's limited economic opportunities create the feeling that the city is in a constant struggle for an economic rebirth: "Like a lot of cities in Massachusetts, we're a gateway community. And gateway communities take the people at the bottom of the totem pole. The housing fits that, the rents fit that, the jobs fit that. We are the last vestige of labor-intensive, low-wage jobs. So what you have in Fishertown is a dependent population and the population that deals with it that makes the Fishertown middle class. . . . Fishertown has never been, in my lifetime, successful. But people here don't live beyond their means. That's how we weather it."

Stan's description of Fishertown as made up of a "dependent population" and the people who serve it points to a somewhat compressed socioeconomic class structure within the community. A position in state government paying $25,000 to $35,000 per year (2001 dollars) is considered a good job in Fishertown. Hospitals, schools, the welfare department, and numerous other government and nonprofit human service agencies employ almost one quarter of the Fishertown labor force, funded largely by the federal and state government.[5] Its median household income was $29,014 in 1999 while the statewide median was $50,502.[6] Its homeownership rate in 2000 was 34.9 percent compared with the statewide average of 61.7 percent.[7] In 1999, 21.7 percent of families with children under the age of eighteen were impoverished, compared with the statewide average of 10.1 percent.[8] Hence, although they are considerably poorer than Fishertown's middle class and often residentially concentrated in the city's public housing developments, welfare recipients do not exist in a social or physical space that is isolated from their better-off community members.

Fishertown's grim prospects are not news to workers at the city's welfare office. In fact, many welfare office workers acknowledge having friends and family members who struggle to make ends meet, and several of the office's staff members have been on the other side of the desk themselves. Debbie Bailey, a white supervisor with thirty years in the department, recognized that in a city where any job really is "a good job," the welfare office takes on increased relevance as a community agency: "We're just lucky in Fishertown to have this job, any job—living in Fishertown in the economy we have. We can go out to dinner in Fishertown for $6 a person. We can have a decent apartment for under $500 a family. We live very reasonably here. My income is excellent for a woman in Fishertown. So this agency becomes very important. A lot of people in the city have walked through these doors, whether they admit it or not. Some for just a month or two of help, others years of help, generations of help."

Although Fishertown may not boast the employment opportunities of central cities, it does have one resource that makes it an attractive relocation site for someone like Trina—affordable housing. The combination of a very strong labor market for workers, the elimination of rent control, and high rents in that state's larger cities has created an exodus of the poor from these areas and into places like Fishertown where the cost of living is lower and public housing is more plentiful and quickly available (Salamon 2003). Although Trina reported hearing about Fishertown from her own friends, housing advocates and other human service providers in larger cities are considered by many Fishertown natives to be important agents in this migration trend, encouraging many of their clients to move. There is definitely some truth to this. For example, Sundra, a black caseworker in the Staunton DTA office, was increasingly becoming a booster for places like Fishertown as she described the struggles her clients face:

SUNDRA: Housing. You still hear a lot of rumors that there isn't adequate housing. Unfortunately, the city lost its rent control. So, there isn't a large market of affordable housing.

INTERVIEWER: Do you hear a lot about clients from this office going to Fishertown and other smaller cities for housing?

SUNDRA: Yes, because there's more housing out that way. I've had clients leave the area. I've said to some of them that if you're willing to relocate, you might be able to find affordable housing someplace else and I've told them about Fishertown and other places. Some of them have [moved].

Sundra was aware that recommending to her clients that they relocate to places like Fishertown had its risks. These communities had much less racial and ethnic diversity, and there was no guarantee that jobs would await them. In addition, moving could disrupt one's social network. Nevertheless, Sundra tried to convince many of her clients that the challenges would be worth overcoming for the allure of available housing:

Sometimes it's difficult because if they have family ties in the city, they want to remain in the city. They feel more comfortable. Sometimes if you go to another community, it could be a predominantly white community and they might not be comfortable. Some have never lived in a mixed community setting . . . a predominantly white setting can become overwhelming. I've had parents even say that. They've [moved to different areas within the city], which has had its questionable areas. They'll say, "My child has had a racial slur said to them, had bricks thrown at them." That's right here in the city. If they deal with that here and then you take them to someplace that's almost totally white, they'll feel alienated. I don't think they're made to feel comfortable in a lot of those places.

Pushed out of urban housing markets, many poor families, including a number of Hispanic and black families, nevertheless took the advice of Sundra and others and began migrating in larger numbers. Sharon Bass, a white administrator in the office, was starting to see a shift:

Fishertown has always had a very high number of public housing units per capita. And many of the Fishertown natives would choose not to live in public housing and make every attempt to go into Section 8 or private housing, because [the] cost of living isn't that outrageous here even if you live in a private house. So this became a place for people to come to for housing. When you realize what an important issue housing is, you realize that people will come from almost anywhere for a place to stay, and when they get here, they find out they can afford to live, and they find out that, for a city of roughly one hundred thousand, it is not an outrageously violent city. It is not overrun with violence and drugs. It could be an okay place to bring up your kids. So we receive a lot of transfer cases from the bigger cities.

In 1990, Fishertown was 97.2 percent white, 1.7 percent Hispanic, 1.03 percent black, and 1.33 percent Asian.[9] In 2000, those numbers had shifted to make Fishertown 91.2 percent white, 3.3 percent Hispanic (of any race), 2.5 percent black, and 2.2 percent Asian.[10] The proportion of minorities in Fishertown has more than doubled in recent years, partly due to immigration and the migration of families from U.S. central cities. The absolute numbers and even the percentages of minorities in the community remain very low; they still represent less than 10 percent of the Fishertown population. The growth trend has, however, put the intersection of race and poverty on the community's radar screen as a salient but highly controversial issue. In addition, the economic concentration and residential segregation of newcomers in several of the city's public housing projects has marked their presence.[11]

Even though not all of the migrants are poor or minorities, a perception of shifting racial and economic demographics in the community has quickly made its way into the Fishertown welfare office. The historically white client base of the Fishertown DTA office has indeed seen a shift. In 1990, the Fishertown's office caseload was 72 percent white, 10 percent Hispanic, 10 percent black, and 8 percent Asian. By 2001, the office's caseload was 64 percent white, 13.1 percent Hispanic, 13.6 percent black, and 9.0 percent Asian.[12] These are not dramatic changes—and caseloads across the country, for various reasons, are becoming increasingly concentrated with racial minorities (Lower-Basch 2000). However, staff members in the Fishertown office attribute the minority percentage increases primarily to the migration of families from urban areas and secondarily to immigration in general. From their point of view, this shift suggests that there is an unprecedented trend under way that is racially diversifying a historically white town and its welfare office.

The Welfare Office as a Site for Integrating Newcomers

With regular influxes of new immigrants, poor-relief bureaucracies have historically gone beyond the traditional task of distributing benefits to fulfill a deliberate role in the assimilation of these families into host communities (Gordon 1994). The Fishertown office is no exception. In the last several decades, as waves of Cambodian refugees arrived in the city in the late 1970s and continuing through the early 1990s, many applied for and received public assistance. The office hired three Cambodian-born workers to assist this population, and one worked his way up to become an administrator. Sharing a common language and culture, these bureaucrats helped their countrymen and women access welfare services and assimilate into the Fishertown community. Similar approaches have been adopted by the office for Portuguese- and Spanish-speaking Latino clients. As bilingual and bicultural caseworkers have developed ties with several established members of these ethnic communities, they have acquired information about community resources and passed them on to their clients.[13] As a result, Fishertown's immigrant families have traditionally had access to ethnic social support networks vis-à-vis the welfare department. This has proved useful as they transfer their skills and integrate into the community.[14]

DTA office administrators did not replicate the approach used for integrating immigrant newcomers over the years with the increasing numbers of migrating families who have moved into the area from the state's biggest cities. The office has not created the kind of institutional supports in terms of new services or reassigned staff, nor have office leaders suggested that these demographic shifts might require extra attention on the part of the agency. The conventional wisdom in the office is that caseworkers should not deny services to newcomers, but they need not make special accommodations for them either: migrating clients should learn to navigate Fishertown just as natives do.

But there is a problem with this logic. The stated intention among organizational leaders for adopting this minimalist approach to community integration has been to treat everyone equally, and perhaps to quell any potential racial tensions that might result from openly acknowledging the arrival of migrating black and Latino families. Yet there are some consequences to this that place the office's newest clients at a disadvantage. There is an assumption built into welfare reform that social networks and nonprofit service providers will be instrumental in facilitating the welfare-to-work transitions of recipients and will take up the slack when government assistance is limited. For many families, tapping into these networks and institutional resources is critical, and the welfare office is a logical place to facilitate these connections.

Yet recently migrated clients who are English speaking are assigned to workers according to availability, not on the basis of language, as is the case for non-English-speaking Cambodian, Portuguese, and Hispanic newcomers. As a result, they are spread across a worker population that has varying knowledge of the resources available to new residents and disparate commitments toward brokering resources for them. As the migratory trend continues, the differences that emerge between workers who see their professional identities as efficiency experts versus those who view themselves as social workers take on even bigger implications. Furthermore, with no African American caseworkers and only one Spanish-speaking caseworker (who is of Portuguese descent), the welfare office largely fails to serve as an entry point for access to ethnic-based social networks for migrants in the ways that it does for immigrants. Sharon went on to describe what this may mean for clients:

I think that people on my side of the fence can forget that the person they are talking to might not know anything about this area except how to find their apartment and this building, because right now, we are their lifeline. You aren't dealing with a Fishertown native any more. You can't assume. They don't know how to go to WIC and get coupons for their children, they don't know where the Salvation Army is, they just don't know. So, we may not be giving out enough resource information, because we are not believing that these people don't know where they are, we aren't assimilating them. So we might be short-changing them in that respect. I think if they asked, "Where is the Salvation Army?" we would tell them, but we can't assume that they know.

Sharon's point affirms the notion that welfare offices are catch-all bureaucracies for low-income families. By situating the Fishertown office in its community context, we see that it is the first institutional representative of the community for poor newcomers. When this relationship is acknowledged, formal and informal strategies can go a long way toward integrating families coming from larger cities and introducing the resources and culture of their host communities. One might not equate the immigrant waves that gave rise to agency changes in previous years with the more recent migrant waves, or one may assume that migrants will and should rely on their own resourcefulness or budding networks in their host communities to learn the new environment. What is noteworthy for our analysis is how the combination of this demographic shift and the administration's limited response to this round of newcomers has left caseworkers to decide for themselves once again whether and how they would define their professional roles and dispense services to these newcomers.

Members of the central office have been observing this trend play out in offices all over the state. As families move their cases from the state's largest cities to midsize and small towns, Bob has a clear sense of how workers should respond:

It's the workers [that should help in this transition]. But it's [also] who prepares them and how they're supported. Some offices are very good because they're so tied in to the broader community. They are like the 211 connection; they know where everything is.[15] You need a job, you need housing, you're not eligible for TAFDC, we have other options for you. There are folks who spend a lot of time developing resources within local offices. But they tend to be small offices [where this happens]. But I think what you discover in the migration of families to certain larger offices [like Fishertown]—the office personnel hasn't changed much. But the neighborhood around the office is changing because of the influx of new people. How are they dealing with that? I think it will depend upon the office and its staff and how they serve the community at large.

Just as we saw in previous chapters, disparities in service delivery abound in the Fishertown office, in large measure due to the differences in how staff members define their professional identities. Some caseworkers see serving as a gateway to community integration as part of the welfare office's continuing function and of their responsibility as professionals. Although they are not ethnically matched in the way that Cambodian and non-English-speaking Portuguese clients are, they believe that it is part of their job to provide information, lend support, and ease the acculturation process. Molly Templeton, a white Fishertown caseworker, represents this kind of welfare professional. She is sympathetic to newcomer clients' needs for housing and expresses concern about the social support problems that they may encounter in their new communities:

We have a lot [of clients] that come [here] from the bigger cities. I find that a lot of them are here just for housing. You really can't blame them because you can't find affordable housing there. It must be really hard to relocate to an area especially when you may not have roots or family here. I have made referrals to a support group for people who are from other areas. I have made other referrals as well so that they can find out what's going on with the new community, what services that they may be entitled to here in Fishertown.

But Bob's desire and Molly's strategies to help make the transition as smooth as possible for newly migrated clients were not shared by all of the welfare caseworkers at the Fishertown office. Lisa Twain, a white caseworker in the office for seventeen years, was less comfortable in this role:

LISA: I refer them to wherever [services] I refer everybody else. Well, I know that there's some Hispanic organizations in the area. Like agencies that have Spanish-speaking staff and help people connect with services in the area. Peggy [Lipscomb, the Spanish-speaking worker] knows a lot about them, so I might send a client to her.

INTERVIEWER: What if Peggy isn't available? Do you feel like you know enough about them to tell clients who they are and what they do?

LISA: Kinda, but not really. I know there's a few of them and I just haven't had time to investigate and figure out what's what.

At first glance, it appears as though whether workers invest in orienting newcomers to services falls right along the social worker versus efficiency engineer continuum outlined in previous chapters. Those who see themselves as social workers are likely to spend more time and energy in providing referrals and recommendations to newcomer clients, and efficiency engineers are reluctant to engage in this way. The remedy would appear simple: if one wants to integrate migrating families into communities so that they can gather resources and increase the likelihood that they will be successful in their transitions through and eventually off the welfare system, caseworkers' professional identities need to be aligned with what they call social work so that these individuals can assist in brokering resources for these families.

Upon closer inspection, however, there is more to the story. As I spoke to workers about the changes in the office, it became clear that differences among caseworkers on the migration question could not be completely attributed to yet another representation of the philosophical and practical differences between social workers and efficiency engineers. Even some of the most firmly avowed social workers were oddly silent around the issue of integrating newcomers into the community, and I observed some efficiency engineers shift from their focus on speed and accuracy to tell a new client where she could find the WIC office or some other neighborhood service that she thought might be helpful to a mother whose social networks were in another city. Something else seemed to be informing how caseworkers thought about their responsibilities toward newcomer clients. In fact, their own views about what these shifts meant for not only the agency but for the community at large figured into many workers' views about how to fashion their professional identities and discretionary tools in light of these changes.

Welfare Offices as Politicized Spaces in Residential Migration Debates

Just as welfare offices can serve as sites for *community integration*, they can also become sites for *community discord*, when anxieties arise about its future. By serving as a default gateway to an insular community for its poorest newcomers, the Fishertown welfare office is a space in which frontline workers wrestle with questions of community transformation and potential encroachment. As most office employees both live and work in Fishertown, community-based tensions over the demographic changes in the town's population permeate the agency in a way that is simply not on display in Staunton's big-city office where both workers and clients are residentially dispersed. Julie Jacobs, a central office administrator, is seeing this dynamic play out in so many different mid-sized offices across the state that she has a name for it:

I called it the turnstile office, because you've got a lot of new people coming out of bigger cities in the state because they can't afford the housing, thinking "if I move [to a place like Fishertown], I'll be able to get a job and afford it, but [it] is close enough to still be near my social network." And it's not always working. But you also have the older community that's been there forever, that's well established, and . . . they're mashing up against each other consistently. And they're just now on the verge of where they're settling a little bit, but anything that happens—culturally, ethnicity, jobs, whatever—any competition brings the tensions right to the surface again.

Some newcomers in fact complete their revolution through "the turnstile" and return to their home communities after jobs become too difficult to find and the distance from their social networks becomes too great. Others opt to try to persevere in their new homes. Regardless of their tenure, welfare caseworkers assigned to assist them in Fishertown have begun to politicize these families in ways that differ from how they understand indigenous clients. When I first visited the office in 2001, about two-thirds of the interviewees either directly voiced uneasiness about these newer residents or reported that they had heard their co-workers express negative feelings about the migration of families from larger cities. When I returned several years later, there were fewer people who expressed these views, but the anxieties and negative attitudes still surfaced in my conversations with some of the staff. Some worry that the growing ranks of impoverished families in the community further tax a city that is already struggling to provide for its "native" poor; others lament that newcomers damage the social fabric of the community; and still others believe that these particular newcomers—minority, poor, and urban—bring problems to the city.

When Clients and Outsiders Are One and the Same:
Welfare Caseworkers and the Politics of Community Change

The fear that poverty is being imported to a city struggling for its own economic viability plagues many of the issues around the migration. Although Stan at Community Cares didn't outright oppose the transition taking place, the fact that the city is working with such scarce resources causes him to talk passionately about the issue:

So, that's why when you're sending poor people here, there's a ceiling. You can only go so far. You are either going to go from a poor person on welfare to a working poor person. That doesn't really resolve your economic problem. . . . They are moving people here without the resources to deal with it. Fishertown has had a double-digit unemployment rate, double the state, my entire life. We don't need a whole bunch more poor people; I can't even deal [as a service provider] with the ones I've got! The problem is here, there are no jobs. They are sending them here for the housing, but there is nothing else. My complaint is that I am getting overwhelmed. . . . You have to give me something to deal with these people, because there's no such thing as dealing with somebody on one problem. When somebody's poor, the world's caving in on 'em and you gotta get 'em out. Then you've gotta get them daycare, then you've gotta get them some job training. There's a number of issues. And they just send these people here.

The concern over whether Fishertown has enough resources has also morphed for some into concerns about whether the city's resources should be used on *these* newcomers. Martine, a white caseworker, describes what she has heard from some of her co-workers in the DTA office:

Workers are frustrated. Workers don't like it. . . . A lot of workers have property in the city. A lot of workers know that we're getting everybody else's poor people; we are getting everybody else's "unproductive people." Eventually this city is going to be very distressed. They say, "People are coming here with no skills, they are not producing, they are not doing anything." And in a way it's true because they do arrive with few skills, but in another way, the reason why [my family] came here was because nothing was happening for my father [in Portugal]. And you know how courageous it was for my father just to pick up his family and go to another country where he didn't even know the language?

Defining Fishertown DTA workers as the very property owners who supposedly stand to lose, Martine connects the anxieties in the city to the attitudes brewing in the welfare office. The notion that newcomer clients are being constructed in the minds of some workers as "unproductive people" harkens back to old labels of "the undeserving poor," who are believed to threaten everything from property values to the quality of life of Fishertown (Katz 1996; Gans 1995). As Tina D'Angelo, a white caseworker, contrasts older versus newer migrants, her statement offers a window into how she understands not only the changes under way in Fishertown but also who the newest clients are: "Well, I'm just thinking back that years ago when people came to this country, you had to be sponsored. You had to have a job waiting. And now it seems like a lot of people come over here and they're right down in the [DTA] office. I don't really think there's any contributing to the community."

Billie, a white supervisor in the Fishertown office who spoke about seeing herself as a social worker in previous chapters, nevertheless saw what many termed "the influx" of families as problematic. Born and raised in Fishertown, she describes a strong sense of community, with extended family living within the city or in a nearby area and former school classmates serving as co-workers and close friends. Billie wondered whether these newest migrants from the city would be able to adopt Fishertown as more than just their physical place of residence, but rather as their symbolic home:

Basically nobody leaves Fishertown—I have my mother here, my grandmother here, no one's ever left. My husband's family, the same thing. Every generation has still been here. We have lots and lots of families like that. We have also seen lots and lots of new families that have come in and done very well. We've had lots of immigrants come in—not just from the Azores but Spain; we've had some from Jamaica that are doing very, very well. The problems that we're seeing are the transients that are coming, wherever they come from. They have never come from one particular place, that's their problem. They have never had a home or a family. The mother was living in Boston or New York or New Haven when she had that baby and now she has moved to Fishertown.

Billie's idea of Fishertown's newest inhabitants as "transients" who "have never come from one particular place" suggests how she differentiates among newcomers—immigrants versus migrants from central cities. She sees Fishertown's immigrant populations as being made up of close-knit family units, similar to the way she views her own family and in-laws: hard-working people who came to Fishertown as outsiders and pulled themselves up. She adds Jamaicans to her list of groups that have come to Fishertown and done well, belying potentially simplistic racial undertones in her thinking about the city's dynamics. Newcomers from other cities, according to Billie, are without family and the perseverance necessary to settle in one community and buckle down to work. Fishertown for them is just a stop on a continual movement from city to city, potentially bringing these values and problems to her community.

As Billie's comments suggest, newcomers are perceived by some as threatening the social fabric of Fishertown. This concern is grafted onto their ideas about what the change means for the DTA office. For example, some welfare office employees contend that safety is compromised by the newcomers and that the migrants bring with them a set of social problems and sensibilities that not only threaten the community but also make their caseloads harder to manage. Public bureaucracies often have one group of clients who are deemed, for whatever reason, unfavorable. In welfare offices, clients labeled "aggressive" or "hostile" tend to be the ones to avoid. As workers describe it, these undesirable clients try to assert power in every aspect of service delivery, from when they show up for appointments to their reluctance to comply with the requests of welfare workers. To protect themselves against problems and uncertainties, workers informally categorize clients and create narratives about them based on their perceptions. For Fishertown staff members already struggling with the changes in their community, these categorizations have become geographically informed and sometimes even racially tinged.[16]

Some workers describe a schism between what they characterize as "aggressive" urban culture versus Fishertown culture, and they believe that migrants import the former into the city and the welfare office.

171

Lucy Mitchell, a white Fishertown office supervisor, explains that it is based not on race but on the differences between big city and small city sensibilities:

For the most part, our clientele grew up in Fishertown. . . . It's like city mouse and country mouse. I think that most people who work here have always treated everyone basically the same. I find that people who are coming from other areas oftentimes are the ones who come with an attitude attached. When I would go up to the city and stay with family and you go into downtown, you take the subway, my aunt who lived there would be much more aggressive than I would ever be. Aggression, that's how you got onto the subway, that's how you were going to get a seat. So I think that when people come from the city and they come down here [to the welfare office], they think that they are getting a seat on the subway and they have to be aggressive to get it, when in reality they don't have to. So sometimes their aggressive attitude makes it appear to be confrontational when maybe it really isn't and we're not quite used to it.

Billie makes a more pointed observation. "They come ready for battle because that's all they know," she commented. "This office isn't that type of an office. I think we're a friendly office. We're not hostile. We've never had to be. Maybe with a couple of clients once in a while. In that respect, there's been a big change." For whatever reasons these families have come to Fishertown, workers agree that a stronger urban influence than in previous years has been making its way into the community and not necessarily for the better. One might argue that savvy, assertive clients are best able to assert their legal rights and discourage mistreatment by the welfare department. However, Billie and Lucy see this stance as contrary to the ways in which business in the welfare office is typically handled in Fishertown. Their fears and anxieties about "aggressive" clients loom even larger when the behavior is coming from newcomers who are seen as different and unfamiliar.

As these bureaucrats have grappled with how to interpret and talk about the changes taking place in their office and community, race has worked its way explicitly into the narratives and discourse of a handful of respondents. Because the town's main source of racial and ethnic diversity up until this point had come from Cambodian refugees and waves of white European immigrants, Fishertown's history as an overwhelmingly white community has been treated as a largely taken-for-granted yet coveted aspect of the community ethos. With the high number of blacks and Hispanics among the newcomers, this presumption has been disrupted and the Fishertown community and its DTA staff have been catapulted into a debate about diversity. As Conrad, a white supervisor, comments, "[the numbers of] black families have just increased tremendously. It was odd to see a black family in Fishertown. It was very heavily Portuguese and that was normal, you expected that. But we definitely have a lot more black and Hispanic families coming to the area." Such a demographic shift has not gone unnoticed in Fishertown. As Stan explains: "Well, yeah, they're saying that we're getting too many 'out-of-towners,' code word for black people. This is a city that where I went to high school, Stevenson High School, there were three thousand kids in it, three black kids. We don't have a lot of black population now. But when you go from zero to one hundred, one hundred seems like the hordes are coming."

As workers voice their feelings about the migration to each other informally and theorize about how their neighbors and friends have been interpreting the shifts in Fishertown's population, they have begun to take opposing sides on the politically charged issue. Sharon expresses concern about the negative attitudes of some of her colleagues: "Well, because we are near more interracial cities there are a lot of folks coming for housing who just happen to be black. But they also happen to have a culture, and happen to have a history, that I'm not sure that our people here in Fishertown truly understand. We do talk about diversity, but it has been a long time since the back of the bus, and I'm not sure that we've all come quite that far with it." Similarly, Conrad makes this observation: "People don't like it, the influx. They say stuff like the crime has increased because of the influx of people from the bigger cities. The influx of the Hispanics, because people don't speak English, services are being demanded of the city. 'These people don't belong,' some say. You're talking basically about a very small-minded group because this is an old mill city and there are people who still expect it to stay Mayberry. It's not going to stay Mayberry."

The reputation of inner-city minority communities as high crime, persistently poor, and culturally antagonistic has worried others. They have not seen this influx as a positive or neutral trend. It has been, instead, the tip of an iceberg that will not be a blessing for the community. A handful of staff members talk explicitly about the relationship they see between race, poverty, and urban culture, and express clear antipathy toward clients of color for this reason. As these workers speak about their newest clients, their comments focus less on the concerns we heard earlier about resource constraints or an intimidating style of interaction that they believe was gleaned from living in big cities and more on the social group memberships of the families themselves.

Debbie was one such respondent. She expressed great concern about the impact that these new families would have on not only the quality of life in Fishertown but also on her own safety:

The population has changed. More ethnic, much more so. When I went to high school, Fishertown had one black family and a lot of Portuguese. The population has completely changed. My street was all white and now it's a quarter black. Still, it's higher up enough that they have to work, you now what I mean, they're good people. But right down the street it's starting to come up that there are more crimes, more fights. They seem to bring their Bloods and their Crips with them, things like that, you know. All those people. I think the crime is expanding. I never used to be afraid to go out at night. We might have had two rapes a year at the most. We're generally people that knew people. I think that's changing. House breaks. I don't know the statistics, my point of view as an older woman is it's not as safe. There are a lot of carjackings; who ever heard of that? The population has changed, be it ethnic, or race, or just a population [that's] poor coming in because of the low-income housing. The population is poor and desperate.

Fear of crime has long been associated with the racial composition of people's neighborhoods (Stinchcombe et al. 1980), and whites living in close proximity to blacks tend to be more fearful of crime (Skogan 1995). Further, consistent with social disorganization theory, "residents' perceptions of signs of deterioration and decay in their neighborhoods increase levels of fear and perceived personal risk of victimization, while negatively influencing [their] neighborhood safety ratings. Perceptions of neighborhood disorder do seem to cause people to fear more or be more concerned with crime in both personal and general ways" (Kanan and Pruitt 2002, 544). Debbie's comment reveals how the foundation is laid for community anxieties to make their way into the welfare office. Living on a block that is now one-quarter black suggests to her that the neighborhood has "completely changed." Debbie makes clear class distinctions between her working black neighbors who are "good people" who "have to work" and the "baggage" that "other" black families seem to bring with them—jobless friends and family, crime, and social decline in Fishertown. Her description of employed blacks is racially tinged, suggesting some kind of exceptionalism that makes them very different from their poorer counterparts.

Debbie's next set of comments reveal the complexities of these moments as bureaucrats try to square their views with their beliefs about their appropriateness. Despite her strong words, we see her grappling with the idea of explicitly linking her attitudes about the newcomers to race. She then struggles to disentangle race from class, perceived by her as a much more comfortable platform from which to speak:

Well, if I had a family to feed and no way to feed it, I'd be doing the same thing. I wouldn't die. The Irish had to do it—it doesn't have anything to do about race; the Portuguese had to do it. It's not—they're not black, they're not Puerto Rican— they're desperate. They wanted something and they got it. . . . I think it's poverty and I think that uneducated people may put it toward ethnic, but I think it's poor. I've seen a hell of a lot of scary white men, just as tough, just as desperate.

For Debbie and others, the fact that these newcomers are minority, urban, *and* poor is what creates problems for the city. Although all of her ideas about the city's decline and its link to this population are based on her perceptions rather than any factual information that she could present, Debbie is sure that this kind of diversity has meant a deterioration in the quality of the city. In fact, violent crime rates have fluctuated between 1990, when many contend the migration of families from big cities began in large numbers, and 2005, with a low of 596.1 per 100,000 people in the year before I interviewed Debbie (2001) and a high of 1,269.1 in 2005.[17] Property crime rates have held steady since a spike between 1987 and 1990 when the rate was around 7,000 to 8,000 per 100,000 people. In 2001, the rate was 3,523.7 per 100,000 people. In Debbie's sense-making strategies, however, stereotypes of the minority urban poor enter into her constructions of her newest neighbors. To her, the newcomers don't really belong in Fishertown:

For me, to be very honest, I didn't want my city to change that much. I guess we have to, you can't move, you can't tell someone not to live in your town. That's ridiculous but I want them to be able to add something to the community, not wreck it. Don't put any more graffiti in my town. Different cultures and different ways of doing things. Different rules about respecting property, it's tough. They didn't respect property [where they came from]. It's going to take a lot for people that were born here to learn the different things. I don't think we have the discrimination they have other places, as far as I know. Nobody would say anything, I don't see any discrimination whatsoever because of color. . . . But Fishertown residents are low income too and they need as much help as the people coming in. It's not right.

The distinctions that Debbie makes on the basis of class and her stated antipathy toward lower-class blacks suggests that she views negative class-based perceptions as more acceptable to express than those made on the basis of race. This perhaps explains why she was so willing to talk about race with me as a black researcher. My own "middle class-ness" likely explains why staff members in general were so forthcoming about talking about race in the office even though I am African American. Surely as a black female researcher, I was not likely privy to all of the respondents' attitudes about the movement of blacks and Latinos into their city. But the greater level of candor around these issues than I expected suggests that perhaps my class status was fully operational in those moments, creating the space for them to talk about sensitive topics while allowing them to remain fully cognizant of my race.[18]

Steven and Margaret, the front-desk clerks whom we met in chapter 1, were also working hard to negotiate this intersection of race, place, and class that had become an undercurrent in the office. They had worked for years in the office and came from two of the oldest black families in the city. Their co-workers in the Fishertown office got to know them well, and both garnered a great deal of affection in the office. Steven often talked about his privileged upbringing as a member of one of Fishertown's prominent black families and joked that because of that history and visibility, "people saw us as the 'nice colored people.' You know, we were the nice ones." Yet caught in the crosshairs of the migration debate, he shared feelings that were eerily similar to those of many of the black and Latino employees in the Staunton office. After talking about watching the local news and hoping more and more not to see a black face in the latest reports on Fishertown crime, I asked him this:

INTERVIEWER: So do you feel like the migration that people are talking about has implications for you?

STEVEN: Yeah, I do. I got to be honest. One of my best friends, a white woman, used to be married to a black man. We were riding in the car one day. I live in one of the nice neighborhoods. She said, "Now I'm going to show you something," She is no racist, doesn't have a racist bone in her body. And she took me on a tour of the ghetto, the new ghetto [in Fishertown]. She said, "I'm going to tell you something. This affects my biracial kids. My kids are going to be reflected in these fools hanging out, selling drugs." And drugs is a big thing. She said, "Look at this." And I locked the car door. I say to myself, "Am I my brother's keeper?" And I don't know . . . it's a race thing, but sometimes it is a class thing.

How did these complexities and tensions around race, place, and class shape interactions within the DTA office? These events can be difficult to observe and parse out during participant observation, particularly when the researcher is herself a member of a minority group and overtly negative behaviors are viewed by employees as politically incorrect. Although Debbie asserts that discrimination is a nonissue in Fishertown, she admits to bringing many of her concerns about the community into the welfare office. She is convinced that Fishertown's newest inhabitants bring with them a set of styles, attitudes, and behaviors that are difficult to respond to at work. In her mind, these new clients represent the "aggressive" and therefore harder-to-serve contingent of her caseload:

I've been scared a couple of times; we have no police officer here. We have no glass on that window [in the front desk area]. Those locks on those doors [that separate the client waiting area from the worker area] are stupid because anyone who wants to get in can just jump over the counter. We have no security here; some offices have a glass, why can't we have a glass, why can't we have some safety here? Wherever they came from, they are not respectful of us trying to help them. They don't see us as trying to help. We're the law, and they're the criminal. It's like that to them. We're not used to that, we're used to someone coming in and saying, 'What can I get?' 'How can you help me?' Not, 'Hey, you're going to help me now.' It's just so different. . . . We don't expect to keep our guard up and be aggressive, we're here to help and get the job done.

Secondhand accounts provide even more evidence of racial antipathy. For example, Sharon was troubled by the idea that some of her coworkers seemed to equate being urban, minority, and poor with having a culture that was aggressive, problematic, and incompatible with Fishertown. Although she had not seen it reach palpable levels, she believes that this tension is bubbling just beneath the surface:

You can hear that kind of thing: "I don't know how she does it; she's got the Hispanic caseload. I wouldn't want to have all of them, you know they all lie." That's not something that's prevalent in the office, but it might be an undercurrent. And, I don't even think it's malicious; it's like learned behavior. This has changed. If you came in here years ago and looked in our waiting room, you could probably sit here for three days before you would see someone of color walk in. So not everyone here has been able to check their perceptions at the door.

Martine offered these observations about what she has heard about clients of color and how they are treated in the office:

MARTINE: It's the comments people make. Which I don't think is appropriate for the office. Everyone has a right to their own beliefs, but do it in the privacy of your own home. Also, sometimes people deal with the newer clients [poorly]. True, we [workers] are not going to become so friendly, we are not going to take them home to dinner. I'm their worker and that's the way it is. But some workers will have an attitude that "we're also not going to show them, by facial expressions or body movement, that [they] belong here." But sometimes a facial change or a body change says more than any words, and I think that's what you have in this office.

INTERVIEWER: Can you give me an example?

MARTINE: Offensive things are being said about Hispanics, Puerto Ricans. Not so much [about] Cape Verdeans because Cape Verdeans were at one point Portuguese, and because of the people of Portuguese descent in this office, because it's a group that had the same language. I think it's the Puerto Ricans and the Hispanics—they refer to them as a "dirty group." Making small indications in front of clients, it's sometimes very subtle, but there.

Although some caseworkers express fears, anxieties, and even antipathy toward their newest clients to co-workers, they know better than to openly express them. In fact, workers strongly assert that their views on the migration and the newcomers do not affect welfare service delivery. They understand that they are expected to be fair, and, besides that, the fear that clients might lodge formal complaints should they feel mistreated keeps these workers in check.

But more subtle maneuvers give them the opportunity to express their views without incurring the wrath of clients or management. No one described incidents of overt discrimination against minority clients; in fact, Steven, the black former front-desk worker, commented that if he had seen any, "I would have rung that bell long ago." But some, as Martine told me, have witnessed instances in which their co-workers have not been very welcoming, either. As an administrator, Sharon worries that workers sometimes express their behind-the-scenes discomfort by finding crafty ways to manipulate those things over which they have control, such as waiting room time: "I think there's always a certain fear of the unknown, and it's really hard not to make inappropriate snap judgments. So if you had a day where you just had two aggressive, difficult African American clients, and you peek out into the waiting room, and there's four people, all African American, and you're a smoker, you might figure you need a smoke break before you go deal. But maybe that person doesn't need to sit there another ten minutes."

Because the agency administrators have never directly addressed the issue of the changing caseload with the staff, they have not created outlets for staff members to grapple with the change as an office and put in place measures to address workers' attitudes, perceptions, and stereotypes. This has left workers to deal with the changes on their own, deciding what this environmental shift means for how they understand their jobs, their clients, and the change in their workplaces. Phyllis Conley, a white Fishertown caseworker, had this to say:

> Oh, definitely a lot of workers are having difficulty dealing with the diversity. Sometimes going for help means weakness, and people don't want to say that they are having problems. . . . But their negativity comes out in their approach. They're short with the clients. They don't want to hear it. You can hear it in their interview, their curtness. They don't mean to be. I've worked with these people for years, and I know how nice they can be, but the stresses of the job turn them into being abrupt and not as compassionate to some of the feelings of certain clients coming in. Client misses an appointment because she was in [another] city with her family, they don't want to hear it. I know they're not meaning to be that way, but they are so overwhelmed.

Most of these views were expressed by interviewees during the initial round of fieldwork in 2001. When I returned to the office years later, these stances were less widely expressed. Perhaps it had become apparent that the newcomers had not brought the catastrophic community change with them that some believed they would. Few workers could recall incidents when the "aggressive" urban culture of newcomer clients was dangerously on display. And many of the staunchest opponents of the migration had retired. Perhaps the newcomers have become more familiar to workers with time; perhaps the newcomers have found ways to navigate Fishertown's culture. Regardless of the reason, by 2007 most workers seem to have settled into the belief that these are simply families who are seeking relief from the limited housing markets in their home areas rather than ominous threats to their way of life. This does not mean that workers have welcomed the newcomers with open arms and few reservations. But the high levels of anxiety and even antipathy that I heard in 2001 were certainly not as widespread in 2007.

Ironically, Steven answered his own rhetorical question about whether he was his brother's keeper. When I returned to the field years later, Steven had left the welfare department and was working for one of its contracted job placement centers. Despite his anxieties about Fishertown's newcomers, Steven began engaging in the kind of racialized professionalism described in the previous chapter:

This one guy, good guy, straight as an arrow. He looks like a gang banger, you know, bald head, the whole look. And I tell him, "When you go in for a job interview, I want you in a shirt and tie." He looks at me like I'm crazy. I said, "Michael, there's an orphanage, a boys' Catholic orphanage. They're going to hire you. Because they've got kids in there of color and they're going to want a man of color, a strong, educated man of color. They're going to hire you as a group leader." He called me this morning, he says, "They hired me." What did I tell you? And I always say when they tell me [that they're worried about racism], "You're going to face discrimination until the end of the earth. You have to go in there . . . " and this is what my grandmother used to say. She'd say, "You have to go in there and prove you're not just as good, but you're better." . . . But part of that I think is they need a lot of self-esteem. If you've been beaten down all your life, you're not going to have a lot of self-esteem.

Nevertheless, six years later, negative and stereotypical views about minority clients have not completely disappeared even though they are less widely expressed. Although many workers in both Fishertown and Staunton describe their belief that their clients regularly lie to them in order to maximize their resources (Edin and Lein 1997), Myrtle's racialized assessment of this issue is striking. It came up as we discussed the migration trend and the increasing number of Latino clients in her caseload, and Myrtle, a white Fishertown caseworker, did not mince words in her assessment: "They're a bunch of liars. They don't tell you the full truth of anything. And they don't report things on time. They're all [clients] the same way. I shouldn't say that, but a lot of it . . . they're demanding, too."

With the continuing migration and new waves of immigrants coming into Fishertown, this issue is likely to continue to reemerge as caseworkers and clients, old-timers and new residents negotiate the boundaries of community. Conrad sums it up: "I don't see the dynamic [the migration] changing. We're on this boat now where it's gotten to the point where there's nothing—even if they eliminate public housing and Section 8—that can change it. There's still going to be an influx of people because this is still, for someone with a very limited income, where they can get the most for their dollar."

Fishertown bureaucrats are slowly coming to terms with the reality that their office and community are changing. Whether they are coming from Portugal, Mexico, or the nearest urban metropolis, Martine argued that newcomers *should* be able to make a home in Fishertown: "We're so selfish in terms of thinking, 'These people are going to live here? Our city is going to be in total distress!' Well, wouldn't it be wonderful if life didn't call for changes?"

Negotiating Race, Class, and Place
within Postreform Welfare Offices

The issues that Fishertown is facing are not unique. Considering the history of residential segregation in the country (Massey and Denton 1989; Grant 2000), it is not surprising that racial anxiety and antipathy were expressed by some members of the Fishertown DTA staff. In a 1992 Los Angeles-based survey, Bobo and Zubrinsky (1996) found that hostile attitudes toward the out-group shape views on residential integration more powerfully than mere in-group preferences. Timberlake (2000) similarly found that negative racial stereotypes and perceptions of group threat continue to plague integration efforts in Atlanta. Despite an overall decline in expressed support for racial discrimination and increased agreement on the *principle* of racial integration, we still see that it is nevertheless slow and fraught in *practice* (Schuman and Bobo 1988). As a midsized city, Fishertown appears to be wrestling with similar dynamics as, to borrow a phrase from Sonya Salamon (2003), newcomers come to old towns and have to navigate the existing social order.

As a companion to the previous chapter, this chapter explores an important set of relationships that inform how bureaucrats understand their work as race, resources, and politics collide in welfare offices. While these individuals encounter policy and environmental shifts, interests and investments related to their own social positions shape how they (re)formulate their interests and investments as professionals. Attendant politics give rise to a set of beliefs, attitudes, and behaviors that are incorporated into discretionary toolkits as workers try to determine just how much time they will spend plugging a recently migrated client into the resources of the community, whether the new client's interaction style is too "aggressive" and therefore unappealing or even dangerous, or whether one is troubled by the "bad rap" newcomers are receiving to the point that one works particularly hard to make sure one's new clients get a fair shake. None of these statuses operate in deterministic ways. Caseworkers and supervisors *decide* how they will interpret the political implications embedded in the demographic makeup of their offices and whether they will find ways to incorporate those views into service delivery. In this respect, the welfare office serves as a filter through which situated bureaucrats understand community dynamics and, in some cases, the agency operates as a vehicle with which to express or challenge these social anxieties and concerns.

A critical difference between the workers studied in this and the previous chapter should be noted. Minority workers saw themselves as attempting to *combat* a set of systems that systematically undermined their power and standing: the structure of a labor market that seemed to limit the opportunities of both themselves and their clients and a policy that was rooted in a political discourse that stereotyped and demonized less-privileged members of their racial groups. White workers in Fishertown were grappling with the question of how to *protect* the social fabric and resources of both the office and the community at large. At the same time, the majority of the interventions around race and class by bureaucrats of color appeared to take place *during* the interactions that they had with minority clients as they advised, coached, and regulated them through the welfare system. For white bureaucrats in Fishertown, the majority of their debates around race and class took place with *each other,* as they articulated their views about the migration and what it would mean for the town and the office. Anticipating negative consequences from management should they explicitly allow racial views to shape their interactions with clients, these workers quietly created narratives about their new clients and made choices about how these views would inform their work.

It is important to note, as sociologists Monica McDermott and Frank Samson suggest, that white racial identity is "rooted in social and economic privilege, and its meaning and import are highly situational" (2005, 247). We therefore cannot assume that whiteness operates in the same way for all bureaucrats in all welfare offices. Whiteness is largely understood by Fishertown staff members through a fairly recent connection to a European country of origin, a working- or lower-middle-class background, and an interpretation of themselves as culturally opposite of poor, minority urban newcomers. Such a status grants access to durable employment, housing, and social connections in the city through strong white ethnic networks. Meanwhile, although white networks and privileges thrive in the city where the Staunton DTA office is located, the long-standing racial and ethnic diversity in both the office and the city mean that minority groups have a foothold claim on the area's resources. Further, as Staunton's staff members and clients are spread out all over the city, the connections in these bureaucrats' minds between the office and their residential communities are fuzzy. Because of this, white workers in Staunton tended in my observations to talk about the diversity of both the staff and clients in the office positively and rarely described race as an important piece of the institutional landscape.[19] The relatively stable and diverse racial makeup of the office does not carry a social meaning to them that is directly tied to their sense of community-based security, quality of life, or resource abundance. This suggests that community context is an important determinant in how whiteness plays out in welfare offices.

With the community anxiety and downright racial antipathy toward new clients of color expressed by some workers in Fishertown, it becomes clearer why the drive for welfare offices to facilitate clients' integration into their communities in order to secure resources for self-sufficiency and for bureaucrats to see their roles as resource-brokering social workers becomes even harder to achieve. The responsibility that some workers feel toward some clients is diluted when certain attitudes persist, and the interaction becomes limited in what it can accomplish. There is hope, however, for those who believe that the office should take on these more strategic roles. Time certainly has appeared to salve some of the most vitriolic attitudes in the Fishertown office. If a case can be made that the professional and residential interests of caseworkers are not only conjoined but also better served should the office emphasize the successful integration of newcomers into the community, workers may be more inspired to fully participate in the process. Families that are well connected to the city's resources and networks may be more likely not only to be successful clients in their journeys through the welfare system and into the labor market but also thriving community members who are visible contributors to small and tightly woven communities like Fishertown (see also Small 2009). Otherwise, black and Hispanic newcomers run the risk of feeling like, and being treated as, perpetual outsiders. As Bob in the central office commented: "You know, it depends on the workers, how they're trained and how they're prepared. I remember having some workers who I don't think ever saw a black person before in their life. But watching them provide services indicated to me that they were just so driven as *humanitarians* that they felt it was their *moral duty* to be as helpful as possible . . . and whether or not they know the resources that might be helpful."

Rather than fall into a dynamic of detachment or even discrimination, the Fishertown DTA office, like many local catch-all bureaucracies, has the opportunity to put in place services and staff that are tailored to the community context. Rather than systematically downplaying or ignoring how community changes might affect staff members and shape caseworker-client relations, organizational leaders can proactively think through how these shifts might inform how caseworkers understand the work that they do and the clients that they serve. "Turnstile" offices are not likely to go away anytime soon, and the demands of the new welfare system encourage clients to establish the institutional and personal ties necessary to find and maintain work. Catch-all bureaucracies such as welfare offices can play critical roles in community integration by helping these families to gather the resources and navigate the community in order to be successful. Rather than thinking of demographic shifts in the office as interesting but ultimately irrelevant changes to the institutional landscape, this chapter shows the dangers of such thinking. Socially situated street-level bureaucrats, working to reconcile their views and investments gleaned from their professional roles and social group memberships, may in fact clash on how best to work with those who are newcomers to both the office and the community at large. The result is an institution that is caught between facilitating community integration and allowing community antagonisms to simmer within its borders.

SIX

The Crisis of Identity
in Catch-All Bureaucracies

Many have declared, quite convincingly, that the revolution that was welfare reform is over. The social safety net has undergone massive restructuring, the rolls have declined substantially, and low-income mothers have entered the labor force in record numbers. Looking at a variety of measures, many policymakers and influential members of the poverty research community have pronounced that, by and large, the goals of this reengineering of social policy have been successfully accomplished. Ron Haskins, once a senior adviser for welfare policy to President George W. Bush, has gone so far as to call the 1996 Personal Responsibility and Work Opportunity Reconciliation Act "a spectacular piece of legislation" (Haskins 2006, ix).

Whether this is truly the case is a topic for others to discern. There are volumes of research describing the experiences of low-income mothers in ways that both support and refute this assessment. A larger question has been virtually ignored, however, one posed in the introduction of this book. As government institutions continue to serve millions of desperately poor families every day, how do we ensure that these agencies reflect the bridge, rather than the gulf, between what we want to be as a nation and where we actually are—politically, socially, culturally, and economically? In every decade, there are defining moments that frame the question of how we will deploy public bureaucracies (and increasingly private institutions that receive public monies under the contracting system) to help address the needs of the disenfranchised. Not coincidentally, these also tend to be occasions that highlight not only our economic disparities but also our societal shortcomings with regard to racial equality. The 1996 welfare reform and Hurricane Katrina and its aftermath are such events. The United States is facing an economic crisis that will be felt most severely by those whose resources are the most precarious. The implications of all of these events will reverberate for decades. The public declarations that our welfare system, representing our most systematic institutional network for responding to the needs of the poor, has been successfully "reformed" seem stubbornly at odds with those raw moments in 2005 when we witnessed Katrina-related natural and unnatural disasters unfold and as we anticipate how the economic crisis will affect low-income families.[1]

Against this backdrop, this quote by Vicki Hawthorne, a supervisor in the Staunton office, perhaps best represents the central preoccupation of this book:

Just like everything else, there are [caseworkers] that are terribly interested in [in-depth casework] and like to do it and think of it as certainly part of their jobs. It's now integrated into their jobs. There are other people that have no idea about it and don't want to really. . . . And then the responsibility is largely on the client to figure out what to do. It often leaves the client dangling. . . . It's more difficult for the client when their TANF worker is not knowledgeable or not forthcoming with all the reams of knowledge that we have in this department. If they're not forthcoming with that, "Gee, here's what you could do. How about if you do this? We know that there's this [opportunity] over here, would you be interested in that?" A lot of caseworkers don't take the time for that. [For example,] daycare. They often give misinformation like, "No, you can't do that. You can't have daycare" —which is totally at times erroneous. . . . So the service that you get largely depends on who your worker is at the end of the day.

Vicki was discussing the implementation of the "work-first" thrust of our current welfare system, but she could have been talking about any number of issues explicated in this book: integrating impoverished newcomers into a community and connecting them to its resources, using messages prominent in racial-uplift struggles to encourage poorer race-mates to engage in certain behaviors, or using one's own personal history of economic strife to convince clients that they can be successful. This book investigates how the differences among street-level bureaucrats that Vicki lays out emerge and are permitted, in fact encouraged, to persist in two catch-all bureaucracies, differences that have important consequences for low-income families.

Our analysis ultimately rested upon questions around the relationship between identity and discretion. How are professional identities constructed, and how are they informed by institutional dynamics? Do the social locations of organizational actors (e.g., race, class, gender, community residence, and so forth) inform their professional identities, and how does this become incorporated into how institutions work? How does the interweaving of professional and social identities shape institutional transformation and the administration of the public's resources through service delivery?

In the book I have therefore aimed to offer not only a sociological analysis of welfare systems but of discretion in human service delivery. In my exploration of those whom Michael Lipsky (1980) describes as the intermediaries, gatekeepers, and resource brokers between citizens and the state, I offer an overarching framework to explain how bureaucrats think about their use of discretionary power. Unsatisfied with stopping at the well-known consensus among students of human service bureaucracies that "caseworker discretion matters," in this book I have sought to explore from where it emerges and what social forces inform its form and content. Discretion helps to shape more than whether a welfare caseworker gives a client extra time to complete a document or overlooks a policy rule. Discretion also shapes how bureaucrats communicate with clients stylistically, the issues they choose to address during their interactions, and how they school clients in the expectations of the organization and the outside world. Discretionary acts, therefore, are much more systematic than previously recognized. They are products of workers' discretionary toolkits, the set of beliefs, ritual practices, habits, skills, and styles that they draw upon to interact with the social world (Swidler 1986). Although tweaked to fit whatever context bureaucrats find themselves in at the moment, discretionary acts are patterned, socially formulated, and have their roots in certain understandings that bureaucrats hold of themselves as professionals. By the time we witness the exercise of discretion in street-level bureaucracies, staff members have already created a scaffolding made up of personal histories, social and political attitudes, perceptions of clients, and beliefs about the job that form the basis through which these seemingly random and "of-the-moment decisions" are made.

Whereas prior to the 1996 welfare reform the role of the caseworker was primarily to ensure program eligibility, in the new world of welfare service delivery bureaucrats perform a wider range of frontline services. They are also exposed to many more of their clients' strengths and challenges, their triumphs and roadblocks, as families are now navigating a welfare system controlled by time limits and work requirements. For welfare caseworkers, the question becomes how they understand themselves as professionals in a changing environment and how they will use their interpretations to shape the discretionary tools at their disposal (and vice versa). They are presented with various options for interpreting their professional roles, each with its own set of organizational cues suggesting that social work, efficiency engineering, or mere bureaucratic survival is an optimal goal to pursue in the agency. Each constellation has its own social norms, incentives, risks, and drawbacks, and frontline workers deploy their own logics to decide which they will pursue. Although workers create a steady state through which to approach their jobs—what I have been calling their professional identities—the needs of a particular client, a set of supervisory directives, or other everyday variables have the potential to lure these bureaucrats to adopt a different approach at any given time. As such, the path between identity and behavior is not always a straight and uncontested one.

To be sure, social workers, efficiency engineers, and bureaucratic survivalists existed in the agency prior to welfare reform (and they arguably exist in most human service agencies). In the present era, however, the actions of individual caseworkers are increasingly important as they are expected to shepherd clients through the new system and ensure that they have the tools to survive without the safety net of ongoing cash assistance. Recognizing their importance, organizational leaders have sent cues to frontline staff in order to advocate for a professional constellation that they believe will succeed in the pursuit of the desired political outcomes of welfare reform as well as fulfill their hopes for the fortunes of low-income families. Nevertheless, when those cues become contradictory and inconsistently enforced, each frontline worker decides which approach is most compatible with her professional and personal goals. The result is a high level of variation among caseworkers—in terms of their stylistic approaches, surveillance and enforcement tactics, and the tangible and intangible resources offered to clients—helping us to understand exactly what is at stake when Vicki comments that "the service that you get largely depends on who your worker is at the end of the day." It is not simply about whether one is assigned worker A or worker B to manage one's case; how worker A versus worker B *define* themselves as professionals, and the discretionary toolkits that they wield in the service of those self-definitions, become critically important for the operation of caseworker-client relations and service delivery in general.

How do bureaucrats decide which professional identity suits them? Although this is difficult to predict, by emphasizing that policy implementers are "situated bureaucrats" who have their own personal, occupational, and group-based interests, we gained a sense of how individuals' social locations contribute to their choices around the constructions of their professional identities. The intersection of the professional and social identities of street-level bureaucrats is best conceptualized as a negotiation between (1) their perceived institutional power vis-à-vis superiors, co-workers, subordinates, and clients to bring their own investments into the institutional fold; (2) the unique sets of politics surrounding the policies bureaucrats are called to implement and the social contexts in which these policies are embedded; and (3) whether and how bureaucratic actors choose to simultaneously operationalize a defined set of group interests and professional considerations—concerns that may compete or coalesce. The social and professional identities of organizational actors are crucial to the operation of caseworker-client relationships, help drive intra- and interorganizational variation, and inform policy implementation more generally as bureaucrats struggle with apparently conflicting dispositions to both embrace and resist institutional change in a larger environmental context. This complex identity construction is not simply a symbolic exercise; it has consequences for clients in terms of what they receive from service organizations and when and how services are rendered. As such, the intersection of the social and professional identities of bureaucrats is a crucial part of the story of not only policy reform but organizational change.

More specifically, a personal history of poverty provides a set of tools and experiences that caseworkers can draw upon in their interactions with clients and can be used to set tones of benevolence, malevolence, or something in between, depending on the worker. Although human service staffs are growing more racially diverse, we knew little before this study, with the notable exception of Gail Lewis's work in the United Kingdom, about what the substantial incorporation of racial and ethnic minorities into the bureaucratic ranks of welfare agencies means for the levers of discretion and bureaucrats' professional identities (Lewis 2000). We saw in chapter 4 how caseworkers and supervisors of color engage in "racialized professionalism" as they integrate race (and class and gender) into their understanding of their work and their goals for what it should accomplish. They then actively deploy these constructions by shaping the content and tone of their interactions with clients of color in ways that reflect both key priorities in welfare reform implementation and a set of intragroup politics within black and Latino communities. In chapter 5, we saw how client migrations out of central cities as a result of shifts in economic and residential opportunities add a new dimension to previous observations about race, class, and bureaucratic relations in the human services. When street-level bureaucrats see the institution as a reflection of the community in which they both live and work, perceived negative changes in the client caseload are seen as threats to both the organization and to the community at large. Caseworkers and organizational leaders express their concerns about community change and racial diversity by framing newcomer clients, and their professional responsibilities to them, in discourses tied to service delivery. They in turn deploy bureaucratic power as a filter through which to interpret, and sometimes as a vehicle to protect, defined group interests. In this book I suggest that both inter- and intra-group anxieties, concerns, investments, and interests contribute to the formulation of bureaucrats' understandings of their clients and how they should work with them. The debates taking place within bureaucrats' respective communities give rise to ideologies, collective memories, and interactive styles that these individuals can then use to interpret organizational power dynamics, the implications of certain policies for particular groups, and the goals and resources they should incorporate into their service delivery. This integration of professional and social identities helps to narrow and specify the instruments bureaucrats use as they interact with clients and with each other.

All of this occurs in an institutional context that can be characterized by the term *catch-all bureaucracies*. As the "first responders," "last resorts," and perhaps many things in between for disadvantaged families, these institutions are confronted by the individual-, family-, and community-level challenges that arise as individuals navigate the bottom of our economic, political, and social system. This population's problems are not necessarily unique or confined to their social group. But whereas more privileged individuals might negotiate undesirable situations by purchasing high-quality services and accessing socked-away bankrolls, the truly disadvantaged, as sociologist William Julius Wilson (1987) once termed them, approach (or are sent to) these institutions to have their grievances heard and their conflicts resolved. Often, there are few other places to go for the financial assistance, physical and mental health services, education, or housing that they so desperately need. What makes catch-all bureaucracies a distinct subset within the population of street-level bureaucracies from which goods and services are delivered to citizens are the ways in which intersecting challenges related to economic, political, and social marginalization and exclusion are readily apparent within their territorial borders. As such, bureaucrats working in these agencies are often asked to go beyond their job descriptions and use their discretionary toolkits to respond to a range of issues that may be only indirectly related to their institutional missions.

Other key features of catch-all bureaucracies have been uncovered in previous work and are important to keep in mind (Lipsky 1980). The relationship between bureaucrats and clients often comes with a level of apprehension and skepticism on the part of both parties that can be derived from years of interfacing with multiple and overlapping government systems. For clients, bureaucratic incompetence, finding an unreceptive ear, or simply "slipping through the cracks," are real, legitimate, and often substantiated fears, and are often difficult for clients to find the proper channels to address (Lens 2007; Lens and Vorsanger 2005). Further, associations with catch-all bureaucracies often come with a high level of stigmatization. Catch-all bureaucracies are sites at which some of our most controversial issues—poverty, single motherhood, personal vs. collective accountability, race, and money—converge and are confronted by a workforce that has diverse backgrounds, education levels, work experiences, and political attitudes. Clients' access to services often hinges upon their laying bare very complex, often devastating, and sometimes humiliating circumstances as they request help, mindfully subjecting themselves to the judgments of bureaucrats. They must battle the underlying assumptions that palpably swirl that they— through their choices, attitudes, and behaviors—are the ones wholly responsible for the circumstances that brought them through the agency's doors. The service-delivery apparatus within catch-all bureaucracies is often geared around the idea that clients are the rightful targets of change, rather than any structural, environmental, or even bureaucratic factors that may be actual impediments to change. The limited political and economic clout that clients garner outside of the agency sets the stage for them to be institutionally marginalized within these settings, relegated to the lower limits of organizational power. The stigmatization embedded in this position consequently can discourage individuals from fully investing in the agency and mounting effective efforts for change (Seccombe 1998; Seccombe, James, and Walters 1998). Merely accessing necessary resources becomes an exercise in one's ability to deploy her bounded power effectively and strategically.

But the current analysis uncovers an additional feature of these institutions: the critical interchange between community politics and organizational power. Where the agency ends and the external landscape begins extends beyond the question of how public and quasi-public institutions secure economic resources and political support for survival, an important and well-traveled road in the study of organizations (Marwell 2007). Similar to what scholars have been arguing since Philip Selznick's ([1949] 1980) classic study of the Tennessee Valley Authority, localized government bureaucracies do not operate as mere satellite outposts of a social welfare system where the political battles are fought at a distance at the federal, state, and county levels.[2] To the contrary, this book argues that street-level employees import their own sense of neighborhood histories and indigenous territorial battles into these organizations, shaping the form, content, and discourse around service delivery to reflect their investments, anxieties, and visions for both policy and the world around them. This often takes place without the knowledge or input of organizational leaders and thus remains "under the radar screen" within catch-all bureaucracies. When employees on the ground invoke notions of "the neighborhood," "this town," or what sociologist Mary Pattillo (2007) calls a "racialized we" to either lower or raise boundaries between themselves and clients, they are essentially playing politics, signifying notions of community that are based on shared experiences and often hard-fought political, social, and economic struggles and grounded in a symbolic connectedness invested in protecting or gathering precious resources. The boundaries and contours of these struggles are strategically invoked within local catch-all bureaucracies as actors pursue certain political and social ends vis-à-vis service delivery and assert conceptions of themselves as professionals, community residents, mothers, race-mates, and any number of other relevant social roles. This self-fashioning of bureaucrats' identities reminds us that catch-all bureaucracies, like all institutions, are raced, gendered, and classed even when these topics are not explicitly brought to the fore in organizational interactions. Frontline caseworkers confront, propagate, or assuage these issues in their everyday interactions with low-income families. Although certain values, beliefs, and interests may stimulate the creation of policy, it is in these institutions where these arrangements come to life at their most intimate level—via the dynamic between the impoverished who seek benefits and the bureaucrats who respond.[3]

In this book I demonstrate how catch-all bureaucracies become sites where homegrown community concerns—and larger national debates on the struggles, opportunities, and futures of certain social groups—filter into the agency vis-à-vis clients and institutional staff, take up residence within agency walls, and encourage bureaucrats to deploy the institution and its power in ways that express a certain politics or point of view as benefits are distributed, policies enforced, and aspects of clients' lives monitored. Agency interactions become important spaces in which a *range* of resources are strategically distributed, political ideas are exchanged, and social support and regulation are wielded as valuable tools to encourage certain outcomes. These relations are historically grounded, reinforced by both these institution's cultural reputations and decades of formal structures and policies and informal norms that have become part of a collective understanding of what the particular catch-all bureaucracy is about. Catch-all bureaucracies such as welfare offices therefore serve as critical institutional terrains on which individuals are negotiating and acting upon some of our most complex societal issues: race, class, gender, neighborhood integration, and even the transformation of parochial industrial towns into inviting regional metropolises. Power here is *situated* in that it is largely bestowed based on one's organizational position and "anchored" by that association; but it is also *situational* in that social hierarchies existing outside of the agency are imported into the agency and assign varied levels of status within both the bureaucratic and client ranks. If "all politics are local," beliefs about what is good for "the community," however defined, shape how bureaucrats interpret and operationalize their professional roles and negotiate their interactions with other organizational actors.

Because I adopt an analytic framework that places the professional identities of employees at the center and views these formations as key drivers of discretion, examining these individuals' social locations proved critical to the analysis. Mindful of analytic perspectives that privilege either institutional structures or actor agency to explain organizational events, I wanted to show how bureaucrats delicately operate at the intersection of formal mandates and the need to "make do" when exposed to a wide swath of issues. The responses of bureaucrats are situated not simply within a certain organizational milieu but are also located within a broader social, political, and economic context that employees draw upon to operationalize what they think "helping the poor" looks like. These maneuvers may or may not align with the stated policy goals of the organization and thus have the potential to contribute to or thwart institutional change.

The in-depth interview and observation data presented in the book leave no doubt that the challenges around working in catch-all bureaucracies in this postreform era are immense. Having summarized the main empirical findings and theoretical contributions of the book, the next three sections of this chapter offer insights into the theoretical, policy, and programmatic implications of what this analysis has uncovered.

Shaping Professional Identities, Changing Organizational Cultures: Theoretical Implications

Thomas Kane and Mary Jo Bane (1994) famously argued that pre-1996 welfare offices were plagued by an "eligibility-compliance culture" that was in opposition to a "self-sufficiency culture" that the authors argued was more likely to successfully transition low-income women from welfare to work (see also Corbett 1995). The lack of an institutional culture geared toward client self-sufficiency is a harder claim to make in today's era of time limits and work requirements. Most workers will now tell you that their goal in almost every interaction with nonexempt clients is to help them achieve economic self-sufficiency (although we know that there is disagreement among caseworkers about what this actually means and whether low-income families relying on low-wage work are truly "self-sufficient") (Hays 2003).

Prevailing approaches to the study of institutional culture offered by organizational scholars help us to specify how we might think about welfare office "cultures" in this postreform era.[4] By looking at the evolution of institutional dynamics over time, such as the underlying values and assumptions held by members, their meaning-making strategies regarding institutional processes, and the symbolic elements embedded in the everyday rhythms of their work lives, we are able to gain an insider's point of view on the culture of an agency (Denison 1996; Martin 2001; Schein 2004). The intraagency variation highlighted in this book suggests that perhaps our first revision is that we should be talking about a welfare office in terms of having multiple cultures. It was the shared but competing meanings that arose from a negotiated set of interaction patterns among agency actors that seemed to define the essence of the offices that I studied (Denison 1996). When we explicated the *manifestations* of assumptions, beliefs, values, or perspectives of actors and how they shaped patterns of interaction (Sackmann 1992), we were able to witness multiple cultures in play.

A 1992 article by Sonja Sackmann is instructive in this regard. She argues that while an organization-wide "cultural overlay" may be identifiable, several cultural subgroups may exist that are based on different kinds of organizational knowledge. Sense-making at the individual level gives way to "collective sense-making" whereby interrelated and interconnected cognitions—interpretive structuring devices for labeling things or events, prescriptive lessons, event explanations, and a perceived causal understanding of events—are generated. Cognitions are possessed by a group of actors in a given agency, "even though members of the same cultural group may not be aware in their daily activities of what they hold in common. In the process of enculturation, cognitions become rooted in the group and ultimately exist independently of an individual group member, even though individuals are the carriers of culture" (Sackmann 1992, 141). Individuals in these groups share similar kinds of organizational knowledge, based on their accumulated cognitions, which are then manifested within the agency through artifacts and behaviors.[5]

Some subgroups form on the basis of what Sackmann calls functional domains, which "are tied to people's professional role perceptions and perceived responsibility in their professional roles rather than to such structural manifestations as departments or prescribed roles in an organization chart" (Sackmann 1992, 147). Similarly, I found at least three cultural groups among street-level bureaucrats, based on their professional identities and accompanying discretionary toolkits. Social workers, efficiency engineers, and survivalists were clearly organized around a particular approach to policy implementation. These collective identities and toolkits added up to an agency-wide understanding of the institutional enterprise, despite the differences among the groups about how this should be carried out. In other words, although there appeared to be a shared understanding around a mission connected to client self-sufficiency, there were multiple interpretations of what this meant, how it should be pursued, and what tools should be brought to bear. Beneath the surface of an overlying culture of the office lay several subcultures within the agency, each with its own assumptions, beliefs, ideologies, artifacts, and behavioral patterns.

The intersection of Sackmann's notion of multiple cultures and my extension of Swidler's cultural toolkit framework allows us to move beyond the impasse around the question of culture in welfare offices. What observers are seeing in TANF offices are the results of *multiple* professional identities and accompanying discretionary toolkits in action. They coalesce into cultural subgroups and are bound together by an overarching institutional culture. An institutional culture that represents the pursuit of client self-sufficiency vis-à-vis eligibility-compliance enforcement has achieved dominance in the Fishertown and Staunton offices, bolstered by contradictory cues within the organization that ultimately support the enforcement of benchmarks rather than the use of in-depth casework to encourage exits from the welfare system. It would be imprecise, however, to crown efficiency engineering as *the* culture of the welfare office because of the presence of a subculture that is invested in social work and another that is invested in bureaucratic survivalism. We must not negate the presence of these subcultures and the workers within them that possess clearly defined professional identities and have collected discretionary toolkits to help them do their jobs in the ways they believe they should be done— within the parameters of the overarching culture of the office.

When both the dominant culture and the various subcultures within an institution are not considered and addressed, efforts to change will likely fail (Johnson 1990; Pascale, Milleman, and Gioja 1997). Changing organizational *cultures* within welfare offices requires that actors' discretionary toolkits be altered in ways that expose them to a different range of plausible and desirable attitudes, decisions, and practices to do their work (as well as by removing some existing tools). Focusing on behavioral change as a start to longer-term cultural change has been identified as a more viable option than the direct targeting of assumptions and ideologies (Heracleous 2001; see also Beer, Eisenstat, and Spector 1990 and Burke 1995). Nevertheless, as organizational scholar Loizos Heracleous writes, "it is important for clinicians to identify the organization's governing assumptions and ensure that the new behaviors, values, and beliefs the organization pursues do not conflict with, and are supported by, these governing assumptions" (2001, 440). Therefore, how workers understand their missions and clients should be addressed as well. "To adopt a line of conduct," Swidler offers, "one needs an image of the kind of world in which one is trying to act, a sense that one can read reasonably accurately (through one's own feelings and through the responses of others) how one is doing, and a capacity to choose among alternative lines of action" (1986, 275). In other words, altered toolkits and professional orientations require reinforcements from structural resources that encourage actors to adopt certain strategies of action. Welfare offices, therefore, must consistently put organizational cues in place to persuade workers to adopt discretionary tools and interpretations of their roles that are consistent with desired agency cultures. As workers grow more comfortable leveraging these revamped discretionary powers, well informed, "state-of-the-art" professional identities are strengthened and become more deeply embedded within institutions. Subcultures are formed that are consistent with this mission and, if supported, can add up to underlying changes to the overarching culture of the agency.

A question for further study is the degree to which the processes that I have laid out are present in other bureaucratic settings. The disconnects between policy, prescribed roles, and presented roles that we witnessed in the Staunton and Fishertown offices are not unique. Similar processes have been written about in connection with other kinds of catch-all bureaucracies (Lipsky 1980). For example, in her case study of dropouts in an urban high school, Michelle Fine (1991) paints a portrait of an institution organized around efficiency and control, complete with institutional rituals that exclude and silence both students and teachers who want to assert a different model for doing their jobs but who are ultimately ignored and marginalized by the school administration. Steven Maynard-Moody and Michael Musheno (2003) point to how police officers, teachers, and vocational rehabilitation specialists negotiate a duality between law abidance and cultural abidance when doing their jobs. The former refers to the demand that workers apply laws, rules, and administrative practices in accordance with formal mandates while the latter reflects their own moral values and beliefs about how the job should be done as a result of who they believe their clients to be in terms of identity and moral character.

The coexistence of this duality defines the tensions inherent in human service work. Ruth Horowitz's (1995) work on a program designed to provide GED exam and job preparation to teenage mothers suggests that it is not unusual for social service providers within a setting to have disparate approaches to their jobs, largely based on their ideas about what clients can and should contribute to society, how these providers should enforce social control toward those ends, and how they should instill a level of self-control in their clients in ways that produce measurable outcomes. Horowitz calls these phenomena of disconnects between policies, service delivery, and informal messages "loosely coupled cultures." These books suggest that the sociologies and politics of human service delivery involve connections between organizational cultures, professional and social identity construction and performance, and discretionary acts as mediators and shapers of employees' efforts in ways that must be continually examined and addressed.

Additional research can also explore human service clients more deeply using the frameworks offered in this book. Are clients able to parse out differences among bureaucrats who represent different organizational cultures, and how do clients respond to workers' deployment of discretionary tools that represent these cultures? Do clients alter their strategies for navigating the institution when they encounter an efficiency engineer versus a social worker versus a bureaucratic survivalist? Do client outcomes differ depending on the professional identities of the bureaucrats assigned to assist them? How do they interpret racialized professionalism and other maneuvers within the agency whereby racial or other identity politics are brought to bear in service delivery? Future research can explore how clients interpret messages coming from bureaucrats from their or other racial groups, whether they adopt certain behaviors as a result, and whether this ultimately shapes outcomes. All of these questions suggest that integrating frameworks within organizational theory, African American studies, and poverty studies offers a whole new avenue into research on identity, power, and professions within public policy.

Transformation from the Top Down: Recommendations for Policymakers and Welfare Administrators

In chapter 1 we learned that despite the variation in state and local policies, many of the changes in Fishertown and Staunton mimicked those adjustments reported in other work on welfare offices across the nation (Holcomb and Martinson 2002; Hays 2003; Riccucci 2005; Ridzi 2004; Austin 2004). Waiting rooms and client service areas underwent cosmetic changes, complete with signs and placards that exalted work and reminded clients of the seriousness of time limits. Welfare service delivery was transformed from a largely paper-driven enterprise into one that is computerized and networked to other agencies in unprecedented ways. This allows for greater surveillance of clients' personal records, on the one hand, and strengthened connections between service providers, on the other (Lurie 2006). Job training, employment search, child care, and transportation services are integrated into welfare offices in ways that would have been unimaginable in previous years. Managers have engaged in new practices and behaviors and set up new organizational structures in order to reinforce policy goals (Lurie 2006; Riccucci 2005). "Overall," the Urban Institute reported in its analysis of the Massachusetts system, "it appears that state and local flexibility, combined with ample financial resources and the shared goal of creating a work-oriented system, led to [a] new programmatic and organizational environment" (Kaye et al. 2001, 1).

Although this book has focused on the delivery of services on the ground, it has also uncovered several key issues connected to policymakers and high-level welfare administrators that affect the abilities of street-level bureaucrats to do their jobs. Work requirements, time limits, sanctions, and increased resources devoted to child care and job placement and training have injected a range of tools and tactics into postreform welfare offices. Yet events in the Staunton and Fishertown DTA offices suggest that many of the state's goals for welfare reform—increased labor force participation by low-income mothers, increased child support enforcement, and reduced caseloads—have been achieved in large part by the enforcement of eligibility and compliance benchmarks. Helped greatly by the often-cited favorable labor market conditions and the increase in the Earned Income Tax Credit that accompanied welfare reform in the 1990s, organizational actors could meet agency expectations largely by ensuring that their cases were accurately and efficiently processed and that time clocks, work requirements, and sanctions were actively managed and enforced. In-depth case management, complete with extensive service referrals, engaged problem-solving with clients, and frequent follow-ups to ensure that client service plans are fully executed, was the ambition of only a fraction of the workforce.

One could argue that as long as bottom-line targets are met—decreased caseloads, increased work among some low-income mothers, and greater child support enforcement—the welfare system is running optimally. Furthermore, with the pressure to produce certain outcomes while under such heavy scrutiny during welfare reform's early years, bureaucrats from the outset had an incentive to stick to an identity more akin to efficiency engineering rather than time-consuming and potentially draining social work. However, for those with greater ambitions about how public policy and catch-all bureaucracies can respond to the needs of low-income families, these benchmarks feel hollow. Researchers continue to capture disconcerting stories about individuals who live below, at, or just above the poverty line, and child poverty rates in the United States remain among the highest in the industrialized world. Moreover, the ways in which stigma, distrust, and outright hostility continue to frame too many of the interactions between bureaucrats and clients run against the argument that these government institutions are truly effective at serving families. Pragmatically speaking, there is likely little political will to return to cash entitlements or to eliminate sanctions and work requirements. But what if our goals, the standards by which we measure success in welfare offices, are more ambitious and comprehensive? Can these agencies do more to encourage longer-term economic stability, promote mobility from low-wage jobs, and address the service needs of clients that go beyond the "critical basics" of cash assistance, child care vouchers, and job placement and training program referrals? Are there ways in which our current system can be altered to improve how it delivers the critical basics and better function as a catch-all bureaucracy?

Consistency among bureaucrats can be difficult to achieve, especially in the human services where clients' circumstances shape much of what goes on (Schein 1978; Hill 1992). Professional identities, as interpretations of formally prescribed job designs, will always be infused with actors' own meanings, goals, and commitments as they create day-to-day capacities of action. Individuals therefore may never wholeheartedly adopt institutional decrees or may offer competing presentations of them. But if it is the case that orientations used to assist clients produce variations in welfare offices, this is a potentially useful area to target for organizational effectiveness.

With the uneven provision of services and the narrow definitions of client self-sufficiency, the current welfare policy and its institutional infrastructure have not fully lived up to the promise of successfully restructuring the poor-support system. My recommendations focus on expanding the offerings of and eliminating some of the disparities in service delivery by addressing the professional identities of frontline staff. Hogg and Terry (2000) remind us that this is not an easy transformation as identity reflects the cognitive processes by which people categorize themselves and the organization to reduce uncertainty. However, identities are nevertheless manageable and changeable through changes to behavior.[6]

Discretion Can Generate Inequalities in Service Delivery,
But It Is Too Important to Be Eliminated

This book does not recommend that bureaucratic discretion be eliminated. Despite its dangers, it is a critical tool that allows workers to fit the agency to the complex circumstances of clients rather than the other way around. Less discretion would essentially tie the hands of workers, and severely limit their discretionary toolkits. As such, it would likely have devastating consequences for their professional identities, which are essentially the creative outlets through which they personalize their occupations. Often, it is the unspoken collusion between bureaucrat and client that makes these organizations run effectively. As Jim Thomas's (1984) illustrative research on prisons makes clear, loose coupling results as bureaucrats and their charges (in Thomas's case, guards and inmates) negotiate interpretations of the social order that may differ from agency mandates and control techniques, but still constitute a level of formality and structure.[7] Formal rules are decoupled from the behaviors intended to carry out those rules and give way to "discretionary behaviors, alternative rules, tacit understandings, and strategic interaction techniques" through give-and-take between institutional actors (215). In these moments, through their power to assess and treat, bureaucrats are able to define not only the conditions of clients but of their own professional practice (Gubrium and Buckholdt 1979). We saw numerous instances throughout the book in which discretion, while allowing some workers to move in punitive and limiting directions in service delivery, allowed others to provide the crucial resources, words of encouragement, and interpersonal contact that were needed for a client at a critical time.

Bureaucratic Survivalists Are in Every Bureaucracy and Should Not Be Ignored

In the course of my fieldwork, I became highly concerned about the presence of a number of what I call bureaucratic survivalists among the ranks of the DTA frontline staff. Few new changes will stick if survivalists, in both the local and central administrative offices, remain uninvested in the institutional enterprise and encourage co-workers to do the same. This breed of worker has likely always existed in welfare offices and other catch-all bureaucracies, and even the most dedicated social workers and efficiency engineers will tell you that they adopt survivalist tendencies at various junctures. But in this era of holding clients accountable for certain outcomes during their time on the system, we are falsely assuming that all the bureaucrats with whom they work are actively involved in helping them in their transitions. The bitter cynicism of the survivalists can be a destructive force for both clients and co-workers and can lead clients to feel as though the welfare office cannot be counted on to offer the resources that it has at its disposal for their day-to-day survival and eventual movement into the labor market. "They act like the money is coming out of their pockets" is a charge that I frequently heard lobbed at survivalists by frustrated co-workers, signaling that these bureaucrats' interactions with clients have become corrosive, tense, distrustful, and highly stigmatizing.

Those feelings are unlikely to be productive as these same clients are then expected to trust these individuals enough to reveal barriers to their success and rely on them to provide necessary tangible and intangible support.

For their co-workers, survivalists who cope by missing multiple workdays for noncritical reasons, showing up daily but managing to do little until quitting time, passing off work to already overburdened co-workers, or doing just enough to clear the low expectations of the agency, threaten to engulf the entire office in antipathy and apathy, stalling any efforts to launch new and innovative initiatives that may improve the system but threaten the survivalist way of life. Local office managers reported believing that their ability to remove survivalists from the agency was limited due to employee protections institutionalized in civil service; therefore, central office administrators would be wise to look more closely at how bureaucratic survivalism emerges and what can be done to address it once it arrives.

In moments of massive organizational change, frequent rollouts of retirement packages give bureaucrats who are struggling to meet new organizational expectations the opportunity to gracefully exit the agency while simultaneously giving the agency the opportunity to re-shuffle responsibilities among staff within the protections of civil service guidelines. Considering that many survivalists in the DTA offices that I studied reported "waiting for the next package to be offered," there is little reason to believe that these individuals will resist the opportunity to retire. In cases where the agency wants to launch ambitious policy and institutional changes to improve its engagement with clients, retirement packages may be the only way to successfully pursue these initiatives with a staff that is motivated and up to the challenge. Early packages may seem expensive, but they are likely to offer cost savings over time. Launching new initiatives that are ultimately thwarted by roadblocks erected by survivalists will be an even more expensive undertaking in the long run in terms of the financial cost, the political capital wasted on a failed initiative, and the blow to worker morale after another unsuccessful attempt to make needed changes to the organization.

Train the Staff to Meet the Needs of Clients More Comprehensively

A second recommendation coming out of this research reflects the importance of having a staff that is well trained to meet the expanding demands of the caseworker role and the complex problems that clients face. Finding or developing individuals with backgrounds that are more aligned with the present mission of the welfare system rather than its prior claims-processing function is likely to increase their ability to do the kind of in-depth work with clients that many, including those in the central office, would like to see. Evidence from this book clearly indicates that more significant efforts are needed to retrain frontline staff in comprehensive case management that includes client assessment, referral, and ongoing follow-up rather than simply processing the financial aspects of their cases. Training in policy rules, implementation procedures, and computer skills has so far predominated in the agency. The profession of social work has its own complex history and struggles around professional identity, so I want to be careful about advocating that welfare caseworkers be trained social workers. Caseworkers should, however, possess many of the skills that trained social workers possess around client evaluation, social service referrals, counseling, and follow-up.

To this end, continual in-house training of caseworkers should be mandatory and targeted toward changing client needs, and outside professional development should be strongly encouraged and incentivized. Experts on welfare reform often call for increased funding to improve the skills and capabilities of clients as they transition into the labor market. Equally important is increased funding toward subsidizing caseworker training and education (with the understanding that workers receiving educational subsidies will remain in the welfare department for a period of time afterward to prevent a "brain drain"). Newly hired caseworkers should be required to have a bachelor's degree at a minimum in a field related to human services, as the demands of the job are no longer simply focused on the technical tasks of financial assistance. In addition to improving their educational credentials, offering caseworkers incentives to obtain bachelor's and master's degrees in social work and relevant fields also allows them to make connections with other area service providers in order to expand their networks and knowledge base.

With the abundance of schools of social work and social policy in the areas surrounding the Fishertown and Staunton DTA, partnerships also could be formed between the DTA and these institutions to facilitate the direct hiring of staff and the continuing education of the DTA workforce. As turnover often makes it difficult to foster the kinds of relationships between clients and caseworkers and the level of client follow-up that I am proposing, it is not recommended that student interns or others with short-term commitments to the office engage in client case management. Nevertheless, these individuals could be stationed within the agency to assist in facilitating the procurement of child care, transportation, work clothing, and other ancillary needs for clients under the direct supervisions of caseworkers who are ultimately responsible for ensuring that such needs are met. This would encourage a constant flow of new energy into the institution, introduce possible hires to the organization, and provide caseworkers and supervisors with low-cost assistance to help them assemble and distribute a package of services for clients. It would also provide an outlet for educational institutions looking to arrange internships for their students.

Enforce All Aspects of a Comprehensive Worker Evaluation System

Agency leadership should ensure that the caseworker evaluation structure as it is currently written, with its balance of accountability toward social work and efficiency engineering, is implemented and enforced in such a way that it does not undermine either thrust. It became clear that supervisors and local office administrators deemphasized the "softer" measures of caseworker performance in part because they believed that it was of secondary importance to the central office behind the efficient and accurate processing of cases. This is likely done to ensure that the state's performance measures stay on par with those in other states and align with national trends. The expiration of the state's waiver and its mandate to follow federal accountability guidelines will make these "softer" measures of case management even harder to prioritize. If it becomes clear, however, that the central office places great importance on those measures most tied to what bureaucrats define as "social work," local administrators, supervisors, and caseworkers are likely to follow suit. In fact, this change actually has the potential to increase the employment rate among clients even further as more and more individuals receive the assistance necessary to be successful in this endeavor.[8]

Creative Compensation: Rewarding a Civil Service Staff

A hallmark of civil service employment is the standardized compensation of the staff, negotiated through collective bargaining agreements. Pay raises come as a result of seniority rather than performance. This is for a good reason: civil service jobs often involve interactions and behaviors that are difficult to measure objectively, and artificial measures of performance often ring hollow to the employees who do the job every day. However, informal awards are possible within these institutions and central office administrators would be wise to budget resources toward that end. Otherwise, there is little incentive for caseworkers, regardless of professional orientation, to go above and beyond the call of duty to do the highest caliber of work possible. Workers in my observation often gave superior service out of their own sense of pride, but even this sense of internal motivation must be nurtured and not taken for granted. Creating opportunities for individuals to feed that inner sense of inspiration and feel acknowledged for the work that they do is critical to the long-term success of the agency and its ability to prevent workers from embracing bureaucratic survivalism. Putting in place local office administrators who understand the importance of this and providing these leaders with the resources required to reward and encourage staff in these ways will likely go a long way toward improving the organization.

Some of my recommendations advance the direction in which the agency is already headed, while others offer significant course corrections to address policies and processes that I view as potentially detrimental to both clients and caseworkers. Some are low cost while others will require more resources in order to implement. Cynics will argue that changes on the order of what I propose are not possible for a variety of reasons, starting with the inherent difficulties of organizational change. But welfare reform itself, with its sweeping policy shifts and changes within welfare offices, suggests that widespread organizational changes are possible and that institutional inertia is not an adequate explanation for unambitious or unsuccessful policy reforms. Regardless of the policy's shortcomings, caseworkers, supervisors, and administrators in local offices were given a tall order with the advent of welfare reform, and these bureaucrats took the charge to change seriously and participated in the most sweeping transformation to the social safety net in decades. My conversations with street-level bureaucrats find that many are hoping for the kinds of changes that I have outlined above, suggesting that many of these recommendations, if properly implemented, would find support on the ground. Lastly, the political history of the state, in terms of the relative generosity of its social policies for low-income families and a liberal-leaning electorate, suggests that Massachusetts possesses the kind of political climate in which support could be generated to engage in these interventions on behalf of low-income families.

Transformation from the Bottom Up:
Recommendations for Direct Service Providers

Welfare reform was not only about clients but about the professional futures of street-level welfare bureaucrats as well. With the policy shift came a change in their job descriptions (from an eligibility-compliance model that focused on claims processing to a welfare-to-work case-management model), but without reinforced steps to facilitate a long-term change to their professional identities. This has resulted in inequalities among staff members as they operationalize disparate understandings of their professional roles. In order to reduce these differences, I again do not advocate the elimination of discretion in service delivery; such a tool can be beneficial or detrimental, depending on its use and the perspectives of those involved.[9] Its elimination could prove destructive for families if not organizationally impossible within the offices. Rather, my prescriptions target lessening disparities in the knowledge, resources, and overall support to which clients have access as they navigate the welfare system. This means making substantial investments in developing and sustaining the workforces of these institutions so that they are equipped to take on such an endeavor.

Help Workers Improve Their Client Assessment, Referral,
and Follow-up Skills and Capabilities

One way to address some of the concrete struggles of clients is to arm human service professionals with the tools necessary to deliver tangible and intangible resources to help improve the conditions under which clients live. Clients who are assigned to caseworkers who are less informed about opportunities, and who do not see imparting this information as a key part of their jobs, are likely to be highly disadvantaged. The tone, frequency, and content of their interactions, as well as the skillfulness with which both parties manage their relationships, become critically important organizational tools that can be positively or negatively exploited as recipients navigate the current welfare system.

The improvement and enhancement of client assessment, referral, and ongoing case management services could go a long way in this respect. At present, assessment is a one- or two-step process that includes an initial interview to determine client eligibility, a quick probe for any barriers to work, and assignment to a job placement or training site along with a child care voucher if the client is required to work. Clients who report domestic violence, physical disabilities, or learning disabilities are sent by the DTA to specialists for further screening and evaluation and may receive some in-depth attention there. The external employment and training programs to which clients are sent vary as to whether and how they do in-depth client evaluations of clients' skills and needs, and the results are often not communicated back to the caseworker. With this system, there is a high probability that clients will "slip through the cracks," and this leaves the DTA heavily reliant on outside contractors to identify barriers that both hinder clients and diminish the ability of the agency to reach its own federal work-participation rates. In addition, the reality that clients often move from program to program further lessens the likelihood that an outside contractor can serve as the point person who gathers in-depth information about a client and properly ensures that any issues are addressed.

If state welfare officials allocate a larger portion of their block grant toward the education and training of their workforces, improving the diagnostic and troubleshooting skills of caseworkers is a worthy place to target. It is unlikely that welfare offices will ever be able to address all client issues. They can, however, certainly improve their capabilities so that staff members are highly trained to assess problems, identify possible solutions, and make the appropriate social service referrals. Logistically, caseworkers could maintain the eligibility determination focus of the initial client visit by conducting an inventory of her financial situation and eligibility for various economic assistance programs. After this is determined and cash benefits, food stamps, and Medicaid cards are issued (i.e., the case is opened), a subsequent series of meetings should be reserved solely for evaluating clients' skills, interests, and barriers; troubleshooting; and providing service referrals with the goal of putting together a plan and package of tangible and intangible supports that will assist the client in both her transition into the labor market and her juggling of work and family, should she not qualify for an exemption from work requirements and time limits. Attempting to complete both routine case maintenance and in-depth case management in the same meeting with clients is proving difficult for caseworkers, and too often their focus shifts to the former with the latter receiving much less attention.

Effectively requiring caseworkers to separate these functions into different meetings will increase the likelihood that, during at least one interaction, the focus of both caseworkers and clients will be on assessing existing resources and barriers and assembling a set of governmental, nonprofit, and private resources so that the client can find and maintain employment and meet family demands. Previous research suggests that having one caseworker focus on eligibility-compliance enforcement while another focuses on welfare-to-work services is less effective than having an integrated model whereby one worker completes both tasks (Hill 2006; Scrivener and Walter 2001). Maintaining the integrated model, but refocusing the purpose of each client-caseworker interaction to ensure that eligibility-compliance enforcement does not form the crux of the encounter each time creates a space in which clients can raise any concerns they might have and allows caseworkers the time and focus to help address those concerns.

Until these offices have assembled a frontline staff where all caseworkers are well-trained and can truly do both case maintenance and in-depth case management at a high level, detailed assessment, troubleshooting, and service referrals should be conducted by a specialized and highly trained subset of DTA employees.[10] This would ensure that clients continue to receive the proper inter- and intra-agency services in the interim while the agency retrains the staff. Mark Jacobs's observations about the importance of intercessions on behalf of clients between street-level bureaucrats working in different agencies are critical and come up again in more recent work by sociologist Mario Small on child care centers as interinstitutional brokers for mothers (Jacobs 1990; Small 2006, 2009). Specialized caseworkers in DTA offices could be trained to help address easily hidden problems such as drug abuse and domestic violence by being well versed in the variety of related services in the area and with the interpersonal skills to negotiate this often-delicate dynamic. These staff members should therefore be among the most highly experienced or highly educated in the office, hand-selected and trained for this special task.[11] To be sure, certainly not all clients will require this level of assistance; child care vouchers and job placement and training referrals are just what some may need in order to be successful. But under the model I am proposing, *all* clients, not simply those privileged enough to be assigned to caseworkers who see it as part of their job to perform this role, would have *access* to frontline staff members who take seriously the need to parse out challenges facing clients and connect them to the web of resources both in the agency and in the area.[12]

After the initial assessment and referral process is complete, service plans would be designed for each client, and caseworkers would be expected to continually follow up with clients to address any problems, encourage clients, and offer revisions to the plan. Whereas current client service plans tend to very vaguely outline a plan for the client to look for a job or complete a training program, these more comprehensive plans will address any barriers to clients' abilities to juggle work and family. Periodic "case meetings" between the caseworker, client, and other relevant staff such as a specialized caseworker could focus on marrying the requirements of policy with the service needs identified in the assessment process. Coupling caseworkers with specialized case managers also ensures that at least two DTA office employees are versed in the specifics of a particular case and can marry their perspectives to ensure that clients receive all of the resources and services available while meeting the benchmarks set forth by policy. This will decrease the likelihood that any client is exposed solely to one professional approach. The best outcome is likely to result when a client is exposed to a range of perspectives from staff members.

Increasingly, working with these kinds of engaged bureaucrats is becoming a necessity rather than a luxury. As low-income families approach welfare offices seeking refuge from unemployment, underemployment, and a host of other social ills in a context of ticking time limits, they require not only financial support but also assistance connecting to an array of private, nonprofit, and government services and survival resources. As we saw in chapter 1, regardless of how strongly policymakers argue that welfare offices need to serve a very limited function in the present era, many of society's poor and working-poor families see these institutions as critical places to go when they need help, broadly defined. Welfare offices will likely continue to play the role of catch-all clearinghouse as clients bring issues to them, so it will be wise for these agencies to constantly develop in order to meet this charge head-on. If the goals of these catch-all bureaucracies include moving to a more holistic organizational identity, one that moves in the direction of providing a variety of helping resources—monetary and otherwise—to society's most disadvantaged, changes that speak to the core of caseworkers as professionals are in order.

Improve upon Interorganizational Networks and Client Access to Services

The revised assessment, troubleshooting, and service-referral process assumes that an expansive network of external service providers awaits clients in order to effectively address challenges that are revealed. Massive amounts of dollars have gone toward funding vendors who provide employment and training, remedial education, drug and alcohol rehabilitation, and other services to welfare recipients. The extensive amount of faith that workers, supervisors, and administrators have placed in these outside vendors was a troubling finding, as most assumed that high-quality services were being provided to their clients. Efficiency engineers especially tended to rely solely on the referral system to address client needs outside of financial benefits. Staff members reminded me that the central office evaluates these service providers annually in order to determine whether their contracts with the DTA should be renewed, but we know from previous work that performance-based contracting often covers a whole host of problems on the ground that become gaps in service delivery (DeParle 2004; Johnson-Dias and Maynard-Moody 2007). Therefore, if certain services are to be "farmed out" to nonprofit or private agencies, regular quantitative and qualitative accountability measures should be in place that track client progress as well as the continued professional development of the contracted workforces to meet changing and complex client needs (Smith and Lipsky 1995). Perhaps the best evaluators of a program are clients themselves, and finding ways to effectively capture their views and opinions about these services can be an important organizational tool that could be used to ensure that caseworkers are making referrals to the appropriate outside vendors.

In order to ease some of the burden on caseworkers to identify all of the necessary services and resources for clients, the office could put resources in place to train clients in this skill. In my research with Sylvia Domínguez, we have been struck by the ability of some impoverished mothers to amass a web of social service resources while others languish and struggle to find supports for everyday survival and when crises loom (Domínguez and Watkins 2003; see also Small 2009). This latter group does not appear to have a clear understanding of whom to call for what services, what to ask for, how to interact with service providers in ways that lead to accessing the right tangible and intangible resources, or how to address gaps and mistakes in service delivery. Deftly negotiating a community's interagency human services apparatus is a skill (Lareau 2003), and increasingly important in this era of limited government assistance and the expanding role of private and nonprofit service providers. Providing clients with training to teach them how to navigate these waters would likely go a long way toward assisting families to develop the skills to barter for their own services and resources so that they can be successful. Such skills also would likely assist with the community integration issue that we heard about in Fishertown and families' everyday management of resources and services overall.[13]

Lower the Number of Cases Assigned to Each Caseworker

The interventions that I am suggesting require that caps be placed on the caseload sizes of individual workers. Caseloads of over one hundred make it virtually impossible for workers to have in-depth knowledge of their clients and to provide high-quality and thorough assistance to them. Granted, many clients in the caseloads of current DTA workers are exempt from work requirements and time limits for any number of reasons and thus see their workers only annually or semiannually. However, with the advent of federal work-participation requirements as a result of the expiration of Massachusetts's waiver, the office will likely have to grant fewer exemptions to meet these goals. In order to ensure that these families receive a high quality of service as they enter the ranks of work-mandated and perhaps time-limited clients, caseworkers will likely have to spend a great deal of time with these clients, many presumably of the "harder-to-serve" variety, in order to help them be successful. Coupled with their currently work-mandated and time-limited clients, workers should be responsible for working with fewer cases in order to provide the in-depth case management that I am advocating.

Understand the Local Context of the Office

We tend to think of welfare offices as locales for dispersing benefits that have been determined by high-level policy. But if we consider these institutions in their environmental context, we realize that, especially in places like Fishertown, they are the first institutional representatives of the community for poor newcomers. These agencies also reflect the changing distribution and location of poverty within states. In order to ensure that community politics do not graduate into discriminatory practices and indirect biases, program officers would be wise to revisit recent work that calls for the installation of performance measures to ensure racial equality in the system (Gooden 2003). Furthermore, by sharing information with clients on where and how to access community resources, these agencies can help families assemble a support web through which to facilitate their adjustment to a new area and their ability to successfully juggle work and family. The ways in which specific caseworkers were assigned to handle the cases of immigrant newcomers, with the indirect effect of helping them to integrate into the host community, is a model that can be replicated in these offices, whether newcomers are migrants from other cities or immigrants from other countries.

The present study also highlights both the importance of and the complexities related to racial diversity among the staffs of street-level bureaucracies. Increasing the presence of people of color in the administrative ranks is crucial because it offers varying perspectives as central and local office leaders make policy and programmatic decisions. Moreover, integrating and moving qualified minority candidates up the managerial ranks will likely improve the morale of local offices and communicate the agency's commitment to fair and balanced promotions and hiring, regardless of race.

In addition, this work has also revealed the unique complications faced and resources wielded by some minority street-level bureaucrats of color. For those who actively engage in what I call racialized professionalism, perceived group interests help to shape how they interpret and operationalize their roles as policy implementers. They deploy frames common within marginalized communities to communicate the functions, goals, opportunities, and pitfalls of policies and procedures in ways they hope will resonate with clients. Their interactions hinge on the acknowledgement of racial sameness, and this frames their work, even if the frame is recognizable only through words of encouragement, admonishments against certain activities, or explanations of the unspoken implications of certain policies for communities of color. Yet we must not assume that a singular racial agenda characterizes the views and actions of these bureaucrats, as they clearly make choices about whether and how to inject their social group memberships into the bureaucratic context. Furthermore, we must also be mindful of the ways in which the exercise of power on the basis of gender, class, or other statuses might be problematically downplayed or unaddressed because it is assumed that shared racial minority status between bureaucrats and clients permits a level of policing and regulation that may not be appropriate. As it is not yet clear what impact this has on clients, it would be irresponsible on my part to offer prescriptions around whether or how to address this dynamic.

Organizational sociologist Philip Selznick (1996) once observed that "our society desperately needs organized ways of dealing with social problems; we cannot rely solely on market strategies. Yet the spectre of bureaucracy still haunts and repels, still saps public confidence and weakens support for collective action" (276). If we are to improve the everyday delivery of poor-relief services, public institutions must be given the mandates and resources necessary to be effective. I remain optimistic about the power of institutions to help change lives. Certainly most of us can point to institutions that have provided us with the tools necessary to improve our own human capital, that have shaped our professional and personal identities, or that have helped us take care of our loved ones in improved ways. Why, then, do we expect so little from the institutions charged with responding to the needs of the poor? Great institutions are not created simply through cosmetic changes such as physical renovations or programmatic changes through policy reforms; they are created through building and sustaining a workforce that is prepared, empowered, and rewarded for rising to the occasion. They are created by shaping the terrain of services for the better by addressing their biggest resources—their staffs. Welfare offices, and catch-all bureaucracies more broadly, remain critical institutions in the current era. By nurturing the professional identities of their workforces, and marrying this to concrete resources, we can create and implement effective strategies that endow people with the tools they need not only to survive but to thrive.

Appendix A

Professional Identities in the Making:
A History of the Profession of Welfare Casework

Edna Singletary is a stout brown-skinned woman with graying hair and a quiet dignity. When she graduated from high school in 1971, she worked for a camera manufacturing company for about five years before she was laid off. As the head of the family after her mother's death, Edna found herself struggling to take care of herself and three younger siblings. "My mother and I were excited that I got that job," Edna reflected, "and when she passed I got kind of depressed."

Edna collected unemployment for a few months, but knew that things had to change after navigating the behemoth unemployment office proved to be just too frustrating, "It was not me. And that's when they used to have the lines down the street, the old unemployment lines. I mean it was literally down the street." But Edna knew someone who might be able to help. She approached her cousin, who at the time was working for a community-based agency that helped people find jobs. "I told him, 'I cannot collect unemployment another day. If you have anything, I just want to give this up because this is not me.' He said, 'Okay, what do you want to do?' I said, 'I want to be a social worker.'"

Edna's cousin enrolled her in a state-run training program, and within months she was placed in the McClain office of the Massachusetts Department of Transitional Assistance. She arrived as a trailblazer. "When I first went into the office," she explained, "I was the first black woman to walk through the door." It was January 4, 1976.

It is difficult to fully appreciate the complex and evolving identities of today's public welfare workers without also gaining a sense of their professional histories. Numerous texts have tracked the historical evolution of the welfare system and the ways in which administrators and caseworkers in local offices have both supported and regulated the contours of work, family, and citizenship for poor women from its inception (Katz 1996; Nadasen 2005; Trattner 1999; Abramovitz 1996; Gordon 1994; Neubeck and Cazenave 2001). Yet Edna's story reminds us that these actors have their own stories to tell. They play critical roles in translating abstract policy into concrete rules and directives, have often operated as foot soldiers in ongoing battles between powerful lawmakers and impoverished families, and frequently, in the words of political scientist Joe Soss (2000), "dull the sharpest edges of poverty and inequality" by offering economic sustenance to families in need (12).

Nevertheless, public welfare work's ancestral roots in social science research, social work, and volunteer charity suggest that these individuals have also been active players in contests over their own professional legitimacy and futures. The presence of high numbers of women and people of color in these jobs suggests that these actors have historically been at the forefront of debates about the appropriate roles of women in not just the receipt but also the administration of public services, and the terms by which racial minorities enter into government work. In short, disputes over boundaries and access—professional, community, racial, gender, and class—have been central to the formation of street-level welfare bureaucrats and, in turn, the internal workings of welfare offices. As policy shifts and societal events usher in prescribed changes to their formal roles, these actors in turn negotiate professional identities that reflect their debates about the contours, opportunities, and limits of not only poor support but the work involved to carry out such ambitions.

Public and private poor-support workers from the outset have been actively engaged in trying to delineate their professional identities, political relevance, and social contributions while inextricably linked to a population that has been subject to decades of castigation and has had almost no political clout.[1] The job of supporting and regulating society's economically marginalized exists in a context of staunch investments by the public in questions such as who is "deserving" or "undeserving" of our sympathy and resources; what is the proper role of women and men in families, labor markets, and states; and to what degree should racial minorities have access to state protections and resources (Katz 1996; O'Connor, Orloff, and Shaver 1999; Orloff 2002). Local officials have served as agents of the often conflicting wishes of the public and those occupying the highest positions in welfare's administrative and policymaking power structure over the years. Through their everyday provision of services, poor-support workers have weighed in on some of the most controversial issues of our time.

Creating a Profession: Poor Relief's Early Years

Prior to the passage of the 1935 Social Security Act, which created the Aid to Dependent Children Program (ADC), localities were largely responsible for addressing the needs of the poor within their own borders.[2] Local officials distributed outdoor relief—money, food, clothing, and other goods—throughout the colonial period and into the early nineteenth century, until this practice was briefly replaced in several communities with almshouses and poorhouses beginning in the mid-nineteenth century and continuing into the early twentieth century (Katz 1996; Wagner 2005).[3] State charity boards later began coupling scientific analysis with humanitarian concerns for wards of the state (Trattner 1999). Casework became a central aspect of this budding professional orientation, and agents incorporated investigation, diagnosis, preparation of case records, and treatment into the service-delivery process.

As casework became more formalized, similar practices were simultaneously being refined by private charitable societies, which held similar ambitions to adopt a more studied and organized approach to poverty relief work. Starting in the 1870s, the "friendly visitors" of scientific charity doled out limited financial help and extensive personal advice encouraging economic self-reliance, moral discipline, and reduced dependence on government support (Myers-Lipton 2006). Social historian Michael Katz (1996) writes, "Charity organization society agents and visitors were supposed to be both investigators and friends. They were to inspire confidence and radiate warmth as they intruded into the most intimate details of their clients' lives" (70). Interactions therefore involved screening applicants on the basis of perceived "deservingness" for resources, keeping detailed records of recipients' family histories, and coupling support with heavy behavioral monitoring.

The Progressive Era's expansion of social services beginning in the 1890s became a way for social workers and other reformers to address what many viewed as the dangerous underbelly of unbridled capitalism and the unintended consequences of rising industrialization, immigration, and urban geographic, residential, and economic expansion.[4] Settlement house workers joined the community of social welfare workers, although they were less apt to criticize government-based assistance for "encouraging dependency" and instead advocated for more state engagement in order to help transform communities and help individuals navigate the urban wilderness. Invested in promoting virtue, morality, and good conduct as a result of religious influences, settlement houses under reformers such as Jane Addams at the same time grappled with and often critiqued the paternalism and hierarchy already entrenched in the emerging field of social welfare work. They were among the first to inject social activism for social and economic justice into their social welfare missions (Addams 2002; Katz 1996).

As contests over the values embedded in the profession echoed throughout its development, its organized work was also taking root. The provision of educational, medical, and financial assistance to the needy became increasingly formalized during the Progressive Era. Charity, relief, and reform workers formed new associations, published books and articles in start-up journals dedicated to social welfare work, and created and enforced professional standards (Katz 1996). Individuals began developing a shared understanding of their occupational roles, cultivating what historian William Trattner (1999) describes as "a systematic body of knowledge, a monopoly of skill obtained from higher education and training, and a subculture whose members shared a group identity and common values" (233).

The links between private social work and public welfare work were tentative, however; each struck its own path toward professionalization based largely on its critique of the other field.[5] The growing bureaucratization of public welfare stripped away some of the autonomy that private social work enjoyed during this period while at the same time increasing its public accountability. According to Katz (1996): "The state government threatened their authority, took away some of their responsibilities, and demanded more and more paperwork; private charities criticized the way they ran their institutions, castigated them in public, and judged them by impossibly high standards. . . . They were trapped between county boards of supervisors who wanted to keep expenses as low as possible, constituents who wanted more relief for their friends and relatives, and reformers who attacked their competency and integrity" (173). Partly in response, public welfare officials asserted an increasingly professionalized identity by adopting civil service regulations and in 1930 forming the American Association of Public Welfare Officials, which lobbied for federal relief during the Great Depression. Although they still lagged behind private social workers in terms of prestige, training, educational infrastructure, and the development of national associations, public welfare officials remained responsible for the care of more people than their rivals in private charity and continued that dominance with the advent of New Deal social policies. Promoted by a growing coalition of reformers who wanted to see assistance to the poor instituted on a national scale, ADC (eventually to become AFDC) was created by Title IV of the Social Security Act. Public welfare workers were designated to provide cash assistance for children in need of economic support due to the death, continued absence, or incapacity of the primary wage earner (typically the child's father).

Despite their successful collaborative efforts to achieve federal legislation, the status of public welfare workers would remain below that of private social workers. "State and local bureaucrats handing out welfare [were] eclipsed by the private social workers who adjusted personalities and dispensed services, not money" (Katz 1996, 174). While professional social workers worked in schools and hospitals, public relief workers struggled for prestige and power in welfare offices and were implicated in the backlash against the welfare system that began shortly after its creation. Over the next several decades, the welfare system would become increasingly bureaucratized on the local level as administrators carved out systems to distribute resources in ways that attempted to address the concerns of multiple constituencies who demanded cost-effective and well-allocated support (in terms that were often quite subjective) to poor mothers and children.

ADC, like its smaller-scale forerunner, mothers' pensions, encouraged mothers to focus their energies on taking care of their children in the home rather than on entering the labor market.[6] If, as feminist scholars have argued, activists, policymakers, and powerful constituent groups constructed a gendered social welfare system that set clear expectations for women as homemakers and mothers and for men as breadwinners, it was in the local offices where those expectations were reinforced through the provision of resources and the enforcement of rules consistent with those prescribed roles.[7] Long-standing expectations for women were grafted onto equally venerable moral distinctions between the "deserving" and "undeserving" poor as "disreputable" single, deserted, and divorced women made up increasing proportions of the rolls after many "respectable" widows left the ADC system when they became eligible for their husband's Social Security benefits in 1939. By 1960, twenty-three states had some form of "suitable home" provision, which stipulated that welfare workers could end or reduce welfare grants should they determine that their grantees were not supplying morally proper homes for their children, according to the standards set by welfare officials themselves (Neubeck and Cazenave 2001). These criteria were often linked to women's sexuality; caseworkers could close a case on the basis of the presence of a man's hat or suit in the closet.[8] In theory, workers' latitude to investigate everything from their clients' household partners to the cleanliness and safety of their homes gave them the ability to ensure that the children for whom the state provided assistance were in healthy environments. It was, however, through the enforcement of "suitable home" provisions that, according to Winifred Bell (1965), workers could also exercise the greatest discretion and even enforce racial inequalities through administrative ambiguity: "The very vagueness of the 'suitable home' eligibility conditions guaranteed their adaptability to local and regional mores, and, as the evidence shows, statutes rarely made any pretense of spelling out the meaning of 'fit' or 'proper' parents or 'suitable homes.' Local workers were relied upon to infuse the terms with meaning, and, in doing so, they tended to restrict the programs to nice Anglo-Saxon widows and to move separately but in concert to protect their young programs from Negro and unmarried mothers who might well attract criticism" (18–19).

This provided public welfare workers with the power to enforce moral, gender, and racial hierarchies through their everyday professional practices. They disproportionately denied or limited access to benefits for mothers of color (including widows whose husbands worked in jobs excluded from Social Security benefits), serving as not only economic but also political gatekeepers who could block access to state resources.[9] Piven and Cloward (1971) took this argument a step further by offering a neo-Marxist reading of the professional roles of street-level welfare officials, describing them as operatives for capitalist interests who, over time, adapted access to relief to regional economies and local political interests in order to incentivize low-wage work at some times and quell political conflict in others. Others have constructed these bureaucrats as agents for gendered racism, subjugating women of color, and subsequently all women who seek welfare, through restrictive policies and procedures (Neubeck and Cazenave 2001). Workers' enforcement of "suitable home" provisions, other formal and informal controls that barred women from the rolls, and disparities in the cash allotment of benefits served as everyday practices in welfare offices that called into question the claim, especially by mothers of color, to the nation's entitlement promise. Despite any benevolent intentions welfare workers may have had, the organization of poor-relief work helped to define a professional identity for welfare workers that emphasized surveillance, gatekeeping, and facilitating national and local inequalities through the provision of services.

Professional Change in an Age of Turmoil: Welfare Rights and the Remaking of Poor-Support Work

The civil rights movement, urban unrest in blighted communities, and growing scholarship on poverty's causes and scope increased the public's awareness of the economic deprivation plaguing many American communities in the 1960s, and many political leaders came to the consensus that in-depth attention was needed in response. President Johnson's implementation of the War on Poverty, originally conceptualized by advisers to President John F. Kennedy, created programs designed to improve the health, education, and well-being of families. Many viewed local services as key locales through which to do this work, and there was increased emphasis on utilizing the skills of both professionally trained social workers and community members who were thought to intimately understand the issues facing their neighborhoods (Naples 1998).[10]

Formally trained social workers, who were never completely absent from the ranks of public welfare employment, would therefore enter the field in larger numbers in the 1960s. The Public Welfare Amendments of 1962 were another major contributor to the professional shift toward "social work" in local welfare departments. The recognition of the need for "services" in public assistance accompanied interest in a professional social-work-based doctrine in welfare offices that assigned discretionary power to workers to conduct in-depth casework (Gilbert 1966). This required them to complete extensive paperwork on the mental and physical health, school performance, and well-being of the children on the AFDC rolls and to create plans to respond to their needs. They could offer clients opportunities to access counseling services, job training, and education, while at the same time continuing their mission of "moral uplift" by espousing the value of family stability and, in some cases, employment. The assumption remained that the economic struggles of impoverished families could and should be solved through interventions at the individual and family levels rather than through any major economic redistribution efforts.[11]

This shift in caseworkers' roles also had teeth: welfare workers in many states could initiate court proceedings to remove children from their homes, giving them the power to serve as both child welfare and

AFDC workers. Welfare workers also continued to enforce man-in-the-house rules and monitor family purchases to prevent welfare fraud. They enforced residency requirements until they were struck down in 1969, delineating and verifying the boundaries of who belonged to a community, and thus had access to its resources.[12] Caseworkers interviewed clients' neighbors, school personnel, relatives, and children— seemingly preserving the paternalistic practices of the scientific charity of the late 1800s (Kane and Bane 1994; Orleck 2005). There was a clear and ever-present belief that one's right to privacy was surrendered as a condition of public aid, and rules regarding benefit levels and recipients' rights were unclear.

The surveillance role that the welfare department still expected workers to undertake made building supportive and empathetic relationships difficult. Workers engaged in home visits, starkly underscoring the schism between desperate clients and the limited programmatic, financial, and training resources available to caseworkers to respond.[13] Welfare administrators were expected to reduce the caseloads of individual workers to meet the more expansive demands of casework and to closely supervise employees to ensure a high quality of service (Kane and Bane 1994). This often did not happen. Rolls grew unevenly as caseworkers overpaid benefits or gave payments to ineligible families when confronted with the intensity of the poverty that some mothers faced, while denying or reducing benefits for other families through often discriminatory practices. The increased access of blacks and other racial minorities to the rolls in this period made caseworker discretion particularly problematic as mothers of color found themselves strongly under the white gaze. Through the configuration of welfare casework, black women's home lives, and their abilities to be by extension "respectable women," were highly scrutinized by the state. In sum, although workers were encouraged to dig deeper into clients' lives, it was not clear whether this probing led to the amelioration of poor families' suffering or the expansion of their stifling regulation. In all likelihood, workers accomplished both.

The contentious politics of welfare offices in the 1960s reached a boiling point as welfare rights groups challenged the toxic mix of unrelenting scrutiny, ostensibly capricious benefit denials, and what social historian Annelise Orleck describes as "quick, impersonal, and hostile" encounters between clients and caseworkers that often became highly confrontational (Orleck 2005; Nadasen 2005; Piven and Cloward 1971; Katz 1996). Quoting a welfare rights leader in the community activist group Mothers for Adequate Welfare (MAW), historian Premilla Nadasen (2005) writes:

> It is the way in which many social workers do their jobs that arouses great bitterness and anger in the MAWs. To begin, the workers are accused of being arbitrary and unfair: One worker may allow such things as a new living room set or fluoride treatments, while another does not, and workers often refuse to grant allowances which are clearly deserved. Even worse, from the MAW's viewpoint, are the worker's attitudes. These are characterized as "sick," "condescending," "insufficiently interested in humanity," "manipulative" and "punitive." "Everything the social workers do screams out that they still love the fact that they have people under their control" (53).[14]

Welfare and grassroots civil rights activists, often working in tandem and sharing many key players, successfully challenged the harsh and often discriminatory practices of welfare administrators and their staffs in ways that would have long-term implications for how caseworkers did their jobs.[15] They pressed to expand local access to welfare benefits, educated poor women about their legal rights and entitlements, escorted them on visits to the welfare office to ensure an appropriate level of service, and pushed to curb local offices' surveillance techniques, which seemed to do little to support recipients and much to police them (Orleck 2005; Nadasen 2005; Piven and Cloward 1971).[16] Their successful agitation, along with several court cases that challenged restrictive rules, made welfare caseworkers more accountable to implement AFDC as a true entitlement program and to restructure the staunch gatekeeping function that had arguably become the core of their occupational identities.

An Abiding Presence: Blacks in Social Welfare Work

What is often omitted from the historical charting of the changing roles of public welfare officials are the ways in which racial minorities were actively engaged in shaping their professional identities not simply as external agitators but as inside agents. For African Americans, their history in social welfare work has been informed by their unique social, economic, and political positions vis-à-vis the legacy of slavery, Jim Crow, the sharecropping system, the Great Migration, de jure and de facto racial segregation, economic subjugation, and eventual integration. Their presence in the field can be traced all the way back to the benevolent societies, clubs, and churches that blacks organized to assist newly freed slaves during the post–Civil War Reconstruction of 1865 to 1877. These efforts in essence represented early human service institutions, organized attempts by African Americans to provide for the poor, sick, aged, and disabled among them. Later, as blacks were routinely denied access to public services such as outdoor relief, orphanages, homes for the elderly, clinics, and settlement houses serving whites, black women reformers responded by establishing more benevolent institutions to offer those resources to those on the lowest rungs of the social ladder within their communities (Ross 1976; Hunter 1997; O'Donnell 1994; Gordon 1991).[17]

Black social welfare organizations were not simply focused on the distribution of resources and services for the sake of responding to discrete cases of indigence; these efforts also reflected aspirations toward a larger mission. Historian Linda Gordon writes, "Race uplift work was usually welfare work by definition, and it was always conceived as a path to racial equality" (1991, 580; also see O'Donnell 1994). For black social workers, this was critical for how they understood themselves as volunteers and eventually as professionals in the early years of organized human services. Quoting Eugene Kinckle Jones, executive director of the National Urban League, in a 1928 article, Kevin Modesto writes, "While the Black social worker has to do all the work of a typical social worker, they also have the responsibility of bringing the whole Negro group as a separate entity up to a higher level of social status" (2004, 85).[18] Black social welfare workers viewed their efforts not as charity given to a socially distanced few, but important self-help work with broad community implications for collective survival and mobility.

There were few opportunities for black social welfare workers to distribute resources and services within government agencies until well into the history of these institutions. There was a small contingent of blacks who worked for the Bureau of Public Welfare and the Juvenile Court in Chicago, especially during the Depression when the numbers of African Americans on relief and in the child probation system swelled.[19] Sandra O'Donnell highlights that "by the beginning of 1933, the Cook County Bureau of Public Welfare employed 102 African-American workers, 5.7 percent of its employees, and had two African-American supervisors" (2001, 461). In Georgia, black and white social welfare workers formed a coalition in the aftermath of World War I and gained a significant foothold in employment in state government and city public welfare programs by leveraging federal support (Wilkerson-Freeman 2002). Black caseworkers were hired by the Georgia Department of Public Welfare to conduct needs surveys, administer assistance, and direct projects under the leadership of white female social reformers Gay Bolling Shepperson and Louisa FitzSimons. Theirs was a radical vision of social welfare at the time, "requiring social workers to present themselves as clients' allies and address each as 'Mr.,' 'Mrs.,' or 'Miss,' regardless of race, a practice denounced by local politicians as part of the New Deal's agenda for 'social equality' of the races" (Wilkerson-Freeman 2002, 144).

Despite some enlightened strides made in the New Deal era, racial discrimination in the hiring, promotion, and assignment of staff in public welfare agencies remained the norm until the civil rights era. Blacks who worked for state agencies often saw their duties targeted to designated tasks with an all-black caseload, despite protest from the National Association for the Advancement of Colored People (NAACP), other civil rights organizations, and individuals working within these agencies (King 1999).[20] The supervisory structure within these welfare offices functioned the same way, as blacks rarely if ever oversaw white employees. "In the South," contend Kenneth Neubeck and Noel Cazenave (2001), "it meant that it was unlikely that African Americans would be hired as welfare caseworkers, and almost unimaginable that black caseworkers would be assigned to investigate and determine the eligibility of white mothers for ADC" well into the 1970s (48).[21] Further, it was not unusual for the impartiality of blacks in these positions to be questioned.[22] For instance, when both the rolls and the number of African American welfare caseworkers grew in areas such as the District of Columbia, Senator Robert Byrd sought to undermine these providers' professional legitimacy by charging in 1962 that it was their favoritism and laxity toward black recipients that caused the increase in the rolls (Neubeck and Cazenave 2001).

Beginning in the 1960s, political and social pressures increasingly challenged government organizations, including those offering human services, to diversify their workforces and ensure that their staffs better reflected the demographics of the citizenry. The welfare rights and civil rights movements, along with the War on Poverty's requirements for maximum feasible participation of the poor, created a climate in which there was great pressure to increase access to jobs in community-based agencies, and some former clients were integrated into service delivery roles (Naples 1998). Legal prohibition of job discrimination through the Civil Rights Act of 1964 and the creation of the Equal Employment Opportunity Commission (EEOC) also increased access to human service work for blacks. The Civil Service Reform Act of 1978 called for a public sector that "reflects the nation's diversity" and put in place accountability measures to track agencies' success. As a result of these social movements and legislative reforms, public agencies became the first institutions forced to open their doors to workers of color and to offer a salary, promotion, and job protection structure less open to discrimination (Dobbin et al. 1993). In fact, public sector employment, with its formalized merit and seniority-based promotion system as well as affirmative action policies, has subsequently served as an important means of expanding the black middle class, playing a more significant role in intergenerational mobility for blacks than it has for whites (Eisinger 1982; Greene and Rogers 1994; Hewitt 2004).

"The Good Old Days": Becoming a Caseworker in the 1970s

Several of my respondents came into their jobs shortly after this tumultuous era of professional and political upheaval and reform. Edna remembers that being in the McClain office as a racial pioneer was freighted with complexity. She made important inroads with her coworkers and eventually felt like a part of the organization, but her professional legitimacy was frequently undermined: "I loved the job. I loved the people at the office and the clients. But at that time in '76, I was going through the big 'N' word. Knocking at doors, doing home visits, having doors slammed in my face. And actually these were absent parents that were opening the door and they would say, 'There is a [nigger] at the door.' You know, I went through all that for years."

White caseworkers who arrived around the same time as Edna recounted few occupational hazards of this sort and instead recalled the early 1970s as one of the best eras of welfare service delivery. When Fishertown supervisor Lucy Mitchell started as a caseworker, the job still had its clear orientation toward social work, complete with home visits and the requirement that caseworkers have at least a bachelor's degree. Lucy thought of herself as among the caseworkers at the time who were sympathetic to clients' needs and had a philosophical belief that casework could be performed in such a way as to be helpful rather than intrusive and punishing to clients.[23] Clients' financial services were delegated to specialists within her office, making clear the professional distinction between caseworkers and benefit technicians in the organization. Although she dreamed of being a lawyer or a teacher while she pursued her degree in psychology from a nearby university in the late 1960s, the availability of a job upon graduation was what attracted Lucy to work for the welfare department in 1971. Such a professional move was not incongruous with Lucy's personal career goals and background because of how she understood the orientation of the job:

Personally I came to this job because I wanted to be able to help people. I had this doll when I was young; it was called a Poor Pitiful Pearl doll. That was my favorite doll and my mother said she knew I was going to be a social worker because only somebody who had those aspirations could possibly like that doll. I'm rooting for the underdog. I went to school in one of the poorest parts of Fishertown . . . so I would see people work so hard and get nowhere. That's what I guess I bring to the job.

Similar to the ways in which bureaucrats would understand the term decades later when I conducted my fieldwork, most, like Lucy, recognized that they weren't speaking of social work in the formal sense, complete with its educational credentials and grounding in social scientific and therapeutic knowledge.[24] In fact, despite the enthusiasm with which Lucy and her veteran co-workers took on the professional identities of social workers, few of them were formally trained or licensed in the field. Rather, "social work," as workers defined it, signified a more supportive orientation toward clients, featuring moderation in the use of surveillance and the more punitive aspects of policy. Personalized prescriptions and "addressing the whole client" through in-depth casework were how they defined social work.

Caseworkers were professionals in the early 1970s—trained and educated, responsible for major decisions, and relatively autonomous as they traveled from home to home. Fishertown employee Sharon Steven's unequivocally characterized her early years in the agency as "the good old days":

There was a lot to be said for seeing people in their environment and their comfort level, because you were on their turf. If you went to a house after 2:30 or 3 o'clock when kids were out of school, you saw what was going on between that parent and those kids. You saw what kind of bonding was going on. You saw what kind of parenting was going on. . . . I was after the era when they would open the refrigerator and the cupboards and look for food and under the bed for men. . . . We also saw what people were living with and contending with when we were talking with them about getting out and getting a job. It was a real big picture. So there was a lot of good to that.

This professional model ultimately was not sustained.[25] Pressure to reduce the rolls reached a boiling point, and state and local welfare officials were encouraged by the federal government to abandon the "social work" model of service delivery that constructed caseworkers as in-depth case managers, counselors, and rehabilitators.[26] In 1969, the federally established college degree requirements for new caseworkers and caseload size limits were dropped, coinciding with the advent of a deemphasis on services that would roll across the nation. Policy officials emphasized that local welfare bureaucrats should actively guard the public purse, and welfare administrators as a result widely adopted what became known as an *eligibility-compliance model* of service delivery (Brodkin 1986; Bane and Ellwood 1994).[27] Caseworker-client interactions became increasingly focused on rule enforcement and accuracy as the federal government imposed fiscal penalties for benefit overpayment. States pulled workers out of the field and shifted the sites of worker-client interactions back to welfare offices. The eligibility forms that became the basis of interaction were thought to curb discrimination, but they also prevented workers from making exceptions to the rules or acting on their sympathies. The increased paperwork also controlled the pace and content of service delivery. Staff was neither trained nor rewarded by federal or state politicians for helping welfare applicants or recipients achieve economic self-sufficiency or for alleviating problems outside of determining whether they qualified for benefits. In fact, local administrators, under pressure from state and federal governments, encouraged caseworkers to make interactions with recipients as regimented as possible and rewarded them for enforcing eligibility and compliance rules to reduce errors and guard vigilantly against fraud. Discretion existed only to the degree that caseworkers could slightly reduce or add to the web of verification requirements. "Social workers," consequently, need not apply for the job.

Redefining Casework: The Eligibility-Compliance Model of Welfare Administration at the Dawn of PRWORA

This dramatic "about face" in the prescribed roles of welfare caseworkers eventually reached the Massachusetts offices. Caseworkers were now to focus on assessing clients' eligibility for benefits, helping them to complete applications for cash assistance, collecting necessary verifications, processing accompanying paperwork, and recertifying clients' cases annually. What welfare implementation scholar Evelyn Brodkin (1986) calls "administrative reform" quietly restricted access to welfare via the standardization of benefits, the relegation of social service provision to a much smaller proportion of the staff, and quality control reviews of welfare payments. At the same time, it remade staff members such as Lucy and Sharon, transforming them from "social workers" into claims processors. Accuracy, efficiency, and impersonality became the new benchmarks of welfare worker success, upending the content, purpose, and even the prestige of their work. As Lucy explained, "When I was hired, we had to have a college degree. I think they stopped that in the mid–'70s and started having people promoted who were clerks or came in through the CETA program. They really didn't do the [social work] part of the job."[28]

Caseworkers such as Lucy struggled with their professional identities when this slightly less educated group came into the job. Prior to the state's restructuring of casework, staff members sorted themselves out based on their professional assignments. "Social workers" tended to have college degrees and were "out in the field" conducting home visits. They left it to "technicians" to determine families' budgeted cash assistance. When these groups were combined in the 1980s and all frontline workers began issuing checks, their collective professional identity was suddenly up for grabs. Massachusetts put its weight behind the technician model, following national trends. Instead of raising the human capital of the existing office technicians, they deprofessionalized the social workers. Lucy and her veteran colleagues found not only that fulfilling the dual roles of "counselor" and "technician" was logistically difficult but it also seemed to contradict the therapeutic model of the profession. If they were to survive, it was Lucy and Sharon who would have to adapt.

This did not mean that the technicians had an easy time with the transition. Now they would have to deal with clients. Robert Prince, who started as a courier for the office and eventually became a data entry technician, came to welfare work though the CETA program after an injury suffered while working in a textile mill prevented him from returning to industrial work. He described the shift from processing budget documents to interacting with clients as "a big change. There's very few good days because nobody comes in here that doesn't have a problem. So you're with that all the time." Nevertheless, Robert would soon realize that the job in its current configuration suited his professional orientation much better than it did that of his co-workers Lucy and Sharon. It was accuracy and efficiency that seemed to matter, not his ability to "connect" with clients and help find them services.

Other employees would join the fray throughout the 1980s and 1990s. Government work became quite alluring, with its steady work schedules, union-negotiated salaries, guaranteed pensions, and generous vacation and sick days. Jane Braddock had a very clear goal in mind when she agreed to become a caseworker in the early 1990s:

JANE: I mainly took the job to finish school, because I could never do it as a store manager. You try to leave for school and, you know, somebody doesn't show up, you can't leave. You miss God knows how many classes, you can't finish. So that's mainly why I took it.

INTERVIEWER: Was it the case that you could've ended up in any government agency that was hiring and offered stability? It could've been the Department of Motor Vehicles or something else?

JANE: Yes, anything 9 to 5. Yeah, so I didn't really [take this job] for altruistic reasons [chuckles].

For the overwhelming majority of Fishertown and Staunton staff members, welfare work was a backup choice. It was supposed to tide them over until they were able to do the kind of work they really wanted to do, often teaching or starting a business. Among several respondents, it was the job that their social connections were able to get them after they suffered layoffs or a lack of available positions in their initial fields. Although most described a desire to help others as something that ultimately made the job attractive, it was their limited opportunities to do other kinds of work, and their need to do something to survive their own economic struggles, that first drew most respondents into the department. As a result, the professional identities that these bureaucrats may have imported into the agency are likely to have been influenced by any number of factors rather than by a distinct antipoverty agenda. This book suggests that, once welfare workers were hired, institutional factors played a central role in how they came to see their work.

Regardless of what brought them into the job, it is perhaps surprising that so many have stayed. Of the twenty-nine Fishertown office employees interviewed in 2000–2001, eighteen were still there when I returned in 2007, most having started in the 1970s and 1980s. In Staunton, twenty-three of the twenty-seven original interviewees were still working for the department in 2006. Many of the newcomers that I met during the second round of data collection were actually transfers from other offices, and most departures were due to retirement. The perks of government work that drew many decades earlier help to explain why so many remain. A state hiring freeze during much of the period covered in this research also contributed to the low numbers of newcomers, a notable difference from accounts in other research (Hays 2003). As we saw throughout the book, fighting the demons of burnout as this current cohort moves slowly toward retirement became an additional consideration as we traced their professional self-conceptions. Sundra, who started working in the office in 1988, described welfare work as a "trap," a term usually reserved for welfare receipt itself:[29]

In the years that I've been here, we have even said to some of the younger, brighter workers, "Look, don't give this place your life. You have the ability to do better in the private sector or whatever. Don't marry, have children, and buy a house because then you're locked in welfare." Years ago, my Mom used to say, "You've got a government job, you're set for life." That was my thought, but it's not [all it's] cracked up to be. There's not a lot of opportunities to move up, so a lot of times some of the young ones will come and go and rightfully so. They don't stay like we do anymore. There are people who've been here thirty years and are maybe at job level two. They see no way out because they don't have the retirement age. Or in my case, I'll have the age but not the years in the job. So I'll probably be forced to work until I'm sixty-five, but hopefully not here. I don't think I could do this until I'm sixty-five.

Sundra's imploring newbie workers *not* to "marry, have children, and buy a house" because they will be financially locked into the welfare system as employees drips with irony. Clients under welfare reform are now being instructed to do the exact opposite: to pursue those golden rings of work and marriage as avenues to financial security. Welfare, therefore, is constructed in Sundra's mind as a trap on two levels: as she described in chapter 4, for clients who run the risk of making it their "lifestyle" and for employees who hazard wasting their professional talents in a job that offers few opportunities to do more.

During the 1980s and into the 1990s, a staff of long-term employees would eventually settle in at the Staunton and Fishertown welfare offices. They greeted newcomers who occasionally funneled in and out in much smaller numbers and grew comfortable with a professional identity that was largely focused on eligibility-compliance enforcement. They navigated the waves of incremental policy reforms as the state experimented with introducing opportunities for work, education, and training for clients into local offices. From the outside, the stance on client employment appeared to generate a contradiction in the professional identities of AFDC caseworkers: balancing eligibility-compliance enforcement with a drive to encourage clients to participate in employment and training programs. In practice, however, although there was hope that welfare recipients would leave the rolls for work, Massachusetts, like many states, did not consistently or strongly enforce a welfare-to-work program that would have an impact on the order of PRWORA.[30] Bureaucrats had the discretion to encourage work, but had few tools to enforce the recommendation. Clients who desired work or educational opportunities prior to 1995 were immediately sent to meet with these offices' Employment Services staff.[31] Ivy Scott, who has worked in the Staunton office since 1987, reflected on what this meant for her day-to-day work:

> It used to be: See if they're [clients] eligible and put them on [the welfare rolls] until their babies moved out. . . . We saw them for reviews. "Hi, how are you? How are the kids? Has anything changed that I need to know about—your address, assets, number of people in the household? Interested in a job or training? Yes? Go see Employment Services. No? Okay, fine, maybe next time. Sign these papers. Okay, see you later." They leave; I make sure all my documents are straight. With that, some folks were on for only two, two-and-a-half years, and then gone. Others, lifers. Yeah, it was good to see people leave welfare, but we didn't care that much either way. We didn't have the pressure.

As a result, caseworkers overwhelmingly clung to a shared professional identity that focused on accuracy and efficiency in issuing cash benefits and food stamps. They interpreted their professional roles as claims processors, focused almost exclusively on the technical aspects of the financial lives of the poor. Transforming clients was simply not a part of their professional DNA. Overwhelmingly, they failed to define themselves as employment counselors, advocates, social workers, or anything other than conduits through which clients accessed their monetary benefits. Their responsibility was to keep the paperwork errorless and efficiently channeled through the bureaucracy so that clients could receive their checks, and their job titles of financial assistance workers unambiguously drove this point home.

Uncharted Territory: Reform and the Birth of the Welfare-to-Work Professional

As Massachusetts continued to try to tweak its poor-relief system, it became one of several states in the years prior to PRWORA's passage that experimented by obtaining waivers from federal government regulations.[32]

The Transitional Aid to Families with Dependent Children (TAFDC) program started in 1995 and stresses work as a means to self-sufficiency through its expanded Employment Services Program, largely made up a network of contracted private and nonprofit agencies to which clients are referred for job training or placement. The TAFDC program provides up to twenty-four months of cash benefits within a five-year period and enforces a twenty to thirty hour per week work requirement for adult recipients whose youngest child on the TAFDC grant is two years of age or older.[33] To add teeth to the directive that clients find work, sanctions for noncompliance were instituted, and a variety of other actions can trigger sanctions such as missing appointments with caseworkers, failing to provide paperwork requested by the department such as child immunization records, and having a child in the home who is truant.[34] In addition, the state instituted a "family cap" policy, barring additional funds for children born to current recipients (with exceptions in extraordinary circumstances). To be eligible for benefits, teen parents under the age of twenty are required to have a GED or high school diploma or to be in a program to receive one, and they must live either with a parent or in a supervised setting approved by the department. Lastly, adult program participants are required to assist in the identification of the absent parent of children on TAFDC grants so that the Department of Revenue can pursue child support enforcement.

When welfare reform began in Massachusetts, workers were encouraged to revise their professional roles yet again. In order to fulfill expectations for a "new" welfare office and operationalize policy changes that included time-limited benefits, work requirements, expansive work supports, and sanctioning power, the Massachusetts DTA adopted what Hill (2006) calls unified case management (also see Hargen and Lurie 1995; Rothman 1985). This model assigns responsibilities to eligibility-compliance caseworkers that include "assessing the client's need for services, working with the client to develop an employability plan, arranging and coordinating services, and monitoring client progress."[35] For employees like Lucy and Sharon, these behaviors represented a promising possibility of a return to "the good old days," with rhetoric suggesting that although they would not conduct home visits, these bureaucrats would rekindle in-depth casework to help clients train for and find work. For those like Robert, this shift felt somewhat jarring, but the push toward employment and more stringent rules appealed to his black-and-white understanding of what clients needed to be doing. The pendulum that swung between a job defined as social work in some moments and technical services in others was in motion yet again. Vicki Hawthorne, a Staunton supervisor, explained what this meant in terms of the changing professional expectations placed on caseworkers:

[Previously] we had the Employment Support Program (ESP) unit that helped to direct the client in areas that they voluntarily wanted to go in. Say somebody wanted to go to college; it was ESP's job to tell them about the best colleges available, how to get financial aid and all that kind of stuff. The repository of knowledge was in ESP workers. The TAFDC workers never even cared about that. All they cared about was to get people on assistance, check their assistance, the usual things that they actually do now. But when the client at all said, "I'm thinking of going to school," immediately they would then tell them to go to the ESP and make an appointment. They had absolutely no knowledge of any of that kind of stuff, nor did they have any knowledge of how to [refer people to] daycare, and all that stuff. So, when welfare reform came [and] we got the time-limit rules, what happened was that then [clients] became time limited and then the whole culture of welfare changed to jobs, jobs, jobs, work, work, work. . . . They also spread the ESP job out to every single TAFDC worker, to say that they now had to encompass the ESP part. Suddenly you didn't refer anybody to ESP, you had to know. All TAFDC workers suddenly had to know all the resources, all of the places people could go to get jobs, to go to get training, how to get daycare.

Vicki describes a pivotal moment when caseworkers were being given the opportunity to change how they understood themselves as professionals once more. Along with their previous duties around benefit distribution, the role expectation would now encompass getting a sense of the occupational interests of clients, matching those interests to appropriate programs and services, completing the referrals to those services, and addressing any problems that may arise as clients take advantage of those resources and try to transition into jobs and off the welfare rolls. As we saw throughout the book, these shifts brought major changes to workers' assigned professional roles, the expectations placed on them as employees, and to their professional identities.

Appendix B

Demographic Data

Table 1. State and national demographics.

Characteristic	Massachusetts			United States		
	2000–1	2006–7	% Change	2000–1	2006–7	% Change
Population characteristics						
Population (A1, A2, A3, A4)	6,349,097	6,437,193	1.4	281,421,906	299,398,485	6.4
Percent under age 18 (A1, A2, A3, A4)	23.6	22.5	-1.1	25.7	24.6	-1.1
Percent living in poverty (C1, C2, C3, C4)	9.3	9.9	0.6	12.4	13.3	0.9
Percent white [1] (A1, A2, A3, A4)	86.2	84.3	-1.9	77.1	75.7	-1.4
Percent black or African American [1] (A1, A2, A3, A4)	6.3	7.0	0.7	12.9	13.1	0.2
Percent American Indian and Alaska Native [1] (A1, A2, A3, A4)	0.6	0.6	0.0	1.5	1.4	-0.1
Percent Asian [1] (A1, A2, A3, A4)	4.2	5.2	1.0	4.2	4.9	0.7
Percent native Hawaiian and other Pacific Islander [1] (A1, A2, A3, A4)	0.1	-0.1	0.0	0.3	0.3	0.0
Some other race [1] (A1, A2, A3, A4)	5.1	4.7	-0.4	6.6	6.8	0.2
Percent Hispanic or Latino (of any race) (A1, A2, A3, A4)	6.8	7.9	1.1	12.5	14.8	2.3
Percent noncitizen immigrant (B1, B2, B3, B4)	6.9	7.4	0.5	6.6	7.3	0.7
Percent nonmarital births [2] (D1, D2, D3)	28.3	29.9	1.6	33.1	36.8	3.7
Percent teen births [3] (D1, E1, D3, E2)	6.5	5.9	-0.6	11.6	10.0	-1.6
Fertility rates [4] (D1, E1, D3, E2)	57.2	55.6	-2.8	67.5	66.7	-1.2
Birth rates females ages 15–19 [5] (D1, E1, D3, E2)	25.8	21.7	-15.9	48.5	40.5	-16.5

State Economic Characteristics

Per capita income (C1, C2, C3, C4)	$25,952	$30,686	18.2	$21,587	$25,267	17.0
Unemployment status (C1, C2, C3, C4)	3.0	3.9	0.9	3.7	4.1	0.4
Civilian employment status (C1, C2, C3, C4)	63.1	63.4	0.3	59.7	60.4	0.7
Percent employed in manufacturing [6] (C1, C2, C3, C4)	12.8	10.5	-2.3	14.1	11.6	-2.5
Percent employed in service sector [6] (C1, C2, C3, C4)	46.5	49.8	3.3	42.0	44.3	2.3
Percent employed in public sector [6] (C1, C2, C3, C4)	4.3	3.8	-0.5	4.8	4.7	-0.1

Family Characteristics

Percent children living in married-couple family household (G1, G2, G3, G4)	69.3	71.9	2.6	66.0	68.0	2.0
Percent children living in female household, no husband present (G1, G2, G3, G4)	19.0	22.3	3.3	18.4	24.4	6.0
Percent children under 18 years in poverty (C1, C2, C3, C4)	11.8	12.4	0.6	16.2	18.3	2.1
Percent adults 18 years and over in poverty (C1, C2, C3, C4)	8.5	9.2	0.7	10.9	11.6	0.7

(continued)

Table 1: (continued)

Politics	Massachusetts			United States		
	2000–1	2006–7	% Change	2000–1	2006–7	% Change
Governor's party affiliation (H1, H2)	R	R	0.0	(2001) 19D 29R2I	22D 28R0I	15.8D -3.4R -100.0I
President's party affiliation (I)	R	R	0.0	R	R	0.0
Party composition of Senate [7] (J, K, L)	33D 7R	34D 6R	3.0D -14.3 R	(2001) 50D 50R	44D 55R	-12.0 D 10.0R
Party composition of House of Representatives [8] (M, K, L)	130D 27R 1l 2V	138D 21R 0l 1V	6.2D -22.2 R -100.0 l -50.0 V	(2001) 211D 221R	201D 231R	-4.7D 4.5R

[1] Race alone or in combination with one or more races. The six numbers may add up to more than the total population and the six percentages may add to more than 100 percent because individuals may report more than one race.

[2] Females ages 15–44.

[3] Females ages 15–19.

[4] Fertility rates are live births per 1,000 women aged 15–44 years in a specified group.

[5] Birth rates are live births per 1,000 population in a specified group.

[6] Manufacturing, service sector, and public sector percentages calculated according to U.S. Census definitions (F).

[7] Massachusetts's numbers reflect state Senate members, U.S. numbers reflect the senators at the federal level.

[8] Massachusetts's numbers reflect State House of Representative members, United States' numbers reflect the House of Representatives at the federal level, V = vacancy.

Sources:

2000–1 Massachusetts, United States Data

A1. U.S. Bureau of the Census. United States Census 2000. 2007. "Table DP-1: Profile of General Demographic Characteristics: 2000." Geographic area: Massachusetts. Retrieved November 5, 2007 (http://censtats.census.gov/data/MA/04025.pdf).

B1. U.S. Bureau of the Census. United States Census 2000. 2007. "Table DP-2: Profile of Selected Social Characteristics: 2000." Geographic area: Massachusetts. Retrieved November 5, 2007 (http://censtats.census.gov/data/MA/04025.pdf).

C1. U.S. Bureau of the Census. United States Census 2000. 2007. "Table DP-3: Profile of Selected Economic Characteristics: 2000." Geographic area: Massachusetts. Retrieved November 5, 2007 (http://censtats.census.gov/data/MA/04025.pdf).

A2. U.S. Bureau of the Census. United States Census 2000. 2007. "Table DP-1: Profile of General Demographic Characteristics: 2000." Geographic area: United States. Retrieved November 5, 2007 (http://censtats.census.gov/data/US/01000.pdf).

B2. U.S. Bureau of the Census. United State Census 2000. 2007. "Table DP-2: Profile of Selected Social Characteristics: 2000." Geographic area: United States. Retrieved November 5, 2007 (http://censtats.census.gov/data/US/01000.pdf).

C2. U.S. Bureau of the Census. United State Census 2000. 2007. "Table DP-3: Profile of Selected Economic Characteristics: 2000." Geographic area: United States. Retrieved November 5, 2007 (http://censtats.census.gov/data/US/01000.pdf).

D1. Commonwealth of Massachusetts Department of Public Health. Center for Health Information, Statistics, Research, and Evaluation: Division of Research and Epidemiology. 2007. "Massachusetts Births 2000." Retrieved November 5, 2007 (http://www.mass.gov/Eeohhs2/docs/dph/research_epi/birth_report_2000.pdf).

D2. S. Ventura (personal communication, January 8, 2008)

E1. J. A. Martin, B. E. Hamilton, S. J. Ventura, F. Menacker, M. M. Park. 2007. Births: Final Data for 2000. National Center for Health Statistics: National Vital Statistics Report, vol. 50 no. 5. Hyattsville, Md.: U.S. Department of Health and Human Services. Retrieved November 5, 2007 (http://www.cdc.gov/nchs/data/nvsr/nvsr50/nvsr50_05.pdf).

F. S. Laue (personal communication, July 3, 2008)

G1. U.S. Bureau of the Census. United States Census 2000. 2007. "Summary File 1 (SF1) 100-Percent Data. P28: Relationship by Household Type for the Population under 18 Years." Geographic area: Massachusetts. Retrieved November 5, 2007 (http://factfinder.census.gov).

G2. U.S. Bureau of the Census. United States Census 2000. 2007. "Summary File 1 (SF1) 100-Percent Data. P28: Relationship by Household Type for the Population under 18 Years." Geographic area: United States. Retrieved November 5, 2007 (http://factfinder.census.gov).

H1. National Governors Association. 2008. "Massachusetts Governors." Retrieved July 3, 2008 (http://www.nga.org/portal/site/nga/menuitem.8fd3d12ab65b3048a2781105001010a07submit=Submit&State=MA).

H2. U.S. Bureau of the Census. Statistical Abstract of the United States 2007. 2007. "Section 7: Elections. Table 398: Number of Governors by Political Party Affiliation: 1975 to 2006." Retrieved November 5, 2007 (http://www.census.gov/prod/2006pubs/07statab/election.pdf).

I. White House. 2007. "Presidents of the United States." Retrieved November 5, 2007 (http://www.whitehouse.gov/history/presidents/).

(continued)

Table 1. (*continued*)

J. State Library of Massachusetts. 2007. "State Senate Political Complexion (1867 to Date)." Retrieved November 5, 2007 (http://www.mass.gov/lib/facts/spc.htm).

K. U.S. Bureau of the Census. Statistical Abstract of the United States 2007. 2007. "Section 7: Elections. Table 394: Composition of Congress by Political Party Affiliation—States: 1999 to 2006." Retrieved November 5, 2007 (http://www.census.gov/prod/2006pubs/07statab/election.pdf).

M. State Library of Massachusetts. 2007. "State House of Representatives Political Complexion (1867 to Date)." Retrieved November 5, 2007 (http://www.mass.gov/lib/facts/hpc.htm).

2005–6 Massachusetts, United States Data

A3. U.S. Bureau of the Census. 2006 American Community Survey. 2007. "Table DP-5: ACS Demographic and Housing Estimates: 2006." Geographic area: Massachusetts. Retrieved November 5, 2007 (http://factfinder.census.gov).

B3. U.S. Bureau of the Census. 2006 American Community Survey. 2007. "Table DP-2: Selected Social Characteristics in the United States: 2006." Geographic area: Massachusetts. Retrieved November 5, 2007 (http://factfinder.census.gov).

C3. U.S. Bureau of the Census. 2006 American Community Survey. 2007. "Table DP-3: Selected Economic Characteristics: 2006." Geographic area: Massachusetts. Retrieved November 5, 2007 (http://factfinder.census.gov).

A4. U.S. Bureau of the Census. 2006 American Community Survey. 2007. "Table DP-5: ACS Demographic and Housing Estimates: 2006." Geographic area: United States. Retrieved November 5, 2007 (http://factfinder.census.gov.

B4. U.S. Bureau of the Census. 2006 American Community Survey. 2007. "Table DP-2: Selected Social Characteristics in the United States: 2006." Geographic area: United States. Retrieved November 5, 2007 (http://factfinder.census.gov).

C4. U.S. Bureau of the Census. 2006 American Community Survey. 2007. "Table DP-3: Selected Economic Characteristics: 2006." Geographic area: United States. Retrieved November 5, 2007 (http://factfinder.census.gov).

D2. S. Ventura (personal communication, January 8, 2008)

D3. Commonwealth of Massachusetts Department of Public Health. Center for Health Information, Statistics, Research, and Evaluation: Division of Research and Epidemiology. 2007. "Massachusetts Births 2005." Retrieved November 5, 2007 (http://www.mass.gov/Eeohhs2/docs/dph/research_epi/birth_report_2005.pdf).

E2. J. A. Martin, B. E. Hamilton, S. J. Ventura, F. Menacker, M. M. Park. 2007. Births: Final Data for 2005. National Center for Health Statistics: National Vital Statistics Report, vol. 56 no. 6. Hyattsville, Md.: U.S. Department of Health and Human Services. Retrieved December 5, 2007 (http://www.cdc.gov/nchs/data/nvsr/nvsr56/nvsr56_06.pdf).

F. S. Laue (personal communication, July 3, 2008)

G3. U.S. Bureau of the Census. 2006 American Community Survey. 2007. "Table S0901: Children Characteristics." Geographic area: Massachusetts. Retrieved November 5, 2007 (http://factfinder.census.gov).

G4. U.S. Bureau of the Census. 2006 American Community Survey. 2007. "Table S0901: Children Characteristics." Geographic area: United States. Retrieved November 5, 2007 (http://factfinder.census.gov).

H1. National Governors Association. 2008. "Massachusetts Governors." Retrieved July 3, 2008 (http://www.nga.org/portal/site/nga/menuitem.8fd3d12ab65b304f8a278110501010 a0?submit=Submit&State=MA).

H2. U.S. Bureau of the Census. Statistical Abstract of the United States 2007. 2007. "Section 7: Elections. Table 398: Number of Governors by Political Party Affiliation: 1975 to 2006." Retrieved November 5, 2007 (http://www.census.gov/prod/2006pubs/07statab/election.pdf).

I. White House. 2007. "Presidents of the United States." Retrieved November 5, 2007 (http://www.whitehouse.gov/history/presidents/).

K. U.S. Bureau of the Census. Statistical Abstract of the United States 2007. 2007. "Section 7: Elections. Table 394: Composition of Congress by Political Party Affiliation—States: 1999 to 2006." Retrieved November 5, 2007 (http://www.census.gov/prod/2006pubs/07statab/election.pdf).

L. Kenneth G. Morton and Papalinka Paradise. 2006. Massachusetts Political Almanac. Annual ed. Centerville, Mass.: Center for Leadership Studies.

Table 2. Area demographics for the Staunton and Fishertown offices.

Characteristic	Staunton			Fishertown		
	2000–1	2006–7	% Change	2000–1	2006–7	% Change
Population Characteristics						
Population (A1, A2, A3, A4)	589,141	575,187	-2.4%	91,938	91,867	0.1
Percent under age 18 (A1, A2, A3, A4)	19.8	19.2	-0.6	24.1	22.1	-2.0
Percent living in poverty (C1, C2, C3, C4)	19.5	19.8	0.3	17.1	18.6	1.5
Percent white [1] (A1, A2, A3, A4)	56.8	58.7	1.9	93.3	91.0	-2.3
Percent black or African American [1] (A1, A2, A3, A4)	27.7	26.4	-1.3	3.2	5.8	2.6
Percent American Indian and Alaska Native [1] (A1, A2, A3, A4)	0.9	0.7	-0.2	0.6	1.0	0.4
Percent Asian [1] (A1, A2, A3, A4)	8.1	8.5	0.4	2.5	2.2	-0.3
Percent native Hawaiian and other Pacific Islander [1] (A1, A2, A3, A4)	0.3	0.1	-0.2	0.3	N	N
Some other race [1] (A1, A2, A3, A4)	10.9	8.4	-2.5	2.8	3.4	0.6
Percent Hispanic or Latino (of any race) (A1, A2, A3, A4)	14.4	14.9	0.5	3.3	5.2	1.9
Percent noncitizen immigrant (B1, B2, B3, B4)	16.2	15.2 (2005)	-1.0	9.2	9.5	0.3
Percent nonmarital births [2] (D1, D2)	44.0	44.7	0.7	49.0	50.5	1.5
Percent teen births (D1, D2)	10.0 [3]	7.5 [4]	-2.5	13.0 [3]	11.7 [4]	-1.3
Crude birth rates [5] (D1, D2)	13.7	13.5	-1.5	12.9	13.0	0.8
Birth rates females ages 15–19 [6] (D1, D2)	35.3	28.6	-19.0	51.5	49.5	-3.9

Local Economic Characteristics

Per capita income, $ (C1, C2, C3, C4)	23,353	29,243	25.2	16,118	18,456	14.5
Unemployment status (C1, C2, C3, C4)	4.6	4.3	-0.3	4.1	5.6	1.5
Civilian employment status (C1, C2, C3, C4)	58.9	62.5	3.6	54.9	56.6	1.7
Percent employed in manufacturing [7] (C1, C2, C3, C4)	6.1	4.9	-1.2	24.3	19.4	-4.9
Percent employed in service sector [7] (C1, C2, C3, C4)	55.6	59.5	3.9	38.1	39.0	0.9
Percent employed in public sector [7] (C1, C2, C3, C4)	5.1	4.4	-0.7	4.1	3.1	-1.0

Household Characteristics

Percent households with married- couple family and own children under 18 (A1, A2, B3, B4)	11.8	10.9	-0.9	17.0	14.2	-2.8
Percent households with female, no husband present, and own children under 18 (A1, A2, B3, B4)	9.5	9.1	-0.4	11.0	12.7	1.7
Percent children under 18 years in poverty (C1, C2, C3, C4)	25.3	27.3	2.0	25.3	27.2	1.9
Percent adults 18 years and over in poverty (C1, C2, C3, C4)	17.9	18.0	0.1	14.3	16.2	1.9
Mayor's party affiliation (F, G)	D	D	0.0	D	D	0.0

[1] Race alone or in combination with one or more races. The six numbers may add up to more than the total population and the six percentages may add to more than 100 percent because individuals may report more than one race.

[2] Females ages 13–49.

(continued)

Table 2. (*continued*)

[3] Females under the age of 20.

[4] Females ages 15–19.

[5] Crude birth rates represent the number of births per 1,000 residents.

[6] Birth rates are live births per 1,000 population in a specified group.

[7] Service sector and public sector percentages calculated according to U.S. Census definitions (E).

Sources:

2000–01 Staunton and Fishertown Data

A1. U.S. Bureau of the Census. United States Census 2000. 2007. "Table DP-1: Profile of General Demographic Characteristics: 2000." Geographic area: [Staunton], Massachusetts. Retrieved November 5, 2007 (http://censtats.census.gov/). Source available on request.

B1. U.S. Bureau of the Census. United States Census 2000. 2007. "Table DP-2: Profile of Selected Social Characteristics: 2000." Geographic area: [Staunton], Massachusetts. Retrieved November 5, 2007 (http://censtats.census.gov/). Source available on request.

C1. U.S. Bureau of the Census. United States Census 2000. 2007. "Table DP-3: Profile of Selected Economic Characteristics: 2000." Geographic area: [Staunton], Massachusetts. Retrieved November 5, 2007 (http://censtats.census.gov/). Source available on request.

A2. U.S. Bureau of the Census. United States Census 2000. 2007. "Table DP-1: Profile of General Demographic Characteristics: 2000." Geographic area: [Fishertown], Massachusetts. Retrieved November 5, 2007 (http://censtats.census.gov/). Source available on request.

B2. U.S. Bureau of the Census. United States Census 2000. 2007. "Table DP-2: Profile of Selected Social Characteristics: 2000." Geographic area: [Fishertown], Massachusetts. Retrieved November 5, 2007 (http://censtats.census.gov/). Source available on request.

C2. U.S. Bureau of the Census. United States Census 2000. 2007. "Table DP-3: Profile of Selected Economic Characteristics: 2000." Geographic area: [Fishertown], Massachusetts. Retrieved November 5, 2007 (http://censtats.census.gov/). Source available on request.

D1. Commonwealth of Massachusetts Department of Public Health. Center for Health Information, Statistics, Research, and Evaluation: Division of Research and Epidemiology. 2007. "Massachusetts Births 2000." Retrieved November 5, 2007 (http://www.mass.gov/Eeohhs2/docs/dph/research_epi/birth_report_2000.pdf).

E. S. Laue (personal communication, July 3, 2008).

F. City of [Staunton]. 2007. "Biography of [James Smith]: Mayor of [Staunton]." Retrieved November 5, 2007 (http://www.[staunton].gov/mayor/bio.asp).

G. City of [Fishertown]. 2007. "Mayor [Scott's] Biography." Retrieved September 7, 2007 (http://www.[fishertown].org/pressarticles.asp?ID=112). Source available on request.

2005–6 Staunton and Fishertown Data

A3. U.S. Bureau of the Census. 2006 American Community Survey. 2007. "Table DP-5: ACS Demographic and Housing Estimates: 2006." Geographic area: [Staunton], Massachusetts. Retrieved November 5, 2007 (http://factfinder.census.gov).

B3. U.S. Bureau of the Census. 2006 American Community Survey. 2007. "Table DP-2: Selected Social Characteristics in the United States: 2006." Geographic area: [Staunton], Massachusetts. Retrieved November 5, 2007 (http://factfinder.census.gov).

C3. U.S. Bureau of the Census. 2006 American Community Survey. 2007. "Table DP-3: Selected Economic Characteristics: 2006." Geographic area: [Staunton], Massachusetts. Retrieved November 5, 2007 (http://factfinder.census.gov).

A4. U.S. Bureau of the Census. 2006 American Community Survey. 2007. "Table DP-5: ACS Demographic and Housing Estimates: 2006." Geographic area: [Fishertown], Massachusetts. Retrieved November 5, 2007 (http://factfinder.census.gov).

B4. U.S. Bureau of the Census. 2006 American Community Survey. 2007. "Table DP-2: Selected Social Characteristics in the United States: 2006." Geographic area: [Fishertown], Massachusetts. Retrieved November 5, 2007 (http://factfinder.census.gov).

C4. U.S. Bureau of the Census. 2006 American Community Survey. 2007. "Table DP-3: Selected Economic Characteristics: 2006." Geographic area: [Fishertown], Massachusetts. Retrieved November 5, 2007 (http://factfinder.census.gov).

D2. Commonwealth of Massachusetts Department of Public Health. Center for Health Information, Statistics, Research, and Evaluation: Division of Research and Epidemiology. 2007. "Massachusetts Births 2005." Retrieved November 5, 2007 (http://www.mass.gov/Eeohhs2/docs/dph/research_epi/birth_report_2005.pdf).

E. S. Laue (personal communication, July 3, 2008).

F. City of [Staunton]. 2007. "Biography of [James Smith]: Mayor of [Staunton]." Retrieved November 5, 2007 (http://www.[staunton].gov/mayor/bio.asp).

G. City of [Fishertown]. 2007. "Mayor [Scott's] Biography." Retrieved September 7, 2007 (http://www.[fishertown].org/pressarticles.asp?ID=112). Source available on request.

Appendix C

Methodology

A central goal in my research is to integrate scholarly debates across disciplines and bring their various analytical tools to bear on the study of poverty, social policy, and formal organizations. I am fundamentally interested in deconstructing how street-level bureaucrats maneuver in institutions that cater to disadvantaged populations and how the policies that these actors implement come to life at the ground level. Marginalized individuals are often resourced, regulated, and restricted in street-level bureaucracies in ways that affect their experiences, both directly and indirectly, in economic, political, and social life. As such, the frontline workers who facilitate these processes are central to our understanding of avenues through which inequalities can be mitigated.

My approach to the in-depth study of public bureaucracies is grounded in the tradition of early organizational sociologists such as Philip Selznick (1980), Peter Blau (1972), and Michel Crozier (1964), as well as political scientist Michael Lipsky (1980).[1] These scholars sought to develop rich understandings of the informal practices, structures, and cultural forms that guide behavior and contribute to the production of public goods and the implementation of public policies. Because their focus was on the bureaucrats who perform this work, I considered them as guides for the present analysis, which delves deeply into organizational life through extensive participant observation, interviews, and archival work. My task has been to use these techniques to formulate a conceptualization of an agency's inner workings that extends beyond solely documenting and describing events related to Clinton-era welfare reform and moves toward theorizing the complex ways in which policy is re-created and politics are negotiated on the ground in what I call catch-all bureaucracies.

Organizational ethnography has gained increased attention in recent years. John Van Maanen (1979) writes that, as a methodology, its aim is to "uncover and explicate the ways in which people in particular work settings come to understand, account for, take action, and otherwise manage their day-to-day situation" (103). Calvin Morrill and Gary Alan Fine (1997) highlight five areas in which the use of ethnography has been particularly effective for organizational sociology: uncovering informal and often hidden interactions that may or may not undermine agency goals; articulating the ways in which organizational actors generate, share, and revise systems of meaning (what Anselm Strauss and his colleagues [1963] called a "negotiated order"); examining how environmental conditions and arrangements shape internal dynamics; documenting processes of organizational change; and revealing conventional behaviors within "deviant" or unconventional organizations and "deviant" behaviors within more conventional locales. All of these goals allow us to capture individuals in the "natural contexts" of their everyday work lives.

The ethnographic approach to organizational dynamics has several methodological strengths. First, because I have employed the research strategy of a longitudinal case study, I have been able to look at the experiences of my respondents not as snapshots in time but rather as processes through which they develop strategies to implement policy (Eisenhardt 1989). Second, ethnographic data, collected through participant observation and in-depth, semistructured interviews, is multidimensional in that it allows us to capture not only what respondents say but also what they do and to cross-reference data to tease out consistencies and inconsistencies. Third, ethnographic field observations are particularly useful for explicating the cultural aspects of organizations and capturing events that often go unaccounted for in survey research (Schein 1996). Thus, this approach to questions of organizational culture and change gleans insights that directly reveal important ideas not only about the implementation of welfare reform but also about the ways in which issues around race, migration, occupational reward and evaluation systems, and professional identities interact in public bureaucracies.

Access to Research Sites

Access to the institutions was less difficult to obtain than I had expected it to be. Welfare office employees were eager to tell their stories
about implementing such a massive policy shift and to "set the record
straight" about what they do and why they do it. Access was facilitated
by William Julius Wilson, one of my dissertation committee members.
Bill is well known within the state's antipoverty community and was
kind enough to send a letter to the Massachusetts welfare commissioner requesting that access be granted to me. I met with the commissioner to explain the purpose of my study and to assure her that
while I would be critical in my analysis, my intentions were to present
a scholarly portrait of organizational dynamics rather than to engage
in muckraking (a key concern for such a public institution). I also provided a copy of my research prospectus and a sample of the kinds of
questions I was interested in asking.

After the state's welfare commissioner gave her approval, she introduced me to key regional and office directors to discuss my study. I
requested access to offices based on size, the racial composition of the
workforce and clients, and the demographic characteristics of the cities in which they were situated. I met with the directors and assistant
directors of each of the two offices, explained my study, and invited
inquiries into my research design and vision for the final product. Having received approval from each of the directors, I began my fieldwork.

Data Collection

Welfare offices are much-maligned organizations and I knew that it
would be tempting to go into my research sites and simply uncover
various examples of what readers would consider problematic behavior. I was, however, committed to capturing the positions of frontline
workers and to be fair to the research endeavor and the goodwill of my
respondents who let me into their work lives. The driving push was
to depict the complexity of these institutions as accurately as possible.
Therefore I utilized three different techniques of data collection: participant observation, in-depth interviewing, and archival research.

The welfare commissioner and her staff allowed me to carry out my
research largely unsupervised. I typically visited my research sites during normal business hours, Mondays through Fridays. Feeling quite
conspicuous early on, I connected with a few employees in each of-

fice who allowed me to observe them during their workday and who began to describe the informal lay of the land in the offices. While the directors or assistant directors in each office introduced me individually to employees during an office tour, these key informants would facilitate secondary introductions that were much more informal and allowed employees to ask more questions about my background and my project. Within days, I was invited to join workers for lunch, which provided me with many opportunities to get to know them outside of the office and to hear about many of the "behind the scenes" dynamics taking place in the agency.

I began in-depth interviews with employees a few weeks after starting fieldwork, and they typically lasted between forty-five minutes and two hours. I sought to interview as many employees connected to the TAFDC program as possible, informally approaching them in the hallways and asking for some of their time. I interviewed caseworkers and supervisors in each of the TAFDC supervisory units and targeted employees among the DTA's administrative ranks, and ensured that I had a good mix of respondents in terms of seniority, age, gender, race, and ethnicity. To encourage a conversational flow, I tape-recorded every interview and reserved extensive note taking until after the session concluded. After explaining and answering questions about the parameters of the study and having interviewees sign consent forms, I typically began by asking how they came to work for the welfare department. I asked about their education, places of birth and residence, past work histories, and lengths of time working for the department. I had workers describe a typical day and asked questions about administrative practices; perceived strengths and weaknesses of the organization; the evaluation, reward, penalty, and surveillance techniques to which they were subject; their feelings about welfare reform; and attitudes toward clients. Interviews followed a format that I designed, but they often veered in other directions depending on the comments made by interviewees. It was by allowing this kind of flexibility that I learned about the dynamics that would become the basis for chapter 5—the relationship between race, class, migration, and welfare service delivery.

Although workers were eager to share insights into their jobs during casual conversations, when the possibility for formal one-on-one interviews came, a few were reluctant to participate. Some were suspicious of my motives. Was I some kind of evaluator or mole who would report their opinions and ideas directly to organizational leaders or to the central welfare office? Was my presence the organization's way of discerning who was happy with welfare reform and who was not? To assuage these fears, I spent the first few weeks of fieldwork simply getting to know the caseworkers and the jobs that they performed without approaching anyone for in-depth interviews. My relationships with key informants in the office served as a kind of "authenticity" test, demonstrating that if particular workers openly talked to me about the job, then I was "okay." I also experienced something very similar to what Peter Blau (1972) describes in his book, *The Dynamics of Bureaucracy*, whereby my ignorance of the intricacies of policy and of the service-delivery process demonstrated that I certainly didn't have any prior relationship to the welfare department. As our relationships grew, workers became convinced that I was simply a graduate student conducting dissertation research with no ulterior motives related to policing them for the welfare department. As a result, I was able to conduct more than eighty in-depth interviews with over seventy DTA employees, forming the database I draw upon here.

I also conducted participant observation, shadowing caseworkers and other employees to get a better sense of their everyday work lives and also to see how policy is implemented and politics are negotiated at their most intimate level—through the interactions between frontline welfare workers and their clients. It is here that workers would make on-the-spot decisions that operationalized their professional identities and reshaped policy through their use of discretion. I observed service-delivery meetings between clients and workers and sat in cubicles with workers as they spent hours balancing stacks of paperwork while taking frequent calls and holding impromptu meetings with clients. To make myself useful to my informants, I performed miscellaneous copying and filing tasks for workers. Rather than relying solely on procedural manuals that dictate what workers should do, I could observe firsthand what actually occurred. I was also able to discern inconsistencies between what respondents said during their interviews and what they actually did in their relationships with clients, their demonstrated knowledge of policies, and the job functions that they emphasized and deemphasized in the course of the day. In other instances, bureaucrats contextualized and explained in greater detail in interviews what I had observed while shadowing them.

Archival research was particularly helpful in developing an understanding of many of the policies that I observed workers implementing. For secondary sources, I collected newspaper stories related to the department and welfare reform. For primary sources, I read protocols and procedural documents generated by the organization. During one of my earliest days of fieldwork, I spent hours in the "forms room" in the Staunton office, a small room lined on all four sides with shelves that extended to the ceiling with stacks of documents piled high. These were the forms that guided service delivery during my observations. I also analyzed worker evaluation documents and memos from the central office regarding policy changes. This cross-comparison of data gathered through different research techniques allowed me to check the reliability of my arguments and to uncover the errors and false assumptions that I made early in the process.

These research techniques allowed me to interact with staff members on multiple occasions over a long period of time and to develop the kind of rapport that, I hope, encouraged them to have some level of comfort with my presence as a "fly on the wall." Much of this was predicated upon institutional staff's tolerating my essentially "being in the way," something ethnographers almost invariably ask of their subjects as they study them over long periods of time. However, as Mark Jacobs (1990) aptly describes in relating his fieldwork experience in the juvenile court system, I found that "reflexive professional curiosity and concern" greatly encouraged my subjects to share their experiences with remarkable candor. Quite simply, these bureaucrats wanted to tell their stories.

Data Analysis

Although I analyzed what I was learning throughout my time in the field, after I felt that I had learned enough about both the Staunton and Fishertown offices to achieve what is known as "immersion," I focused my full attention on the data analysis process.[2] It was a tedious back-and-forth operation aimed at getting the story "right," to the degree that any outsider can do so. Famed anthropologist Clifford Geertz (1973) writes, "What we call our data are really our own constructions of other people's constructions of what they and their compatriots are up to" (9).[3] I coded all field notes and interview transcripts after each round of fieldwork using emergent themes and categories, refining my codes as the process went on (Glaser and Strauss 1967). I triangulated my data within and across methods—in-depth interviewing, participant observation, archival research—in order to increase the internal validity of the findings. I also conducted what are known as "member checks," discussing with a few key informants, both during and after the first round of data collection, some early conceptualizations that I was developing so that they could help me determine whether I should view them as representative of the organization or outlier events that rarely occur.[4] When I found deviations within and across methods, I followed up by asking respondents to discuss them so that I could make sense of what I had heard and seen.

In the second round of data collection, during interviews, I explored my preliminary arguments in greater depth with respondents, modifying them as I interacted with subjects. By the end of my follow-up round of fieldwork, I was quite forthcoming about what some of my key formulations were with all of my respondents, inviting further detail, agreement, and even critique from them. During the entire time that I worked on this project—thinking about and rethinking data points, theoretical frameworks, and interpretive analyses—it was not unusual for me to pick up the phone and ask more questions of informants who would allow such intrusions. Through these interactions, I heard many different interpretations from organizational actors of the major policy and programmatic shifts that continued to be under way after I officially exited the field, allowing me to keep abreast of the evolution of the agency and to ensure that my findings were constantly updated and current. As a result, my subjects were critical resources in my data analysis process and my grounded theory approach.[5]

Of course, I do not propose to know, or convey here, *exactly* what it is like for welfare caseworkers as they navigate these institutions and implement such a major policy shift as PRWORA. Van Maanen (1979) reminds us that:

In the final analysis, fieldworkers can never fully apprehend the world of their informants in its "natural" form. Even though ethnographers may sense the situated meanings various informants attach to the objects of their concern, such meanings will remain largely exhibits of how informants think rather than the "true" meanings such objects have to informants. . . . [But] a fieldworker is not interested solely in what things are for themselves . . . but . . . specifically in what things "stand for" to the people observed. (542)

I hope that, through my ongoing conversations with street-level bureaucrats along the DTA hierarchy and from diverse walks of life, I did justice to their stories and their generosity. It is these individuals who grapple daily with the complexities, opportunities, and challenges of organizational life in the social world.

Notes

1. For an extensive social scientific treatment of Hurricane Katrina and its aftermath, see Hartman and Squires (2006) and the spring 2006 edition of the *DuBois Review,* vol. 3, no. 1. For a more detailed analysis of the bureaucratic problems that hindered the preparation leading up to Katrina and its aftermath, see Schneider 2005.

2. According to the report, in 2004 poverty rates in Alabama, Louisiana, and Mississippi were among the highest in the country (16.1%, 19.4%, and 21.6%, respectively). The national poverty rate at the time was 13%. Thirty-five percent of black households did not have a vehicle (59% among poor black households), compared with 15% of white non-Hispanic households that lacked a vehicle.

3. President George W. Bush, for example, was widely criticized for asserting, "Brownie, you're doing a heck of a job," during a visit to tour Louisiana's damages, referring to Federal Emergency Management Agency (FEMA) director Michael Brown. Brown was widely criticized for his handling of Katrina and eventually resigned. http://www.whitehouse.gov/news/releases/2005/09/20050902-2.html DOR: 9-1-06.

4. This field is roughly grouped into the following categories: welfare implementation research that tracks policy and administrative outcomes and explores the institutional maneuvers that undergird citizenship, gender, and race in these agencies; comparative and historical welfare regimes; the evolution of U.S. welfare politics and state policy choices; public opinion toward the system and its recipients; the effectiveness of various welfare policies; and the everyday experiences of recipients. Blank and Ellwood

2002; Cherlin, Bogen, Quane, and Burton 2002; Ellwood 1988; Hancock 2004; Handler and Hasenfeld 1991; Hargen and Owens-Manley 2002; Katz 1996; Korteweg 2003, 2006; Mead 1997; Rank 1994; Riccucci, Meyers, Lurie, and Han 2004; Schram, Soss, and Fording 2003; Somers and Block 2005.

5. For more on the politics behind the passage of PRWORA, see DeParle 2004 and Haskins 2006.

6. PRWORA also replaced the Job Opportunities and Basic Skills (JOBS) training program. The 1998 Workforce Investment Act (WIA) replaced the Job Training Partnership Act (JPTA), consolidating and streamlining the nation's employment and training programs by allowing the federal government, states, and local communities to develop comprehensive systems to provide workers with job search assistance, training, and counseling services. In order to receive their block grants, states no longer have to "match" the federal contributions as was the case under the AFDC system. Rather, states and localities must spend a specified percentage of their block grants on "qualified state expenditures" (known as maintenance of effort), can keep the rest, and must pay for any cost overruns.

7. A June 2006 fact sheet produced by the Urban Institute comprehensively summarizes many of the national trends related to welfare reform. There was a decline in deep poverty (income below 50% of the federal poverty level) by 18 percentage points between 1997 and 2002. Child support receipt among low-income families is up (from 31% to 36% from 1996 to 2001 among poor children who are eligible, living with their mothers, and have fathers living elsewhere). There were also slight declines in the share of low-income children living in single-mother families between 1997 and 2002, following a pattern similar to what was happening for all children at that time. A larger proportion of children in low-income families were living in families with unmarried cohabiting partners (from 6% to 8% from 1997 to 2002) compared with the 48% share of low-income children living in married-couple families.

8. Many studies have examined exactly how reduced rolls and increased work among poor mothers across the country came about, evaluating the quantitative impacts of macro-level changes to welfare policy, the booming economy of the 1990s, the expansion of the Earned Income Tax Credit, and the increase in the minimum wage. Ziliak et al. 2000 conclude that the decline in per capita AFDC caseloads in the early to mid-1990s was attributable largely to the economic conditions in states and not to waivers from federal welfare policies. Nationwide, they attribute 66% of the caseload decline to the macro economy.

9. This merger of stricter behavioral rules and expansive administrative powers of enforcement was something that Mead had been calling for in prior years as a remedy for what he saw as the lack of work ethic and appropriate civic behavior among the poor (Mead 1992).

10. Many current and former welfare recipients work in low-wage jobs (often without employer-provided health benefits) and are very vulnerable to the fluctuations of the labor market. Further, significant barriers to employment are both apparent and hidden among many welfare recipients, such as the lack of a high school diploma or GED, poor physical and mental health, language barriers, very limited work histories, and the need to care for a child with disabilities (although the share of those reporting two or more barriers still worked in higher numbers after welfare reform). About a tenth of those that leave welfare report no working spouse, employment income, or other government benefits, raising questions about the experiences of those who are what the Urban Institute calls "disconnected." Mental and physical health problems are thought to account for much of this disconnection. The Urban Institute also reports a small but statistically significant increase in the number of children living without parents (4.7% to 5%).

11. In a study of low-income women subject to Michigan's "work first" program, Danziger and Seefeldt (2000) found that high percentages of unemployed respondents lacked transportation, had physical or mental health problems, or had been on welfare for five or more years—although these barriers were underestimated by "work first" program managers who were asked to identify the most common of their clients' barriers to employment. High levels of depression, drug and alcohol dependency, learning disabilities, and past and ongoing sexual, physical, and emotional abuse are just some of the issues that welfare observers have identified as critical contributors to the paralysis of many low-income families. Additional initiatives are also necessary, this group recommends, for welfare offices to offer better supports for the heads of poor families who are working and whose families no longer receive cash assistance.

12. Complicating the desire to offer generalizations about what is occurring in restructured welfare offices is the variation in different states and localities as each has adopted a distinct approach to reform, assembling different configurations of supports and penalties to assist clients and promote rule compliance. This has encouraged implementation researchers to speak in a language of qualified generalities, talking in broad strokes about what states are doing, but eventually situating their observations in a context of policy and environmental specifics.

13. This focus is due in part to the continuing emphasis on limiting errors in the federal food stamps program. There has been a long-standing quality control (QC) system operating in welfare offices whereby federal officials monitor over- and under-benefit payments and financially penalize states for making excessive errors. While the high level of federal oversight of individual cash benefit levels subsided with the advent of welfare reform, QC in the food stamp program is still very much in effect and continues to be monitored by the Department of Agriculture.

14. One of the most cited aspects of what was essentially a bifurcated social welfare system for decades is the way in which Social Security, at its inception, excluded domestic and agricultural workers from eligibility in order to appease white Southern cotton interests. This largely relegated black families to work for whatever wage they could get with few receiving pensions or disability protections under the Social Security system or the right to pursue benefits through the AFDC program (formerly known as Aid to Dependent Children). While the Social Security system was centrally administered at the federal level, and therefore thought to be less subjective and discriminatory, AFDC was a locally administered program with a number of provisions that relied on the subjective assessments of caseworkers. This localized administrative structure is widely thought to be a key mechanism through which racial discrimination proliferated in the welfare system for decades (Lieberman 1998).

15. For books on this subject, see Lurie 2006, Riccucci 2005, and Hays 2003.

16. I define both terms in more depth later, but the notion of socially situated bureaucrats is meant to highlight the subjectivities that give rise to a general framework through which bureaucrats approach their work. Catch-all bureaucracies are institutions whose work is intimately tied to responding to a variety of individual- and family-level issues and concerns that are directly or indirectly related to severe economic and social inequality.

17. The current work uses an analytic starting point similar to Maynard-Moody and Musheno's 2003 book *Cops, Teachers, and Counselors: Stories from the Front Lines of Public Service*. In it, the authors analyze the narratives of street-level bureaucrats in an effort to understand how they "make sense of their world and account for what they do" (9). Although my work ultimately offers a different explanation of that process, one that emphasizes social group membership in the formulation of professional identities, both *Cops, Teachers, and Counselors* and the present text are interested in discerning how employees interpret their professional roles in the face of institutional constraints.

18. Pseudonyms often sound contrived to the reader, but protecting the anonymity of my respondents was paramount. Therefore, while I identify the state in which this study was conducted in order to offer readers some sense of the political, social, and economic context in which this work is embedded, I assign pseudonyms to the offices, the towns in which they are located, and the employees within them. My sense of the "typicalness" of these offices was confirmed when reading other fieldwork-based accounts of welfare offices in different areas of the country. For example, Sharon Hays's description of a local outpost in a midsized town in the Southeast mirrors my own impressions of the Fishertown DTA office, "mimic[king] the style of the town in which it is located, offering the feel of community and of a place where people know and trust one another" (Hays 2003, 26).

CHAPTER ONE

1. The Department of Transitional Assistance has both male and female clients; however, because approximately 93% of the caseload household heads are female, I will use female pronouns throughout the book to refer to clients.

2. For more discussion on identity in organizations, see the special 2000 issue of the Academy of Management Review (vol. 25, no. 1).

3. By examining the transition of the Hungarian welfare system as the country moved from socialism to capitalism, Lynne Haney (2002b) explores how shifting conceptions of "need" over several decades were embodied in both social policies produced at the national level and institutional practices in local offices serving clients. Haney's "layered" approach, connecting discursive elements and redistributive policies produced at the national level to local implementation practices and distributed benefits, demonstrates how state actors from different locales in the state apparatus effectively co-create the conditions of redistribution and the meanings associated with them as a loosely coupled system. Haney offers a strong case for these layered, contextually based approaches: "While feminists who view the state as a policy regime are well positioned to illuminate who the state targets and its redistributive effects, they are less able to analyze gender as an interactive, negotiated process. While studies of national-level political struggle reveal how welfare politics are infused with gender meanings, they frequently miss the concrete manifestations of these constructions. And while accounts of welfare implementation expose the dynamics of caseworker/client interactions, they are ill-equipped to situate these local interactions in broader contexts" (15).

4. Early organizational sociologists that were influenced by the work of pioneers such as Max Weber and Robert Merton were, of course, among the first scholars to illuminate what were essentially catch-all bureaucracies. Peter Blau's (1960) work represents, for example, one of the first explorations of the orientations of caseworkers toward clients in public welfare agencies.

5. It is important to acknowledge that social work's interest in cultural competence signals an acknowledgment of the importance of race, ethnic, gender, and other social identities in not only the caseworker-client relationship but also in the attitudes that bureaucrats bring to the job. For examples, see Uttal 2006 and Dunn 2002.

6. Emphasis added.

7. Steven Maynard-Moody and Michael Musheno (2000) describe employee narratives gleaned from interviews as "highly textured depictions of practices and institutions" (29) where individual actions and motives are prominently featured. To be sure, narratives "do not assume that the stories are historically accurate accounts," although they might be (336).

Rather, narratives give us a sense of the norms and beliefs that drive social interaction. Another caveat that Maynard-Moody and Musheno cite is applicable here. These stories cannot help us understand the prevalence of a problem or issue: "Stories are biased toward the memorable and, therefore, the nonroutine and dramatic; they exaggerate the good and egregious and downplay the everyday" (336). The use of what amounts to participant narratives is also discussed by sociologist John Van Maanen (1979), who is noted for his in-depth studies of police officers: "The information as recorded by the fieldworker is then primarily talk, not only because this is what occupies the vast majority of the ethnographer's time but also because . . . understanding the concrete activities taking place in the field is grounded largely upon what members have to say about what such activities mean to them. Moreover, because the ethnographer focuses on both behavior and the symbolic worlds within which such behavior is located, the meaning and significance of the events of interest to one's informants can not be known merely by analyzing the number of times such events are observed to take place. . . . But, it is nonetheless true of fieldwork that when it comes to the events one's informants regard as significant, one must often lean far more on what one hears than on what one sees" (543).

8. Special operations workers included Employment Services Program (ESP) workers, technical support staff, and special investigations unit workers. Respondents were interviewed for approximately one to one-and-a half hours on a variety of topics, including but not limited to their work histories; how they came to work for the organization; attitudes about welfare and welfare reform; perceptions of clients; assessments of the transitions in their jobs and the office over the years; and their beliefs about how their racial, gender, and class backgrounds influence how they approach their work and are perceived within the organization. Interviewees were asked how they define their class, racial, and ethnic backgrounds, and subsequent discussions of the role that these social locations played in how they approached their jobs helped me to assess just how salient these identities seemed to be for interviewees in their everyday lives and work. Interviews were tape-recorded and transcribed. Each took place in an enclosed meeting room in the DTA office.

9. During this round in Staunton, I conducted interviews with fifteen staff members (two administrators, three supervisors, nine caseworkers, and one SO staff member). I had previously interviewed nine of these fifteen second-round respondents during the first round of data collection. In the Fishertown office, I interviewed eleven staff members (one administrator, three supervisors, five caseworkers, and two SO staff members). I had previously interviewed nine of these eleven second-round respondents. During both follow-up visits, I also conducted additional observations with several employees at each site. Initial interviews conducted between 2000

and 2001 allowed me to generate hypotheses and themes that I explored again during the second round of data collection in 2006 and 2007. I confirmed previously reported dynamics and interviewed institutional newcomers to determine whether what I had heard and seen had persisted in cases of staff turnover and other organizational changes. This kind of involvement also provided the opportunity to build the relationships necessary to encourage staff members to discuss organizational interactions that often took place under the radar of organizational leadership. The perhaps unusual nature of staff turnover in these offices—particularly the low numbers of new hires and the longevity of existing employee careers—helped to facilitate this follow-up and will be addressed in other chapters of book.

10. I deliberately reserved these interviews for the end of my fieldwork because I wanted to focus on capturing the experiences of caseworkers and supervisors from their vantage points, allowing my insights into their professional lives to evolve organically. As I was conducting my fieldwork, I wanted to come to know "central office" as the caseworkers had—as a distant entity that sent commanding orders from on high and turned out to indirectly contribute a great deal to the professional identities of street-level workers. In other moments, central office was remarkably absent from the process by which local office employees squared the work that they did within an immediate context of community concerns, personal histories and investments, and professional evolutions. When I eventually interviewed central office figures, not surprisingly I gained insights that challenged how many caseworkers and supervisors portrayed these high-level administrators; however, I also saw some of the ways these perceptions could have been formulated and become solidified over time.

11. For more content analysis of the conversations between caseworkers and clients, see Lurie 2006.

12. In January 2006, 39.3% of the office's caseload family heads were black, 37.3% Hispanic, 18.6% white, and 3.7% Asian. At that time, the office had eighteen white TANF caseworkers and supervisors, ten black caseworkers and two black supervisors, and nine Hispanic and three Asian caseworkers.

13. When I returned in 2006, Fishertown had gone from five to four units administering TAFDC (one of which is a two-caseworker teen parent unit).

14. The Emergency Aid to the Elderly, Disabled, and Children (EAEDC) program provides state-funded assistance to disabled adults who cannot access Social Security, caretakers of disabled individuals, elderly people awaiting federal funds or who are ineligible for Social Security, unrelated caretakers of children, children unable to receive TAFDC, and legal immigrants who do not qualify for TAFDC or SSI (Supplemental Security Income). Also, while TAFDC caseworkers oversee food stamp benefits for their clients, each local DTA office also maintains a cadre of workers who

administer the service to families who do not qualify for cash assistance. In recent years, the state launched an initiative to actively encourage families to apply for food stamps, sending advertisements written in English, Spanish, and other languages to radio, television, and print mediums and community-based social service agencies. This intervention was coupled with a reduction in the paperwork required to gain access to the program to make it more user-friendly.

15. In support of this effort, I did something about which I am sure ethnographers have differing opinions. I shared the entire manuscript with members of the DTA before it went to press. I offered this as a condition of my access, and the DTA accepted it as an opportunity to review what might be said about them. But I had other motives. Not only did this give-and-take relationship allow me to do some necessary fact checking on the intricacies of TAFDC policies, but I believe that it also set a tone of constructive feedback on both of our parts. I firmly believed throughout this project that while it was my responsibility to be critical and reveal the tensions and dilemmas embedded in the organization, giving my respondents the opportunity to see what I had written about them before it went to press would hopefully open up a dialogue rather than making them feel as though I was delivering a treatise in such a way as to limit their power (and buy-in) in the process. Upon the book's release, I did not want my respondents to be consumed with "damage control," feeling burned by someone who had come in and essentially offered up a "gotcha" exposé. Such tactics are often necessary to expose rampant and even criminal wrongdoing, but I did not feel such measures were warranted or necessary in this case. When respondents do not have opportunities to read and comment on what has been written about them before it goes to press, I believe that their focus has the potential to problematically move to a place of protecting institutional and professional reputations at all costs by disputing the analysis rather than accepting some of the offered prescriptions and taking seriously critiques in the spirit in which they were offered.

16. In my analysis of welfare offices, I sympathize with anthropologist Philip Bourgois's (1998, 1999) concern that one might, in fact, create policy prescriptions that "control" marginalized individuals even more than what they already experience (also see O'Connor 2001 for a similar critique of the poverty research community). In his work on intravenous drug users, Moore (2004) wrestled with this concern, attempting to bridge the divide between what many define as "applied, problem-oriented work commonly described as sociology in or for . . . policy versus highly theoretical research that explores the sociology of . . . policy" (1547, emphasis added). As Moore explains, "in the former, the aim is to employ sociological perspectives and methods in order to refine or improve . . . policy whereas, in the latter . . . policy itself—its theories, methods, and ideological

bases—becomes the object of inquiry. Those engaged in the analyses of . . . policy criticize those engaged in applied research for their collusion in expert-driven social control. The refinements or improvements made to . . . policy are portrayed as little more than new forms of governmentality. Those engaged in more applied . . . research sometimes characterize the 'of' research as being theoretically elegant but of little practical value" (1547–48). I agree with Moore's conclusion that his analytical goal is to present ideas that, in the words of Bourgois (1999), may "produce less social suffering." I borrow from both scholars' proposed remedy of explicitly linking a sociology of welfare offices with a sociology for welfare offices.

17. Department of Transitional Assistance website: www.ma.gov/dta. DOR 11-15-05.

18. Fishertown had stopped using the call number system by the time I did follow-up data collection in 2007 and now summons clients by name.

19. Although the rolls declined starting in the mid-1990s, a hiring freeze and several staff retirements kept worker caseloads high. When I went back for the second round of data collection in 2006 and 2007, caseworkers had an average of 140 cases each.

20. Pay stubs are critically important as they document wages and hours worked so that a caseworker can adjust a client's benefits, verify that she is meeting the work requirement, and continue approving her eligibility to receive day care.

21. Only office directors have completely enclosed workspaces. Supervisors' cubicles are enclosed in Plexiglas that extends from the floor to about two feet from the ceiling. Ironically, supervisors and directors have the least amount of client contact in their workspaces.

CHAPTER TWO

1. Employment and training programs to which recipients are sent by their TAFDC caseworkers offer job search, job training, and job readiness classes that usually include assistance with résumé and cover letter preparation, mock interviews, and sometimes even motivational-type training that focuses on "soft skills."

2. Two-parent households are eligible for benefits as long as their combined earnings fall below a financial threshold.

3. "Settled" cultures create continuities in style or ethos that permeate strategies of action. "Although internally diverse and often contradictory," Swidler (1986) contends, "[settled cultures] provide the ritual traditions that regulate ordinary patterns of authority and cooperation, and they so define common sense that alternative ways of organizing action seem unimaginable, or at least implausible" (284).

4. Multiple identities within individuals are organized into what organizational behaviorist Blake Ashforth calls a "hierarchy of salience." Those identities that fall highest in the hierarchy—reflected in actors' behaviors and views—most frequently speak to workers' *steady states*. Although workers might exhibit a variety of complex and at times contradictory behaviors to meet organizational expectations and to navigate constraints, steady states allow them to perform with some degree of consistency. It is the frequency of action, and the social meanings that individuals assign to these actions, which tells us something about their professional identities, approaches to the job, and organizational processes such as service delivery (Ashforth 2001).

5. This wasn't always the case. In the early years of welfare reform, interviewees reported that they often argued about whether they should buy in to the stated goals of welfare reform. When I studied them, however, workers had mostly come to accept the overall goals of the new policy regime. Of course, workers who strongly opposed the policy may have left, and it seems that many of the recent retirees indeed left happily because of the massive policy, technological, and administrative changes that were ushered in with welfare reform. But for the most part the attrition statistics suggest that many workers stayed working for the office.

6. Learnfare requires that children between the ages of five and eighteen listed under the TANF grant attend school. Should children not attend, the mother's portion of the grant is removed.

7. Clients whose youngest child in the grant was between the ages of two and five were limited to twenty-four months of benefits but not mandated to work or participate in a job program in the initial years of welfare reform in Massachusetts. That has since changed, and those clients are now mandated to engage in twenty hours of work-related activities per week.

8. Perhaps most notably, from the policy's inception, a very high percentage of the Massachusetts caseload has been exempt from the work requirements and time limits. A report by the Urban Institute put the percentages of TAFDC adult recipients exempt from work requirements at 92%, and 70% of the adult caseload was reportedly exempt from time limits in 2000 (Kaye et al 2001). A report issued by the Welfare, Children, and Families Three-City Study found that in 2004, 74% of the family caseload of 47,834 in Massachusetts was exempt from work requirements and time limits. "After Welfare Reform: A Snapshot of Low-Income Families in Boston." Welfare, Children, and Families Three-City Study; http://www.innovations .harvard.edu/showdoc.html?id=4909. DOR: 1-6-08. Although who makes up this percentage fluctuates as some parents become nonexempt once their children turn two, this is a much larger percentage than that permitted for states operating under federal guidelines, where only 20% of a state's

monthly caseload can be exempt from time limits (Urban Institute 2002). The mismatch between the federal participation requirements and the state's actual numbers did not come under heavy scrutiny until almost ten years into the Massachusetts program because the state was under a waiver and still significantly reduced caseloads, even receiving the federal caseload reduction credit.

9.   My interviews with administrators in the Staunton and Fishertown office in the early stages turned up few negative comments about the overuse of disability supplements by some of the workers. In fact, the vast majority of both offices' caseloads were exempt. Some of this was due to the age of the youngest child in the grant or other factors, but much of it was likely due to the use of disability supplements. As Massachusetts was not subject to the federal guidelines until almost ten years into welfare reform due to its waiver, administrators may not have felt pressure to curb this. In fact, Massachusetts's strong client advocacy community likely created an environment where officials erred on the side of leniency in this regard. Later, administrators described a desire to see more disabled clients pursue employment.

10. The program is also open to those caring for nonrelated disabled children or other disabled individuals.

11. But again, without systematically analyzing likely hundreds of interactions between caseworkers and clients, we must be cautious about such conjectures. Although future work can assess whether these differences are widespread and statistically significant, this chapter has highlighted the often unspoken differentiation that exists among workers and helps us to chart how workers' conceptions of their work likely influence multiple dynamics on the ground. In addition, without systematic data collected from clients over time on a range of outcomes, taking myriad other intervening factors into account and assuming that clients work with only one caseworker during their entire time on welfare (a scenario somewhat unlikely for a variety of reasons), we should be cautious about making the analytic leap by suggesting that one kind of professional identity is "better" or "more effective" than another. This study did not set out to determine whether having workers who see themselves as "social workers" or "efficiency experts" are best for the clients or the administration of policy in the long run. Moreover, the identity-shifting on the part of workers that is explored in the next chapter also means that we are well advised to use caution in considering the complications of conducting that kind of analysis. Rather, I was interested in how workers' professional self-conceptions—historically grounded, socially situated, and methodical—represent differing views of how best to help poor families. What this chapter demonstrates is that these varying models exist within the same agencies, are operationalized in different ways, and encourage bureaucrats to pull different

discretionary levers in ways that are often systematic and consistent with who workers believe themselves to be as professionals.

12. For a historical overview of this tension, see appendix A.

CHAPTER THREE

1. For more on this court case, see Tina Cassidy, "US Faults State, Says It Discriminated against 2; Cites Case Involving Impaired Women," *Boston Globe* (January 23, 2001), B1.

2. I will hereafter dispense with scare quotes to refer to caseworkers who see social work as an important dimension of their jobs and to differentiate them from the so-called efficiency engineers identified in the previous chapter, unless the context calls for a distinction between these would-be and actual social workers.

3. Also see Hasenfeld 2000.

4. Monet's boyfriend is not the father of her son, so he is not responsible for child support. Also, it is not against the rules of TAFDC for him to stay overnight.

5. Although Massachusetts was one of the first states to institute comprehensive reform, Wisconsin received more press and research attention. Under the leadership of Republican governor William Weld, Massachusetts applied for and received federal waivers in early 1995 to create a sweeping new state welfare program, approved through September 30, 2005, after a renewal was granted at the five-year mark. Earnings and asset disregards in Massachusetts are among the highest in the country, meaning that a larger portion of applicants' incomes are not counted when determining benefit levels, and recipients are permitted to keep more of their earnings while collecting benefits (Holcomb and Martinson 2002). Recipients in the state are permitted to own a motor vehicle with a fair market value up to $5,000 (up from a $1,500 equity value). Recipients are also allowed to have up to $2,500 in assets, up from $1,000 before reform. For those subject to the time limit, the policy disregards $30 and one half of earnings as long as recipients are earning up to $1,050 a month. The state significantly increased its spending on child care beginning in 1998, enabling a higher percentage of TAFDC recipients to access child care vouchers for up to twelve months after they no longer receive cash benefits if they are working or attending training programs. Massachusetts fully funds the supplemental food program for Women, Infants, and Children (WIC), the only state in the country to do so. MassHealth—a mixture of federally funded Medicaid, State Children's Health Insurance Program (SCHIP), and state funds—insures low-income adults and children, rendering just 3.4% of children in the state without health insurance in 1999, compared with the national average at that time of 12.5% (Kaye et al. 2001). Along with generous standards for eligibility, Massachusetts has tradition-

ally had some of the highest benefit levels in the country ($565 to $579 a month for a family of three in 1999). In fact, Massachusetts is one of only fourteen states that provides over $4,000 per family under its TANF block grant on average while eighteen others provide less than $2,000 per family. Block grant distributions are determined in part by the historical allocations that states have given to welfare recipients (Urban Institute 2002). Furthermore, the state policy allows recipients to pursue skills training and postsecondary education with greater ease than in many other states—in terms of both TANF program rules and the resources that it provides to clients toward such efforts. After receiving an additional one-year renewal, Governor Mitt Romney opted not to apply for another extension. As a result, the state adopted federal guidelines and is now more accountable to the welfare reform performance measures to which many other states have been subject since 1996.

6. Cellucci was acting governor from 1997 to January 7, 1999, and was elected in 1998 for a term beginning January 1999. http://www.mass.gov/lib/facts/governors.htm#present. DOR: 8-8-07.

7. See Hays 2003 for an analysis of how other welfare offices attempted to communicate this shift.

8. It should be noted that caseworkers were hired around the time of my second round of data collection. However, most were stationed in the food stamp program because caseloads are even higher there than in the TAFDC program.

9. Unlike other states that instituted diversion programs—offering one-time cash payments in exchange for not completing an application for TANF, sending applicants first to private agencies or other government programs such as SSI for help, or requiring proof of a job search and/or attendance at a work-focused orientation session prior to receiving cash assistance—Massachusetts allows immediate access to the rolls for applicants who meet the policy's financial and paperwork requirements. Caseworkers have twenty-eight days to authorize cash benefits, but the most efficient workers could have cash benefits and food stamps in the hands of applicants within days after they submit the necessary verifications.

10. In 2007, the central office was in the process of devising a client customer service survey that would be available in local offices and mailed to a representative sample of clients.

CHAPTER FOUR

1. See, for example, *Black Scholar* (2004, vol. 34, no. 4); Dyson (2004); and West (2004). Cosby has continued to make these critiques in various public addresses and media appearances. In 2007, he published a book with noted psychiatrist Alvin Poussaint, *Come on People: On the Path from Victims to Victors* (Nashville, Tenn.: Thomas Nelson Publishing).

2. In January 2006, 39.3% of the office's caseload family heads were black, 37.3% Hispanic, 18.6% white, and 3.7% Asian. At that time, the office had eighteen white TANF caseworkers and supervisors, ten black caseworkers and two black supervisors, and nine Hispanic and three Asian caseworkers.

3. All but one of the ten black respondents identified themselves as African American in interviews (the tenth is Trinidadian). Place of family origin is noted in the case of the seven Latino employees in this analysis, all of whom were first- or second-generation migrants from Puerto Rico or immigrants from Central or South America. None of the Latino respondents identified themselves as black Hispanics, and thus I describe respondents in this chapter as black *or* Latino.

4. My understanding of group solidarity is more politically inflected than the principle of homophily, the notion within organizational studies that "birds of a feather flock together" and social networks tend to be made up of people of similar races, ages, and other characteristics (McPherson, Smith-Lovin, and Cook 2001). Group solidarity also differs from in-group preferences in that the latter suggests the presence of preferential treatment, which does not universally apply to the descriptions that these workers are providing for how they relate to clients of their same race or ethnicity.

5. Kimberlé Williams Crenshaw (1991) is widely credited for introducing the term "intersectionality," positing that it "denote[s] the various ways in which race and gender interact to shape the multiple dimensions of Black women's employment experiences" (1244). Intersectionality of course encompasses many more social domains among its areas of interest, including families, politics, and public policy, while maintaining its central focus on the relationships among race, gender, and class. The majority of this work explores what Evelyn Simien describes as "the ways in which race and gender operate in tandem to produce and maintain the unequal distribution of power and privilege" (2007, 264). As both political project and intellectual intervention, researchers placed black women at the center of analyses in order to parse out the simultaneity of racial and gender oppression and what Patricia Hill Collins (2000) has called the "interconnections among systems of oppression" or "interlocking systems of oppression" (18). More recent work has gravitated toward a wider-ranging understanding of intersectionality, positing it as a "normative and empirical research paradigm rather than a content specialization" (Hancock 2007a, 249; McCall 2005). As such, any group can be the subject of an intersectional analysis, not solely black women or particularly marginalized groups. Leslie McCall (2005) describes intersectionality as encircling "the relationship among multiple dimensions and modalities of social relations and subject formations" (1771). Acknowledging an important intellectual, political, and often personal debt to previous intersectional

research coming out of women's, ethnic, and critical race studies—what Hancock (2007a) calls "rich, deeply nuanced examinations of groups and populations living at the marginalized crossroads of various categories of difference"—this perspective nevertheless pushes intersectionality to be more comprehensive (and potentially less political) in its approach to the relationship between social location and access (or lack thereof) to power, wealth, privilege, justice, and other resources.

6. The increasing incorporation of blacks and Latinos into government and quasi-government employment such as welfare administration complicates this issue even further. While introducing important but traditionally excluded actors into the implementation of public policy, the incorporation of blacks and Asians into social work by local authorities in the United Kingdom in the 1980s and 1990s, Gail Lewis argues, was done precisely because these agents would be expected to monitor and regulate black and Asian families who were constructed as "deviant," "pathological," and "dysfunctional" (2000). Placing black and Asian social workers in positions of "normalizing" and "moralizing" families of color, Lewis asserts, becomes positively classified within the field as a movement toward "ethnically sensitive" services. Even harsher critics (Reed 1999) contend that African Americans in public service are largely operating as cue takers from the policy priorities of the white majority and acting as complicit agents within bureaucracies of "race relations management."

7. 2001 dollars.

8. Carlos's specifying of "Anglo whites" is telling as well. He appears to want to differentiate this group from Hispanic whites, whom he arguably sees as part of his social group despite any differences on the basis of class, skin color, or country of origin that might exist.

9. Like their white co-workers, black and Latino workers have diverse educational backgrounds. Some have bachelor's degrees, while others have worked their way up in the organization by starting as data entry clerks with high school diplomas. Seniority and civil service exam scores, rather than educational credentials, put one in the running for supervisor positions, but interviews and the recommendations of past supervisors typically get one the job. Positions higher than supervisor typically rely even more heavily on those qualitative measures.

10. Collective memory contributes to some black bureaucrats' racially informed readings of the welfare system, creating another symbolic link between themselves and race-mate clients. The localized administration of welfare benefits allowed many communities over the years, particularly in the South, to prevent blacks and other racial minorities from gaining access to the rolls prior to the late 1960s (Neubeck and Cazenave 2001; Lieberman 2001). Constance therefore remembers the ways in which the system had for decades undermined the political rights and economic survival of other African Americans: "I'm originally from [the South],

from a very small town. When I was a child, I was not aware of welfare. I grew up in a time when segregation was big. I have heard my parents and older people say, 'Of course you weren't aware of welfare because you had to know somebody to be on welfare.' I don't mean you had to know somebody on welfare. I mean you had to know someone to get you on a state roll. Otherwise, they'd find a reason to turn you away. I knew poor people, but not people on welfare."

11. In this study, I rely heavily on frameworks initially developed to explain black politics because many of them appear to be pertinent to the Latino interviewees as well. However, I recognize that the experiences of black and Latino staff members in street-level bureaucracies are likely to differ because each group has a distinct history, a unique way that it was incorporated into government work, and variation in the amount of resistance that marked its entrance. Therefore, when appropriate and available, I incorporate literature that specifically addresses politics within Latino communities.

12. This didn't mean that Sharlene would allow someone to pull institutional levers with motives that she viewed as racist. She had the power to play the waiting game: "When she came in, I had her sit a little while . . . because, don't say that about the clerks. And then she came in, 'Oh, hi, Sharlene.' And I stood and said, 'Hi, how you doing?' but in the back of my mind I was like [makes gagging noise] but I didn't let her bring my evilness out." For Sharlene, her waiting game and unaffected air were subtle but crucial ways for her to regain her professional authority. Regardless of her race, her occupational status granted her the ability to not only control the terms of her interaction with this client but also to demand a level of respect in her dealings with whites.

13. This finding is reminiscent of Royster's (2003) study comparing the job acquisition strategies of black and white working-class men. She describes white teachers who adopted a differentiated approach to counseling white versus black students in a high-school training program. Yet the crucial difference here is that black and Latino bureaucrats did not appear to offer a different set of tangible resources such as leads on lucrative jobs in the way this occurred in Royster's analysis, nor can the interventions made by black and Latino bureaucrats with minority clients be deemed universally preferential treatment.

14. Unlike some other states, this state allows time-limited recipients, under certain conditions and within certain limits, to attend school for the first twelve months of their allocated twenty-four months of benefits.

15. Political scientist Katherine Tate writes: "Welfare mothers have long served as easy scapegoats, and this has been the case even in the black community. . . . While blacks had emphatically rejected the anti-welfare language of Ronald Reagan during the 1980s that included the stereotypical black 'welfare queen' who owned furs and drove Cadillacs, many in

the 1990s found persuasive the more subtle attack on black welfare *mothers* as irresponsible, who, instead of striving to provide for their children, were actually damning them to a lifetime of crime and welfare dependency" (1999, 355, emphasis added). Considering the increasingly conservative political attitudes of blacks toward the welfare system, as documented in Tate's analysis of the National Black Election Study (NBES), such reactions are perhaps not surprising (1999, 2003). There was, until late in the debate, minimal protest against welfare reform from top political and civil rights leaders that represented large constituencies of racial minorities. Barker, Jones, and Tate (1999) point out that "Congressional Black Caucus members voted overwhelmingly against the bill, and some condemned the legislation as a betrayal of core Democratic principles. But on the whole, public criticism was muted" (287).

16. Seeking to navigate oppressive white-dominated political, social, and economic structures and processes, the politics of racial respectability rely heavily on the modification and policing of individual behaviors and the promotion of mainstream norms and values within black communities in an effort to prove worthiness for social uplift and equality. These politics, scholars have pointed out, have historically focused on the social regulation of more economically and educationally disadvantaged race-mates by individuals who have the weight of private and public institutions behind them (Cohen 1999; Gaines 1996; Higginbotham 1993).

17. Previous sociological work suggests that many poor women have their own justifications for their decisions around motherhood, relationships, and work. For example, Edin and Kefalas (2005) suggest that many poor women believe that childbearing and rearing under extreme conditions of poverty provides opportunities to "prove their worth" and help turn their lives around, whether their children's fathers are available or not.

18. Other research suggests that many low-income mothers actually share these critical perceptions of welfare use, offer measured support for welfare reform, and focus their efforts on demonstrating, even if superficially, that their behavior falls within socially accepted norms (Hancock 2004; Hays 2003; Seccombe, James, and Walters 1998). There also seems to be an important generational component to these interactions. In 2006, the average age of agency employees was fifty-six years old. The average client was 26.2 years old. Timothy is alluding to the ways in which older clients might contest these more supervisory interventions.

19. Immigrant status may be another social location that complicates racialized professionalism. There is some evidence to suggest that recently arrived Latino immigrants do not hold the same views about the prevalence of racial discrimination as blacks and Latinos who have lived in the United Stats for longer periods of time (Domínguez 2008). I found few differences between the black and Latino bureaucrats in this study, yet this may be because most of the Latino respondents have been in the United

States for more than fifteen years. They are therefore more likely
to have experienced race-based discrimination and include it as a key
factor in describing their opportunities and experiences in the labor
market.

CHAPTER FIVE

1. The national unemployment rate rose to 4.7% in 2001. Current Population
Survey, United States Bureau of Labor Statistics, "Unemployment Data:
Civilian Labor Force." http://data.bls.gov/servlet/SurveyOutputServlet.
DOR: 2-7-03.

2. Current Population Survey, United States Bureau of Labor Statistics, "Unemployment Data: Civilian Labor Force, Massachusetts." http://data.bls
.gov/servlet/SurveyOutputServlet. DOR: 2-7-03.

3. Extremely low income was defined as earning $19,560 or less annually,
30% of the area median income of $65,200. *Out of Reach 2001: America's
Growing Wage-Rent Disparity,* National Low Income Housing Coalition.

4. There is reason to believe that area politics continue to play a role in both
the creation and implementation of state and local welfare policies. For
example, recent work finds that states and localities with the largest
concentrations of blacks on the welfare rolls tend to adopt the most punitive welfare policies and racial disparities in welfare service delivery
continue to be discovered (Soss et al. 2001; Gais and Weaver 2002;
Gooden 1998).

5. U.S. Census Bureau, "Profile of Selected Economic Characteristics: 2000."
http://factfinder.census.gov/ DOR: 1-29-03.

6. U.S. Census Bureau, Census 2000 Summary File 3, "DP-3. Profile of Se-
lected Economic Characteristics: 2000," matrices P30, P32, P33, P43, P46,
P49, P50, P51, P52, P53, P58, P62, P63, P64, P65, P67, P71, P72, P73, P74,
P76, P77, P82, P87, P90, PCT47, PCT52, and PCT53.

7. U.S. Census Bureau: State and County QuickFacts. Data derived from
Population Estimates, 2000 Census of Population and Housing, 1990
Census of Population and Housing, Small Area Income and Poverty Esti-
mates, County Business Patterns, 1997 Economic Census, Minority- and
Women-Owned Business, Building Permits, Consolidated Federal Funds
Report, Census of Governments. http://quickfacts.census.gov/ (full source
available on request). DOR: 9-1-07.

8. U.S. Census Bureau: State and County QuickFacts. Data derived from
Population Estimates, 2000 Census of Population and Housing, 1990
Census of Population and Housing, Small Area Income and Poverty Esti-
mates, County Business Patterns, 1997 Economic Census, Minority- and
Women-Owned Business, Building Permits, Consolidated Federal Funds
Report, Census of Governments. http://quickfacts.census.gov/ (full source
available on request).DOR: 9-1-07.

9. United States Census Bureau, 1990 Census. Database: C90STF1A.

10. U.S. Census Bureau, Census 2000 Redistricting Data (Public Law 94–171) Summary File, matrices PL1, PL2, PL3, and PL4. http://quickfacts.census .gov/(full source available on request). DOR: 9-1-07.

11. It is also important to note that many city leaders and observers of the migration trend theorized that families were moving into the city for a short time until housing became available in central cities, potentially underestimating the count of migrant families, and particularly minority families, in Fishertown over time.

12. Massachusetts Department of Transitional Assistance Caseload Statistics.

13. The Fishertown DTA office has one caseworker who serves the Portuguese-speaking caseload and one Spanish-speaking worker of Portuguese descent.

14. As Sharon explained:

   By the very nature of having just arrived in this country with no language skills, if they had job skills, they no longer had viable job skills—farmers, fishermen, or military people—and there just wasn't a big need for that in the area. So they did come on assistance. Many of them, who were probably more middle to upper class when they came here, went right into education, left the rolls, became advocates in the community, and opened up a lot of avenues. And the others had extremely large families in many cases and language barriers . . . some of them might have been older, not a lot of job skills. Many of them are still on the rolls, but many more of them got help from the resources that the more educated people from their country shared with them.

15. The 211 connection is a phone number that connects people to human services in the area. Callers can receive referrals and information on human services such as counseling, financial management, food, shelter, and affordable housing.

16. The discussion of urban newcomers as "aggressive" could be read as reminiscent of what Kinder and Sears (1981) call "symbolic racism," new stereotypes that have arisen in an era of expanded rights for people of color. Although views toward certain groups are less often expressed as arguments about inherent inferiority or in terms of overt support of segregation, other attitudes abound: blacks are described as pushy, pressing for illegitimate demands, and benefiting from overreliance on government. "Such symbolic racial beliefs," Schuman and Bobo (1988) write, "thus become the new basis for opposing implementation changes that benefit blacks" (275). Interestingly, between the first and second rounds of fieldwork, not only did workers express less antipathy toward blacks and Latinos moving into Fishertown but there were fewer instances of clients from larger cities being called "aggressive."

17. U.S. Department of Justice Bureau of Justice Statistics, www.ojp.usdoj .gov/bjs/ DOR: 12-29-07. Despite the migration, Fishertown's population remained close to ninety thousand between 1990 and 2005.

18. Other respondents were quite reticent to talk in the office about race or the migration of families, commenting that "it's not something that I've

noticed." This could certainly be the case, but such color blindness in an institution where these dynamics seem so salient to others does raise important questions about (a) whether respondents were opting not to engage in the debate for fear of its repercussions; (b) whether respondents were simply opting not to engage in the discussion with me; or (c) whether the migration truly was a nonissue for them.

19. This is not to suggest that race is inconsequential in Staunton. Not only did the black and Latino staff members in the previous chapter describe how race mattered both inside and outside the office, white and minority Staunton workers report that clients occasionally expressed that they expected a more favorable outcome if they or their caseworkers were of a different race. Part of the professional socialization process for these street-level bureaucrats therefore is to deflect such attempts to deploy race, a tactic considered a desperate move on the part of clients. Rhoda Anderson, a white caseworker in Staunton, has her scripted response at the ready: "I have heard clients say, 'Well, if I was black or foreign, I'd get all sorts of benefits and you're denying me those benefits and I'm a U.S. citizen or I'm white.' If they say that to my face, I look at them and I say, 'Ma'am, policy is policy, and it has nothing to do with race, sex, national origin.' And they'll say, 'Well, that's not fair because if I was black, I'd be getting . . .' and I look at them and I say, 'If you were black, you'd be getting exactly what you're getting now, because I'm following policy. Either you're eligible or you're not, based on policy. And it has nothing to do with race.'" Again, this has happened to black and Latino caseworkers as well. Each racial and ethnic group within the caseload seemingly held a perception of whom the welfare system favored, and they wanted their workers to turn the tables to their advantage.

CHAPTER SIX

1. This reference to Katrina is not meant to characterize welfare reform as a literal or figurative disaster. Welfare reform arguably has brought with it some desirable outcomes, both for individuals and for the system more generally. Moreover, where welfare reform has failed, it has not done so as spectacularly or with such devastating immediate effects as Katrina caused. But the economic hardships that were revealed during Katrina and its aftermath might be seen as evidence of the failure of welfare reform as well, insofar as the welfare system under reform was supposed to provide not only a temporary safety net for society's neediest people but also a route to economic stability that would allow people the resources to respond to such a crisis more effectively.

2. Institutional approaches in the vein of Philip Selnick's landmark *TVA and the Grass Roots* (1949) of course represented the movement of early organi-

zational sociologists toward a focus on the "macrosociological background structure behind firms" (Stinchcombe 1997) and the ways in which change processes could be thwarted by local politics, the vested interests of organizational actors, and unreconciled conflicts.

3. For more on the politics of the welfare system in general, see Abramovitz 1996; Piven and Cloward 1971; Neubeck and Cazenave 2001; and Hays 2003.

4. In a 1985 *Annual Review of Sociology* article, William Ouchi and Alan Wilkins point out that "the contemporary study of organizational culture appears to amalgamate several points of view, rather than to constitute one branch of a single disciplinary family of scholarship. There is no single dominant point of view or method but rather a rich mixture of ideas and of approaches" (459). More than twenty years later, this is still a fair characterization of the field.

5. This is distinct from self-defined subgroups that coalescence around a set of beliefs and practices that are distinct from the larger culture.

6. For more discussion of this point, see the symposium on professional and organizational identities published in the *Academy of Management Review* in 2000 (vol. 25, no. 1, p. 141).

7. Thomas's work on loose coupling and negotiated order is informed by the work of sociologists such as Anselm Strauss and Karl Weick. See also Zimmer 1987.

8. In the coming years, there will be a ratcheting-up of the focus on recipient employment, including finding ways to increase the number of adult caretakers required to work by limiting the number of exemptions given and encouraging job placements for exempt recipients. A letter from the state commissioner in 2004 written to a committee convened to evaluate the implications of the expiration of the federal waiver and the adoption of federal guidelines makes this clear. John Wagner writes, "Expanding the limited participation of the current program to a universal engagement model will be a significant challenge, but one that will help thousands of recipients move toward self-sufficiency, while aligning state policies with those of the federal government." Letter to Jeffery J. Hayward, vice president of public policy for the United Way of Massachusetts Bay, from John Wagner, commissioner of the Massachusetts DTA, November 4, 2004.

9. Of course stronger alignment between organizational goals and evaluation and reward structures is most beneficial when it is connected to well-thought-out policies. In the case of policies that are viewed as detrimental to clients on the ground, it may be helpful for workers to have the ability to subvert certain goals (Maynard-Moody and Musheno 2003).

10. The Massachusetts DTA has Employment Services Program (ESP) workers who presumably do some of this work. Under the earlier ET Choices program, they were the main employment support counselors for clients who expressed an interest in returning to work, but their responsibilities

were folded into the jobs of traditional caseworkers under welfare reform.
Although it would have been impossible for the three to five ESP workers
per office to provide the welfare-to-work services for the entire caseload
of work-required clients after 1995 reform, reducing their contact with
clients and effectively having them serve as consultants to caseworkers
removed from their jobs a critical feature of many of their skill sets—their
ability to communicate with, assess, and encourage clients. Later, their interactions with clients were increased as many were reassigned to be "full
engagement workers." Here, however, their responsibilities are largely to
hold orientations for large numbers of clients, reinforce the message that
they must return to work, and introduce them to the menu of job training
and placement programs in the area. The solution that I am proposing effectively restores the one-on-one interactive role that they once had with
clients and makes individual assessment, referral, and follow-up the main
thrust of what they do.

11. Employees' pay grades should reflect this level of skill and specialization.
An additional staff member could focus solely on building the network of
providers to which clients are referred for a variety of services, maintaining those relationships, gathering data from clients and caseworkers about
the strengths and weaknesses of these vendors, and communicating this
back to vendors so that changes can be made in a nimble way rather than
during the annual assessments conducted by the central office.

12. An ad hoc committee convened in 2004 to evaluate the implications of
the expiration of the federal waiver and the adoption of federal guidelines. Chaired by the vice president of public policy for the United Way
of Massachusetts Bay and Ed Sanders-Bay of the DTA, the group offered
up similar recommendations that the client assessment capabilities of the
office be expanded, although it failed to offer a comprehensive plan for
doing so (a similar point about the lack of an in-depth assessment plan
for clients was made in a dissenting comment submitted by the Massachusetts Immigrant and Refugee Advocacy Coalition). Welfare Reform Ad-
visory Committee, "A Report to the Commissioner of the Massachusetts
Department of Transitional Assistance: Recommendations Post-Waiver
and in Anticipation of the Reauthorization by the Congress of the United
States of the Personal Responsibility and Work Opportunity Reconciliation Act of 1996," November 2004. Departmental leadership responded
in kind by underscoring the importance of this issue. John Wagner, DTA
commissioner in 2004, makes this clear in a written response to the committee: "The recommendations of the Committee concerning assessments
for recipients are also illuminating. The themes of identifying necessary
supports at earliest opportunity, and searching for strengths, rather than
deficits, on the part of recipients, are ones that I fully support and intend
to work towards as we strive to adapt and improve the TAFDC program."
Letter to Jeffery J. Hayward, vice president of public policy for the United

Way of Massachusetts Bay, from John Wagner, commissioner of the Massachusetts DTA, November 4, 2004.

13. In the case of finding child care, for example, clients are often given a list of providers and perhaps a list of questions to ask providers. However, they are not told how to tailor questions to certain unique needs such as nontraditional work hours and finding additional child care for older children. Nor are families assisted in how to create ongoing relationships with these service providers so that mothers can constantly interface and negotiate with them in the face of work and other demands.

1. There are clearly historical exceptions where welfare recipients were able to agitate for policy and organizational changes in the system. See Nadasen 2005; Orleck 2005; Abramovitz 1999; Valk 2000; Kornbluh 2007.

2. This locally financed and administered structure was heavily influenced by the Elizabethan Poor Laws of 1601 (and their initial versions of 1597 and 1598), which refined the responsibilities of overseers of the poor in England and Wales and incorporated the "correction" of the poor into service provision. William Trattner (1999) writes that the poor laws in England "defined three major categories of dependents—children, the able-bodied, and the impotent—and directed the authorities to adapt their activities to the needs of each: for needy children, apprenticeship; for the able-bodied, work; and for the incapacitated, helpless, or 'worthy' poor, either home ('outdoor') or institutional ('indoor') relief" (11). This framework would influence U.S. models of poor relief starting in the colonial period.

3. Staff members within poorhouses were tasked with providing resources and supervision in an effort to "rehabilitate inmates," who were largely thought to be responsible for their own circumstances. Bad conditions inside—overcrowding, uncleanliness, health risks, poor management, inadequate funding, and a lack of both assistance and useful work for their residents—eventually led to a return to a focus on outdoor relief.

4. Other Progressive Era reformers focused on related issues such as the creation of Societies for the Prevention of Cruelty to Children and Children's Aid Societies, the replacement of institutional care for children with foster homes, the reformation of juvenile justice through the introduction of probation and juvenile courts, advocacy for mothers' pensions to provide a subsidy to families with dependent children but without an adult male income, and public health measures to reduce infant mortality and the rise of certain illnesses. These measures also signaled a focus on the professionalization of agency-based social welfare and human service work (Katz 1996).

5. For an in-depth accounting of these paths, see Katz 1996 and Trattner 1999.

6. Administered between 1911 and 1935, mothers' pensions had their roots in the juvenile court system, women's groups, and the Progressive Era. As a result, financial provision was coupled with a focus on monitoring mothers to ensure the safety and well-being of children. The administration of mothers' pensions was closely aligned with immigrant socialization as many officials in northern cities targeted poor southern and eastern European immigrant families for aid. As Linda Gordon (1994) points out, the award of aid allowed mothers' pensions officials to assist immigrant families with their "Americanization," which often meant the adoption of middle-class cultural habits and values. Social workers administering the pension system could penalize women for using a language other than English in the home, for failing to keep an orderly and clean home, for allowing relatives deemed unsavory to stay in their homes, or for living in objectionable neighborhoods. For more on the history and implementation of mothers' pensions, see Skocpol 1992; Katz 1996; Goodwin 1997; Gordon 1994; Orloff 1991.

7. As large numbers of men were able to access economic resources through Social Security, unemployment insurance, and General Assistance in some localities, the focus of most public welfare workers was almost exclusively on indigent women and children. Alice Kessler-Harris (2001) contends that by preventing welfare recipients from coupling work and welfare in the policy's early years, the system discouraged women's economic self-sufficiency through employment. By defining women as "family members" and white males as "workers," the state distributed or withheld social benefits such as welfare, unemployment insurance, old-age pensions, and worker protections in ways that created and sustained "the sexual division of labor; disparate wages for male and female jobs; the feminization of poverty; protective labor legislation for women only; [and] women's dependence on government welfare" (3). Programs that targeted recipients along gender lines provided unequal resources and opportunities. Kessler-Harris reminds us that while these policies and practices sustained a comforting vision of family life and social order by enforcing the notion of women as caretakers and men as economic breadwinners, they deprived women of economic equality, relegated them to dependency, and hindered their access to full citizenship. For additional feminist analyses of the development of the welfare system in the United States and its role in the shaping of service provision, see Abramovitz 1996; Gordon 1994; and Mink 1995.

8. Some states argued that unmarried mothers, by definition, could not provide morally suitable homes. In other states, having sexual relations with anyone other than one's legal spouse was deemed promiscuous, a violation of the stable moral environment key to a suitable home (Neubeck and Cazenave 2001).

9. In welfare's earliest years, southern Congressmen successfully resisted nationally set welfare standards that could have provided an alternative to

the desperately low wages that many of their constituents offered to the working poor. In addition, they were able to get agricultural and domestic work (populated mostly by blacks) excluded from eligibility in the early years of Social Security entitlements, leaving these workers to labor well into old age (Neubeck and Cazenave 2001; Lieberman 1998; Quadagno 1994).

10. The War on Poverty had several programs that were overseen by the Office of Economic Opportunity (OEO). They included the Job Corps; the Community Action Program, which funded local private or public agencies; Head Start; and the Volunteers in Service to America (VISTA) program. Federally administered War on Poverty initiatives included Medicaid and Medicare, expansions of Social Security, Title I of the Elementary and Secondary Education Act of 1965, the Neighborhood Youth Corps, loans to low-income farm families for business initiatives, and services for migrant farmworkers (Katz 1996).

11. For more on the role of paternalism in social welfare work, see Stone 1977 and Ryan 1971. Both authors highlight the ways in which social welfare work in street-level bureaucracies is organized in a way that focuses on trying to change clients and help them adjust to their life circumstances rather than seeking to change external factors that may contribute to or even produce their conditions.

12. Several states abolished residency requirements prior to 1969. See Trattner 1999.

13. Handler and Hollingsworth (1971) also point out that partly because of high worker turnover and large caseloads, home visits were often infrequent, brief, and often performed by many different caseworkers in the span of a client's welfare spell. See also Kane and Bane 1994; Katz 1996.

14. Nadasen is quoting Brumm 1968 here.

15. Community activists also participated in efforts at the federal, state, and local levels to challenge government policies that indirectly curbed access to resources or subjected women to high levels of surveillance in local offices. For historical overviews of these protest efforts, see Orleck 2005, Nadasen 2005, and Piven and Cloward 1971.

16. Because state and federal welfare manuals were often written in extensive and often confusing ways, recipients were at the mercy of caseworkers to tell them the rules. However, in some areas, welfare rights organizations created simplified manuals.

17. The levers of government worked very differently for blacks throughout much of the twentieth century, and they struggled to make inroads to shape social policies and services on the local, state, and national levels. There were some exceptions. "In Chicago," Linda Gordon writes, "white settlement and charity workers joined black reformers in campaigning for public services for dependent children, establishing the Chicago Urban League, and responding to the 1919 race riot" (1991, 564). African Ameri-

can nurses pushed to expand eligibility for mothers' pensions, a forerunner to the Aid to Dependent Children program that provided a subsidy to families with children without an adult male income between 1911 and 1935 (O'Donnell 1994). African American campaigning also contributed to the formation of the Office of Negro Health and Work in the United States Public Health Service (Gordon 1991).

18. The quote originally appeared in E. K. Jones, "Social Work among Negroes," *Annals of the American Academy of Political and Social Science* 140 (1928): 264–71.

19. Racial discrimination in employment was rampant at this time and African Americans were left to rely heavily on the personal service industry for work, which was vulnerable to the whims of whites and economic downturns. As a result, abject poverty was a way of life for many African Americans and led to their disproportionate representation on the relief rolls in areas where they could gain access. "In 1931," Sandra O'Donnell writes, "African Americans made up 6.0 percent of Chicago's population but fully half of the population on relief rolls" (2001, 459).

20. Some saw black social workers as uniquely qualified to serve black clients and teach and supervise other black professionals. Although recognizing the importance of interracial efforts, the coalitions of black and white social reformers in Georgia emphasized the unique role that black caseworkers could play in addressing many of the challenges facing black communities. Others saw the practice of segregating work as racist and one-sided. It was assumed that white clients would be humiliated, and possibly become violent, if black workers were administering their cases, and most offices acquiesced to this belief (Wilkerson-Freeman 2002). Yet black cases were routinely handled by whites, and rampant discrimination through the denial of benefits and the disparate enforcement of rules was routine in welfare offices throughout the twentieth century (Neubeck and Cazenave 2001; Piven and Cloward 1971; Lieberman 1998; Bell 1965).

21. See also Gooden 1995.

22. As black workers struggled for professional legitimacy within these mainstream institutions, the criticism of these agencies did not come solely from whites. Even Mary McCloud Bethune, perhaps the most historically celebrated of African American human service agents as Franklin Delano Roosevelt's director of the National Youth Administration's Division of Negro Affairs, had to navigate a difficult institutional terrain. Likely summing up the experiences of blacks in the hierarchy of social welfare institutions, Desmond King writes, "An African American employee in Bethune's position had herself to maintain a difficult balance between satisfying Black Americans who looked to her as a defender of their interests and her immediate (white) colleagues by whom she had been appointed and with whom she had to work" (1999, 367).

23. These caseworkers represented, according to Nadasen (2005), a "significant minority" during the activism of the 1960s. Just six years before Lucy's entrance into welfare services, welfare workers represented by the Social Service Employees Union in New York went on strike for improvements for themselves and their clients.

24. Of course, social work has been embroiled for decades in its own battles over professional legitimacy and identity. A central question has been the degree to which social work should emphasize social activism and reform, therapeutic intervention, or assisting clients with navigating their communities in order to access resources. For overviews of these debates, see Ehrenreich 1985; Katz 1996; and Trattner 1999.

25. My description of the transformation in welfare casework in the 1970s and 1980s is based largely on Kane and Bane (1994) as well as Brodkin (1986). However, Brodkin (1997) disputes Bane and Ellwood's (and Kane and Bane's) point in *Welfare Realities* that changes throughout the 1970s eliminated discretion. She argues that discretion is inherent in welfare delivery, even in the most apparently rule-bound system. Brodkin points out that discretion is neither good nor bad but contingent on contextual conditions. It can free street-level bureaucrats and administrators from red tape, or it can be used to discriminate and offer preferential treatment, as Handler and Hollingsworth (1991) argue.

26. Katz (1996) highlights several reasons for what he calls the "war on welfare." First, economic turmoil—rising inflation, high unemployment, and oil shortages—raised anxiety about downward mobility and challenged the assumption of a permanent abundance of public resources to absorb and resolve social problems. Second, a rise in women's labor force participation led to hard questions about why welfare recipients should be permitted to stay at home with their children while many working and middle class mothers were at work. Third, the assumption that voluntarism and the nonprofit sector would replace and improve upon federal government services if public-sector resources were reduced fueled former President Reagan's anti-welfare-state policies in the 1980s. Evelyn Brodkin (1986) highlights important assumptions that also strengthened the case for such a move. First, it was thought that welfare recipients would cheat the system or be slow to point out errors that worked in their favor, so reform needed to take place at the administrative level to ensure accuracy. Second, conservatives blamed caseworker discretion and their heavy involvement in clients' lives for the explosion in the welfare rolls in the 1960s and sought to restructure that relationship. See Handler and Hollingsworth (1971) for more on this point. On the other hand, the changes to casework received support from liberals as well. The National Welfare Rights Organization and many of its local chapters largely viewed home visits as an imposition rather than as a service. These groups wanted to see fewer "diagnoses" of the perceived moral and social deficiencies that

supposedly kept people poor and more inroads toward addressing their monetary needs through a set of standardized procedures (Nadasen 2005). The change to a more bureaucratized structure for service delivery likely served as a partial remedy to discrimination in welfare service delivery by reducing a great deal of caseworker discretion. State-to-state variation notwithstanding, individual workers could no longer selectively wield rules as easily or use their power to allocate different benefit amounts in the same office to families of the same size with the same income.

27. The notion of welfare workers as guardians of the public purse is taken from Corbett (1995).

28. The Comprehensive Employment and Training Act (CETA) served as the vehicle through which an additional wave of my respondents came to work for the department. Enacted by Congress in 1973, CETA was designed to provide unemployed, underemployed, and disadvantaged individuals with job training and placement in the public sector. The CETA program (which was later replaced by the 1982 Job Training Partnership Act) brought together welfare recipients, disadvantaged youths, and unemployed older adults to access state and locally subsidized jobs that were funded in part through a federal block grant.

29. Catherine Kingfisher (1996) makes a similar observation about the "trapped" status of both clients and caseworkers in the welfare system. Nevertheless, it is important to note that long-term association with one employer is how many American workers of Sundra's generation conceptualized work. This trend has changed among later cohorts of workers.

30. For an extensive overview of the history of Massachusetts welfare reforms, see Peck 1998. In the article, Peck connects the roots of the federal and Massachusetts welfare reforms of the mid-1990s to initiatives that began in the previous decade and outlines a diffusion process whereby "reform strategies, mechanisms, and policies [flowed] both vertically, between federal and state levels, and horizontally, among the states themselves" (71). Along with benefit cuts and eligibility restrictions, the Reagan administration's 1981 Omnibus Budget Reconciliation Act expanded the scope of state and local discretion to conduct reform experiments via local demonstration projects that introduced various combinations of work, training, and community service requirements into the welfare system. After conservative Democratic governor Edward J. King launched a Work and Training Program (WTP) with aggressive work requirements in Massachusetts that would prove unsuccessful, his successor Michael Dukakis (who was first unseated in 1978 by King and then elected again to the governorship in 1982) ushered in the Massachusetts Employment and Training (ET) Choices program in 1983. The program was voluntary and provided a service-intensive approach that initially saw a reduction in the rolls and increased work among participants, but it proved quite costly to run and was criticized as a program whose successes were largely attributable to

a booming economy. The Family Support Act of 1988 brought workfare to the federal level under the Job Opportunities and Basic Skills (JOBS) program. The mandatory work provisions of the FSA were weakly enforced at the local level, however, and rising rolls at the state and federal levels created increased momentum to move to a tougher mandatory work program that was not as service intensive as initiatives such as ET Choices strove to be.

31. As Bane and Ellwood (1994) point out, when clients did express interest in work, they often presented a challenge to the bookkeeping system, which tended to treat welfare and work as mutually exclusive.

32. For more on the importance of the political role of experimental welfare pilot programs in shaping the 1996 welfare reform, see Rogers-Dillon 2004. In it, the author argues that the existence of these pilot programs helped to define policy ideas related to welfare reform and set the terms of the ensuing political debate. They also structurally changed the welfare service-delivery apparatus in the states in ways that broke down many institutional barriers to reform.

33. Rather than implementing the federal sixty-month lifetime limit that would become standard in states across the country, Massachusetts instituted a twenty-four-month time limit within a sixty-month period in December 1996. In other words, instead of providing five years of benefits over a recipient's lifetime, the state restricts her to twenty-four months of cash benefits within each five-year span. During the first round of data collection in 2000–2001, Massachusetts implemented its "work first" emphasis by requiring nonexempt parents whose youngest child in the grant was school age or older to work twenty hours per week during their entire twenty-four-month benefit allotment, with the first sixty days allowed for a job search. Recipients whose youngest child in the grant was between the ages of two and five were time-limited but only strongly encouraged rather than required to participate in a job search or training program. Those whose youngest child in the grant was under the age of two were exempt from work requirements and time limits until the child turned two. During the 2004 state fiscal year, the almost ten-year-old policy changed by extending the twenty-hour-a-week work requirement to parents with children between age two and school age. However, these parents could participate in education or training programs to fulfill this requirement. The state fiscal year 2005 budget expanded work require-ments again, and these mandates were in place during the second round of data collection and at press time. Recipients whose youngest child in the TAFDC grant is between the ages of six and eight are now mandated to work twenty-four hours per week, and those whose youngest child in the TAFDC grant is nine years of age or older are required to work thirty hours per week. Work hours remain twenty hours a week for parents whose youngest child is between two and five, and those whose youngest

child in the grant is under two years of age remain exempt from the work requirement (although there has been talk of limiting exemptions to parents whose youngest child in the grant is less than one year old). That year also saw an expansion of the activities that count toward the work requirement to include education and training for up to twelve months and housing searches for homeless recipients. Other work activities continue to count, such as paid work, community service or internships at public or nonprofit agencies, college work study, providing child care for a recipient subject to work or teen parent school requirements, substance abuse program participation at a residential treatment site, job search during the last three months of time-limited benefits, and participation in a DTA-funded work program. Employment and training services are supplied by a network of providers who regularly contract with the DTA and include one-stop career centers; agencies offering basic and structured job search classes, skills training, teen parent programs, and twenty-hour-a-week community service assignments for those unable to find work; community colleges and GED programs; and municipalities offering subsidized transportation for clients returning to work. Massachusetts also offers a subsidized Full Employment Program, but participation in these programs is low for various reasons (Wen 2007). Subsequently, most clients work in unsubsidized jobs or are given community service assignments. Those exempt from both work requirements and time limits include disabled parents; parents caring for a disabled child or spouse; parents with a child receiving benefits who is under the age of two; those in their third trimester of pregnancy; parents with any child under three months (regardless of whether the child is on the benefit grant); parents under twenty attending high school; those sixty years of age or older; and relatives who care for a child receiving TAFDC who are not on the grant themselves. Although Massachusetts's waiver expired by my second round of fieldwork, officials still ran the TAFDC program using the old law.

34. Sanctions in Massachusetts are initially applied against the parent's portion of the grant and then expand to include the children's portion of the grant if the sanction is not "cured" by engaging in certain behaviors for two weeks, such as attending a training program. Massachusetts is one of only twelve states that lifts sanctions in a relatively short time after recipients become compliant, rather than applying months long or even permanent sanctions. The state also requires that recipients show evidence that their children have been immunized, and it will remove or reduce the parental portion of the grant if verification is not provided, since immunization is required by the Massachusetts schools. Parents and then children can also have their portions of the grant reduced if children under the age of fourteen receive unexcused absences from school over the three-month allotment (Learnfare). Clients with outstanding warrants are ineligible for

benefits, and the department recoups money through recipients' wages or future benefits and/or disqualifies them from receiving benefits in cases of fraud.

35. The state has several local DTA office outposts that administer TAFDC, EAEDC, and food stamps, each of which reports to one of four regional directors located at the central office headquarters in Boston. Caseworkers are responsible for educating applicants about the department's programs and indicating whether and how clients can receive benefits; approving recipients' receipt of cash benefits, child care, transportation assistance, and food stamps; tracking compliance with program rules (including work hours and training program attendance); issuing and lifting sanctions for noncompliance; determining exemptions from work requirements and time limits; and accepting requests for extensions to benefit time clocks (and forwarding those requests to the office administrator who ultimately makes these decisions). These same workers are also expected to engage in both immediate triage and ongoing coaching and assessment in order to identify employment-related goals with each client, assemble a set of services to help them pursue those goals, and offer encouragement and problem-solving as clients navigate these plans (keeping in mind each client's unique attributes, skills, interests, barriers, and concerns). Caseworkers are also responsible for identifying and helping clients address barriers such as learning, mental, and physical disabilities; limited English proficiency; drug and alcohol problems; domestic violence situations; and child care and transportation issues that may hinder employment. This includes connecting clients to the web of community-based programs in their area; helping them find employment, job training, child care, and other services; and even providing motivational coaching to encourage clients to engage in desired behaviors. Employment Services Program (ESP) workers, who used to provide these employment-focused services before welfare reform, now serve in a support role: authorizing childcare services, helping caseworkers identify transportation and other work-related resources for clients, assisting with the department's computer system, serving as language interpreters, and working on any other problems or issues on an "as needed" basis.

APPENDIX C

1. Of course, all of this work was taking place around the time that sociologists were also increasingly conducting in-depth case studies of for-profit institutions as well. See Morrill and Fine 1997 for a review of this early work.

2. Morrill and Fine describe this as the point at which the researcher feels that she has "enough insight into the scene that data collected are unsurprising and redundant" (1997, 442).

3. Giddens (1993) calls this the "double hermeneutic" in social science and Van Maanen (1979) refers to this connection as "first- and second-order concepts" in ethnography.

4. Morrill and Fine describe member checks as instances whereby "an ethnographer asks participants to assess the plausibility of the ethnographer's interpretations and conclusions. The recognition by members of a setting that an ethnographer's interpretations are plausible reconstructions of the members' own experiences enhances the authenticity of an ethnography and helps to control for research bias" (1997, 440).

5. Hammersley and Atkinson (1995) highlight these processes as key validating criteria for ethnographic research.

Works Cited

Abramovitz, Mimi. 1996. *Regulating the Lives of Women: Social Welfare Policy from Colonial Times to the Present.* Boston: South End Press.

———. 1999. *Under Attack, Fighting Back: Women and Welfare in the United States.* New York: Monthly Review Press.

———. 2001. "Learning from the History of Poor and Working-Class Women's Activism." *Annals of the American Academy of Political and Social Science* 577:118–30.

Acker, Joan. 2006. "Inequality Regimes: Gender, Class, and Race in Organizations." *Gender and Society* 20, no. 4: 441–64.

Addams, Jane. [1902] 2002. *Democracy and Social Ethics.* Chicago: University of Illinois Press.

Aiken, Michael, and Jerald Hage. 1966. "Organizational Alienation: A Comparative Analysis." *American Sociological Review* 31, no. 4: 497–507.

Albert, Stuart, Blake Ashforth, and Jane Dutton. 2000. "Organizational Identity and Identification: Charting New Waters and Building New Bridges." *Academy of Management Review* 25, no. 1: 13–17.

Albert, Stuart, and D. A. Whetten. 1985. "Organizational Identity." In *Research in Organizational Behaviour, Volume 7,* ed. L. L Cummings and B. M. Staw, 263–95. Greenwich, Conn.: JAI Press.

Anderson, Elijah. 1999. "The Social Situation of the Black Executive: Black and White Identities in the Corporate World." In *The Cultural Territories of Race: Black and White Boundaries,* ed. Michele Lamont, 3–29. Chicago: University of Chicago Press.

Anderson, Erin, and Jerry Van Hoy. 2006. "Striving for Self-Sufficient Families: Urban and Rural Experiences for Women in Welfare-to-Work Programs." *Journal of Poverty* 10, no. 1: 69–91.

Ashforth, Blake. 2001. *Role Transitions in Organizational Life: An Identity-Based Perspective*. Mahwah, N.J.: Lawrence Erlbaum Associates.

Ashforth, Blake, and Fred Mael. 1989. "Social Identity Theory and the Organization." *Academy of Management Review* 14, no. 1: 20–39.

Austin, Michael. 2004. *Changing Welfare Services: Case Studies of Local Welfare Reform Programs*. New York: Haworth Social Work Practice Press.

Bane, Mary Jo, and David Ellwood. 1994. *Welfare Realities*. Cambridge: Harvard University Press.

Barker, Lucius J., Mack H. Jones, and Katherine Tate. 1999. *African Americans and the American Political System*. 4th ed. Englewood Cliffs, N.J.: Prentice-Hall.

Barnett, William P., James N. Baron, and Toby E. Stuart. 2000. "Avenues of Attainment: Occupational Demography and Organizational Careers in the California Civil Service." *American Journal of Sociology* 106, no. 1: 88–144.

Barnum, Phyllis, Robert C. Liden, and Nancy DiTomaso. 1995. "Double Jeopardy for Women and Minorities: Pay Differences with Age." *Academy of Management Journal* 38, no. 3: 863-80.

Beckerman, Adela, and Leonard Fontana. 2001. "The Transition from AFDC to PRWORA in Florida: Perceptions of the Role of Case Managers in Welfare Reform." *Journal of Sociology and Social Welfare* 28:29–48.

Bedolla, Lisa Garcia. 2007. "Intersections of Inequality: Understanding Marginalization and Privilege in the Post–Civil Rights Era." *Politics and Gender* 3, no. 2: 232–48.

Beer, M., R. A. Eisenstat, and B. Spector. 1990. "Why Change Programs Don't Produce Change." *Harvard Business Review* (November–December): 4–12.

Behr, Joshua G. 2000. "Black and Female Municipal Employment: A Substantive Benefit of Minority Political Incorporation?" *Journal of Urban Affairs* 22, no. 3: 243–64.

Bell, Ella L. J. E., and Stella M. Nkomo. 2001. *Our Separate Ways: Black and White Women and the Struggle for Professional Identity*. Cambridge: Harvard Business School Press.

Bell, Winifred. 1965. *Aid to Dependent Children*. New York: Columbia University Press.

Blank, Rebecca, and David T. Ellwood. 2002. "The Clinton Legacy for America's Poor." In *American Economic Policy in the 1990s*, ed. Jeffrey A. Frankel and Paul Orszag, 25–50. Cambridge: MIT Press.

Blank, Rebecca, and Ron Haskins. 2001. *The New World of Welfare*. Washington, D.C.: Brookings Institution.

Blau, Peter M. 1960. "Orientation towards Clients in a Public Welfare Bureaucracy." *Administrative Science Quarterly* 5, no. 3: 341–61.

———. [1962] 1972. *The Dynamics of Bureaucracy: A Study of Interpersonal Relations in Two Government Agencies*. Rev. ed. Chicago: University of Chicago Press.

Blumer, Herbert. 1969. *Symbolic Interactionism: Perspective and Method.* Berkeley: University of California Press.

Bobo, Lawrence, and Camille Charles Zubrinsky. 1996. "Attitudes on Residential Integration: Perceived Status Differences, Mere In-Group Preference, or Racial Prejudice?" *Social Forces* 74, no. 3: 883–909.

Bourgois, Philip. 1998. "The Moral Economies of Homeless Heroin Addicts: Confronting Ethnography, HIV Risk, and Everyday Violence in San Francisco Shooting Encampments." *Substance Use and Misuse* 33:2323–51.

———. 1999. "Theory, Method, and Power in Drug and HIV Prevention Research: A Participant-Observer's Critique." *Substance Use and Misuse* 34:2155–72.

Boyd, Michelle. 2006. "Defensive Development: The Role of Racial Politics in Gentrification." Unpublished manuscript, Department of African American Studies, University of Illinois at Chicago.

Brinkley, David. 2007. *The Great Deluge: Hurricane Katrina, New Orleans, and the Mississippi Gulf Coast.* New York: Harper Perennial.

Brodkin, Evelyn. 1986. *The False Promise of Administrative Reform: Implementing Quality Control in Welfare.* Philadelphia: Temple University Press.

———. 1997. "Inside the Welfare Contract: Discretion and Accountability in State Welfare Administration." *Social Service Review* 71, no. 1: 1–33.

Brown, Michael K. 1999. *Race, Money, and the American Welfare State.* Ithaca: Cornell University Press.

Brubaker, Rogers, and Frederick Cooper. 2000. "Beyond 'Identity.'" *Theory and Society* 29, no. 1: 1–47.

Brumm, Gordon. 1968. "Mothers for Adequate Welfare—AFDC from the Underside." In *Dialogues Boston* (January): 1–12. William Howard Whitaker Papers, Ohio Historical Society, Columbus, box 3, folder 3.

Burawoy, Michael. 1991. "Reconstructing Social Theories." In *Ethnography Unbound: Power and Resistance in the Modern Metropolis,* ed. Michael Burawoy, Alice Burton, Ann A. Ferguson, Kathryn J. Fox, Joshua Gamson, Nadine Gartrell, Leslie Hurst, Charles Kurzman, Leslie Salzinger, Josepha Schiffman, and Shiori Ui, 8–27. Berkeley: University of California Press.

Burbridge, Lynn C. 1994. "The Reliance of African-American Women on Government and Third-Sector Employment." *American Economic Review* 84, no. 2: 103–7.

Burke, W. W. 1995. *Organizational Development: A Process of Learning and Changing.* 2nd ed. Reading, Mass.: Addison-Wesley.

Campbell, Elaine. 1999. "Towards a Sociological Theory of Discretion." *International Journal of the Sociology of Law* 27:79–101.

Carby, Hazel. 1992. "Policing the Black Woman's Body in an Urban Context." *Critical Inquiry* 18, no. 4: 738–55.

Cerulo, Karen. 1997. "Identity Construction: New Issues, New Directions." *Annual Review of Sociology* 23:385–409.

Cherlin, Andrew J., Karen Bogen, James M. Quane, and Linda Burton. 2002. "Operating within the Rules: Welfare Recipients' Experiences with Sanctions and Case Closings." *Social Service Review* 76:387–405.

Chong, Dennis, and Reuel Rogers. 2005. "Racial Solidarity and Political Participation." *Political Behavior* 27, no. 4: 347–74.

Cohen, Cathy J. 1999. *The Boundaries of Blackness: AIDS and the Breakdown of Black Politics.* Chicago: University of Chicago Press.

Collins, Patricia Hill. 2000. *Black Feminist Thought: Knowledge, Consciousness, and the Politics of Empowerment.* New York: Routledge.

Collins, Sharon. 1983. "The Making of the Black Middle Class." *Social Problems* 30, no. 4: 369–82.

———. 1997. *Black Corporate Executives: The Making and Breaking of a Black Middle Class.* Philadelphia: Temple University Press.

Combahee River Collective. 1982. "A Black Feminist Statement." In *All the Women Are White, All the Blacks Are Men, But Some of Us Are Brave,* ed. Gloria Tull, Patricia Bell Scott, and Barbara Smith, 13–22. New York: Feminist Press.

Combs, Gwendolyn. 2003. "The Duality of Race and Gender for Managerial African American Women: Implications of Informal Social Networks on Career Advancement." *Human Resource Development Review* 2, no. 4: 385–405.

Corbett, Thomas. 1995. "Changing the Culture of Welfare." *Focus: A Newsletter of the Institute for Research on Poverty* (University of Wisconsin—Madison) 16, no. 2: 1–15.

Cosby, Bill. 2004. "Remarks at Fiftieth Anniversary Commemoration of the *Brown v. Topeka Board of Education* Supreme Court Decision." *Black Scholar* 34, no. 4.

Crenshaw, Kimberle. 1991. "Mapping the Margins: Intersectionality, Identity Politics, and Violence against Women of Color." *Stanford Law Review* 43, no. 6: 1241–99.

Crozier, Michel. [1954] 1964. *The Bureaucratic Phenomenon.* Chicago: University of Chicago Press.

Danziger, Sandra, Jodi Sandfort, and Kristin Seefeldt. 1999. "What FIA Directors Have to Say about Welfare Reform." *Policy Brief,* University of Michigan Program on Poverty and Social Welfare Policy.

Danziger, Sandra, and Kristin Seefeldt. 2000. "Ending Welfare through Work First: Manager and Client Views." *Families in Society* 81:593–604.

———. 2003. "Barriers to Employment and the 'Hard to Serve': Implications for Services, Sanctions, and Time Limits." *Focus* 22:76–81.

Davis, Angela. 1981. *Women, Race, and Class.* New York: First Vintage Books.

Dawson, Michael. 1995. *Behind the Mule.* Princeton: Princeton University Press.

Denison, Daniel R. 1996. "What Is the Difference between Organizational Culture and Organizational Climate? A Native's Point of View on a Decade of Paradigm Wars." *Academy of Management Review* 21, no. 3: 619–54.

DeParle, Jason. 2004. *American Dream: Three Women, Ten Kids, and a Nation's Drive to End Welfare.* New York: Penguin Books.

Dhingra, Pawan. 2007. *Managing Multicultural Lives: Asian American Professionals and the Challenge of Multiple Identities.* Stanford: Stanford University Press.

DiTomaso, Nancy, Corinne Post, and Rochelle Parks-Yankee. 2007. "Workforce Diversity and Inequality: Power, Status, and Numbers." *Annual Review of Sociology* 33:473–501.

DiTomaso, Nancy, and Steven A. Smith. 1996. "Race and Ethnic Minorities and White Women in Management: Changes and Challenges." In *Women and Minorities in American Professions,* ed. Joyce Tang and Earl Smith, 87–110. Albany: State University of New York Press.

Dobbin, Frank, John R. Sutton, John W. Meyer, and Richard Scott. 1993. "Equal Opportunity Law and the Construction of Internal Labor Markets." *American Journal of Sociology* 99, no. 2: 396–427.

Dolan, Julie, and David Rosenbloom. 2003. *Representative Bureaucracy: Classic Readings and Continuing Controversies.* Armonk, N.Y.: M. E. Sharpe.

Domínguez, Silvia. 2008. "Race, Immigration, and Cognitive Frames in the Integration of Public Housing." Unpublished manuscript, Department of Sociology and Anthropology, Northeastern University.

Domínguez, Silvia, and Celeste Watkins. 2003. "Creating Networks for Survival and Mobility: Social Capital among African-American and Latin-American Low-Income Mothers." *Social Problems* 50, no. 1: 111–35.

Drake, Sinclair, and Horace Cayton. [1945] 1993. *Black Metropolis: A Study of Negro Life in a Northern City.* Chicago: University of Chicago Press.

DuBois, W. E. B. [1899] 1995. *The Philadelphia Negro: A Social Study.* Philadelphia: University of Pennsylvania Press.

Duncan, Greg J., and P. Lindsay Chase-Lansdale. 2002. *For Better and for Worse: Welfare Reform and the Well-Being of Children and Families.* New York: Russell Sage.

Duneier, Mitchell. 1992. *Slim's Table: Race, Respectability, and Masculinity.* Chicago: University of Chicago Press.

Dunn, Clare. 2002. "The Importance of Cultural Competence for Social Workers." *New Social Worker* 9, no. 2: 4–5.

Dutton, J. E., and J. M. Dukerich. 1991. "Keeping an Eye on the Mirror: Image and Identity in Organizational Adaptation." *Academy of Management Journal* 34:517–54.

Dutton, J. E., J. M. Dukerich, and C. V. Harquail. 1994. "Organizational Images and Member Identification." *Administrative Science Quarterly* 39:239–63.

Dyson, Michael Eric. 2005. *Is Bill Cosby Right? Or Has the Black Middle Class Lost Its Mind?* New York: Basic Civitas Books.

———. 2006. *Come Hell or High Water: Hurricane Katrina and the Color of Disaster.* New York: Basic Books.

Edin, Kathryn, and Maria Kefales. 2005. *Promises I Can Keep: Why Poor Women Put Motherhood before Marriage.* Berkeley: University of California Press.

Edin, Kathryn, and Laura Lein. 1997. *Making Ends Meet: How Single Mothers Survive Welfare and Low-Wage Work.* New York: Russell Sage Foundation.

Ehrenreich, John. 1985. *The Altruistic Imagination: A History of Social Work and Social Policy in the United States.* Ithaca: Cornell University Press.

Eisenhardt, K. M. 1989. "Building Theories from Case Study Research." *Academy of Management Review* 14:532–50.

Eisinger, Peter. 1982. "The Economic Conditions of Black Employment in Municipal Bureaucracies." *American Journal of Political Science* 26, no. 4: 754–71.

Ellwood, David T. 1988. *Poor Support: Poverty in the American Family.* New York: Basic Books.

Elsbach, K. D., and R. M. Kramer. 1996. "Members' Responses to Organizational Identity Threats: Encountering and Countering the *Business Week* Rankings." *Administrative Science Quarterly* 41:442–76.

Esping-Andersen, Gosta. 1999. *Welfare States in Transition: National Adaptations in Global Economies.* London: Sage Publications.

Fine, Gary. 2004. "Adolescence as Cultural Toolkit: High School Debate and Repertoires of Childhood and Adulthood." *Sociological Quarterly* 45, no. 1: 1–20.

Fine, Michelle. 1991. *Framing Dropouts: Notes on the Politics of an Urban Public High School.* Albany: State University of New York Press.

Foerster, Amy. 2004. "Race, Identity, and Belonging: 'Blackness' and the Struggle for Solidarity in a Multiethnic Labor Union." *Social Problems* 51, no. 3: 386–409.

Fox, Cybelle. 2004. "The Changing Color of Welfare? How Whites' Attitudes toward Latinos Influence Support for Welfare." *American Journal of Sociology* 110, no. 3: 580–625.

Fraser, Jim, Edward Kick, and Kim Barber. 2002. "Organizational Culture as Contested Ground in an Era of Globalization: Worker Perceptions and Satisfaction in the USPS." *Sociological Spectrum* 22, no. 4: 445–71.

Frazier, E. Franklin. [1957] 1997. *The Black Bourgeoisie.* New York: Free Press.

Gaines, Kevin. 1996. *Uplifting the Race: Black Leadership, Politics, and Culture in the Twentieth Century.* Chapel Hill: University of North Carolina Press.

Gais, Thomas, Richard P. Nathan, Irene Lurie, and Thomas Kaplan. 2001. "Implementation of the Personal Responsibility Act of 1996." In *The New World of Welfare,* ed. Rebecca M. Blank and Ron Haskins, 35–64. Washington, D.C.: Brookings Institution.

Gais, Thomas, and R. Kent Weaver. 2002. "State Policy Choices under Welfare Reform." Welfare Reform and Beyond Policy Brief #21. Washington, D.C.: Brookings Institution.

Galligan, D. J. 1990. *Discretionary Powers: A Legal Study of Official Discretion.* Oxford: Clarendon Press.

Gans, Herbert. 1995. *The War against the Poor: The Underclass and Anti-Poverty Policy.* New York: Basic Books.

Garkinkel, Irv, and Sara McClanahan. 1988. *Single Mothers and Their Children: A New American Dilemma*. Washington, D.C.: Urban Institute.

Geertz, Clifford. 1973. *The Interpretation of Cultures*. New York: Basic Books.

Giddens, Anthony. 1993. *New Rules of Sociological Method*. 2nd ed. Stanford: Stanford University Press.

Gilbert, Charles. 1996. "Policy-Making in Public Welfare: The 1962 Amendments." *Political Science Quarterly* 81, no. 2: 196–224.

Gilens, Martin. 1999. *Why Americans Hate Welfare: Race, Media, and the Politics of Anti-Poverty Policy*. Chicago: University of Chicago Press.

Ginwright, Shawn A. 2002. "Classed Out: The Challenges of Social Class in Black Community Change." *Social Problems* 49, no. 4: 544–62.

Gioia, Dennis A., and James B. Thomas. 1996. "Identity, Image, and Issue Interpretation: Sense-Making during Strategic Change in Academia." *Administrative Science Quarterly* 41, no. 3: 370–403.

Gioia, Dennis A., James B. Thomas, Shawn M. Clark, and Kuman Chittipeddi. 1994. "Symbolism and Strategic Change in Academia: The Dynamics of Sense-Making and Influence." *Organization Science* 5, no. 3: 363–83.

Glaser, Barney, and Anselm Strauss. 1967. *The Discovery of Grounded Theory: Strategies for Qualitative Research*. Hawthorne, N.Y.: Aldine Transaction.

Goffman, Erving. 1959. *The Presentation of Self in Everyday Life*. New York: Anchor Books.

———. 1961. *Asylums: Essays on the Social Situation of Mental Patients and Other Inmates*. Harmondsworth: Penguin Books.

Goldsmith, Pat Carlos. 2004. "Schools' Racial Mix, Students' Optimism, and the Black-White and Latino-White Achievement Gaps." *Sociology of Education* 77, no. 2: 121–47.

Gooden, Susan Tinsley. 1995. "Local Discretion and Welfare Policy: The Case of Virginia (1911–1970)." *Southern Studies* 6:79–110.

———. 1998. "All Things Not Being Equal: Differences in Caseworker Support toward Black and White Welfare Clients." *Harvard Journal of African-American Public Policy* 4:23–33.

———. 2003. "Contemporary Approaches to Enduring Challenges: Using Performance Measures to Promote Racial Equality under TANF." In *Race and the Politics of Welfare Reform*, ed. Sanford F. Schram, Joe Soss, and Richard Fording, 254–75. Ann Arbor: University of Michigan Press.

Goodsell, C. 1980. "Client Evaluation of Three Welfare Programs." *Administration and Society* 12:123–36.

———. 1981. "Looking Once Again at Human Service Bureaucracy." *Journal of Politics* 43:763–78.

Goodwin, Joanne. 1997. *Gender and the Politics of Welfare Reform: Mothers' Pensions in Chicago, 1911–1929*. Chicago: University of Chicago Press.

Gordon, Linda. 1991. "Black and White Visions of Welfare: Women's Welfare Activism, 1890–1945." *Journal of American History* 78, no. 2: 559–90.

———. 1994. *Pitied But Not Entitled: Single Mothers and the History of Welfare, 1890–1935*. New York: Free Press.

Gouldner, Alvin. 1954. *Patterns of Industrial Democracy*. Glencoe, Ill.: Free Press.

Greene, Michael, and John E. Rogers. 1994. "Education and Earnings Disparities between Black and White Men: A Comparison of Professionals in the Public and Private Sectors." *Journal of Socio-Economics* 23, nos. 1–2: 113–30.

Gubrium, Jaber, and David Buckholdt. 1979. *Caretakers: Treating Emotionally Disturbed Children*. Newbury Park, Calif.: Sage Publications.

———. 1982. *Describing Care: Image and Practice in Rehabilitation*. Boston: Oelgeschlager, Gunn, and Hain.

Gubrium, Jaber F., and James A. Holstein. 2001. *Institutional Selves: Troubled Identities in a Postmodern World*. New York: Oxford University Press.

Hall, R. H. 1977. *Organizations, Structure, and Process*. 2nd ed. Englewood Cliffs, N.J.: Prentice-Hall.

Hammersley, M., and P. Atkinson. 1995. *Ethnography: Principles in Practice*. 2nd ed. London: Routledge.

Hancock, Ange-Marie. 2004. *The Politics of Disgust: The Public Identity of the Welfare Queen*. New York: New York University Press.

———. 2007a. "Intersectionality as a Normative and Empirical Paradigm." *Politics & Gender* 3, no. 2: 248–54.

———. 2007b. "When Multiplication Doesn't Equal Quick Addition: Examining Intersectionality as a Research Paradigm." *Perspectives on Politics* 5, no. 1: 63–79.

Handler, Joel F., and Yeheskel Hasenfeld. 1991. *The Moral Construction of Poverty: Welfare Reform in America*. Newbury Park, Calif.: Sage Publications.

Handler, Joel, and Ellen Hollingsworth. 1971. *The "Deserving Poor": A Study of Welfare Administration*. Chicago: Markam Publishing.

Haney, Lynne. 2002a. "Homeboys, Babies, and Men in Suits: The State and the Reproduction of Male Dominance." *American Journal of Sociology* 61, no. 5: 759–78.

———. 2002b. *Inventing the Needy: Gender and the Politics of Welfare in Hungary*. Berkeley: University of California Press.

Hargen, Jan L., and Irene Lurie. 1995. "Implementing JOBS—A View from the Front-Line." *Families in Society—The Journal of Contemporary Human Services* 76:230–38.

Hargen, Jan L., and Judith Owens-Manley. 2002. "Issues in Implementing TANF in New York: The Perspective of Frontline Workers." *Social Work* 47, no. 2: 171–82.

Harrington, Michael. [1962] 1997. *The Other America: Poverty in the United States*. New York: Scribner.

Hartman, Chester, and Gregory D. Squires, eds. 2006. *There Is No Such Thing as a Natural Disaster: Race, Class, and Hurricane Katrina*. New York: Routledge.

Hasenfeld, Yeheskel. 1972. "People Processing Organizations: An Exchange Approach." *American Sociological Review* 37, no. 3: 256–63.

————. 2000. "Organizational Forms and Moral Practices: The Case of Welfare Departments." *Social Service Review* 74:329–51.

Hasenfeld, Yeheskel, and Dale Weaver. 1996. "Enforcement, Compliance, and Disputes in Welfare-to-Work Programs." *Social Service Review* 70, no. 2: 235–56.

Haskins, Ronald. 2006. *Work over Welfare: The Inside Story of the 1996 Welfare Reform Law.* Washington, D.C.: Brookings Institution.

Hawkins, Keith. 1992. *The Uses of Discretion.* New York: Oxford University Press.

Hays, Sharon. 2003. *Flat Broke with Children: Women in the Age of Welfare Reform.* New York: Oxford University Press.

Heimer, Carol, and Mitchell Stevens. 1997. "Caring for the Organization: Social Workers as Frontline Risk Managers in Neonatal Intensive Care Units." *Work and Occupations* 24, no. 2: 133–63.

Heracleous, Loizos. 2001. "An Ethnographic Study of Culture in the Context of Organizational Change." *Journal of Applied Behavioral Science* 37, no. 4: 426–46.

Hewitt, Cynthia. 2004. "African-American Concentration in Jobs: The Political Economy of Job Segregation and Contestation in Atlanta." *Urban Affairs Review* 39, no. 3: 318–41.

Higginbotham, Evelyn Brooks. 1993. *Righteous Discontent: The Women's Movement in the Black Baptist Church, 1880–1920.* Cambridge: Harvard University Press.

Hill, Carolyn J. 2006. "Casework Job Design and Client Outcomes in Welfare-to-Work Offices." *Journal of Public Administration Research and Theory* 16, no. 2: 263–88.

Hill, Linda A. 1992. *Becoming a Manager: Mastery of a New Identity.* Boston: Harvard Business School Press.

Hindera, John. 1993. "Representation Bureaucracy: Further Evidence of Active Representation in the EEOC District Offices." *Journal of Public Administration Research and Theory* 3, no. 4: 415–29.

Hirsch, Paul M., and Michael Lounsbury. 1997. "Ending the Family Quarrel: Toward a Reconciliation of 'Old' and 'New' Institutionalism." *American Behavioral Scientist* 40, no. 4: 406–18.

Hogg, Michael A., and Deborah J. Terry. 2000. "Social Identity and Self-Categorization Processes in Organizational Contexts." *Academy of Management Review* 25, no. 1: 121–40.

Holcomb, Pamela A., and Karin Martinson. 2002. "Implementing Welfare Reform across the Nation." *New Federalism: Issues and Options for States.* Urban Institute Policy Brief (Series A, No. A–53), 1–7. Washington, D.C.: Urban Institute.

Holcomb, Pamela A., LaDonna Pavetti, Caroline Ratcliffe, and Susan Riedinger. 1998. *Building an Employment Focused Welfare System: Work First and Other Work-Oriented Strategies in Five States.* Washington, D.C.: Urban Institute.

Horowitz, Ruth. 1995. *Teen Mothers: Citizens or Dependents?* Chicago: University of Chicago Press.

Hunter, Terra. 1997. To 'Joy My Freedom: Southern Black Women's Lives and Labors after the Civil War. Cambridge: Harvard University Press.

Ibarra, Herminia. 1999. "Provisional Selves: Experimenting with Image and Identity in Professional Adaptation." *Administrative Science Quarterly* 44, no. 4: 764–91.

Iversen, Robert. 2000. "TANF Policy Implementation: The Invisible Barrier." *Journal of Sociology and Social Welfare* 27, no. 2: 139–59.

Jackall, Robert. 1988. *Moral Mazes: The World of Corporate Managers.* New York: Oxford University Press.

Jackson, John L. 2001. *Harlemworld: Doing Race and Class in Contemporary Black America.* Chicago: University of Chicago Press.

Jacobs, Mark D. 1990. *Screwing the System and Making It Work: Juvenile Justice in the No-Fault Society.* Chicago: University of Chicago Press.

Jewell, Christopher. 2007. *Agents of the Welfare State: How Caseworkers Respond to Need in the United States, Germany, and Sweden.* New York: Palgrave Macmillan.

Johnson, G. 1990. "Managing Strategic Change: The Role of Symbolic Action." *British Journal of Management* 1:183–200.

Johnson-Dias, Janice, and Steven Maynard-Moody. 2007. "For-Profit Welfare: Contracts, Conflicts, and the Performance Paradox." *Journal of Public Administration Research and Theory* 17, no. 2: 189–211.

Jones-Correa, Michael, and David Leal. 1996. "'Becoming 'Hispanic': Secondary Panethnic Identification among Latin American–Origin Populations in the United States." *Hispanic Journal of Behavioral Sciences* 18, no. 2: 214–54.

Jordan-Zachery, Julia. 2007. "Am I a Black Woman or a Woman Who Is Black? A Few Thoughts on the Meaning of Intersectionality." *Politics & Gender* 3, no. 2: 254–63.

Kanan, James W., and Matthew V. Pruitt. 2002. "Modeling Fear of Crime and Perceived Victimization Risk: The (In)Significance of Neighborhood Integration." *Sociological Inquiry* 72, no. 4: 527–48.

Kane, Thomas, and Mary Jo Bane. 1994. "The Context for Welfare Reform." In *Welfare Realities,* ed. Mary Jo Bane and David Ellwood. Cambridge: Harvard University Press.

Kanter, Rosabeth Moss. 1993. *Men and Women of the Corporation.* New York: Basic Books.

Katz, Michael. 1996. *In the Shadow of the Poorhouse: A Social History of Welfare in America.* 10th anniversary ed. New York: Basic Books.

Kaye, Laura, Demetra Nightingale, Jodi Sandfort, and Lynne Fender. 2001. *Changes in Massachusetts Welfare and Work, Child Care, and Child Welfare Systems.* Urban Institute State Update No. 5. Washington, D.C.: Urban Institute.

Keiser, Lael R., Vicky M. Wilkins, Kenneth J. Meier, and Catherine A. Holland. 2002. "Lipstick and Logarithms: Gender, Institutional Context, and Representative Bureaucracy." *American Political Science Review* 96, no. 3: 553–64.

Kennelly, Ivy. 1999. "That Single Mother Element: How White Employers Typify Black Women." *Gender and Society* 13, no. 2: 168–92.

Kessler-Harris, Alice. 2001. *In Pursuit of Equity: Women, Men, and the Quest for Economic Citizenship in 20th Century America*. New York: Oxford University Press.

Kinder, Donald R., and David O. Sears. 1981. "Prejudice and Politics: Symbolic Racism versus Racial Threats to the Good Life." *Journal of Personality and Social Psychology* 40: 414–31.

King, Desmond. 1999. "The Racial Bureaucracy: African Americans and the Federal Government in the Era of Segregated Race Relations." *Governance: An International Journal of Policy and Administration* 12, no. 4: 345–77.

Kingfisher, Catherine P. 1996. *Women in the American Welfare Trap*. Philadelphia: University of Pennsylvania Press.

———. 2001. "Producing Disunity: The Constraints and Incitements of Welfare Work." In *The New Poverty Studies: The Ethnography of Power, Politics, and Impoverished People in the United States*, ed. Judith Goode and Jeff Maskovsky, 273–92. New York: New York University Press.

Kingsley, J. Donald. 1944. *Representative Bureaucracy: An Interpretation of the British Civil Service*. Yellow Springs, Ohio: Antioch Press.

Kirschenman, Joleen, and Kathryn Neckerman. 1991. "'We'd Love to Hire Them, But . . .': The Meaning of Race for Employers." In *The Urban Underclass*, ed. Christopher Jencks and Paul E. Peterson, 203–32. Washington, D.C.: Brookings Institution.

Kleinman, Sherryl. 1996. *Opposing Ambitions: Gender and Identity in an Alternative Organization*. Chicago: University of Chicago Press.

Kondo, D. 1990. *Crafting Selves*. Chicago: University of Chicago Press.

Kornbluh, Felicia Ann. 2007. *The Battle for Welfare Rights: Politics and Poverty in Modern America*. Philadelphia: University of Pennsylvania Press.

Korteweg, Anna C. 2003. "Welfare Reform and the Subject of the Working Mother: 'Get a Job, a Better Job, Then a Career.'" *Theory and Society* 32:445–80.

———. 2006. "The Construction of Gendered Citizenship at the Welfare Office: An Ethnographic Comparison of Welfare-to Work Workshops in the United States and the Netherlands." *Social Politics* 13, no. 3: 313–40.

Kroeger, Naomi. 1975. "Bureaucracy, Social Exchange, and Benefits Received in a Public Assistance Agency." *Social Problems* 23, no. 2: 182–96.

Lacy, Karyn. 2007. *Blue-Chip Black: Race, Class, and Status in the New Black Middle Class*. Berkeley: University of California Press.

Lareau, Annette. 2003. *Unequal Childhoods: Class, Race, and Family Life*. Berkeley: University of California Press.

Lens, Vicki. 2007. "Administrative Justice in Public Welfare Bureaucracies: When Citizens (Don't) Complain." *Administration & Society* 39:82–408.

Lens, Vicki, and S. E. Vorsanger. 2005. "Complaining after Claiming: Fair Hearings after Welfare Reform." *Social Service Review* 79:430–53.

Lewis, Gail. 1996. "Situated Voices: Black Women's Experience and Social Work." *Feminist Review* 53: 24–56.

———. 2000. *"Race," Gender, Social Welfare: Encounters in a Postcolonial Society.* Cambridge, U.K.: Polity Press.

Lieberman, Robert. 1998. *Shifting the Color Line: Race and the American Welfare State.* Cambridge: Harvard University Press.

Lineberry, Robert L. 1977. *American Public Policy.* New York: Harper and Row.

Lipsky, Michael. 1980. *Street-Level Bureaucracy: Dilemmas of the Individual in Public Service Work.* New York: Russell Sage Foundation.

Livermore, Michelle, and Alison Neustrom. 2003. "Linking Welfare Clients to Jobs: Discretionary Use of Worker Social Capital." *Journal of Sociology and Social Welfare* 30, no. 2: 87–103.

Loeske, Donileen. 2007. "The Study of Identity as Cultural, Institutional, Organizational, and Personal Narratives: Theoretical and Empirical Integrations." *Sociological Quarterly* 48:661–88.

Lorde, Audre. 1984. *Sister Outsider: Essays and Speeches.* Berkeley: Crossing Press.

Lower-Basch, Elizabeth. 2000. *"Leavers" and Diversion Studies: Preliminary Analysis of Racial Differences in Caseload Trends and Leaver Outcomes.* Washington, D.C.: U.S. Department of Health and Human Services, Office of the Assistant Secretary for Planning and Evaluation. http://aspe.hhs.gov/hsp/leavers99/race.htm DOR: 1/29/03.

Lubiano, Wahneema. 1992. "Black Ladies, Welfare Queens, and State Minstrels: Ideological War by Narrative Means." In *Racing Justice, Engendering Power: The Anita Hill–Clarence Thomas Controversy and the Construction of Social Reality,* ed. Toni Morrison, 323–61. New York: Pantheon Books.

Lurie, Irene. 2001. "State Implementation of TANF: Where Do We Stand in 2001?" *Evaluation and Program Planning* 24, no. 4: 379–88.

———. 2006. *At the Front Lines of the Welfare System: A Perspective on the Decline in Welfare Caseloads.* Albany, N.Y.: Rockefeller Institute Press.

Lurie, Irene, and Norma Riccucci. 2003. "Changing the 'Culture' of Welfare Offices: From Vision to the Front Lines." *Administration and Society* 34:653–77.

March, James G. 1994. *A Primer on Decision-Making.* New York: Free Press.

March, James G., and Johan P. Olsen. 2005. "The Institutional Dynamics of International Political Orders." *International Organization* 52, no. 4: 943–69.

Martin, Joanne. 2001. *Organizational Culture: Mapping the Terrain.* London: Sage Publications.

Marwell, Nicole. 2007. *Bargaining for Brooklyn: Community Organizations in the Entrepreneurial City.* Chicago: University of Chicago Press.

Massey, Douglas, and Nancy Denton. 1998. *American Apartheid: Segregation and the Making of the Underclass.* Cambridge: Harvard University Press.

Masuoka, Natalie. 2006. "Together They Become One: Examining the Predictors of Panethnic Group Consciousness among Asian Americans and Latinos." *Social Science Quarterly* 87, no. 1: 993.

Maynard-Moody, Steven, and Michael Musheno. 2000. "State Agent or Citizen Agent: Two Narratives of Discretion." *Journal of Public Administration Research and Theory* 10, no. 2: 329–58.

———. 2003. *Cops, Teachers, and Counselors: Stories from the Front Lines of Public Service.* Ann Arbor: University of Michigan Press.

McBride, Dwight. 2005. *Why I Hate Abercrombie and Fitch: Essays on Race and Sexuality.* New York: New York University Press.

McCall, Leslie. 2005. "The Complexity of Intersectionality." *Signs* 30, no. 3: 1771–1800.

McClain, Paula D., Niambi M. Carter, Victoria M. DeFrancesco Soto, Monique L. Lyle, Jeffrey D. Grynaviski, Shayla C. Nunnally, Thomas J. Scotto, J. Alan Kendrick, Gerald F. Lackey, and Kendra Davenport Cotton. 2006. "Racial Distancing in a Southern City: Latino Immigrants' Views of Black Americans." *Journal of Politics* 68, no. 3: 571–84.

McDermott, Monica, and Frank L. Samson. 2005. "White Racial and Ethnic Identity in the United States." *Annual Review of Sociology* 31:245–61.

McIntosh, Peggy. 1988. "White Privilege and Male Privilege: A Personal Account of Coming to See Correspondences through Work in Women's Studies." Working paper. Wellesley College Center for Research on Women.

McPherson, Miller, Lynn Smith-Lovin, and James M. Cook. 2001. "Birds of a Feather: Homophily in Social Networks." *Annual Review of Sociology* 27: 415–44.

Mead, Lawrence. 1992. *The New Politics of Poverty: The Nonworking Poor in America.* New York: Basic Books.

———. 1997. *The New Paternalism: Supervisory Approaches to Poverty.* Washington, D.C.: Brookings Institution.

———. 2004. *Government Matters: Welfare Reform in Wisconsin.* Princeton: Princeton University Press.

Meier, Kenneth J. 1993. "Latinos and Representative Bureaucracy: Testing the Thompson and Henderson Hypotheses." *Journal of Public Administration Research and Theory* 3, no. 4: 393–414.

Meier, Kenneth J., and Jill Nicholson-Crotty. 2006. "Gender, Representative Bureaucracy, and Law Enforcement: The Case of Sexual Assault." *Public Administration Review* 66, no. 6: 850–60.

Meier, Kenneth J., and Joseph Stewart. 1992. "The Impact of Representative Bureaucracies: Educational Systems and Public Policies." *American Review of Public Administration* 22, no. 3: 157–71.

Meyer, Stephen G. 2000. *As Long as They Don't Move Next Door: Segregation and Racial Conflict in American Neighborhoods.* Lanham, Md.: Rowman and Littlefield.

Meyers, Marcia, Bonnie Glaser, and Karin MacDonald. 1998. "On the Front Lines of Welfare Delivery: Are Workers Implementing Policy Reforms?" *Journal of Policy Analysis and Management* 17, no. 1: 1–22.

Meyers, Marcia, Norma Riccucci, and Irene Lurie. 2002. "Achieving Goal Congruence in Complex Environments: The Case of Welfare Reform." *Journal of Public Administration Research and Theory* 11, no. 2: 165–202.

Miller, A. H., P. Gurin, G. Gurin, and O. Malanchuk. 1981. "Group Consciousness and Political Participation." *American Journal of Political Science* 25:494–511.

Mink, Gwendolyn. 1995. *The Wages of Motherhood: Inequality in the Welfare State, 1917–1942.* Ithaca: Cornell University Press.

———. 2001. "Violating Women: Rights Abuses in the Welfare Police State." *Annals of the American Academy of Political and Social Science* 577:79–93.

Modesto, Kevin. 2004. "'Won't Be Weighted Down': Richard R. Wright, Jr.'s Contributions to Social Work and Social Welfare." *Journal of Sociology and Social Welfare* 31, no. 2: 69–89.

Monson, Renee. 1997. "State-ing Sex and Gender: Collecting Information from Mothers and Fathers in Paternity Cases." *Gender and Society* 11, no. 3: 279–95.

Moore, David. 2004. "Governing Street-Based Injecting Drug Users: A Critique of Heroin Overdose Prevention in Australia." *Social Science & Medicine* 59, no. 7: 1547–57.

Morgen, Sandra. 2001. "The Agency of Welfare Workers: Negotiating Devolution, Privatization, and the Meaning of 'Self-Sufficiency.'" *American Anthropologist* 103, no. 3: 747–61.

Morrill, Calvin, and Gary Alan Fine. 1997. "Ethnographic Contributions to Organizational Sociology." *Sociological Methods Research* 25, no. 4: 424–51.

Moss, Philip, and Chris Tilly. 2001. *Stories Employers Tell: Race, Skill, and Hiring in America.* New York: Russell Sage Foundation.

Munger, Frank, ed. 2002. *Laboring below the Line: The New Ethnography of Poverty, Low-Wage Work, and Survival in the Global Economy.* New York: Russell Sage Foundation.

Murray, Charles. 1994. *Losing Ground: American Social Policy, 1950–1980.* 10th anniversary ed. New York: Basic Books.

Myers-Lipton, Scott. 2006. *Social Solutions to Poverty: America's Struggle to Build a Just Society.* Boulder, Colo.: Paradigm Publishers.

Nadasen, Premilla. 2005. *Welfare Warriors: The Welfare Rights Movement in the United States.* New York: Routledge.

Naples, Nancy. 1998. *Grassroots Warriors: Activist Mothering, Community Work, and the War on Poverty.* New York: Routledge.

National Hurricane Center. 2007. "Tropical Weather Summary—2005 Web Final." National Weather Service. http://www.nhc.noaa.gov/archive/2005/tws/MIATWSAT_nov_final.shtml DOR: 1/5/08.

Neckerman, Kathryn, and Joleen Kirschenman. 1991. "Hiring Strategies, Racial Bias, and Inner-City Workers." *Social Problems* 38, no. 4: 433–47.

Neubeck, Kenneth J., and Noel A. Cazenave. 2001. *Welfare Racism: Playing the Race Card against America's Poor.* New York: Routledge.

Newman, Katherine. 1999. *No Shame in My Game: The Working Poor in the Inner City.* New York: Russell Sage/First Vintage.

———. 2006. *Chutes and Ladders: Navigating the Low-Wage Labor Market.* New York: Russell Sage Foundation.

Nkomo, Stella M., and Taylor Cox Jr. 1990. "Factors Affecting the Upward Mobility of Black Managers in Private Sector Organizations." *Review of Black Political Economy* 18, no. 3: 39–57.

O'Connor, Alice. 2001. *Poverty Knowledge: Social Science, Social Policy, and the Poor in Twentieth-Century U.S. History.* Princeton: Princeton University Press.

O'Connor, Julia, Ann Orloff, and Sheila Shaver. 1999. *States, Markets, Families: Gender, Liberalism and Social Policy in Australia, Canada, Great Britain and the United States.* Cambridge: Cambridge University Press.

O'Donnell, Sandra M. 1994. "The Care of Dependent African-American Children in Chicago: The Struggle between Black Self-Help and Professionalism." *Journal of Social History* 27, no. 4: 763–76.

Ogmundson, Richard. 2005. "Does It Matter if Women, Minorities, and Gays Govern? New Data concerning an Old Question." *Canadian Journal of Sociology* 30, no. 3: 315–24.

O'Reilly, C. A., J. Chatman, and D. F. Caldwell. 1991. "People and Organizational Culture: A Profile Comparison Approach to Assessing Person-Organization Fit." *Academy of Management Journal* 34:487–516.

Orleck, Annelise. 2005. *Storming Caesar's Palace: How Black Mothers Fought Their Own War on Poverty.* Boston: Beacon Press.

Orloff, Ann. 1991. "Gender in Early U.S. Social Policy." *Journal of Policy History* 3, no. 3: 249–81.

———. 2002. "Explaining U.S. Welfare Reform: Power, Gender, Race, and the U.S. Policy Legacy Source." *Critical Social Policy* 22, no. 1: 96–118.

Ouichi, William, and Alan Wilkins. 1985. "Organizational Culture." *Annual Review of Sociology* 11:457–83.

Owens, Chris T. 2005. "Black Substantive Representation in State Legislatures from 1971 to 1994." *Social Science Quarterly* 86, no. 4: 779–91.

Pager, Devah, and Lincoln Quillian. 2005. "Walking the Talk? What Employers Say versus What They Do." *American Sociological Review* 70, no. 3: 355–80.

Parker, Martin. 2000. *Organizational Culture and Identity: Unity and Division at Work.* Thousand Oaks, Calif.: Sage.

Pascale, R., M. Milleman, and L. Gioja. 1997. "Changing the Way We Change." *Harvard Business Review* (November–December): 127–39.

Pattillo, Mary. 2007. *Black on the Block: The Politics of Race and Class in the City.* Chicago: University of Chicago Press.

Pattillo-McCoy, Mary. 1999. *Black Picket Fences: Privilege and Peril among the Black Middle Class.* Chicago: University of Chicago Press.

Peck, Jamie. 1998. "Postwelfare Massachusetts." *Economic Geography* 74:62–82.

Peyrot, Mark. 1982. "Caseload Management: Choosing Suitable Clients in a Community Health Clinic Agency." *Social Problems* 30, no. 2: 157–67.

Piven, Francis Fox. 2001. "Welfare Reform and the Economic and Cultural Reconstruction of Low Wage Labor Markets." In *The New Poverty Studies: The Ethnography of Power, Politics, and Impoverished People in the United States,* ed. Judith Goode and Jeff Maskovsky. New York: New York University Press.

Piven, Francis Fox, and Richard Cloward. 1971. *Regulating the Poor: The Functions of Public Welfare.* New York: Vintage Books.

Proctor, Bernadette D., and Joseph Dalaker. 2002. *Poverty in the United States: 2001.* U.S. Census Bureau, Current Population Reports, P60–219. Washington, D.C.: U.S. Government Printing Office.

Prottas, Jeffrey. 1979. *People Processing: The Street-Level Bureaucrat in Public Service Bureaucracies.* Lanham, Md.: Lexington Books.

Quadagno, Jill. 1994. *The Color of Welfare: How Racism Undermined the War on Poverty.* New York: Oxford University Press

Rank, Mark. 1994. *Living on the Edge.* New York: Columbia University Press.

Ravasi, Davide, and Johan van Rekom. 2003. "Key Issues in Organizational Identity and Identification Theory." *Corporate Reputation Review* 6, no. 2: 118–32.

Reed, Adolph. 1999. *Stirrings in the Jug: Black Politics in the Post-Segregation Era.* Minneapolis: University of Minnesota Press.

Reskin, Barbara F. 2000. "Getting It Right: Sex and Race Inequality in Organizations." *Annual Review of Sociology* 26: 707–9.

Reskin, Barbara F., Debra B. McBrier, and Julie A. Kmec. 1999. "Determinants and Consequences of Workplace Race and Sex Composition." *Annual Review of Sociology* 25: 335–61.

Riccio, J., D. Friedlander, and S. Freedman. 1994. *GAIN: Benefits, Costs, and Three-Year Impacts of a Welfare-to-Work Program.* New York: Manpower Demonstration Research Corporation.

Riccucci, Norma. 2005. *How Management Matters: Street-Level Bureaucrats and Welfare Reform.* Washington, D.C.: Georgetown University Press.

Riccucci, Norma M., and Marcia K. Meyers. 2004. "Linking Passive and Active Representation: The Case of Frontline Workers in Welfare Agencies." *Journal of Public Administration Research and Theory* 14, no. 4: 585–97.

Riccucci, Norma, Marcia Meyers, Irene Lurie, and Jun Seop Han. 2004. "The Implementation of Welfare Reform Policy: The Role of Public Managers in Front-line Practices." *Public Administration Review* 64, no. 4: 438–48.

Ridzi, Frank. 2004. "Making TANF Work: Organizational Restructuring, Staff Buy-In, and Performance Monitoring in Local Implementation." *Journal of Sociology and Social Welfare* 31, no. 2: 27–48.

Roberts, Dorothy. 1999. "Welfare's Ban on Poor Motherhood." In *Whose Welfare?* ed. Gwendolyn Mink. Ithaca: Cornell University Press.

———. 2002. *Shattered Bonds: The Color of Child Welfare.* New York: Basic Books.

Rogers-Dillon, Robin H. 2004. *The Welfare Experiments: Politics and Policy Evaluation.* Stanford: Stanford University Press.

Ross, Edyth L. 1976. "Black Heritage in Social Welfare: A Case Study of Atlanta." *Phylon* 37, no. 4: 297–307.

Rothman, Gerald. 1985. *Philanthropists, Therapists, and Activists: A Century of Ideological Conflict in Social Work.* Cambridge, Mass.: Schenkman.

Royster, Deirdre A. 2003. *Race and the Invisible Hand: How White Networks Exclude Black Men from Blue-Collar Jobs.* Berkeley: University of California Press.

Ryan, William. 1971. *Blaming the Victim.* New York: Random House.

Sachs, Judyth. 2001. "Teacher Professional Identity: Competing Discourses, Competing Outcomes." *Journal of Education Policy* 16, no. 2: 149–61.

Sackmann, Sonja A. 1992. "Culture and Subcultures: An Analysis of Organizational Knowledge." *Administrative Science Quarterly* 37, no. 1: 140–61.

Salamon, Sonya. 2003. *Newcomers to Old Towns: Suburbanization in the Heartland.* Chicago: University of Chicago Press.

Sanchez, Gabriel. 2006. "The Role of Group Consciousness in Political Participation among Latinos in the United States." *Hispanic Journal of Behavioral Sciences* 18, no. 2: 214–54.

Sandfort, Jodi. 1991. "The Structural Impediments to Human Service Collaboration: Examining Welfare Reform at the Front Lines." *Social Service Review* 73, no. 3: 314–39.

———. 2000. "Moving beyond Discretion and Outcomes: Examining Public Management from the Front Lines of the Welfare System." *Journal of Public Administration Research and Theory* 10, no. 4: 729–56.

Sandfort, Jodi R., Ariel Kalil, and Julie Gottschalk. 1999. "The Mirror Has Two Faces: Welfare Clients and Front-line Workers View Policy Reform." *Journal of Poverty* 3, no. 3: 71–91.

Schein, Edgar. 1978. *Career Dynamics: Matching Individual and Organizational Needs.* Reading, Mass.: Addison-Wesley.

———. 1996. "Culture: The Missing Concept in Organization Studies." *Administrative Science Quarterly* 41, no. 2: 229–40.

———. 2004. *Organizational Culture and Leadership.* San Francisco: Jossey-Bass.

Schneider, Saundra K. 2005. "Administrative Breakdowns in the Governmental Response to Hurricane Katrina." *Public Administration Review* 65:515–16.

Schram, Sanford, Joe Soss, and Richard Fording, eds. 2003. *Race and the Politics of Welfare Reform.* Ann Arbor: University of Michigan Press.

Schram, Sanford, Joe Soss, Richard Fording, and Linda Houser, 2009. "Deciding to Discipline: A Multi-Method Study of Race, Choice, and Punishment at the Frontlines of Welfare Reform." *American Sociological Review* 74, no. 2 (forthcoming).

Schuman, Howard, and Lawrence Bobo. 1988. "Survey-Based Experiments on White Racial Attitudes toward Residential Integration." *American Journal of Sociology* 94, no. 2: 273–99.

Scott, Patrick. 1997. "Assessing Determinants of Bureaucratic Discretion: An Experiment in Street-Level Decision." *Journal of Public Administration Research and Theory* 7, no. 1: 35–57.

Scrivener, Susan, and Johanna Walter. 2001. *Evaluating Two Approaches to Case Management: Implementation, Participation Patterns, Costs, and Three-Year Impacts of the Columbus Welfare-to-Work Program.* National Evaluation of Welfare-to-Work Strategies. New York: Manpower Demonstration Research Corporation.

Seccombe, Karen. 1998. *So You Think I Drive a Cadillac? Welfare Recipients' Perspectives on the System and Its Reform.* Boston: Allyn and Bacon.

Seccombe, Karen, Delores James, and Kimberly Battle Walters. 1998. "They Think You Ain't Much of Nothing: The Social Construction of the Welfare Mother." *Journal of Marriage and the Family* 60, no. 4: 849–65.

Segura, Gary M., and Helene Alves Rodrigues. 2006. "Comparative Ethnic Politics in the United States: Beyond Black." *Annual Review of Political Science* 9:375–95.

Seipel, Amy, and Ineke Way. 2006. "Culturally Competent Social Work Practice with Latino Clients." *New Social Worker* 13, no. 4: 4–7.

Selden, Sally. 1997. *The Promise of Representative Bureaucracy: Diversity and Responsiveness in a Government Agency.* Armonk, N.Y.: M. E. Sharpe.

Selznick, Philip. [1949] 1980. *TVA and the Grass Roots: A Study of Politics and Organization.* Berkeley: University of California Press.

———. 1996. "Institutionalism 'Old' and 'New.'" *Administrative Science Quarterly* 41, no. 2: 270–77.

Sheridan, J. E. 1992. "Organizational Culture and Employee Retention." *Academy of Management Journal* 35:1036–56.

Sherman, Arloc, and Issac Shapiro. 2005. "Essential Facts about the Victims of Hurricane Katrina." Washington, D.C.: Center on Budget and Policy Priorities.

Simien, Evelyn. 2007. "Doing Intersectionality Research: From Conceptual Issues to Practical Examples." *Politics & Gender* 3, no. 2: 264–71.

Skocpol, Theda. 1992. *Protecting Soldiers and Mothers: The Political Origins of Social Policy in the United States.* Cambridge: Harvard University Press.

Skogan, Wesley G. 1995. "Crime and the Racial Fears of White Americans." *Annals of the American Academy of Political and Social Science* 539, no. 1: 59–71.

Small, Mario Luis. 2004. *Villa Victoria: The Transformation of Social Capital in a Boston Barrio.* Chicago: University of Chicago Press.

———. 2006. "Neighborhood Institutions as Resource Brokers: Childcare Centers, Interorganizational Ties, and Resource Access among the Poor." *Social Problems* 53, no. 2: 274–92.

———. 2009. *Unanticipated Gains: Origins of Network Inequality in Everyday Life.* New York: Oxford University Press.

Smith, Janice Witt, and Toni Calasanti. 2005. "The Influences of Gender, Race, and Ethnicity on Workplace Experiences of Institutional and Social Isolation: An Exploratory Study of University Faculty." *Sociological Spectrum* 25, no. 3: 307–34.

Smith, Sandra S. 2005. "'Don't Put My Name on It': Social Capital Activation and Job-Finding Assistance among the Black Urban Poor." *American Journal of Sociology* 111, no. 1: 1–57.

Smith, Steven, and Michael Lipsky. 1995. *Nonprofits for Hire: The Welfare State in the Age of Contracting.* Cambridge: Harvard University Press.

Somers, Margaret, and Fred Block. 2005. "From Poverty to Perversity: Ideas, Markets, and Institutions over Two Centuries of Welfare Debate." *American Sociological Review* 70:260–87.

Soss, Joe. 1999. "Welfare Application Encounters: Subordination, Satisfaction, and the Puzzle of Client Evaluations." *Administration and Society* 31, no. 1: 50–94.

———. 2000. *Unwanted Claims: The Politics of Participation in the U.S. Welfare System.* Ann Arbor: University of Michigan Press.

Soss, Joe, Sanford F. Schram, Thomas P. Vartanian, and Erin O'Brien. 2001. "Setting the Terms of Relief: Explaining State Policy Choices in the Devolution Revolution." *American Journal of Political Science* 45, no. 2: 378–95.

Sowa, Jessica E., and Sally Coleman Selden. 2003. "Administrative Discretion and Active Representation: An Expansion of the Theory of Representative Bureaucracy." *Public Administration Review* 63, no. 6: 700–709.

Stack, Carol. [1974] 1997. *All Our Kin: Strategies for Survival in a Black Community.* New York: Basic Books.

Stinchcombe, Arthur. 1997. "On the Virtues of the Old Institutionalism." *Annual Review of Sociology* 23:1–18.

Stinchcombe, Arthur, R. Adams, C. A. Heimer, K. L. Scheppele, T. W. Smith, D. G. Taylor. 1980. *Crime and Punishment—Changing Attitudes in America.* San Francisco: Jossey-Bass.

Stokes, Atiya Kai. 2003. "Latino Group Consciousness and Political Participation." *American Politics Research* 31, no. 4: 361–78.

Stone, Clarence. 1977. "Paternalism among Social Agency Employees." *Journal of Politics* 39, no. 3: 794–804.

Strauss, Anselm, Leonard Schatzman, Danuta Erlich, Rue Bucher, and Melvin Sabshin. 1963. "The Hospital and Its Negotiated Order." In *The Hospital in Modern Society,* ed. E. Friedson, 147–69. New York: Free Press.

Swidler, Ann. 1986. "Culture in Action: Symbols and Strategies." *American Sociological Review* 51, no. 2: 273–86.

Tajfel, Henri. 1982. "Social Psychology of Intergroup Relations." In *Annual Review of Psychology* 33, ed. Mark R. Rosenzweig and Lyman W. Porter, 1–39. Palo Alto, Calif.: Annual Reviews.

Tajfel, Henri, and John C. Turner. 1985. "The Social Identity Theory of Inter-group Behavior." In
Psychology of Intergroup Relations, ed. Steven Worchel and William G. Austin, 7–24. Chicago: Nelson-Hall.

Tate, Katherine. 1999. "Welfare Reform: Scrapping the System and Our Ideals." In *African Americans and the American Political System,* ed. Lucius J. Barker, Mack H. Jones, and Katherine Tate, 350–59. Englewood Cliffs, N.J.: Prentice-Hall.

———. 2003. *Black Faces in the Mirror: African Americans and Their Representatives in the U.S. Congress.* Princeton: Princeton University Press.

Thomas, David, and John Gabarro. 1999. *Breaking Through: The Making of Minority Executives in Corporate America.* Cambridge: Harvard Business School Press.

Thomas, Jim. 1984. "Some Aspects of Negotiated Order, Loose Coupling, and Mesostructure in Maximum Security Prisons." *Symbolic Interaction* 7, no. 2: 213–31.

Timberlake, Jeffrey. 2000. "Still Life in Black and White: Effects of Racial and Class Attitudes on Prospects for Residential Integration in Atlanta." *Sociological Inquiry* 70, no. 4: 420–45.

Trattner, William. 1999. *From Poor Law to Welfare State: A History of Social Welfare in America.* 6th ed. New York: Free Press.

Tripi, F. G. 1984. "Client Control in Organizational Settings." *Journal of Applied Behavioral Science* 20:39–47.

Turner, J. C., P. J. Oakes, S. A. Haslam, and C. McGarty. 1994. "Self and Collective: Cognition and Social Context." *Personality and Social Psychology Bulletin* 20:454–63.

Turner, John, and S. Alexander Haslam. 2001. "Social Identity, Organizations, and Leadership." In *Groups at Work: Theory and Research,* ed. Margaret Turner, 25–66. Mahwah, N.J.: Lawrence Erlbaum Associates.

Urban Institute. 2002. "Fast Facts on Welfare Policy: Worst Case Sanctions." Assessing the New Federalism Project. Washington, D.C.: Urban Institute. http://www.urban.org/toolkit/policybriefs/subjectbriefs.cfm?documentty peid=403. DOR: 1-2–08.

———. 2006. "A Decade of Welfare Reform: Facts and Figures." Assessing the New Federalism Project. Washington, D.C.: Urban Institute.

Uttal, Lynet. 2006. "Organizational Cultural Competency: Shifting Programs for Latino Immigrants from a Client-Centered to a Community-Based Orientation." *American Journal of Community Psychology* 38, nos. 3–4: 251–62.

Valk, Anne M. 2000. "'Mother Power': The Movement for Welfare Rights in Washington, D.C., 1966–1972." *Journal of Women's History* 11, no. 4: 34–58.

Vallas, Steven P. 2003. "Rediscovering the Color Line within Work Organizations." *Work and Occupations* 30, no. 4: 379–400.

Van Maanen, John. 1979. "The Fact of Fiction of Organizational Ethnography." *Administrative Science Quarterly* 24:539–50.

Wagner, David. 2005. *The Poorhouse: America's Forgotten Institution.* New York: Rowman and Littlefield.

Waldinger, Roger, and Michael I. Lichter. 2003. *How the Other Half Works: Immigration and the Social Organization of Labor.* Berkeley: University of California Press.

Watkins, Celeste. 2000. "When a Stumble Is Not a Fall: Recovering from Employment Setbacks in the Welfare to Work Transition." *Harvard Journal of African American Public Policy* 6, no. 1: 63–84.

Weick, Karl. 1976. "Educational Organizations as Loosely Coupled Systems." *Administrative Science Quarterly* 21, no. 1: 1–19.

Wen, Patricia. 2007. "Job Program for Welfare Recipients Falls Flat: Employers Say Woes Outweigh State Subsidies." *Boston Globe* (January 15): A1.

West, Cornel. "Cornel West Commentary: Cosby's Comments." *Tavis Smiley Show,* National Public Radio, May 26, 2004.

Whetten, David, and Paul Godfrey. 1998. *Identity in Organizations: Building Theory through Conversations.* Thousand Oaks, Calif.: Sage Publications.

Wilkerson-Freeman, Sarah. 2002. "The Creation of a Subversive Feminist Dominion: Interracialist Social Workers and the Georgia New Deal." *Journal of Women's History* 13, no. 4: 132–54.

Wilkins, Vicky. 2006. "Exploring the Causal Story: Gender, Active Representation, and Bureaucratic Priorities." *Journal of Public Administration Research and Theory* 17:77–94.

Wilkins, Vicky M., and Lael R. Keiser. 2004. "Linking Passive and Active Representation by Gender: The Case of Child Support Enforcement." *Journal of Public Administration Research and Theory* 16:87–102.

Wilson, William Julius. 1987. *The Truly Disadvantaged: The Inner City, the Underclass, and Public Policy.* Chicago: University of Chicago Press.

Zedlewski, Sheila Rafferty. 2000. "Family Economic Well-Being." In *Snapshots of America's Families II: A View of the Nation and 13 States from the National Survey of America's Families.* Washington, D.C.: Urban Institute.

Ziliak, James P., David N. Figlio, Elizabeth E. Davis, and Laura S. Connolly. 2000. "Accounting for the Decline in AFDC Caseloads: Welfare Reform or the Economy?" *Journal of Human Resources* 35:570–86.

Zimmer, Lynn. 1987. "How Women Reshape the Prison Guard Role." *Gender & Society* 1, no. 4: 415–31.

Index